W9-ABR-448

PHILOSOPHY OF EDUCATION

PHILOSOPHY OF EDUCATION

William Heard Kilpatrick

THE MACMILLAN COMPANY · NEW YORK

MACMILLAN NEW YORK · LONDON

A Division of The Crowell-Collier Publishing Company

The Macmillan Company, New York
Macmillan New York, London
Brett-Macmillan Ltd., Galt, Ontario

PRINTED IN THE UNITED STATES OF AMERICA

TO MY WIFE

Marion Ostrander Kilpatrick

FOREWORD

The special aim of this book is to consider critically and constructively the principal problems of general educational theory now confronting modern civilization. It is accordingly designed for a wide range of readers—for students preparing either to teach or to administer, for leaders of youth groups, for teachers and others now actively engaged in educational work, for parents and citizens—in one word, for any and all who are consciously concerned for the intelligent and effective direction of education.

The effort herein made is to sum up in a statement for others the results of the author's thinking in connection with his life work of teaching philosophy of education. While he was actually thus teaching it seemed unwise to publish any such inclusive statement of position; the position itself was always in process of growth, and more, there was the danger that his students would be tempted to accept and give back what they found in his book rather than think creatively for themselves.

The author has, of course, his own position on the various matters discussed and he has not hesitated to say what he thinks. But because future study will surely improve upon our present insight a specific aim of the book is to promote independent and creative thinking in the hope that students and readers, and those whom they influence, may share in bringing about the more defensible future insight.

For the deeper formative influences that entered into the making of the book the author feels most indebted to the intellectual atmosphere created by that second generation who sought to digest and apply Darwin's *Origin of Species* to life and thought, most definitely to C. S. Peirce, William James, and John Dewey, with greatest indebtedness to the last named of these three. The effort here made is to carry that atmosphere, that attitude, that outlook on life, practically and consistently into education, specifically into the problem of the aims which education should pursue and to the search for an educative process adequate to implement these aims.

A very definite indebtedness should also be acknowledged to those students who during the successive years of the author's teaching insisted on raising difficult questions. These he had to think through, either to clarify his own conception and statement or to dig deeper into theory. The accumulations from these efforts make up the most of what is distinctive here.

For help in the actual writing I am deeply indebted to my wife. Marion Ostrander Kilpatrick. She gave much time and effort to reading the entire manuscript and made many helpful suggestions for both content and form. Finally I wish to thank the various authors and publishers from whose books I have quoted. These are listed at the close of the book.

William H. Kilpatrick

New York City
January, 1951

CONTENTS

PART I
Philosophy of Life

CHAPTER I. *The Meaning and Significance of Philosophy of Education: A Preliminary View*

WHAT is philosophy of education? What does it teach us? What does it tell us about education that we cannot otherwise find out? Can it help us, practically, to run a schoolroom? Or a school system? Can it help parents rear their children? Let us keep such questions in mind as we try to get the best preliminary insight we can into the meaning and significance of a philosophy of education. The fuller meaning will come as we go further into the book.

Possibly the word philosophy gives trouble at the outset. The term may sound too abstruse, too highbrow, not within the range of ordinary thinking. Perhaps it is better to begin instead with some simpler term, such as "point of view" or "outlook on life," and reserve until later the term "philosophy."

What is a point of view or outlook on life? What does it do to or for the man who holds it? How does it serve? To answer these questions let us begin with a higher than ordinary instance, say the case of a statesman. What point of view or general outlook does he have? The answer may be clearer if we first contrast the behavior of a democratic leader with that of a dictator, such as Hitler or Mussolini, and see what opposed points of view have respectively guided the two cases.

Every leader of either type well understands that in each important move he must have his people back of him or his effort will not succeed; but the means for getting this backing will differ profoundly in the two contrasted systems. It is just here that the point of view begins to get in its specific work. The truly democratic leader wishes to carry his people along with him of their own reasoning and volition; he knows as a fact and sincerely believes as a principle that final authority in his country lies in the people, in their decisions freely expressed at the polls. He will accordingly help the people study and decide adequately. They on their part will not only vote but will tell him more or less forthrightly and audibly what they think, that he may take their judgment into account. While it is they who must finally decide, he strives through his leadership to help them decide more wisely. Note, for example, this statement by President Franklin D. Roosevelt:

> Government includes the art of formulating a policy and using the political technique to attain as much of that policy as will receive general support; persuading, leading, sacrificing, teaching always, because the greatest duty of a statesman is to educate (123: Mar. 19, 1950).*

The authoritarian outlook and procedure differ fundamentally from this. The dictator's decision is final. He may consult if he wishes, but he need not do so; if he does, he chooses whom he will consult; and he makes up his mind as he sees fit. Next he tells his people what they are to think and do. For this he may use the radio, the press, the moving pictures—all of which he controls absolutely to insure that no contrary opinions are voiced. In getting the support of his people he may browbeat them and threaten them; or he may "throw dust in their eyes" and confuse them; or he may deliberately deceive them as to his real aims and purposes. Both Hitler and Mussolini at times did all these things. Lenin, who preceded both Mussolini and Hitler, was more explicit: "The Communists must be prepared, if necessary, to resort to all sorts of cunning schemes and stratagems, to employ illegal methods, to evade and conceal the truth." (123: *Bk. Rev.*, Apr. 25, 1948)

The fundamental difference of outlook between the democratic leader and the dictator thus shows itself most crucially in their opposed attitudes (i) as regards respect for human personality (whether or not people are to think for themselves and have their choices count) and (ii) as to the location of final authority (whether the people as a whole decide or whether the dictator and his henchmen decide). The really democratic leader believes that human personality as such is to be respected—developed and expressed—as best possible on terms of equality of treatment; and that, on this

* A parenthesis following a quotation refers to the List of References (pages 433 ff.). The first number gives the place of the item on the list; what follows locates the quotation within the item.

basis, government derives its just powers from the consent of the governed. The dictator takes exactly opposite grounds on both points; and his henchmen speak accordingly. Field Marshal Goering thus told German labor: "You must be blind followers of the Fuehrer wherever he may lead us." The Nazi Press Chief, Otto Dietrich, explained to the students of the University of Berlin: "There is no freedom of the individual; there is only freedom of peoples, nations, or races." Mussolini's Minister of Justice said to the same end: "The individual is only the means to achieve the noble purpose of the state." Mussolini himself said: "I spit upon the corpse of liberty."

As our chief concern here is with education, let us see what the autocratic outlook demands regarding education and how this differs from what we know of democratic education. Hitler is reported as saying, "Universal education is the most corroding and disintegrating poison that liberalism ever invented for its own destruction. . . . We must therefore be consistent and allow the great mass of the lowest order the blessings of illiteracy." He also said elsewhere regarding the young men he had chosen to work with him: "I will have no intellectual training. Knowledge is ruin to my young men." The Nazi "Commandments to Youth" had twelve points: No. 1, "The Leader [Fuehrer] is always right"; No. 5, "The program is your dogma; it demands your complete surrender to the cause"; No. 12, "Whatever serves the interest of the movement, and through it, Germany and the German people, is right." (26:xxiii *f.*) A Fascist textbook said: "Religious dogmas are not discussed because they are truths revealed by God. Fascist principles are not discussed because they come from the mind of a Genius: Benito Mussolini." (qtd. in 145:101)

It begins now to come out clearly that each type of world outlook demands its consistent type of education. The autocrat wishes docile followers; he therefore wishes a type of education to build docility and obedience. Democracy wishes all the people to be both able and willing to judge wisely for themselves and for the common good as to the policies to be approved; it will accordingly seek a type of education to build responsible, thinking, public-spirited citizenship in all its people.

In an authoritarian society it is sufficient for the leaders to know what they want, to know the import of their planning and procedures. In a democratic society this will not suffice; leaders and, very importantly, the large majority of people must see clearly the aims of democratic living and the type of education consistent with these aims. In other words, in a democracy it is essential that both leaders and people have a clear philosophy of life and a clear philosophy of education. Any citizen, then, who values democracy, who thinks much, feels deeply, and accepts responsibility for his acts will try to build a consistent and defensible outlook on life and on education. And the higher and finer the character the more likely will the person seek to build through the years a philosophy which has been thought out (so that he knows what values he stands for) and scrutinized for its defensibility (so that he knows how it affects the values of others).

Some may at this point say that of course the very highest type men will seek thus to build a defensible and consistent outlook on life, a philosophy of life; but how is it with lesser people? Can the ordinary teacher be expected to have a philosophy of education, or even a general theory of education, in accordance with which he determines what to do in the classroom? And what about the superintendent of schools? And parents? And members of the school board? And citizens in general? What can be expected of such everyday people? In answer to all such, the fact is that anyone who cares about any disputed matter will build a point of view regarding it; but the points of view so built will differ widely in quality according to the quality of the thinking that goes into them.

An illustration may make this clearer. A certain school system was so proud of the fame it had achieved some decades ago that it rested content on these past-won laurels. It elected a new superintendent and the board assured him that their system was quite "up-to-date." The superintendent was dismayed when he discovered how "behind-the-times" the system seemed to him; many teachers were equally dismayed when they learned what the new superintendent expected and wished. Opposition thus arose, especially among certain older teachers of the upper grades and the high schools. However, certain of the younger teachers, having come more recently from their schools of education, sided with the superintendent. Conflict developed. Parents took sides, some very vigorously. Members of the school board became aroused, some strongly against the new ways. The voters took up the conflict, especially as it began to appear that the two board members next to be elected would determine the attitude of the now divided board.

Whatever else was true of this conflict, this much is clear: each of the people involved did have a point of view from which he acted. It is also true that some of these disputants had thought less significantly than others about the educational problems at issue. In fact, some seemed to fight simply to resist change, as if any change must be evil. Others, on the contrary, seemed to advocate change for no other reason than a wish to be "up to date," as if style holds properly in educational affairs as with women's hats. A number of the participants argued from positions formerly counted valid in competent educational circles, but now no longer so accepted. Certain of the disputants, however, including the superintendent, knew why they thought as they did and could give reasons that seemed to those willing to examine them to be well founded.

It is of course known to all men that ordinary people do have attitudes on matters educational, and that these attitudes are related to what they otherwise think. That some points of view on education are more adequate than others, more defensible, more valid, more worthy to be held, follows as soon as we consider the matter. We can then easily conceive of a scale on which points of view in education are arranged from low to high: at the bottom, the point of view least defensible to careful scrutiny and accordingly less worthy to be held; at the top, the highest, finest, most defensible, the most worthy to be held; in between, all the others arranged in the order of worth and acceptability. The question immediately arises as to the factors that determine position on this scale: What makes one outlook finer? What makes it more defensible?

This question is not easy to answer briefly. It will be discussed in more detail in the next chapter. In fact, the rest of this book is devoted to a consideration of this matter, and in so doing the book will try to help each reader build a philosophy for himself. In all of this, it should be clear that a philosophy can never be stated once for all—any defensible philosophy must be constantly open to scrutiny, re-examination, and revision as new problems arise and new insights are gained. But there are some ways of judging a point of view, a philosophy of education, which may well be indicated at this point.

First, as indicated above, if a point of view has nothing but custom or familiarity to support it, or the selfish wish of its advocates, then that point of view or outlook belongs close to, if not at, the bottom of the scale.* It is a point of view, to be sure, but it is defensible only by mere accident.

Second, a point of view or a philosophy may be judged on the basis of its consistency—does the person uphold some values as "good" and at the same time so act, at few or many points, as to defeat the realization of these values? (For example, verbally uphold democratic living but act in a way to violate it.)

Third, a point of view or a philosophy may be judged as to its inclusiveness—whether it has taken into account a sufficiently wide range of factors to give guidance and validity in meeting the varied significant problems faced by men.

Fourth, a philosophy may be judged on the basis of the values it upholds and acts upon. Philosophies differ widely in the values they accept. Conformity to one set of values cannot be expected of all; nor is it desirable. But it is nevertheless proper and even essential to evaluate a philosophy crucially in terms of the basic value-assumptions it makes (what it assumes and accepts to be "good," what it takes as *its own* criteria for evaluating "goodness"). For example, does the philosophy count the highest possible development of all individuals as a basic value and in terms of this evaluate the "goodness" of all situations and procedures; or does it ignore this consideration; or does it even accept instead a hierarchy of persons, some to be developed to control, with some or most to remain "lesser" and accept direction from "above"? Or, again, does the philosophy accept as a basic value the belief in "equal rights for all, special privileges for none"?

Do these criteria mean that most people cannot have a philosophy, that only "professional" philosophers can have one? The answer is no; any person who is willing to question his present point of view, who is open to critical examination of his own views and those of others, who is earnest in his search for deeper, finer, more defensible values, can build a philosophy. And this philosophy—in the degree to

* Nor can an old way of teaching defend itself simply by pointing to the great men who were taught that way. We should need to know more than that; possibly they were taught by the only way of thinking then known, however inadequate it may have been, and succeeded in spite of it. As regards schooling this seems probably true for George Washington, Andrew Jackson, and Abraham Lincoln, three of the great men of our country. Certainly it was not their formal schooling that made them great.

which he works at it—can give him a more reliable base for his living, his decisions, his choices, than can be expected otherwise. To wish to live by points of view we have not examined is to hide our heads in the sand. Plato said, "The unexamined life is not worth living." It is this process of examining our values, of stubborn search for more and more adequate ones, which we call philosophizing.

As a philosophy is to life so is a philosophy of education to education. Specifically, it should help us evaluate and choose in all matters of school life and management. So broad a claim may surprise some, but an illustration from the past will show how this is true. Contrast, for example, Napoleon Bonaparte and his American contemporary, Thomas Jefferson. From them we can see somewhat of how far a specific philosophy of education goes towards determining both what shall be done in school and the spirit with which it is to be done.

Napoleon's aim for education is thus explicitly stated:

> My principal aim in the establishment of a teaching body is to have a means for directing political and moral opinions (115).
>
> Of all political questions this [one of education] is perhaps of the highest importance. There will be no fixed political State if there is no teaching corps with fixed principles. As long as one will not learn from childhood on whether one must be a republican or a monarchist, a Catholic or an atheist, the State will not form a Nation . . . (114: No. 8:328).

In order to help teach the young "from childhood on" what to think, Napoleon had a catechism made. This told first what duties were owed "towards Napoleon I, our emperor"; then followed this question and answer:

> *Question.* Why are we subject to all these duties toward our emperor?
>
> *Answer.* First, because God, who has created empires and distributed them according to His will, has, by loading our Emperor with gifts both in peace and in war, established him as our sovereign and made him the agent of His power and His image on earth. To honor and serve our emperor is, therefore, to honor and serve God himself . . . (qtd. in 73:I:535)

This shows the attitudes meant to be built in the Napoleonic school,—unquestioning acceptance of Napoleon as emperor, honor to him, willingness to serve him. As to method, "Everything was done in military fashion. The schools were conducted to the beating of the drum. Military law was observed in the schools. Classes were organized into companies with their captains, lieutenants, sergeants, and corporals. A martial spirit pervaded every nook [phase] of the school. . . . " (30:35)

In all the Napoleonic schools everything was authoritatively regulated by the central government "even to the most minute details; for example . . . [it was prescribed] to the professors of law to divide their lessons into dictations and oral explanations, according to an invariable proportion." (100:II:40)

Jefferson of course stood for exactly the contrary attitude. So far from regulating everything from a centralized government he stressed local authority. His inclusive aim was the freedom of the individual, the freeing of each one's mind and soul from the thralldom of ignorance and prejudice for personal decision and action. To be sure, Jefferson gave rather the general principles of a democratic educational outlook than the details of a democratic school procedure. In fact, the bearing of his general principles we can probably better apply in our day than could be done in his. Some of his statements follow:

> A system of general education which shall reach every description of our citizens from the richest to the poorest, as it was my earliest, so will it be the latest of all [my] public concerns. (Letter to Joseph C. Cabell, January 14, 1818)
>
> Above all things I hope the education of the common people will be attended to. (Letter to James Madison, December 20, 1787)
>
> Were it necessary to give up either the Primaries or the University, I would rather abandon the last, because it is safer to have a whole people respectably enlightened than a few in a high state of science, and the many in ignorance. This last is the most dangerous state in which a nation can be (93:267*f.*).
>
> I have sworn on the altar of God, eternal hostility against every form of tyranny over the mind of man. (Letter to Benjamin Rush, September 23, 1800)
>
> This institution [the University of Virginia] will be based on the illimitable freedom of the human mind. For here we are not afraid to follow truth wherever it may lead, nor to tolerate error so long as reason is left free to combat it. (Letter to William Roscoe, December 27, 1820)

Napoleon had no faith in the thinking of the people and no wish for it, counting, on the contrary, that they must be told "from childhood on" what to think. Jefferson, by contrast, believed exactly in the thinking of the people, if they were "respectably enlightened."

With these differences in philosophy before us, is there then any respect in which a Jeffersonian school and a Napoleonic school would agree as to ways of doing any one thing? Would they build their schoolhouses alike? The answer of course is no; for different kinds of activities would go on inside and so call for different planning of schoolrooms, of libraries, of laboratories, of assembly rooms. Would the grounds about the buildings be the same? Again the answer is no; for Napoleon would wish a drill and parade ground, while Jefferson would wish games and plays. Would the school books be the same? Clearly not; they would differ in content and in the ways the classes would study them and therefore would differ in internal arrangement. Would the teachers treat the children alike? Again clearly not; Napoleon's pupils would march about to the drum, Jefferson's would practice going each the way a self-directing and responsible person should learn to go. Would the two schools, in fact, agree precisely in any respect? Students of this book are asked to consider whether the educational systems of Napoleon and Jefferson, if worked out in thoroughgoing consistency, would agree at any point on the details of either aim or procedure. To think through this problem will show better than could any formulated statement (i) what is meant by a philosophy of education and (ii) how far such a philosophy will go toward determining the details of school theory and practice.

Two things seem clear from all the foregoing discussion: (i) any distinctive social-political outlook, as democracy or Hitlerism or Communism or reactionary conservatism, will wish its own kind of education to perpetuate its kind of life; and (ii) each distinctive kind of teaching-learning procedure will, even if the teacher does not know it, make for its own definite kind of social life.

It seems certainly to follow from what has just been said that school people—teachers, superintendents, supervisors—must ask themselves very seriously (i) what kind of social outlook their school management and teaching tends to support; (ii) what kind of social life they ought to support; and (iii) what kind of school management and teaching-learning procedures they ought to adopt in order to support this desired social life.

It is exactly the foregoing questions that this book will study: What kind of civilization shall we seek or, in the technical term, what philosophy of life shall we uphold? And what should be the resulting philosophy of education in order to implement the chosen philosophy and realize the life for which it stands?

CHAPTER II. *The Life Process as Foundation for Philosophy: Contributions of Biology, the Experience Process, and Scientific Method*

IN the preceding chapter a preliminary notion was developed of what philosophy means and how it bears on life. In this chapter the reverse of that order will be followed, namely, beginning with life and its improvement and asking what this process tells us about philosophy and how it should work.

THE LIFE PROCESS

In the life process—of individuals, of groups—is centered all there is to living. Here is whatever life includes of satisfyingness, of consideration for others, of fine values or lesser ones, of adequacy at control, of realization of one's longings, of effect—good or otherwise—on the lives of others. It is essential therefore for philosophy to make the study of the life process central if it is really concerned with the living of people, if it wishes its study of basic assumptions, of values, of worthwhile aims, of means of validating, to flower in more satisfying living. In Chapter XI this problem of what makes a life good to live will be discussed at some length; here it is the biological life process which concerns us.

Bertrand Russell has said:

> Desire, activity, purpose, are essential to a tolerable life, and a millennium, though it may be a joy in prospect, would be intolerable if it were actually achieved (143:138).

In other words, the successful and happy life is active life. This statement gives us a clear clue to the nature of the human organism. Any organism—human or lower—abhors inactivity; its pattern is behaving, activity, striving for something that it prefers or desires. In the human organism purposing is characteristic.

The inclusive word *behavior* brings us directly into the life process as biology sees it. By *behaving* we mean the *responding* of an *organism* to a *confronting situation.* This responding involves an inner *stirring* which in the case of man includes not simply *intellect*, as the older outlook would have it, but the person's whole being, his *whole organism* (to repeat the biologic term); he *feels*, he *thinks*, he makes pertinent *bodily movements.* More precisely, the stirring brings forth or wakes up a *want;* and this want leads to the setting up of *an aim or goal;* and following this the individual puts forth *efforts* to attain this aim and goal so as, we say, to *control the situation* to his chosen end. But there is more to the life process than efforts and control. Along with it all goes *interest*, interest in what one is doing and interest in what it leads to. There is, in fact, positive *enjoyment* in making efforts, provided they promise approved success. And the satisfaction which crowns success is still not all; we enjoy this success the more if there seems more ahead beckoning us on still further; as Wordsworth said,

> Effort, and expectation, and desire,
> And something evermore about to be.—*Prelude*, bk. vi, l. 607.

The life process thus includes both effort and interest: effort to attain goals, interest in the effort itself as truly as in the goals, and further interest in what this leads to.

From what has just been said we can conclude that the unit element for the study of the life process is not simply the organism—still less merely the intellect, as the older emphasis seemed to say. Nor is this unit the environment, nor even the organism and the environment, each viewed as simply a distinct entity. The true unit of study is the organism-in-active-interaction-with-the-environment. While the interacting is in process, both organism and environment are each also in process of becoming somewhat different. This word *process* we shall many times meet hereafter.

HOW LIFE'S VALUES ARISE

When the organism does thus come into interaction with the environment, there typically results, as we saw earlier, a stirring within from which typically arises a want. Now it may happen that two such wants may come at the same time and conflict. My alarm clock goes off; it is 7:30, time for me to get up so as to get to my work by 9 o'clock. But this morning I am sleepy, I wish not to get up. So a conflict arises, and I must choose. Which do I really and finally wish: to get up now and get to work on time, or to sleep longer now and get late to work? What will getting to work late mean as contrasted with getting to work on time? Suppose I think this through and come out, say, with the conclusion that if I am to succeed in life, if I am to amount to anything, then I must not yield to so small a thing as mere sleepiness but must control the sleepiness and subordinate it to *being on time*. When I do so think through a conflict of wants and come out with a criticized principle of action, that principle becomes a *value*. A value in this sense is thus a want which has been critically evaluated and found worthy of choice.

THE LIFE PROCESS, VALUES, AND PHILOSOPHY

Everyone who expects to "amount to anything" must do a good deal of such valuing. And he must live up to the values he sets up. The worthy man will accumulate such criticized values and will live them. In this sense he has, as we saw in Chapter I, a guiding outlook on life; and in the degree that this outlook is consistent, part with part, and defensible to reason, in like degree he has what may properly be called a philosophy of life.

From all the foregoing it follows that philosophizing is the critical turning of thought back upon the life process. Plato, quoted earlier, said that "the unexamined life is not worth living"—unworthy, that is, of anyone who wishes to respect himself. We started above with behaving as a process to be examined. From this we built, step by step, the conception of philosophizing. We saw that out of behaving came wants; out of the conflict of wants came evaluation and resulting values; out of the study of these, through an aggregate consistent and defensible at the bar of reason, came what we have called philosophizing. The cumulative result of this philosophizing is one's philosophy of life, built as we have just seen upon the life process itself. In this way are essentially related the life process, values, and philosophy.

With this preliminary view of the relation of the life process to philosophy in mind, we are now ready to consider critically certain details of the relationship.

A BIT OF HISTORY

The conception of philosophy as just discussed differs greatly from what had come down from the past. This newer philosophy has, to be sure, been in process of making for some centuries, but within the past two or three generations its distinctive differences have come to much clearer consciousness. The older philosophy stems from the Greeks, where it was the intellectual interest of a leisured upper class. These sought a world view satisfying to intellectual contemplation rather than an outlook leading to overt action. In fact, action in the sense of shaping or affecting observable affairs seemed to these intellectuals to belong specifically to the less thoughtful lower classes. Rome continued this same upper-class intellectual tradition; and this, through the Greek and Roman classics, has been handed down to the intellectually interested through the centuries. The Revival of Learning which had great effect on subsequent education consisted precisely of a strong and fresh awakening of interest in this same classic tradition.

In strong contrast with this classical humanist outlook, with its emphasis on deductive and abstract thought, stands the scientific movement begun, we may say, by Galileo (1564–1642). We of our day take the scientific method so fully for granted as the best, if not the only reliable, way of reaching trustworthy conclusions, that we find it difficult to understand the typical thinking of the prescientific age. A glance at the beginning of scientific thinking may help us better to appreciate the change that has taken place.

To understand the typical thinking in the prescientific era it may help to recall our high school geometry. In that subject, the way of proving any theorem is to call on things already accepted as true, either definitions or axioms ("self-evident truths") or propositions previously proved. And the aim is, even with "originals," not so much to establish truths new to the world, as rather to show convincing effectiveness in the process of proving—in the manner just stated—what the well-informed already know. The kind of reasoning used in geometry is *deductive*. Writers on logic call it *a priori* reasoning, that is, reasoning from assumptions known beforehand and typically accepted as self-evident.

In the prescientific university the prevailing activity was disputation. This, like our high school geometry, did not so much aim at establishing new truth as at showing one's skill either in proving in an acceptable manner what was already accounted to be true or in an analogous attack on what was counted to be error. And the method of reasoning was, like that in geometry, *a priori* or deductive, in that it began with definitions or principles counted to be true and from these reasoned (again as in geometry) to supposedly necessary conclusions.

A famous historic instance will illustrate the difference between this older deductive or *a priori* reasoning, on the one hand, and the newer inductive experimental reasoning, on the other hand. The instance cited is that of Galileo and the falling bodies at Pisa. (The story may be apocryphal, but at any rate it shows us the prevalent mental attitude of the Middle Ages.) The Schoolmen at the University there—professors, we would now call them—held that if two unequal bodies be dropped, the heavier will fall faster. Galileo said the two would fall at the same rate. The method of the university people was to "reason" out any question and then if possible clinch their conclusion by quoting Aristotle, the "master of those who know." In this case they said (i) it is "heaviness" that makes anything fall and from this they reasoned (ii) that the greater the heaviness the faster the fall. So that to them the heavier body would of necessity fall faster, and they quoted Aristotle as holding this view (mistakenly it now appears). Galileo had been experimenting with actual balls, and his answer as to the rate of falling was different. Accordingly, so the story goes, he suggested that they try out the two theories by dropping balls of unequal weight from the top of the Leaning Tower of Pisa. The balls were dropped at the same time and they hit the ground at the same time (so far as the observers could tell). Galileo's theory as to falling bodies won out and was so far established. What surprises us most is that the false theory had been taught for nearly or quite two thousand years, and never before had anybody thought to question its correctness, still less to put it to the test of actual trial. To us this seems almost incredible, so completely has the resort to testing been built into our thinking.

Galileo won in establishing how bodies fall, but a principle far more significant than this was that day established, namely, the principle of experimental induction, of beginning with the facts and testing proposed hypotheses by actual experience. This was undoubtedly the greatest intellectual advance made by man since the days of classical Greece.

This principle of experimental induction, it is no exaggeration to say, has since that day at Pisa remade the world. Most obvious has been the remaking of the world of physical affairs, with all that this has meant to the comfort and ease of man. But man's life consists of more than the abundance of things he has to use and enjoy, more even than the surer health which scientific medicine has brought. What concerns us here is the change that has thus come from the new method into outlook on life, how man now thinks and feels and acts differently, and what these things mean for education.

Perhaps the first great moral effect of the new scientific outlook was to give to man a new faith in himself. The prior emphasis, whether theological or humanistic, had been to distrust the present ability of man to do creative thinking in the sense of adding new or significant knowledge or literature. The past had seemingly done all that man could expect to do. Such a view was now no longer acceptable. Man could by his own unaided effort discover significant knowledge hitherto unknown to anybody; and seemingly this new knowledge was reliably true. Concrete experiment or observation verified it. Man could now trust his intelligence as never before.

However, until the middle of the nineteenth century there appeared a division in matters of inquiry, a limit to what man could hope to attack by the scientific method. In the realm of purely physical inquiry man could evidently succeed without any apparent limit; but in the more spiritual aspects of life, wherever life's values were involved, there it appeared, at least to many, that science could not penetrate.

But in 1859 Darwin brought out his epoch-making *Origin of Species*. To be sure, this was no conscious attack on the problem of value. It was, however, in effect an attack upon the older philosophy's attitude on the changeless real. In that older outlook, to *know* was to have (be possessed of) the *changeless*, the *eternal*. Only the changeless and eternal was real or finally significant or worthy of final concern; change was trivial or decadent. Specifically, the older point of view accepted Aristotle's doctrine that any given species of animal or plant was a clear case of the changeless. The egg or seed of this species, wherever it might be put to work, shaped to its one invariable pattern whatever was food to it. And this conception of the rule of a species over material things had by common consent been extended to nature as a whole, that is, to the universe. One overruling purpose explained all observable happenings. Man's philosophic task was to find this goal and aim of nature and help to realize it.

It was this whole outlook that the *Origin of Species* attacked. For Darwin, change—even of the nature of man himself—was the essential conception. And the attack extended itself also to the hitherto dominant theory of knowledge as well as the theories of ethics and politics. Change instead of being considered trivial was now king. Two results from Darwin's position concern us here—as we have already seen in the earlier part of this chapter: first, that process (change) becomes the chief conception for understanding human affairs, both in individual development and civilization; second, that biological behavior, the behavior of man as he faces a situation to control it, becomes the key for the study of the life process, alike of the individual (physiology, psychology) and of the group (sociology, history, politics, economics). Both of these, as we saw above and shall see more fully in a moment, are crucial conceptions in a study of philosophy. That they are equally significant for education we shall find later.

THE CONTRIBUTION OF BIOLOGY TO UNDERSTANDING OF THE LIFE PROCESS

We saw above a brief analysis of the behavior process, with its emphasis on the organism and its responding to a stirring situation. We wish now to see more in detail how biology can help to an understanding of the life process.

Prior to Darwin no discussion of the human individual in relation to the course of life would have begun in this biological fashion. Some, following Aristotelian logic, would have stressed the intellect as man's peculiar endowment, probably speaking of man as *Homo sapiens*. Others, following a widespread interest of the time, would have stressed the "fallen nature" of man, his consequent sinfulness, and punishment visited on him in the way of sickness, plant pests, and the like. Still others, more modern, would have followed Adam Smith and Jeremy Bentham in stressing the opportunity of self-seeking individuals to prosper under a regime of freedom.

But now we start the study of life and of philosophy with the behaving process and see behavior as life itself in action. We find that, while behavior differs from one animal species to another, there are none the less many features in common. Of the eight terms listed below as helpful in the biologic approach to human life and behavior only one, thinking in its fuller sense, is limited to man. However, the descriptions as given best fit man and are so intended; for it is man and his behavior that concerns us in this book.

Consider now in detail the following biological conceptions which were either explicitly or implicitly given just above:

Organism—a living being organized for carrying on life; here a person (technically, an "agent") stirred to action.

Behavior—the effort at control, all that the organism does, inside and out, in response to the stirring; all the thoughts, feelings, physical movements (inside and out) called into play by the disturbing or arousing situation; specifically, all that the organism does to control the situation in order to care for the values felt to be involved or at stake.

The environment—everything, apart from the organism, that affects, either directly or indirectly, the behavior of the organism, including many things of which the organism consciously knows little or nothing.

The situation—this is, in each case of action, the environment-as-the-organism-"sees"-it, including the possible means of action; the "situation" as thus defined will change somewhat as the experience develops.

Goal-seeking—the act and fact of setting up aims and pursuing them; the fact that the agent sees values so involved in the situation as to stir him to defined action in pursuit of them.

Preferences—the crucial factor in any stirring. There would be no response if the organism had no preferences as to what may happen to him, no preferences waiting to be stirred to action by a situation capable of stirring hopes or fears.

Feeling—that aspect of behaving which has to do with pleasure or pain, with satisfaction or dissatisfaction. Normally, feeling or emotion serves as an organic resource to heighten action. Glow of interest and anticipation causes the organism to strive harder and at the same time adds enjoyment to the process. Emotion may, however, as in anger, for example, so overdo the heightening as to bring later regrets.

Thinking—all that the organism (agent) does in advance of overt action to size up the confronting situation and make plans for dealing with it; during action, to evaluate the process and shift the means, if need be, in order the better to effect the aim; and after action to draw lessons for the future from the whole experience.

It may help to see these terms and other related ones at work, so to say, in a specific instance from life itself. Mr. Cox, a truck farmer, finds a new insect pest seriously threatening his bean crop. He is greatly troubled. He cannot afford to lose his beans; he must kill off this pest. But how? Mr. Cox has never seen this pest before; his neighbors know no more than he. The Agricultural Experiment Station comes to mind. It is on the other side of the state, but his crop is worth the effort. Mr. Cox drives to the Station, carrying some of his plants with the insects on them. Fortunately, those in charge at the Station recognize the pest, and give Mr. Cox a well-tested formula. He fills his tanks accordingly, sprays his fields, and saves his crop.

This, we say, is an instance from life itself. To describe it biologically, the farmer, Mr. Cox, is the *organism*, the doer, the agent. The *situation* which *stirs* him is the threat of the pest to the bean crop and all that its loss would mean. Naturally, Mr. Cox has a strong *preference* for a good crop and it is this abiding preference which makes possible the particular stirring. The stirring thus comes from the *interaction* of the situation with the organism possessed of its preferences. It is out of the *want* thus aroused that the person (the organism or agent) sets up the *general* or *guiding goal* of destroying the pest and from this the *particular goal* of visiting the Station to find *means* for attaining his guiding goal and so *satisfying* his *want*. It is clear that the person, the organism, is stirred *as a whole;* there are *feelings*, *thoughts*, and *bodily action*. It is the whole organism that responds to the situation, sets up the goal, and works to attain the goal. The thinking *interpenetrates* the feeling and guides it effectively, and the feeling *suffuses* and supports the thinking, while thinking and feeling *support, direct, and interpenetrate the effort.*

It is this biological way of thinking about life and about the control of the life process which, perhaps more than anything else, has changed the old ways of thinking about education. We must view education differently when we see that the organism responds, is stirred to behave, to act, in terms of his preferences and values as these seem promoted or threatened by interaction with the environment; that he feels, thinks, acts, very importantly, in terms of what the situation means *to him,* and that he estimates success or failure in terms of contribution to his preferences, values, goals. This will become much clearer when we later study the learning process and come to understand it as part and parcel of this biologic life process, part, that is, of the individual's behavior, his actual effort to make life better than otherwise it would be. We shall then see, what common sense has in a way always known, that learning arises in and from behaving in an experience and, typically, comes into being in order to help carry on that same experience. Only when Mr. Cox *learned* what the pest was doing to his beans did the whole affair really begin. And this learning, so to say, got at once to work, spurring and stirring Mr. Cox to make every possible effort to stop the pest. In a word, what Mr. Cox felt and thought and learned about the pest permeated and shaped everything else that he did in the matter from beginning to end, every feeling, every thought, every act.

This is the modern biological way of looking at learning and its relation to the life process—that the organism learns in and through its behavior, through its efforts at shaping a situation to its ends; and that the true unit of study in connection is, as we saw earlier, the person-(the pupil or Mr. Cox)-in-interaction-with-his-environment. This way of thinking about learning and the service of learning in life is quite different from the old way of seeing learning as appropriating, by memorizing, what others have thought. Because the new conception is so different from the old, many used only to the old simply cannot take in the new; the shift is too great.

THE EXPERIENCE PROCESS AND ITS CONTRIBUTION TO THE LIFE PROCESS

Man alone can have true full experience, because he alone can engage in self-conscious activity. Man and the lower animals are alike in striving to get what they wish, but man in his striving *knows* what he is about and knows that he is doing it. A dog, for example, is conscious of the cat he is pursuing, but not (so far as can be told) of himself as doing the pursuing. Mr. Cox, to the contrary, was conscious both of the pest that was ruining the beans and of himself as involved in the affair. And similarly with everything done in connection—he knew what he was doing, that he was doing it, and why he was doing it. It is this ability of man to see what is going on, both as a whole and in its various relations, himself and others included, which distinguishes him from the other animals; and it is this difference which gives to man his peculiar privilege of true experience.

By experience we mean, then, a specific kind of life content, the content of life as a self-conscious being sees it when he is in active interaction with his environment. From this it follows, as we saw earlier, that the unit of study is not the person himself, not even the "whole person" taken alone, but the person-in-active-interaction-with-his-environment. The situation impinges on the person, he undergoes (consciously feels the impinging, which does something to him); he responds actively, first, by feeling stirred, then by sizing up the situation, then by devising goals and means for controlling the situation, finally by attempting the actual control. The person thus actively feels hope or fear according as the future now at work in the present offers promise or threat. Since this is typical of life, we can say that we live precariously or, with Dewey, "we live in a world where changes are going on whose issue means our weal or woe." Experience is thus "a future implicated in a present" and "success and failure are primary 'categories' of life" (42:12, 13), of life as the self-conscious human sees it.

Specifically, Mr. Cox not only could see what was happening but could study it, study each part in its wider relations, actual and possible. He could see pests not as isolated phenomena but as related to his bean crop. In these meanings the future was implicated in the present. Mr. Cox could see that if the pests continued their activity the crop would be destroyed and that this would affect the family budget. With his knowledge of beans, pests, and the Agricultural Station and its possibilities, and with his ability to relate all of these, he could think up the step, as *means* to his *goal,* of going to the Station for advice and help. None of these things could have been done by a dog. The ability thus consciously to devise *means* to an end is at the bottom of man's power to invent. Out of such planning in his early history man devised language and his first crude tools. Civilization had therein begun.

Note that in experiencing, the outcome is precarious. Man can hope but he must also fear. And note further that the early stages of any experience stay with the person (through the process we recognized above as learning) to help shape all else that is done. It was, as we saw, when Mr. Cox *learned* about the new pest that this particular experience began. Because Mr. Cox could learn, this experience was possible to him. What he learned about the pest led him to seek the aid of his neighbors. When he learned that they could not help him, he thought of the Experiment Station. Here both the facts learned stayed with him to shape his further conduct. And the next step—the trip to the Experiment Station—involved various things learned in the past. Experience, then, in a true sense is a kind of life in which the early stages pervade, through learning, the later stages to shape these further efforts.

It has been several times pointed out that the true object of study for the purposes of this book is the organism (here the learner) in active interaction with his environment. The operation of learning gives simultaneously both greater complexity of character to the person (the learner) and greater complexity to the outside world without. The learner thereby becomes more of a person within, and for him the world at the same time takes on more character without. This is a distinctive contribution made by learning from experience to the life process.

In these various ways, then, the factor of self-conscious experience makes at least the following seven contributions to the life process: (i) the person involved is not only active, but he knows what he is doing, and why and how; (ii) through the factor of learning, the early stages of any given experience remain with the person to play their further appropriate part in shaping and directing the effort; (iii) the person also relates what he is now doing with pertinent matters previously experienced so as to use these for better control of the situation at hand; (iv) by self-conscious anticipation the future, with its hopes and fears, its promises and its threats, pervades the present to help shape it to the end sought; (v) this thoughtful effort to shape and control the outcome of the experience "means that success and failure are primary 'categories' of life"; (vi) as man thus attempts to control his life process, he learns from his successive experiences regarding life and the world about him, and these varieties of learning give at one and the same time greater complexity to his own character and a more complex and perhaps better organized character to the outside world; and (vii) from similar experiences man from time to time has invented or discovered or contrived significantly new ways of managing life, the accumulation of which when put to work constitute exactly what we call civilization.

It thus comes about, as Samuel Butler (1835–1902) wisely pointed out, that "every day and every hour" we are engaged in accommodating our changing selves to our changing and changeable surroundings. The life process, he says, is in fact "nothing else than this process of accommodation; when we fail in it a little we are stupid, when we fail flagrantly we are mad, when we suspend it temporarily we sleep, when we give up the attempt altogether we die." In some lives the strain of this accommodation is small, in others great. "A life will be successful or not according as the power of accommodation is equal to or unequal to the strain of fusing and adjusting internal and external changes." (20:329*f*.)

This process of accommodation, because we are conscious of it, we call experience; Butler here gives us an illuminating picture of the life process as we know it who live it. Out of man's successive experiences he builds his insights, his attitudes, his standards, his ideals, his principles of action, his ability to manage. And the quality of this accumulative learning, more than any other single factor, determines the quality of his living. At long last, as we shall later see, man became conscious of the possibility of improving his life process by improving his culture, the content of his civilization. Only two hundred years ago did man thus conceive progress; and the time since then has been short. Of that, more later.

SCIENTIFIC METHOD AND THE LIFE PROCESS

In a true sense science may be said to have had its origin in common sense, the ordinary working of common experience. Throughout human history men working in any given area of practical affairs have cumulatively developed knowledge and skill in dealing with that area superior to that of others less so experienced. The superior knowledge of these artisans, it seems clear, came from watching the results of their specific efforts, whether it was at weaving or making pottery or tending cattle or building houses. They learned from experience somewhat of what was feasible to try, what was reasonable to expect, how to manage effective procedures. Common sense, we may anticipate, is peculiarly the American popular attitude, originally gained partly from the Protestant religion but more definitely from frontier experience.

Scientific method shares typically with this artisan common sense the latter's dealings with tangible materials and its entire reliance on the observable properties (possible types of behavior) of these materials. It differs, however, as to primary aim and accordingly in the degree of care used in operation. The aim of the common-sense artisan is to turn out an immediate material product; science, by contrast, seeks knowledge, knowledge of the behavior of natural objects, and this knowledge must be so accurate and reliable as to be beyond question. It is this last-named demand which accounts for the difference in care with which the typical artisan and the typical scientist work. The artisan is satisfied to please the buyer of his product; the scientist's care must be beyond question.

That common sense is the common life process at work seems clear; but what about scientific method? What has it done for the life process?

We saw above three distinct results of science and scientific method for life:

1. Through science man got new faith in himself. This in time brought the movement called the Enlightenment, out of which came for us of America the Declaration of Independence and much of the 1787 Constitution of the United States, including specifically the Bill of Rights.

2. Science with the aid of technology (itself a product of scientific method) has made the modern world modern. It has brought more changes in life and living within three centuries than all preceding history can show.

3. It has changed the thinking of modern man from main reliance on deductive *a priori* reasoning to main reliance on inductive reasoning. Except for language itself and the development of critical thinking by the Greeks this seems certainly the greatest intellectual advance known among men.

Besides these three important contributions of scientific method to the life process the following further contributions may be named:

4. Science has taught man that the world is not governed by

caprice, but is understandable. This conviction is, in the judgment of Professor P. W. Bridgman, "doubtless, the most important single gift of science to civilization." The result is the growing freedom from superstition formerly found among all classes.

5. The spirit actuating science shows the highest standards of honesty and truthfulness known among men. In 1926, while the writer was in Vienna, a scientist there published a paper on genetics claiming as a fact in his laboratory the biologic transmission of specific acquired characteristics. It was later disclosed that a laboratory assistant had falsified the record, whereupon the scientist in shame committed suicide.

6. Science allows self-interest no place in determining results of research or in reporting thereon.

7. It has provided methods of constructive creative study far and away more effective than any explicitly in use prior to Galileo. Specifically, science has greatly helped conscious experience achieve, along the sixth line above named, the greater knowledge of the actual world with corresponding growth of character possible to the human individual; and has given along the seventh line an amazing list of contributions not simply to material civilization but also to knowledge and insight along all lines of human interest. As Dewey says: "Mankind now has in its possession a new method, that of cooperative and experimental science, which expresses the method of intelligence." (49:83) And he goes on to say: "*There is but one sure road of access to truth*—the road of cooperative inquiry operating by means of observation, experiment, and controlled reflection." (41:32)*

* Two other matters relating to science are so important to later discussions that notice must be taken of them here in spite of the fact that they relate but slightly if at all to the present discussion. They are: (i) the "separation of variables" and (ii) the "law of causation."

Speaking generally, experimental scientific inquiry can succeed only as the experimenting can proceed with no more than two factors allowed to vary: the independent variable, which the experimenter can within limits vary at his will; and the dependent variable, whose resulting manner of variation is the specific subject of inquiry—an inquiry so conducted is said to proceed on the basis of the "separation of variables."

Take the proof of Boyle's Law that with a pure gas the pressure and volume vary inversely. Let the pressure be the independent variable, then all the other possible variables (excepting the dependent variable, the volume) must be kept constant, such as the quantity of gas and the temperature. While

THE LIFE PROCESS AS FOUNDATION OF PHILOSOPHY

The older pre-Darwinian basis of philosophy was, as we have several times noted, *a priori* and deductive. This way of thinking had come down from Plato and Aristotle. To Plato, Greece then appeared headed for chaos unless it could stop its course of reckless change; so he sought a philosophy which permitted no change in fundamental matters. The timeless principles of mathematics, as studied by the Pythagoreans, gave him, it appears, the desired clue; on that model he conceived ideal patterns of thought and institutions true in the nature of things for all time. These he thought were just as absolute and changeless as were mathematical principles. Men must learn and obey these ideal patterns.

In later centuries neo-Platonism, embodying the same essential outlook, became the predominant Greek philosophy; and when the Christian fathers made a formal creed, they stated it in terms of this neo-Platonic outlook, with the change that for them the standard and ideal pattern had been created by God before the foundation of the Earth. Under the dominance of the thought of Aristotle the creed was reformulated in the thirteenth century but on a like basis.

---

the pressure is varied in different ways, the successive volumes are then measured. Actual measurement serves to establish the law. This experimentation proceeded on the principle of the "separation of variables."

The second matter to be considered is the "law of causation." This, as generally accepted by scientists until recently, meant (i) that each event in nature is precisely determined to be what it is by its prior determining "causes"; and (ii) that any given set of causes will always have the same effect. So accepted this "law of causation" has been counted as the principal logical foundation of natural science.

Although this law is even now widely if not generally accepted, certain facts should be stated in connection with it: (i) the term "law" has recently shifted its scientific meaning; an accepted scientific "law" is not now counted as necessarily or finally true, but only as the best formulation yet made by man for describing the known related factor; (ii) the Heisenberg principle of indeterminacy occasions serious doubt among many, perhaps most, scientists as to whether "the law of causation" holds in microphysics; (iii) it has all the while been true that certain philosophers, along with certain moralists and theologians, have doubted that the "law of causation" as scientifically understood holds in regard to human choice and conduct. This is part of the discussion hinted at above in the reference to the pre-Darwinian dispute as to whether science can consider the problem of values. Later discussions will consider these matters more fully.

On this older outlook the body was counted to be a principal source of sin, and the mind or soul was expected to have as little to do with the body as it could. As Plato said: "Thought is best when the mind is gathered into herself . . . when she has as little as possible to do with the body." (*Phaedo:65*) This general attitude of mistrust of the body and its part in the more serious matters of life prevailed without question, we may say, until Galileo; and even after that, as we saw above, it was still powerful in philosophy until Darwin.

An illustration or two of the older reasoning will help us understand better the change that has taken place. When Galileo announced his finding of spots on the sun, this was strongly attacked: the sun is a heavenly body, it cannot have blemishes. Here we see the tendency to reason deductively from certain assumed general principles. In this controversy a certain superior wrote to a subordinate who said he had seen the spots: they "must be on the glass or in your eyes, they cannot be on the sun." And similarly when it was proposed that the earth moves annually about the sun, the reply was that the sun exists to serve the earth, and that the master does not move about the servant. Note in both instances the refusal to study and face the facts.

Galileo, and even more Descartes (1596–1650) and Newton (1642–1727), practically banished this deductive kind of reasoning from any serious study of the physical world; but in matters of ultimate values, where scientific method seemed inapplicable, the *a priori* reasoning held on much longer. This is how Darwin had his impact on philosophy along the two lines named above: (i) the significance of process in understanding human affairs and (ii) the place of behavior in explaining life and experience.

By the time Darwin came, the scientific method of Galileo, Descartes, and Newton had greatly lessened the appeal of *a priori* deductive reasoning. To begin thus with facts immediately at hand and test hypotheses by actual trial—this had an increasing appeal, falling in as it did with common sense. Also this rejection of the *a priori* was strengthened among thinkers by the proof (1829) that Euclidean geometry now had two non-Euclidean rivals, each reasoned with equal logic such that no mathematician can tell which of the three is the true one. Moreover, in Great Britain and America the growth of democracy further helped the tendency. A laissez-faire economy added its influence, and in America frontier experience was a powerful factor. The result was a strong faith in the individual, in social change, and a corresponding lessening regard for fixed-in-advance principles if these were offered to govern life. The story is told that an ignorant American hearing for the first time an account of the doctrine of predestination exclaimed with much vigor, but with a certain discernment: "The American people would never stand for anything like that!"

The older philosophy, as we saw earlier, tried to start with the purpose of the universe or with the ultimate elements of nature, but the modern mind increasingly felt that it knew neither this purpose nor these ultimate elements. Nor could it, as Descartes had tried to do, wipe the slate clean and start afresh. Rather it seemed best to start with life as we know it, study it to learn better how it works, and then try to improve upon the life thus far lived—in one word, study the life process to improve it.

Accordingly, what we learn about biology, the experience process, and scientific method is grist to our mill. They are all just so many ways of understanding the life process. Biology gives the fundamental organic understanding of the life process as such. Study of experience shows various ways in which the life process is lived and enriched on the self-conscious level of man. Scientific method adds critical study to the experience process to improve its efficacy. Education, as we shall later see in detail, improves and enriches the life process for the individual and consequently for society.

What now is philosophy? What is its service in the over-all task of improving and enriching life?

In a way philosophy takes up where science leaves off. Science, we may say, aims at finding more effective ways of satisfying man's specific wants. Philosophy or, better, philosophizing begins when man finds serious questions arising as to what he has hitherto believed or wished, so that he has to ask himself what he really does after all believe and wish.

Consider two simple instances both involving moral obligation. Suppose that a business man confesses in the bosom of his family: "Of course, I cheat my customers more or less, I have to do it. If I didn't I couldn't make enough money to support my family." Clearly this man assumes (i) that the demand for family living at the present standard outweighs the demands of morality, and

(ii) that his present way of making money, as over against any change in it, is to be maintained even at the expense of cheating his customers. If we could get this man really to question these assumptions, he might be on the road to improving the quality of his thought and so the living of surrounding society. In so far as he does come to question these or other assumptions so as to search either for better support or for better assumptions, he has *begun* to philosophize. It was perhaps with something like this in mind that Voltaire said: "Men will continue to commit atrocities as long as they continue to believe absurdities."

As a second instance, a college class is discussing the nature of morality. Certain students say, at the beginning, that to follow the social tradition is to behave morally. Others say that to follow conscience is to behave morally. Again we see two assumptions: (i) that the received tradition adequately embodies a proper morality, and (ii) that the individual conscience is infallible as to moral demands. That any college student could believe either assumption may seem surprising; but clearly there can be no adequate philosophizing about morality until at least these two assumptions are sincerely questioned. And Voltaire's judgment is even more pertinent here.

The philosophizing of these two instances is rather simple. We may sum up so far by saying that philosophizing contributes to the life process by bringing into it greater defensibility and greater consistency of thought and act; and that in general this greater consistency and defensibility begin by consciously examining the assumptions we have hitherto been accepting perhaps without question.

It is, however, both possible and desirable to give to philosophizing, that is, to formal philosophizing, a broader and deeper definition and a fuller statement of its contribution to the life process. Anyone who thinks critically and abstractly about such problems as the foregoing and tries to answer in terms of principles involved; who seeks for as fundamental principles as possible to guide such cases; who searches out the implications of these principles for the life process of individual human beings and of humanity as a whole; who, finally, tries to get his various chosen principles together in one consistent and defensible outlook on life—such a one is philosophizing in the full general sense; and the resulting cumulative outlook, as inclusive and helpful as he can make it, becomes therein his philosophy of life.

The making of a philosophy of education based on study of the life process and directed toward enrichment of the life content—that is the problem with which this book is concerned. The task is not an easy one, but it is a necessary undertaking if the problem of education as related to life is to be attacked with fullness and adequacy.

PHILOSOPHY AND PHILOSOPHY OF EDUCATION

Philosophy, as we have just seen, is the critical study of the conflicting values of life to find out as best possible how to manage life in the face of these conflicts. In this sense, philosophy aims to give a more adequate understanding and conception of life, including a more inclusive ideal of life. Philosophizing and education are, then, but two stages of the same endeavor, philosophizing to think out better values and ideals, education to realize these in life, in human personality. Education, acting out of the best direction philosophizing can give, tries, beginning primarily with the young, to lead people to build criticized values into their characters, and in this way to get the highest ideals of philosophy progressively embodied in their lives. Philosophy of education, we may add, is the study of comparative effects (i) of rival philosophies on the life process and (ii) of alternative educative processes on character building—both undertaken in order to find what management of education is likely to build the most constructive character in young and old. This second aspect of philosophy of education we shall later call "the broad problem of method." As thus considered, philosophy, education, and the philosophy of education all alike aim at the ideal of life, to find this ideal as well as possible, and then to realize it as well as possible.

CHAPTER III. *The Social Nature of Man: None Liveth to Himself; We Are Members One of Another*

How separate and distinct are human beings? How independently of each other can they live? How socially must they live? How independently and yet how socially *should* they live? These questions and their like, our two world wars and our great depression have raised again with greatly renewed force. To these questions, as history and anthropology show, different times have returned different answers. And the differing answers as actually accepted and lived make a great difference to life. It becomes then necessary for a conscious philosophy of life, and consequently for a conscious philosophy of education, to concern itself with a defensible theory as to the relation of the human individual with the group of which he is a member.

Some people seem to think—and many more seem to act—as if the individual need consider only himself and his own interests, or only himself and his family and his immediate group. And many seem to count that such selfishness is both quite natural and defensible. When others object, these people exclaim, "Why should I consider anybody else? I have to live. It is my business to look after myself and my own; if I don't, who will?" It is of course the proper business of each one of us to look after himself; but shall he do this in disregard of others affected by his acts? Is there no necessary obligation to take account of others? Of how his acts affect them? Does the term "duty" have no proper meaning and carry no proper obligation? The answers we give to such questions affect life in infinitely many relationships, all the way from the simple play of a young child to all of humanity brought together in one inclusive world organization.

We begin here with a consideration of how the life of each

human individual is inextricably bound up with others; and we then show, even more fundamentally, how the normal person is, by his very human nature, not purely individualistic, but is in fact inextricably social in his very being.

MAN'S PHYSICAL DEPENDENCE ON OTHERS

It is literally true, even in the most physical sense, that no man liveth to himself alone. To begin with, each one is born of two parents. Without them he would not have been. And further, without them or their substitute, no infant born into the world could possibly stay alive. He must for years be fed and otherwise cared for. In all the animate world the human infant is the most helpless, and he has besides the longest period of infancy. There is, of course, the good side to this, that prolonged infancy under favorable conditions promises the best chance to grow and learn.

But even after infancy each one of us remains dependent on others for any desirable kind of life. In primitive times men lived in small tribes, all working together to secure sustenance and to fight off their enemies. These early tribes, typically, held all things in common. More civilized men live even more certainly in mutual dependence, but now on the principle of division of labor. The typical farmer, assisted by wife and children, raises foodstuffs; these he exchanges with others, through the process we call selling and buying, for house-building materials, for clothes, for farm implements, for medical care, and, by the taxes he pays, for the education of his children—in a word, for all the things he needs which are not supplied by his farm. Nowadays, in fact, even the wheat farmer does not make flour from his wheat, but instead sells his wheat and buys his flour. If the present-day farmer's family had to restrict their life to what comes from the farm, with no help from outsiders through exchange, they would have very meager living. If the farmer were himself alone, without wife and children, his life would be still worse. However, of all workers, the farmer would come nearest to supplying his own needs. No one else could (outside of the tropics) do as well. The fisherman might come next, but to live on fish alone would be poor living.

Thus no man, savage or civilized, can—outside of the tropics—live independent of others; and none does. And because of this shared living, life is both surer and richer. Even religious hermits have generally lived by alms from others; and no one, not even a hermit, upholds this life for all. But even the hermit has always got his idea and ideals of hermit life from predecessors. As stated above, it is literally true that no man liveth to himself alone.

MAN'S CULTURAL DEPENDENCE ON OTHERS

But there is still more. Not only is each human born helpless, as we have just seen, but also ignorant. This helpless, ignorant infant has to learn from others how to live. Each one is born into a group of people living according to the group customs, each group with its manner of living, its language, its government, its moral standards. The child thus grows up among these people, learns their ways of eating, dressing, talking, thinking, acquires their standards of behaving, and ultimately takes his place among them as a mature member of the group to help carry on the group life. Only as the individual has grown up learning all these things from his elders can he live the life of his group.

And the elders of this group got their ways and standards of living and by far most of what they know just as did the child in the preceding paragraph, by growing up in the midst of family, community, society; they learned these particular group ways through the process of living them. True enough, a few members of groups have through the ages thought up, devised, contrived, invented, discovered, created new and different ways of behaving. They thus invented a stone axe, or an earthen pot, or a plow, or a new way of plowing, or a new recipe for making jelly, or a new and more accurate term for thought purposes, or a new kind of engine, or a new theory of government–something new or different which the others in time accepted as a proper addition to life. So that in our day the young people grow up using this new horseless carriage which we call an automobile, or this new music-talking box which we call a radio; and they hand these and their use down to their children.

All the transmitted ways of talking, thinking, behaving, etc., by which a group of people carries on its living we call the group culture. The culture of each group–French, Chinese, American, Mexican, Hottentot, or Malayan–is peculiar to it. No two cultures are exactly alike, though there are always common elements. The term *culture* as here used is relatively new,* having been introduced by anthropology, which studies such phases of life.† Another name for this anthropological culture is "social inheritance," a term made to distinguish its manner of transmission from the biological inheritance with which one is born. The civilization of any group is its culture in action; it is the life of the people as they live their culture.

Suppose by some miracle we should suddenly lose all that has come down to us through the culture. There would then be little left to us beyond the primordial impulses of animal nature. Hunger, for example, we would certainly feel, soon very acutely, and we would look for something to eat; but what to eat, how to find it, how to prepare it—all such knowledge would have gone. And if it went suddenly, practically all of us outside the tropics would starve to death before we could procure enough to eat.

It was stated above that by far the most of what each one knows and does he has got by absorbing the group culture about him. To stress this fact, to "rub it in" so to say, let each reader ask himself how many of the tools or implements of his living he has personally invented, how many of his thoughts and beliefs are not already better stated in existing books, how much addition he has made—beyond what was already better known—to either the theory or practice of a more satisfying life. And if he thinks he can show some useful device he has invented, some new thought he has contrived or discovered, some finer distinction in the quality of living than that previously known—if he has thus added to the race culture, let him ask himself how far, in making this contribution, he has built on what the culture had previously taught him. Finally, let him ask himself what proportion his contribution bears to the whole body of the usable culture. If one will answer these questions honestly, he will see how far the individual is dependent on the group culture for the content both of his thought life and of his practical conduct.

* This use of the word *culture* does not, for example, appear in the main body of the great Oxford English Dictionary (the letter C having been published 1888–92), but only in the supplement (published in 1933).

† This anthropological meaning of the term *culture* must be rather sharply distinguished from an older use, as for example, "a person of culture and refinement," where the emphasis is placed on that part of the (anthropological) culture suggested by the word "refinement." This usage referred, in an earlier time especially, to the personal cultivation distinctively found among the more privileged.

In literal fact, what each one is, has in greatest measure come from the group.

INDIVIDUALITY

The reader may reply to the foregoing that while he has personally contributed little if anything to the group culture, he still has his own individual ways of acting and thinking, his individuality so to say, and this he values in a peculiar sense. Such an answer deserves consideration and probable commendation. To have achieved true individuality is both a personal asset and a social contribution. However, two ways of looking at these private and individual ways of thinking and behaving must be distinguished. With some, these individual ways are mere oddities, which others more thoughtful would refuse to accept as desirable ways of behaving. Many honest old codgers are queer like that; but the rest of us, the more we know of a wider world and the more we think about these matters, count oddity as such to be mere personal idiosyncrasy. There are, on the other hand, desirable individual differences which have been adopted not by chance nor through any mere wish to be different, but chosen consciously and on merit as the person has thought seriously of what is right and defensible. To build this kind of individuality is desirable and commendable creativeness. It not only enriches the quality of individual living, but helps also to raise the standard of group living. The rest of us admire this quality in the individual; we may indeed choose certain features for adoption ourselves. But such an admirably individual character will be among the first to acknowledge his indebtedness to others of the present or past for positive help and suggestion in the building of such a personality.

The more we consider the whole matter, the clearer it becomes that it is by grace of the culture, the social inheritance, that we live decently at all. In plain fact, without the cultural contribution we who now live would be but beasts, a kind of higher beast, if you will, capable of building a culture in generations of time; but until that had been achieved, we could be living only the lives of beasts, not of men as we now know human beings. And this means that for this decent living we are indebted to other men, to those creative ones among our ancestors who through the aeons of years of man's life on earth added now this and now that to the existing culture, eventually to build the cumulative whole thus far got together. To these creative ones and to others who were open-minded enough to appreciate and accept what the inventive ones had achieved—to these two groups each one of us owes the fact that we now live as civilized men. It is in this essential sense that each one of us is dependent on others for the most of what he values in life. Again is it true that no man liveth to himself alone.

OUR VERY SELFHOOD IS DEPENDENT ON OTHERS

But there is a further very significant respect in which man is, if possible, even more dependent on others, namely, for his very selfhood, for the psychological-moral characteristic which distinguishes him from brutes. Most people have thought but little about it; many of the technical psychology books ignore it; but the fact remains that no one is born a self—able to distinguish himself from others, able to recognize that he can effect things, able to think present, past, and future, able to accept personal responsibility for what he does. Such a selfhood, capable of so thinking and feeling, has to be achieved. Man alone has the mental ability to achieve it; no brute can achieve it, though under human tutelage some do approximate in slight measure certain of these distinctively human characteristics. But mere mental ability does not suffice; no individual man achieves his selfhood in its full sense except through association with others who have themselves already achieved such selfhood and so can foster its development in the growing child.* The process of building selfhood, while complex, is in its main outlines easy to see.

First of all, the child—and possibly also the highest brutes—tend to make a "thing" out of any sufficiently related aggregate of experiences. A child thus makes a thing out of his milk bottle experiences: it is first a thing to suck from; then, further, a thing also to feel and hold; then, still further, a thing to see; and finally a thing to name as the unified aggregate of all its meaning. The bottle

* For a fuller treatment than is here possible the reader is referred to the author's *Selfhood and Civilization* (New York, Macmillan, 1941); to George H. Mead, *Mind, Self, and Society* (Chicago, University of Chicago Press, 1934); and to J. Mark Baldwin, *Social and Ethical Interpretations* (New York, Macmillan, 1906).

being thus named, the child is then able to enter into more effective relations with other people. He can ask another to get him the bottle he sees; the other person is implied both in the making of the request and in the granting of it. The Gestalt psychology supports this tendency to make "things" by its doctrine that seeing "configurations" or "wholes" within experience is an inevitable and essential constituent of intelligent experiencing.

In this same way does a child make—at first but dimly—a whole (a thing) of his body, an analogous whole (or thing) of each body among the other people he sees, and—though at first very vaguely—a kind of unity of himself as feelings of hunger or pain and the like arise to demand his attention and as his crying brings the supporting attention of his mother. When this sense of himself as a whole has sufficiently developed, the child begins to relate this whole derived from his "internal" experience with what he knows "externally." His hand he can see from the *outside;* but he can also move it from the *inside*. Sister Mary also has a hand and she moves hers as he moves his. The two sets of childish hands look alike; but these are small, while Father's and Mother's hands are large. But they are all hands. And it is the same with feet, with legs, with arms, with fingers and toes. Further, he drinks milk, Mary drinks milk; he has a name, Mary has a name. He has toys—his toys—and Mary also has toys; and Mother will make Mary give him his toys and make him give Mary her toys. He falls and hurts his head and cries. Mary falls and cries, saying that she hurt her head. Mother says: "Poor Mary, she bumped her head and it hurts her just as yours hurt when you bumped yours."

In these various ways the child begins to relate what he feels on the inside with what appears on the outside, and eventually to see himself, inside and out, as one of those same moving things like Mary and Mother and Father: he has a head, Mary has a head; Mary cries when her head is hurt, he cries when his is hurt; he eats, Mary eats; he has little clothes, Mary has little clothes, Father and Mother have big clothes; Mary knows her clothes, he knows his clothes; Mary knows his clothes, he knows Mary's clothes; he has a little chair, Mary has a little chair, Father and Mother have big chairs. In short, he and Mary are, in our language, small editions of the same thing that older people are.

He begins thus to understand Mary, and less well Father and

Mother, by what he knows in himself of hunger and thirst and pain and of his control over "my" things. And also to understand himself better by what he sees in Mary and in her crying, in her doll playing, and in her eating. And the way the others talk in his presence about him and about Mary helps him in both these ways of understanding: of himself in terms of others, and of others in terms of himself.

He has now begun to form what we call his selfhood exactly by compounding into one these two sets of understanding. The self is thus a working psychological compound of (i) his self understood in terms of others and (ii) of others understood in terms of himself. It may help to say that the true self, the new selfhood, is a compound of a self-other understood self and of self-other understood others. Selfhood is thus doubly a self-other product.

It is out of this growing self-other compounded selfhood that the child builds the facts of conscious "agency" (that is, knowing that he can and does bring things to pass). He comes thus in time to *name* what he does and so to *think* that *he* is doing it. In this process, the social situation is a strong factor. "Look," he says, "look, Mamma." Or, "Let me do it myself." It is through such experiences that the conception of conscious "agency" is formed. As soon as this is accomplished, accountability follows. The child begins to hear, "Who did this?" And Mary will say, "John did it; I told him not to, but he kept on doing it." And Mother will hold John to account for having done it.

The place of language in all this process is very significant. To name whatever is under consideration helps to fasten thinking upon it. Attention to things thus seen and related through naming is the coordinating factor in conscious life. Mind is thus gradually accumulated in terms of conceptions, attitudes, behavior related to idea. For example, references to yesterday, to last week, to last year, to "when you were a baby," to next week, to next month, to "when we were at Grandmother's"—all these cumulatively build, on the one hand, the conception of time, and, on the other, the abiding unity of the self.

One of the most significant developments in connection with this growing selfhood is that of conscious intending. When awareness of "agency" has been reached, as discussed above, the child not only acts and effects—a dog also does the like in his way—but the child now knows—as a dog does not—that he is thus acting and effecting. He next will decide, intentionally, to do things he knows he can do; and he will be the more conscious of his intending if other people notice and take account of the results of his acts and of him as the worthy doer and creator of these results.

One final instance of the bearing on life of the self-other origin of the human personality can be seen in the nature of language as such. The essence of human speech is its self-conscious intent to influence others through the choice and use of appropriate words or signs. The fact of self-conscious intent to use means to achieve ends is peculiar to man, in keeping with the discussion above on the self-other composition of personality, so that language itself in its full sense is possible only for those growing up under the influence of others who have themselves already achieved selfhood. Thus again is man truly man in and through his use of language, and this in its turn is possible only because of the individual's social origin and setting.

At this point, some may wish to ask whether it is true that man alone has language. Is it not true that the hen calls to her chicks as her scratching turns up food? And does she not likewise give unmistakable notice to the other fowls when she sees a hawk? And can we deny that she *intends* her chicks to come and eat the food, and the other fowls to beware of the hawk? For all who know the habits of the barnyard fowl these questions seem plausible and demand our consideration.

To answer the implied argument, consider how a girl's blush differs from language, how her blush may tell us what she would prefer to hide; how in fact her words and her blushing may tell quite different stories: her words, what she wishes us to believe; her blush, what she cannot hide. The hen's call to her young as she scratches and her call to the other fowls regarding the hawk are like the girl's blush. Whether to hen or to girl, these calls all come alike as unbidden responses. A big dog will growl at a little dog and frighten him off. We are not to suppose that the big dog says to himself: "I want him to go away; if I growl fiercely enough, he will go away; so I will growl at him fiercely." No, the dog (it seems clear) does not so think; the sight of the little dog provokes his growl as your questioning makes Mary blush or as the sight of the hawk evokes the hen's warning cry. Similarly will a dog, when his long-absent master comes home, welcome him effusively, showing his gladness all over, his tail wagging furiously. The man sees it all, tail included, understands and appreciates the welcome. Did the dog say to himself, "If I wag my tail vigorously, he will see and appreciate my welcome"? Not at all. It is more probable that the dog did not know that his tail was wagging or even that he has a tail. He was glad, and the gladness, so to say, wagged the tail.

But man's speech, when it is full, true speech, is thought through in advance and chosen to have the desired effect. True enough, one may speak "before he thinks," or more precisely without adequate thinking, and afterwards regret his thoughtless words. But true com-munication, effected as well by a wink or a wave of the hand as by words, is thus a matter of conscious intent, possible only in its full sense in one who has achieved the self-other compounded selfhood. Thus it is that true language is limited to man.

Enough perhaps has now been said to show that the true human characteristics—use of language, conscious intent, conscious conveying of meaning, making responsible decisions, conscience, making distinctions between right and wrong, all the higher aspects of human life—are dependent on the achievement of self-other compounded selfhood; and this is possible in any full sense or degree only through associated living with others who have previously achieved it. Thus does the life of man as man, in its distinction from the merely animal life, depend on the fact of selfhood achieved by the cooperation of others.

The account of the wolf children of India* gives a vivid illustration of what happens when a human infant continues to live with only lower animal companionship. A missionary in India in the year 1920, we are told, took away from wolves two Indian children, one estimated to be about eight years old, the other perhaps a year and a half. The younger soon died, but the elder lived on for nine years in the missionary orphanage at Midnapore. When this Kamala, as the missionaries named her, was taken from the wolves, she had apparently been living for years with the wolves, so long as to show no trace of human rearing. She could neither stand nor walk as any eight-year-old child would, but ran wolf-like on all-

* J. A. L. Singh and Robert M. Zingg, *Wolf-Children and Feral Man* (New York, Harper's, 1942).

fours. She did not in any way use her hands for handling. She lapped water like a wolf and would not drink in any other way. She not only could not talk, but seemingly had no wish to communicate. She shunned humans, preferred darkness to light, ate carrion, and howled in the night after the manner of wolves. As later appeared, Kamala was innately a normal human being of apparently average ability; but when first taken from the wolves she showed exactly the lack of selfhood we have been discussing. To live for eight years does not of itself suffice to bring selfhood. Nor could selfhood come from association with beasts; it can only come by associated living with humans.

In these various ways have we seen how the human individual is not sufficient unto himself. To live in the true human sense each one must live along with his fellows; and in any successful living, each one profits by what he gets from others. Man is inherently and inextricably social in nature. No one lives to himself alone, nor can he if he is to live well. And each one who is fully human includes as an essential part of his fuller being many elements that must come from others: one's very selfhood depends on the essential contribution of others. In these various respects must we understand and accept the social nature of man.

Philosophies of life and of education which give full recognition to this social nature of the human individual are very different from what they would otherwise be. They recognize that the characteristics of the individual are not fixed, but develop instead—on the basis of his own biological inheritance, it is true—according to the opportunities his cultural environment provides. They see that the child who comes to school has grown thus far according to the environment with which he has interacted. They see also that the school, including the insight and understanding of teachers, principal, staff, is part of that cultural environment and that the child's growth from now on depends on the quality of the school environment. They realize, as we shall later discuss, that respect for personality means that opportunity and challenge must be provided to bring out the best in each child. The correlative demands on education are many and clear. Education must be a social process, on the procedural side; and it must aim to bring high-quality social living into effect. These matters are discussed at length in Part II.

CHAPTER IV. *Institutions: Their Nature and Service; The Nature of Rights*

THE preceding chapter showed that only by grace of accumulated culture do men live civilized lives. Let us take now for closer study an important part of this culture, namely, all those social arrangements and commonly accepted understandings—our institutions we shall call them—whereby men order and arrange their mutual interactions in society so as to live better together.

Whenever or wherever human living is studied, there will be found already in operation various customs, laws, regulations, rights, understandings—social arrangements of many varied kinds built up to help people live better together under the conditions then existing. All such social arrangements for regulating the behavior of people with regard to each other, with the intent of thus carrying on life better, we shall here call institutions. (The term is here used in its broad and inclusive sense in contrast with the narrower sense often used to designate certain more important of these social arrangements.) It is by studying these "institutions," these accepted ways of living together and of regulating the resulting common life, that the cultural patterns, the thought patterns, the aims, the ideals of a people, can be seen at work.

HOW TO STUDY INSTITUTIONS

Attention is called to the method stated in the preceding paragraph, that of beginning any study with what is already at work in that area. This will be a fundamental characteristic of the study of philosophy as followed in this book. We do not begin at the beginning of life or of the world; we know too little of what happened then. We do not ask the fundamental purpose of the universe;

we do not know enough about that to begin with it. We do not try to begin at the bottom; we cannot with any certainty dig down far enough to find the bottom. Instead of any of these, we start, as it were, in the middle, where life is now going on. We study what we find there in order to see how life goes on, and to find how to make it go on better. In this way we keep our feet always on the ground. This means that we study inductively—find our ideals, for example, by comparing differing outcomes so as to form a better notion of what to wish and what to work for. For by ideals are meant the most promising goals we can find to pursue. Facts, as distinguished from ideals, give us the necessary conditions to use in pursuit of ideals, tell us whether we are succeeding as we pursue them, and—at times—tell us that we were mistaken in adopting those ideas as ideals. Thus to study institutions we study them "operationally"—as they operate in society today and as people operate with reference to them.

INSTITUTIONS MUST FIT CONDITIONS OF LIFE AND MUST CHANGE AS CONDITIONS CHANGE

To live well men must live in society. This seems clear from two considerations: that men wherever found are living together in society, and that, as shown in Chapter III, man needs other humans in order to develop his full potentialities as man. If men must live in society, each society with its own customs and institutions, an abiding problem appears: how to keep the institutions abreast of the changing conditions or how otherwise to improve institutions to make them serve better. For the institutions, the social arrangements for living well together, must always fit the actual conditions and time in which men live.

How institutions have in fact grown out of actual living conditions is a very interesting and instructive study. In the dawn of civilization, Egypt, it appears, led in the development of culture, because it was protected by sea and desert from hostile tribes and so could give attention, generation after generation, to the building of ever better ways of living. Until recently the island status of Great Britain protected it similarly from attacks from the Continent so that it could from this vantage point develop through the centuries a parliamentary government and greater freedom for the people. France was in this respect not so fortunate, and Germany still less so.

But now the situation seems everywhere different. Until World War II, Great Britain, with its powerful navy, and we of America, through the shelter of the oceans, could feel secure against attack; but now with the airplane, the rocket bomb, and—worst of all—the atom bomb, no country is secure. War has become a crucial danger to civilization and must be abolished if intelligence can effect it. World institutions and a world conscience seem the only way out. Thus has the United Nations—a new institution—come into being, and we must all support it.

In less spectacular ways than these have other new conditions brought other new institutions. The discovery of vaccination brought in time laws compelling all school children to be vaccinated. The coming of the automobile brought traffic regulations, new type roads, Federal aid and direction of important road building, new taxation to support the new roads, and the yet unsolved problem of parking in a way not to obstruct traffic. Always, whether on a grand scale or small, must the conditions of living determine the kind of institutions needed. And if conditions of living change enough, the correlative institutions must change too. This problem of change we postpone for the moment. Now we turn back in history to a problem of theory.

THE RIGHT OF INSTITUTIONS TO BE AND TO CONTROL

In studying the history of human institutions it is not a little surprising to find how men have disputed as to what gives an institution its right to be and to command obedience. In the Middle Ages authoritarianism reigned supreme. In that day all rights were derived, directly or indirectly, either from the king, who was supposed to rule by divine right, or from the church, which was supposed to represent a more direct divine authority. Final right in certain matters was in dispute. A university, for example, might get its charter—its right to be and act—from either king or Pope. From its charter rights a university could grant degrees, which carried the right to teach.

Later, in the seventeenth century, when Charles I, his divine right being denied, was beheaded, Thomas Hobbes (1588–1679) undertook to re-establish the royal authority on grounds other than the "divine" right (in which Hobbes did not believe). He imagined that originally men did not live in society, but as separate individuals, each possessing all rights in himself and exercising them so far as he could against all others. Such a turbulent state of affairs Hobbes described as *bellum omnium contra omnes* (war of all against all) and the resulting life he saw as "solitary, poor, nasty, brutish, and short." Then men, so he further thought, tiring at length of such an unsatisfactory life, came together by nations, and formed, each nation for itself, a "social compact" whereby one man was designated as king and all the rest gave irrevocably into his keeping all the rights they had theretofore individually held. Thus, for Hobbes, monarchy came into existence by social compact; and the monarchy was absolute, for the compact was irrevocable.

Modern anthropologists in their study of primitive peoples know of no such period of purely individualistic life; nor are they disposed to accept such a single authoritative act as founding monarchy among men. And modern social theorists would reject any claim to authority based on such an alleged happening. But we can all join in approving Hobbes's picture of what a society would be without laws to govern it. His words as quoted are indeed aptly chosen.

Later when Charles II, in the eyes of the British majority, turned out not too well and his brother James II much worse, there came the Revolution of 1688; as a result, Parliament, elected by the authorized voters and acting in their behalf, changed by its own law the right of royal succession and brought William and Mary to the throne.

This revolution John Locke (1632–1704) sought to justify, and to this end proposed a revised social compact theory. In this, according to Locke, when the "compact" was formed and the monarchy established, the people had kept back certain "inalienable rights," chief among which was the right to change the government whenever this should seem advisable to the voters. To Americans of today Locke's idea seems more defensible than Hobbes's, partly because it seems more reasonable, partly (some would say) because we are used to the idea. For our own Revolution of 1776 was fought on Locke's theory which appears specifically in Jefferson's wording of the Declaration of Independence.

In this study we cannot, of course, accept a legendary origin or authority for any institution. This leaves us then with the two questions: (i) How did our various institutions come into existence? And (ii) on what grounds can they claim authority over man's acts?

As an illustration, consider the modern practice of using traffic lights. Is such a practice right? What makes it right? And what gives it authority to govern me when I do not wish to obey it?

There appear two lines of argument, the one more general, the other more particular. The more general inquires into the justification of government as such to exist to enforce law and order; the more specific, into the rightness of this particular traffic law.

THE AUTHORITY OF GOVERNMENT

Let us begin with the more general, as to the justification of government to rule, with its laws and its orderly process of making necessary arrangements. An alternative to government would be to leave to each person to decide what he will do and to let him do what he will. When, however, we think of actual thieves and robbers and murderers ready to take advantage of such a situation, it is at once apparent that, as matters now stand, police and laws and courts are necessary to protect us against all such. If we consider further such matters as streets, roads, street lights, water systems, sewers and the like, it is again apparent that we need government either to supply these wants or to see that they are supplied according to proper standards. Such considerations—and there are many more than could here be named—suffice to show that we need government with its orderly processes of making needed social arrangements. And the fundamental reason for having such social arrangements and obeying them is that *with them we live better than without them.*

There are of course many questions which we now postpone, such as the type of government needed, whether monarchy or democracy or whatever, the limitations properly to be put upon governmental action, and the like. All that is necessary for present purposes is to see that some government is essential if men are to live well together. Law and order are necessary to decent living, and for these government is necessary.

THE RIGHTNESS OF TRAFFIC LIGHTS

Now for the particular question, the rightness or wrongness of traffic lights. Having granted the right of government to exist and to make regulations for governing human relations, some might say this suffices for the traffic lights; if the government establishes traffic lights, it is law and that ends it. We would here agree, following the preceding general discussion, that the existence of a law establishing traffic lights gives a presumption in their favor. But laws can be wrong. What we wish here to know is the rightness of this specific law. And it will not suffice to say that the Constitution authorizes the legislature to pass such a law. We will, if necessary, question the wisdom of the legislature and even question the Constitution. We want to get down to the fundamentals that underlie all—law, legislature, and Constitution. Is such a traffic light regulation right? If yes, what makes it right?

The question again turns on the bearing of the lights on the life of the people. Are there conditions of traffic such that the movement of traffic and pedestrians will be helped by the existence of lights? And do the advantages of such regulation outweigh the disadvantages? If yes, then traffic lights are authorized and perhaps required, depending on the degree of advantage over disadvantage. Traffic lights everywhere? At every corner in every village in the land? No; there are plenty of places where traffic lights are not needed. But where they are needed to make life better, yes; there traffic lights are authorized, to be supplied and operated by the authorities and obeyed by the people.

SUMMARY REGARDING THE JUSTIFICATION AND AUTHORITY OF INSTITUTIONS

It is in the way described and with the basis of justification just stated that our regulatory social arrangements—our institutions in the general sense named above—come into existence and demand our support and obedience: *they serve the needs of society*, that is, *they make life better on the whole for all who are affected.*

Is this sufficient justification for any given institution? The answer is yes: if there is real need for this specific institution, that is sufficient justification. And it may be added that the final test is not external to the situation, but internal and inherent in the situation, namely, by the way the institution works. The justifying test is that the total advantages surpass the total disadvantages sufficiently to warrant the expense and effort and annoyance necessarily incurred; and these are practical matters that can be seen by men. The final test always is life itself, that it is made better.

And are men under personal obligation to uphold law and order, to obey the laws duly made? While there is more to be said later in detail, the answer here is yes. If men live better, all things considered, by having a certain regulation to live by, then, once the regulation is duly made, men are under obligation to obey that regulation.

So much so far regarding institutions. They are man-made. They exist to serve. In the degree that the advantages of the arrangement surpass the disadvantages, all things considered, in like degree is that arrangement socially justified and even demanded. For—like all other things that are man-made—institutions are not created out of nothing. On the contrary, they are—and must be—the correlatives of situations that call them forth, of the situation they would serve. In fact, if they are well made, they may be said to be demanded by the situation, man's part then being the creative insight to see what the situation really needs.

In the case of any particular institution many questions must be answered—or answers must be assumed—before advantages and disadvantages can be assessed. Here little more can be done than to raise the questions; answers must come later. One such question is: Advantage how? Better for what? The answer: For the life good to live—to be discussed in a chapter on "The Life Good to Live." Another question is: Advantage to whom? Answer (the democratic answer): To all concerned on terms of ethical equality. Just what this means will be discussed in later chapters on morality and democracy. The question of how to measure or assess advantage and disadvantage must be left to the exigencies of the particular situation.

The principle, however, for the justification of any proposed institution remains as stated above: it is justified by the service it performs; with it we live better than without it. Common sense, critically used, must apply the principle.

THE ORIGIN AND NATURE OF RIGHTS

The foregoing discussion on the justification of social institutions leads almost inevitably to a consideration of rights as such, their nature and origin. A right is of course an institution, a particular kind of institution; it is such an understanding among the members of the social group as lets each one know what he can demand for himself and expect from others; for example, the right to own property, the right to exclude outsiders from one's home. The dictionary defines a right as a just or legal claim, a claim that is ethically right and proper. How have rights originated? What gives to rights their authority? Are there absolute rights?

A bit of history may help. John Locke, as we earlier saw, in his effort to defend the English Revolution of 1688, asserted that certain rights are essential to the proper working of citizen personality, that such rights are therefore "natural," given by the nature of the universe, and so cannot be set aside ("alienated") either by the action of the person himself or of the government. Thomas Jefferson, it seems clear, was much indebted to Locke for the doctrines expressed in the Declaration of Independence. Note how these words repeat Locke's doctrine of inalienable rights: "We hold these truths to be self-evident, that all men are created equal,* that they are endowed by their Creator with certain unalienable rights, that among these are life, liberty, and the pursuit of happiness. That to secure these rights governments are instituted."

Since Jefferson was in religious belief what is often called a Deist, he could write "laws of nature and of nature's God" and mean "natural" laws or rights. In the next chapter we shall see how Plato had given to the world the conception just stated, namely, of ideal patterns of thought and action, eternal and unchanging, the "eternal verities" they were later called. The "laws of nature," as these were understood and accepted by scientists until Einstein, were clear instances of the Platonic "ideas." Plato had said these ideas were "laid up in heaven." The early church fathers, accepting the notion from Plato, said they were ordained of God from before the foundation of the earth. From either point of view

* Jefferson's original draft had "free and equal"; Locke had written "free, equal, and independent" (104: Bk. II, ch. viii, 95).

they were viewed as metaphysical absolutes, timeless and unchangeable. It was in exactly this way that Locke and Jefferson conceived these natural rights which antedated government. In fact, as Jefferson said, it was "to secure these rights" that "governments are instituted."

It may further be remarked, as will later be considered, that before inductive science had upset the *a priori* method of argument these Platonic patterns or "ideas" as metaphysical absolutes furnished the bases from which propositions of law, philosophy, or theology were in general deductively "proved." As discussed earlier, Euclid's geometry was the supreme instance of this deductive *a priori* reasoning, and counted (until 1829) to be absolutely true, the surest truth that man as man had acquired. It was apparently on this Euclidean basis that Jefferson built his logic for the Declaration of Independence: "We hold these truths to be self-evident"—like the axioms in geometry.

Can these rights be accepted as axiomatic or "self-evident," as instances of Plato's "eternal verities" and consequently as metaphysical, *a priori* absolutes? An increasingly negative answer is returned by those who study the question. From the study of anthropology and history, it now seems clear that these so-called "natural" or inalienable rights are the product of long human experience, derived inductively as we considered in Chapter III. As "rights" they were formulated, we must believe, by certain more penetrating minds probably from already existent "trial-and-error" practices more or less crystallized as custom and thereafter subjected through the long years to critical observation as to how well they worked, "all things" considered. Those that thus stood the test have been accepted as "rights" upon which men could rely, rights that others must admit and the courts would recognize.

It may be added, before leaving the question of the validity of asserted "natural" rights, that history shows small ground for accepting as satisfactory proof what any particular age calls "self-evident." A 1566 confession of faith counted that all men are "sunk in depraved desires, averse to good, inclined to every evil, full of every wickedness . . . unable to do or even think any good." (75: ch. 8) And as fine a man as Leibnitz could say of vindictive punishment, though it "aims neither at amendment of the criminal, nor at furnishing an example to others nor at the reparation of an injury," is still "founded in the fitness of things, and satisfies not only the offended party, but all wise on-lookers, even as beautiful music or a fine piece of architecture satisfies a well constituted mind." (qtd. in 87:26)

The final question here asked regarding rights is whether certain rights are to be counted as absolute, that is, as always and absolutely right and authoritative. It seems clear that the answer is no. For example, up to the second quarter of the nineteenth century an employer had the "right" to work his employees twelve or more hours a day and few questioned that he had this "right." Nowadays few would publicly uphold such a right. But to go back to Jefferson's statement that "all men are created equal." As he wrote this, neither he nor the others who accepted the doctrine included woman within its scope. Did they then take "men" in the sentence quoted as literally masculine? It seems more probable that the term *men* meant all humans; but even so the authors of the Declaration did not in any full or active sense mean to include women among the legal voters. It was not until 1920 that our national government did so include women as its recognized voters. In other words, it took a century and a half for this right, which is inalienable, according to both Jefferson and Locke, to be widened sufficiently in this country to include women. It is not unlikely that these leaders, if they had been pressed, would have replied as did a certain American judge paraphrasing Blackstone: "The husband and the wife are one and the husband is that one."

Are there absolute rights? No! Rights in any practicable sense have invariably been interpreted at any one time to fit the accepted doctrine of that time. There are very few if any rights which have not through the years been changed both as to boundaries and content, as times have changed or insight and sensitivity have grown. What the future will bring, no one knows.

For behavior purposes any particular right is a principle of action; but in action rights may, and often do, conflict. Take liberty or freedom, for example, certified as an inalienable right by the Declaration of Independence. This is certainly no absolute right; it may easily conflict with other rights. My right to liberty does not permit me to deprive you of your life or even of your happiness. As Norman Angell (1874–   ) says, "When all demand complete freedom, none has any." (123: Mar. 1, 1942) Or as J. T. Shotwell

(1874–) says, "Freedom is . . . another name for the equilibrium we call justice." (83:272) To the same effect, Edmund Burke (1729–1797) said in 1774:

> The only liberty I mean, is a liberty connected with order; that not only exists along with order and virtue, but which cannot exist at all without them (17:I:441).

As with liberty so with other rights; no one right can claim to be absolute or unchanging. A right is, as stated, a principle of action and so has been built inductively from past experience. Like all principles, it is to be used as an hypothesis, to be taken duly into account, along with all other principles (rights) involved, in seeking that course of action under any given set of conditions which by its total consequences promises best to take care of all the values (rights) involved. It was in the light of such considerations that Phillips Brooks (1835–1893) said, "No man has a right to all his rights." To treat principles and rights as absolute easily opens the door to fanaticism. In fact, to use rights and principles as absolutes often, perhaps generally, leads to their fanatical use.

A CHANGING WORLD DEMANDS CONTINUALLY GROWING INSTITUTIONS

We saw above that any institution, in order to render proper service, must fit the conditions of life then prevailing. The point can hardly be overemphasized, though the principle would deny useless institutional changes as strongly as it demands useful changes. If at any time the original conditions change sufficiently, the institutions built to fit those conditions must themselves be changed to fit the new demands. If the institution is really needed, it should be kept properly abreast of the need.

The term "continually growing institutions" in the heading above perhaps deserves a passing word. This is here used in its dynamic sense to imply continuity amid change. In the degree that the demand which brought forth an institution points to an abiding need in social life, in like degree may the institution be expected to continue, however greatly the conditions of surrounding life may change. But when the changes are sufficient to warrant it, the institution must change enough of its structure, and perhaps somewhat of its original aim. in order to meet the new demands. It is this kind of continuity amid change which authorizes the words "continually growing."

These matters, for example, were not well understood at the time of the French Revolution, when indeed the very conception of the existence and functioning of the culture as above discussed had not been achieved; so that the Revolution was too much conducted on the impossible idea of wiping the slate clean and writing a quite new civilization. Rebuilding any civilization is like rebuilding the house in which the family must meanwhile continue to live: enough continuity must be maintained with the situation hitherto prevailing to permit at one and the same time both the continuance of present living and the current remaking of the otherwise obsolescent institution.

These considerations in no sense uphold the kind of conservation which as reaction would deny a necessary change. They do, however, indicate the existence of a true problem in connection with more fundamental changes. Many immigrant children among us, for example, give up the culture of their parents before they have sufficiently lived the American culture to acquire it effectively; they are therein hurt. The like holds of certain "backward" people in other parts of the world; they have given up their old culture before they have sufficiently digested the new. They thus suffer demoralization, which can be a very serious hurt. The desired formula seems to be: such wise growing as permits adequate continuity amid change.

THE FINAL TEST OF AN INSTITUTION: ITS WIDER INFLUENCE

In considering the tests an institution must meet to be acceptable such phrases as the following were used: "help men live well together," "advantages must outweigh disadvantages," "all effects considered," "all men thereby affected." It is important in connection to note that the indirect and often unintended effects of an institution may be just as significant as the more direct and consciously sought outcomes, at times even more significant. By indirect influences of an institution we mean, for example, the educative effects of a railroad as contrasted with its direct service in hauling freight and passengers. Before the automobile, the radio, and the airplane, the railroad brought very significant educative effects to those living within close reach in comparison with those who lived at great distances. Similarly the moving pictures have brought the prevailing fashions in feminine dress from the city centers to the remotest parts of our country, with notable effects in the appearance of remote country women.

And all these additional effects, so to call them, must be included under "advantages" or "disadvantages," as the case may be. They are to be included among "all effects considered"; and any persons affected by them must be included among "all men thereby affected."

When we consider Ruskin's statement that "there is no wealth but life," we begin to see that all goods, whether material or immaterial, are valuable only as they enhance life. When we consider further that men live as they themselves at bottom are; that this selfhood, this personality, which is thus to decide how one lives and what he gets out of life, is itself always in active process of change, always coming either into fuller being and proportions or into less adequate outlook; and that each experience undergone thus leaves its irrevocable effect to build this individual either up or down—when we consider these things, we will more readily agree with John Dewey that the bearing of an institution on the personalities it affects constitutes the chief test of its fitness to be:

> Just what response does *this* social arrangement, political or economic, evoke, and what effect does it have upon the disposition of those who engage in it? Does it release capacity? If so, how widely? Among a few, with a corresponding depression in others, or in an extensive and equitable way. . . . Are men's senses rendered more delicately sensitive and appreciative, or are they blunted and dulled by this and that form of social organization? . . . Is curiosity awakened or blunted? What is its quality: is it merely esthetic, dwelling on the forms and surfaces of things; or is it also intellectual, searching into their meaning? (52:197)*

The principle here under consideration can be so restated as to make more explicit its bearing in a philosophy of education. By education we mean the cumulative effect of all the successive learning experiences one undergoes. At the moment our concern is the educa-

* John Dewey, *Reconstruction in Philosophy*. Copyright 1948 by Beacon Press, Boston, Mass., and used by their permission.

tive effect of social institutions. Thus, to restate the principle, it can be said unequivocally that *the best single measure of an institution's fitness to serve and to survive*—whether the institution be a government, a railroad, the cinema, an art museum, a law, a newspaper, a city slum, the right to own property, the T.V.A.—*is the total educative effect of that institution on the living of human beings.*

CHAPTER V. *Change: Old Conception vs. New; Significance of the Shift*

THE contrast between the way change was conceived in the pre-scientific days and the way it is now conceived is very great. The difference is especially significant in our present ways of thinking. Let us first get a preliminary view of the matter.

CHANGE IN THE OLD DAYS VS. NOW

In the days before modern science, so few new ways of carrying on life appeared in any ordinary generation that grandparents not only saw their children repeat their own lives but in turn teach grandchildren what the grandparents had taught: to make clothes of the same material and cut (no changes in style), to prepare the same foods in the same or like pots and pans, to serve this same food in the same way in the same kind of dishes, to eat at the same hours (or lack of hours), to cultivate the same crops in the same way and with the same tools, to follow the same artisan trades using the same tools to turn out the same products, to adhere to the same religious ideas and forms, the same folk festivals, the same sort of government, with nearly the same laws, the same methods of communication and transportation (with, however, very few distant journeys). Even today in many regions unchanging custom is still powerful. Among the farmers of India one can find plows of a kind in use for 3,000 years. In Egypt some still use hand methods of raising Nile water for irrigation that were common when the pyramids were being built.

In those early days almost nothing happened to change the culture. The people living at any one time saw changes, but not of a kind to bring new or different ways of living. The changes they saw were such as marriage, births, growing older, disease, death, accidents, quarrels, the wearing out of clothes, the breaking of tools, rain, snow, storms. That there could be what we now think of as progress —any progressive cumulative change in the culture—was then inconceivable even to the best minds. Marcus Aurelius used these words:

> The rational soul . . . traverses the whole universe . . . stretches out into infinite time, comprehends and considers the periodical death and rebirth of all things, and discerns that the men who come after us shall see no new thing, and that they who lived before us saw nothing more than we, but that, so to say, every man who reaches two score years . . . has contemplated all things past and all things future in virtue of the law of uniformity (109:xi, 1).

Of course, with a long enough sweep of historic time we with our present knowledge can find many evidences of change that did come to that historic culture; but, strange as it may seem, it was not until the eighteenth century that men began to think of the kind of change in the culture we now call progress.

Since the Middle Ages many factors have introduced changes, but the most potent factor to break the hold of concrete tradition—blind, binding tradition—has been modern technology working in cooperation with other applications of science. At the beginning of our Republic nine tenths of our people lived on farms. Now one third of this number using modern machinery and other modern ideas suffice to raise our necessary foodstuffs. The other two thirds are at work in largely new ways, and life can thereby be the richer. Industrial life has moved people from the farm to the city, where they have had to learn new ways of making a living and have learned new ways to live. The automobile, the moving pictures, the radio, make a new world; and the whole country now shares almost simultaneously in the same new ideas.

The better to sense the change, go back to the beginning of this section. There in one detailed sentence the word "same" is used eighteen times to describe the similarity of any one generation of that prescientific period with its predecessor. In our day the word "different" would have to be used in almost every one of these specific instances to describe the relation of the present generation to its predecessor: different houses in different localities, different furniture (different often in kind, nearly always in looks), different clothes, of different material and cut (with different styles continually being introduced), different foods prepared in different kinds of pots and pans and cooked on different kinds of stoves with often different kinds of fuel, eaten at different hours, differently served, in different looking dishes, different ways of cultivating both the same and different crops, many different farm tools, many different trades using new and different tools, different religious ideas (though often expressed through the same words and forms), some new and different folk festivals, old ones differently celebrated, a different kind of government (much restricted by the old structural machinery), very different transportation and communication.

Henry Adams, discussing the changes he had himself seen since his boyhood, said:

> In essentials like religion, ethics, philosophy; in history, literature, art; in the concepts of all science, except perhaps mathematics, the American boy of 1854 stood nearer to the year 1 than to the year 1900 (2:53).

and J. B. S. Haldane, writing in 1930 on the same topic, said:

> Today the external conditions of life in civilized communities differ more from those of 1830 than did the conditions of 1830 from those at the time of Noah's flood (71:CLXI:474*f*).

The factor of change has thus become a pervading factor in modern life.

CONTINUAL NOVELTY: EACH EVENT UNIQUE; EACH OUTCOME UNCERTAIN

If we look closely enough at the spectacle of modern rapid change, we see that in our kind of world we face continual novelty. Each event is unique; it never happened before and will never happen, precisely so, again. Under such circumstances we never know for certain and exactly just what to expect. Our world of affairs develops in ever novel and precarious fashion.

Is it true that each event is unique? What about the "uniformities of nature"? Do they not repeat themselves? The answer to the last question is that these uniformities are constituent parts of events, not the events themselves. When Galileo dropped the two balls from the Leaning Tower and the University men, looking on, saw the balls hit the ground together—that whole scene and occasion was (if we accept it as true) an event, a very dramatic event. The falling of the balls together was only part of that historic event—the crucial part, to be sure, but still part only. That event as a whole had certainly never happened before. And that particular event, considering how it came about, what people felt to be at stake, how they all felt about it—that precise event could not possibly be repeated. Suppose the group present had refused to accept the verdict of their eyes and demanded that the experiment be repeated, would the repetition of the experiment have repeated that first event? Innumerable aspects of the second trial would have differed from the first trial; but even if all repeatable aspects had miraculously been the same, it would still have been a different event. The fact that it was a second trial would alone have sufficed to make of it a different event.

The same argument holds, if we look closely enough, for any other event, however trivial. Its repetition is, if nothing else, a repetition; and that makes it a different event. In other words, an event is an event in its setting; and the setting as such can never be the same as it was before.

It is under such circumstances that the stream of affairs develops novelly and must so develop. Here is Mr. Brown, the most methodical business man in the world, if you will. His secretary says she can expect him to enter the outer office at 9:57 A.M. every work day of the year. But does his secretary know that he will come tomorrow morning at 9:57? She does not. Mr. Brown cannot control the railroad or always get a taxi at once; and people, old friends whom he cannot spurn, will stop him in the outer hall. So that in fact his secretary does not know *exactly* when to expect him.

But the unpredictability of Mr. Brown's coming today is but minor in comparison with the unpredictable nature of his business itself. Business conditions vary; Congress is unpredictable; so also is the foreign field. His rivals, too, develop in unexpected ways. And the event is always precarious. When Mr. Brown writes a letter, he does not *know* what effect it will have. For "know" is a strong word. He does feel sure of some things; others he is less sure about; still others are little better than a gamble. As he plans in his office, he does not *know* what may happen in the business world before his plans are realized; that tariff bill he fears may upset his business.

How, then, does a man work when he doesn't know what is going to happen? The answer is that he works on probability. He uses his best judgment, and bets his prospects on his judgment. This again is life. It is so with everyone who carries on affairs. It is so with the farmer; it is so with the business man; it is so with the physician; it is emphatically so with the statesman, with the parent, and with the teacher. We plan as best we can; we do our best; the precise results we never beforehand can know. The event is forever uncertain.

THE NEW VS. THE OLD LOGIC OF CHANGE

Let us now dig a little deeper into theories of change and examine specifically the shift that has come into the logic of change.

It was the Greeks, chiefly Plato (427?–347 B.C.) and Aristotle (384–322 B.C.), who gave to the world the old doctrine of change—or rather of no change. This doctrine, as a metaphysical *a priori* absolute, largely dominated Western thought from its inception until modern science came to modify that thought radically. While this revolution in thought has in certain areas progressed far, we are none the less even yet in the midst of the shift from the old to the new. In many aspects of life, particularly where conservative influence is strong, we still find the old ideas well intrenched. To understand the fundamental difference between the old and the new attitudes toward change becomes thus our first task.

Change, as Plato and Aristotle saw it, was either relatively trivial and accidental, or it was regular and so predictable. The trivial changes were largely "sublunary," that is, belonged on this side of the moon and seemed to the Greeks to be traceable to matter and those aspects of human behavior attributable to the body or to matter. Clouds, for instance, come and go, winds blow and shift and cease, rains and snow come and go; men are born, grow up, live each his kind of life, and die; clothes wear out; wars arise; governments come and go. The regular changes take place above or beyond the moon and were counted to be divine, at least so in some sense: for example, the succession of night and day, the seasons, the length of the year, the annual movement of the zodiac, the diurnal motion of the fixed stars. This last was to the Greeks the most impressive of all. Absolutely without irregularity (so far as they saw) the stars turned in their daily courses; the sphere of the fixed stars seemed more divine, less fallible, than anything else observable to men. In between the quite irregular and the quite regular were such matters as the movements of the moon and the planets, and the growth of animals and plants.

Like all significant philosophers, Plato directed his thinking to the strategic problems of his day. His period was one of disquieting confusion and change, social, political, intellectual. What seemed to him most needed was social order and stability based on justice; for otherwise nothing could either satisfy or last. On many points of Plato's thought current opinions differ; but his principal doctrine stands fairly clear, at least as received through the ages. Back of all shifting *phenomena* stood the *noumena*, the ideal patterns of what should prevail. These he called *ideas*. They were eternal and unchanging. The "laws of nature," as these were until recently conceived by scientists, give an excellent illustration of what Plato had in mind. The early church fathers, as we shall in a moment see, accepted these Platonic ideas as ordained of God from before the foundation of the world—Plato himself had said they were "laid up in heaven."

It was for Plato the duty and business of man to find these ideal patterns and then follow them. To know these patterns was to know the truth; to think them was to be wise; to obey them was to be virtuous; to manifest and appreciate them in the esthetic realm was to exhibit and enjoy beauty. Later thought summed up all these things under the trilogy of the good, the beautiful, and the true. Thus were Plato's system of absolute and unchanging "ideas"—patterns, laws—and the acceptance of their supremacy his answer to the problems of his troubled world.

Aristotle, in a sense, took up where Plato left off, but from another angle. Where Plato dealt with the ideal and the *a priori*, Aristotle was scientific (in the modern sense) and inductive in his personal search for truth. However, the only logic he formulated was the classical deductive kind, which thereafter reigned supreme as the sole system to be taught until John Stuart Mill (1806–1873) formulated the study of modern inductive logic. Aristotle's chief interest, perhaps, was biology. He noticed, what common sense had always known, that each plant and each animal propagated itself after its kind. This kind, or species, or form (εἶδος), was to Aristotle an instance of Plato's absolutes. While individual plants and animals, owing to outside influence, showed each its individual variation, still the abiding species ruled. And the word *rule* in this connection was to Aristotle no metaphor. The species as a spiritual pattern was in the seed literally, controlling its growth at every stage; this pattern took hold of the appropriate stuff—stored-up meat of the seed, soil, moisture, sunlight—and molded all of this to its form, to its pattern.*

When the early church fathers came to formulate the Christian doctrines, they themselves thought in terms of this prevailing Greek philosophy, which had been spread from Athens to Alexandria and other centers throughout the ancient classical world. These fathers chose neo-Platonism—a then current development from Plato—as to them the most usable philosophy at hand, and formulated their doctrines in terms of this as best they could. For in that day and time to be mentally alert and to philosophize in Greek thought meant about the same. The fourth gospel specifically shows this Greek influence. The term *Word* or *Logos* there used is taken exactly from Philo, who in this respect anticipated neo-Platonism. In such ways were the formulated statements of the original church doctrine indirectly based on Plato.

* Many of the words that Aristotle used to describe this phenomenon remain with us today as essential parts of every civilized language. The original seed—whether this term be applied to plant or animal or used in some metaphorical sense—he called dynamis (δύναμις, Latin *potentia*), whence we get our words dynamic and potential. The end product of growth he called entelechy (ἐντελέχεια), a word not now much used in common speech; and the movement from dynamis to entelechy he called kinesis (κίνησις) or energeia (ἐνέργεια), and from these we get kinetic and energy. When the process from *dynamis* to *entelechy* was full, exact, complete, it was called (in Latin) *perfectus* (done through, carried through to the final end), from which we get our English word *perfect*.

There could be successive applications of this teleology (as it is called). The acorn could grow into the full-grown oak; here acorn is dynamis, and oak, entelechy. Then the oak could be sawed into lumber; here tree trunk is dynamis and lumber is the entelechy. Then the oak planks could be made into a desk, with planks and perfected desk respectively dynamis and entelechy. Then I as author may write on this desk to turn out the book which you now read. Here the desk is dynamis and the resulting ms. is entelechy, and so on through other instances until we have as the end result the printed book. This when studied by you as prospective teacher is again dynamis, and what it becomes as thought in your mind is entelechy. This in turn is dynamis as you use it with your students, and they become entelechy to you through your kinetic and energetic efforts. Each instance of kinesis (ideally at any rate) gives a movement from a more material to a more spiritual end until ultimately, so Aristotle thought, God is reached as *actus purus*, pure activity, with no matter involved at all.

During the middle ages when, thanks to the Crusades and the Arabs, the fuller Aristotle had been recovered for European thought, the Christian doctrine was reformulated, most fully by Thomas Aquinas, in terms of Aristotle's logic. It suited the medieval mind and attitude to ignore Aristotle's personal inductive method of study—he had used this, but had not formulated it in his writings—and to center on his logic and his teleology, including the fixed and absolute character of the biological species. With Plato and Aristotle both emphasizing static and absolute ideas as basic to thought, it is easy to see how the medieval mind would seize on both as underwriting what it had other reasons for wishing: an unchanging feudal system to govern the secular affairs of men and an unchanging system of theology embodying an authoritative and unchanging creed. Plato recognized different levels of status among men as regards governing, and Aristotle explicitly asserted that some men are by nature slaves. Both thus supported feudalism. So from the point of view of both church and state the Greek thought was congenial. The theologians were the schoolmasters of that day and they adopted the *a priori* method of reasoning as laid down in Aristotle's logic. Everything was thought through to reasonable consistency on this basis. The Protestant Revolt did not, in theory, change from this. So Plato and Aristotle, with the system of ideal patterns and fixed species, ruled the world until the coming of modern science; and in many respects ruled much later even in science, as for example, in biology until Darwin (1809–1882) and in physics until Einstein (1879–   ).

It will be recalled that Aristotle was most explicit on the eternal and unchanging nature of each biologic species. When therefore Darwin in 1859 published his *Origin of Species*, it would have been impossible to state a more absolute conflict than that between the philosophic thought previously dominant and the succinct title of this book. While the theological opposition to Darwin was perhaps the most vocal of all, the deeper conflict was in philosophy. Change was now explicitly asserted, where formerly it had been most explicitly denied. If natural species are not eternal and unchanging, but have come gradually into existence in the course of geologic time—if such ideas be accepted as true—a revolution in thought had indeed begun.

And that is exactly what recent history has to show; a revolution in philosophic thought had in fact begun. The revolution had begun to take shape in the eighteenth century with the coming of the conception of progress in matters of the culture. It was extended by geologists into the conception of the age of the world; it was continued by Darwin in his theory of the origin of biologic species; it was carried into philosophy and psychology by Charles S. Peirce (1839–1914), by William James (1842–1910), and by John Dewey (1859–). More recently a host of writers and thinkers have carried the new conception into many, many related areas. But the revolution is not yet complete. Numerous implications of the old doctrine remain in current thinking; and, in spite of the fact that the old conception is no longer adequate to the modern demand, many people still think in terms of that old outlook. Indeed, some advocate a revival of the old way of thinking, inviting us to go back to the medieval outlook before inductive thinking had become the rule.

SIGNIFICANCE OF THE NEW DOCTRINE OF CHANGE

What difference does it make to men and to life that this new conception of change has come into the world?

For one thing the new outlook opens a wider door to human effort. It bids men hope and seek and strive, where before they dared not. Under the old view man could do little but accept what was; beyond that he could not hope to go. If the world was evil beyond man's ability to cope with it, discouragement or a sensitive conscience might, and for many did, lead to escape from society for contemplation. But the new opens up opportunities that before seemed forever closed. Man has made great discoveries and inventions, he then can make more and greater. The modern conception of progress (later to be discussed) is itself a human achievement, opening new visions and stirring greater desires and hopes. We can now believe that progress along any particular line is probable if only we work for it hard enough, and net human progress becomes a real possibility. In such ways does the new outlook open new possibilities for the control of life.

The new outlook goes further; it elevates man himself. Not only can man achieve more in affairs than was formerly believed, but man's selfhood has been elevated. He can effect; he now thinks more widely, more creatively, more critically. And the more man learns that effort counts, the less are men disposed to withdraw from society in defeat and the more disposed are they to seek to improve life. If things are wrong at any point it is not withdrawal that is demanded, but better thinking and greater effort. Man now faces the future positively. His effort counts; he can effect; he can bring changes into the world; he can, to greater or less degree, determine what will happen.

But if man thus has greater possibilities, this at once demands a greater sense of responsibility. It was the nuclear physicists working with the atom bomb who saw first and clearest our new responsibility in connection with their science. So also must our statesman accept, as never before, responsibility for abolishing war; and the same obligation extends to all the rest of us. So, with all the problems facing our nation and the world, education must accept a supreme obligation to work for an intelligent and morally effective citizenship. Everything is at stake.

One further advantage on the spiritual side is that the new outlook fits with and supports democracy. The responsible thinking and the greater effort just demanded in behalf of society is exactly democracy at work, intelligently and morally. For man to have faith in himself as he works with others is the psychological foundation of democracy. To accept social responsibility for one's deeds is precisely the moral foundation of democracy. The older point of view on change led easily to obedient acquiescence, which is clearly the psychological foundation of authoritarianism. This the educators now working with the postwar Germans have found as their chief hindrance to bringing a democratic education to Germany.

In conclusion, perhaps the greatest significance of the newer doctrine of change will prove to be the spiritual awakening it brings. From the results of science and the new outlook on change came the eighteenth century Enlightenment with its faith in reason. The advance was great, even though the particular movement tended to restrict itself to the *elite*. But from the Enlightenment, as seen by such men as Locke and Jefferson working on the more individualistic aspects of the Protestant Revolt, came modern democracy, thus spreading the principles of freedom and equality in the spirit of the Enlightenment. Finally, it appears possible that from the concurrence of these several movements there may arise a new devotion to ethics founded on the way that moral principles work themselves out inductively in life rather than on mere obedience to an authoritative code. This inductive ethics we shall study further.

CHAPTER VI. *The Culture: Builder of Men and of Civilization**

MANY references have already been made to the culture and how it operates. This chapter will try to make more explicit the relation of the culture to the development of the human individual and of civilization.

CULTURE DEFINED

By the culture is meant, as previously discussed, all the man-made parts and aspects of the human environment, specifically everything contrived or discovered by man that has made a place for itself in the social process. It thus includes especially such diverse human contrivances as language, tools, customs, accepted procedures, institutions, conceptions, standards, ideals. Another term used to designate this same content is "the social inheritance." For culture is an inheritance from preceding generations to this; without it we who are now alive would, as previously seen, be but higher brutes. But it is a social, not a biological inheritance; we are not born with it, we have to learn it. Also the culture is truly, as it is frequently called, "the funded capital of civilization." It is the valuable contributions of our ancestors saved up and invested as better ways of living.

THE CULTURE AND SELFHOOD

Historically the culture and selfhood have developed together. Each has been at once cause and effect of the evolution of the other;

* For a somewhat fuller discussion of this topic see Chapter v in the author's *Selfhood and Civilization.* The discussion here given is much indebted to that.

any increase or improvement in either has meant a corresponding enrichment of the other. Language and tools furnish the most obvious evidence of the superiority of man over brutes, and both of these are possible only as selfhood and its self-conscious thinking have been present to devise them.

Language in particular seems necessary to any significant cultural accumulation. When Köhler's ape contrived the spliced stick for pulling bananas into his cage, his mental achievement (under the humanly contrived conditions) was sufficient to have added that much to any body of ape culture (had any existed); but it did not so add. On the contrary, the achievement, so far as it concerned him and his ape companions, died with the inventor. Had sufficient language been available among these apes and the situation common enough, the successful spliced stick would have excited comment; and if so, it is hard to believe that some other ape would not have tried it and found it useful, thus helping to perpetuate it. But nothing of the sort happened; only among men did that invention add to the culture. They, not the apes, had the language to describe what happened and so to keep the incident alive.

A somewhat analogous failure is found in the early history of man. The men of the Old Stone Age, having devised their chipped flint implements, went, according to Boas, for thirty thousand years without improving upon them. To us this seems so strange, so different from what we know, that we seem compelled to suppose that their language lacked all words relating to invention and discovery and that the men of that day consequently lacked such thoughts. Probably, as Boas suggests, the original discovery of making such implements was so gradual and took so long to effect that it excited little comment.

It is in the light of such considerations that Professor Dewey has called language "the cherishing mother of all significance." (45:186) "Events when once they are named," he says, "lead an independent and double life." (45:166) When named events are discussed, this comment leads to criticism and further suggestions and possibly also to further additions to the culture. The named thought thus becomes, on its merits, itself an addition alike to the culture and to the personality of those who add it to their thinking. This mutually interactive process has, as was suggested above, been in historic action since the beginning of man as man. In keeping with this view, Hobbes said that without language, "there had been amongst men neither commonwealth, nor society, nor contract, nor peace, no more than amongst lions, bears and wolves." (78:I:iv)

THE CULTURE AND THE DEVELOPMENT OF THE INDIVIDUAL CHILD

The two constituent elements of the educative process are, on the one hand, the child born helpless and ignorant, and on the other hand, the culture embodied in the surrounding group life. This helpless and ignorant child must grow up into an effective member of the social group. This he does, while he matures physically, by gradually acquiring the group culture as he lives in and with the group and takes over progressively its ways of acting and thinking. Whatever the group may be, French, Chinese, or Fiji, that the child normally becomes.

The process of taking on the group culture begins typically in the family, but soon extends to the group in which the family lives. The mother interprets the world to the growing child; the surrounding group helps to reinforce her teaching; and as a result the child comes to accept the group ways as his ways. If the group is unified in customs and outlook the child may grow up believing there is simply no other way of conceiving or doing what his family and his group have taught him. In fact, he may believe, regarding the more important ways and beliefs, that differing ones would be actually wrong. Thus he learns according to the culture he grows up in. Through family, family friends, surrounding group, he learns the language and with it the conceptions of his group. He learns food habits and tastes—to drink milk, to eat blubber or sauerkraut, to eat with his fingers (as in various parts of the world) or to eat with a fork and *never* with his fingers. He may learn to believe that the gods cause or withhold rain, that husbands should have many wives, that "foreigners" or out-groups are persons undesirable or even dangerous; that the republican form of government is the only really good one; that cheating (dishonesty) is wrong, always wrong, or that it is wrong only if practiced within the group, or that it is acceptable and even clever if practiced against customers and within business dealings.

Thus is the group culture maintained. The child learns it as he progressively lives it, then lives it—normally—as he first learned it, until something comes to raise questions and teach him differently. It is in this way, too, that group differences are perpetuated. The child of French surroundings becomes French; the child of Chinese surroundings becomes Chinese. Certain writers of the past have asserted that each child is born with his group traits innate in him, or at least with an innate tendency that way. Thus the child of Irish parents would show Irish tendencies, so to say, irrespective of how he was brought up or where. Anthropology finds no such thing to be true. To be sure, certain racial features are biologically transmitted, as color of the skin and eyes and hair; but the evidence is against any such biological transmission of psychological characteristics. It may be added that the evidence is also against believing any one racial group to be innately superior to another, either in general or in any special ability. Individuals differ innately in such respects, but it does not appear that racial groups so differ. Their group differences are cultural and learned. The culture molds the child to its model.

CERTAIN SIGNIFICANT CULTURAL DEVELOPMENTS

Any complete list of significant cultural achievements would include such items as the use of fire, smelting ore, the wheel. But we know too little of how these originated to attempt any discussion of their development. In the case of fire, it appears that, as regards its European use, this was first found toward the close of the Old Stone Age; but it took the whole ten thousand years of the next period of ground stone implements to develop fire sufficiently for the smelting of copper and the making of bronze implements.

There are, however, three later and highly significant cultural achievements of which we seem to know enough to make their discussion worth-while. In order of their appearance these are, first, the development in Egypt of the conception of the sacredness of human personality, that human personality as such and not social status should determine the ethical treatment of persons; second, the development in Greece of critical thinking (philosophy), arising from the first critical comparison of diverse group cultures; and third, the development in Italy and elsewhere in Europe of modern inductive science experimentally validated. The three accounts will show not only how the culture has significantly grown, but how civilization has thereby been enriched and man elevated.

1. THE SACREDNESS OF HUMAN PERSONALITY

The origin of codes of morals began, we must suppose, very early in human history. And in certain very obvious respects these appear to have developed along similar lines in all cultures. Franz Boas tells us:

> The human code of ethics for the closed social group . . . is everywhere the same: murder, theft, lying, rape are condemned. (13:205*f*.).

Another similarity less admirable, but perhaps equally widespread under conditions appropriate to it, was the development of different codes for upper and lower status. Wars brought subjugation with slavery and, ultimately, differing classes of citizens. As lawmaking was vested in the king and his supporting noble friends, these naturally made it a more heinous offense to assault a high-class man than a low-class man. These and other like differences of status treatment are not yet dead in the world. But it was the Egyptians, it appears, who first rose above this feudal type of morals, and they did this (so Breasted thought) a thousand years before a similar advance by any other known group in the Western world. It was, in probability, the peculiarly protected position of Egypt, with its consequent peace for many successive generations, that allowed this and other instances of higher civilization to arise. According to the *Book of the Dead* (as old as the pyramids), when the soul was examined at death, it was expected to avow that in life it had meted out justice irrespective of social status. This conception, that justice is ethically demanded for personality as such, spread from Egypt to other parts of the world, in particular to Babylon, whence it was later brought to Palestine. The earlier Hebrew code was tribally centered. Certain acts, for example selling tainted meat, were wrong if done within the twelve tribes, but lawful if done to a stranger. In contrast with this, Jesus in the parable of the Good Samaritan defended the Egyptian position. The lawyer who raised the question was apparently willing to limit the injunction, "Love thy neighbor as thyself," to the chosen people and so exclude strangers. Jesus pointedly rejected such a limitation and upheld the obligation to man as man wherever and however found.

Professor Breasted (1865–1935), who most of all has brought the attention of the world to this moral advance of the Egyptians, had this to say on a very important problem, a problem even more important in our day than when he wrote these words in 1933:

> As the oldest known implement-making creature, man has been fashioning destructive implements for possibly a million years, whereas conscience [in the sense discussed just above] emerged as a social force less than five thousand years ago. One development has far outrun the other; because one is old, while the other has hardly begun and still has infinite possibilities before it. . . . Man is morally still a mere child playing in a nursery full of the most dangerous toys (15:ix, 406).

Such a perspective allows us to hope for the future. Possibly the greatly increased danger from our latest war instruments will now help us to develop a conscience demanding ethically equal regard for all, for our "neighbors" as for ourselves.

2. CRITICAL THINKING

Though the Egyptians thus enriched the world's moral outlook by first asserting the sacredness of human personality, it was the Greeks, centered in Athens, who gave to the world its supreme intellectual advance—critical thinking. This advance, in the opinion of Professor Dewey quoted earlier, added a "new dimension" to human intelligence.

Before this contribution by classical Greece, each social group had been sufficiently conscious of its own culture to protect and transmit it. Each group knew its own laws, customs, religious festivals well enough to act on them and to demand the same of all within the group. But as yet no group had become culturally self-conscious in any very active sense. As individuals, members of the group were not critical of what they themselves believed. What they did believe they accepted on tradition, not after, but before, consideration. Thus what they believed they held not as conviction, but as prejudice—as is still true of all who have not developed effective criticism. They had never learned to ask what we now—

since the Greeks—call *fundamental* questions—the *why* of what to think and do and *how* to find this out. For the first time in history a people, the Greeks, did achieve these searching new questions and in consequence did build the conception of cultural criticism.

How this advance came about is too long to tell here in full detail, but too important to omit in essence. When the recording of history first began, the Greeks had settled the islands and peninsulas where Europe and Asia came together in the Mediterranean Sea. In time the thin soil proved unable to support the growing population. Some Greeks then set up colonies in distant parts of the general area, others took to the sea in boats to live by trading. Those who had originally settled on the Asian coast had already come in cultural contact with the "barbarians" previously settled there; others who settled the colonies met new conditions and the culture of other "barbarians." All of these who thus met other groups, and especially those who also met other conditions, became definitely conscious of contrasting group-ways of behaving; and many under these new conditions had had to modify certain of their original cultural ways. Questions thus arose; and Athens, most of all, became the center and focus where these questions were brought forward for consideration. The sons of colonists sent back to Athens for education appear to have been most forward in raising these questions. Those who traveled in trade from one country to another were also sensitive to the problem. This tendency to compare and question and criticize was greatly heightened by the threat, then most seriously felt, that the great empire of Persia might swallow up Greece. Athens led in the war of defense; so that under this threat they studied the Persian ways and Persian ideas for a hundred years as had never before been done by any people in the history of thought.

In the end the Greeks won the war. But even more, in so doing they had discovered themselves *in comparison with others*, and therein had found a new method of thinking. Out of all these various experiences between the Greeks and other peoples, the "other" component of the cultural and self-other mind expanded enormously. "Our" ways and "their" ways were for the first time in history fairly and honestly opposed for thought. "They" behave differently from "us." Which is right? How can we tell? What does "right" mean? Is there really any such thing as right? Or is the mere chance of custom all there is? It was such questions as these that brought self-conscious cultural criticism to the Greeks. Such methods of inquiry led to questioning in every area of thought and life. Treatises were written on every conceivable topic—from cooking, which the Greeks put near the bottom, up to the highest questions of statecraft and philosophy. It is worthy of note that while Athens was the pregnant center of inquiry, practically every great leader of thought at Athens came from some place where the immediate contrast between cultures had forced itself vividly upon consciousness.

Such was the glory of classical Greece. Next after language itself this conception and achievement of critical thinking mark the greatest intellectual advance thus far made by man. In it human personality took an astounding step forward. Many and perhaps most among us agree with the statement of Sir Henry Maine (1822–1888): "Except the blind forces of Nature, nothing moves in this world which is not Greek in origin." Truly the world's intelligence did therein take on a new dimension in both outlook and insight. From this both civilization and man grew in power as never before.

3. EXPERIMENTAL SCIENCE

We have perhaps already sufficiently discussed in preceding chapters this third great advance. It seems strange, and is perhaps discouraging, that after the Greek contribution of critical thought it took man two thousand years to advance to experimental science. Had the world been more orderly, progress might have been more rapid. It seems to us now incredible that men so long after the rise of Greek philosophy remained willing to accept ideas on authority —authority of Aristotle, the "master of those who know"; authority of the church; authority of tradition. As we saw earlier, it was thus taught, supposedly on the authority of Aristotle, that "heaviness" made an unsupported body fall and that the heavier the body, the faster it would fall. This was what Galileo, on the one hand, questioned and what the University of Pisa, on the other hand, upheld. It seems to us astonishing that such a doctrine could be held for two thousand years with no one questioning it and no one thinking to put it to the actual test. Before the time of Galileo to question the received doctrine was bad form if not heretical; now

—among scientists at any rate—to question successfully is to make for one's self a name among the honored.

How experimental science has remade both the mind of man and the world of affairs has already been emphasized. We now believe that man can create both by discovery and by invention. In particular we have discovered how to discover, we have learned how to invent.

We have now considered what seem the three greatest contributions made to the culture within known history. Before men had these three, life was very different. Are men happier than they were before? Different answers have been returned to this question, but some things seem fairly certain. First, these three contributions have so far greatly changed civilization and can yet change it far more. In fact, it may well be that we have so far only begun to exploit the possibilities from these three advances. Second, there is now no turning back. Unless civilization should fail in some manner, man will never willingly give up what these three offer. The only reasonable proposal is to use them better. Further, whether man's happiness is or is not greater than formerly, life has a different quality, and few who have ever truly experienced that quality will consider giving it up. Rather must we see that all have opportunity to experience that quality.

We cannot now say whether man will add other like cultural advances to these three. As Breasted said above, man has for a million years been devising tools of war. But the moral possibilities of the first contribution discussed, the intellectual possibilities of the second, and the practical possibilities of the third must be so put together as to provide an effectively hopeful program for the future. This can be done. The possibilities are here. The task is man's. Philosophy must at each successive stage of growth help men to set up appropriate aims and ideals of life. A suitable philosophy of education must help practical school people find the educative procedures necessary to attain these aims and prepare for still higher. Education must bring up successive generations devoted to making life really good for all.

CHAPTER VII. *The Individual and Society*

OF the many interrelations of the individual and society, various have already been considered. Chapter I, on the meaning of a philosophy of education, turned largely on the contrasted places given to the individual in the respective social outlooks of Jefferson and Bonaparte, and what this difference means for education. Chapter II included a preliminary account of morality as the consideration of others affected by one's decisions and acts. The whole of Chapter III, on the social nature of the human individual, constituted an essential part of the theme of the present chapter. In Chapter IV the discussion of institutions and of their right to control was again a precise phase of the problem of this present chapter. Chapter VI considered the culture as the socially inherited basis whereby men live together in society. These prior discussions must be counted as constituent parts of any full consideration of the interrelationships of the individual and society.

The present chapter will consider first some of the differing kinds and degrees of such interrelationship that history has to show. After that it will consider the kinds of relationship that seem necessary if the individual and society alike are to live best.

INDIVIDUAL FREEDOM IN OTHER TIMES

With primitive man there is little individual freedom. "Custom as a blind king" regulates with great precision the daily round of the individual's acts—bathing, eating, drinking, fasting, hair-cutting, birth, marriage, burial. From the cradle to the grave the individual in primitive life—so anthropology teaches us—is the slave of custom, of ancient usage; and the conscious why of it all is little or no factor in his obedience. In this sense, early man had small freedom of decision, and was hardly if ever original or spontaneous. It is a picture of life that we, as we now are, do not like. We wish freedom, admire originality, prefer spontaneity. Whether we are as free as we like to think we are, is a question later to consider. We can see that custom binds the savage, possibly we do not see what binds us.*

How Greece and Rome have influenced our ideas and practice of democracy and of law and order will be taken up elsewhere. Here we consider the Middle Ages and the place of individual freedom of decision during that period. At that time, as we now see it, a triumvirate (so to say)—tradition, feudalism, and the church—worked consistently together to make decisions for the individual; and these decided without asking him. The individual of that period was born enmeshed in one consistent system of inclusive external control. Feudalism fixed his social status and function: as was his father, so must he be and so remain—serf or artisan or freeman or nobleman. The only way to get out of the feudal order into which one had been born was to enter the church, where one might if fortunate rise according to ability and merit. Along with fixed rank in the feudal order, whether low or high, went corresponding clothes to wear, fitting manners, and suitable training for one's station in life. Even the law varied with status; assault against a higher-class man brought greater punishment than against a lower. Equality of treatment as we know it was conspicuous by its absence.

Further, during this period, what each should believe and think was in greatest measure fixed for him, partly by tradition, partly by the church; and no one was allowed to try to change what was thus handed down. Also, chartered guilds authoritatively fixed conditions of work and resulting pay. In all these various ways, as we now see it, did the Middle Ages severely limit the rights of the individual as to personal choice and judgment, as to the social position he might occupy, and particularly as to his right to try to change any of these authoritarian arrangements. The individual, it seems to us now, existed then largely for society, to support, that is, the three dominant systems of authority.

* John Dewey gave it as his opinion that "the greatest educational power, the greatest force in shaping the dispositions and attitudes of individuals, is the social medium in which they live." (49:91)

THE RISE OF INDIVIDUALISM

After the Middle Ages there followed in the Western world, from the fourteenth to the nineteenth centuries inclusive, a series of powerful movements which increasingly recognized the individual as such, and step by step weakened alike the hold of tradition and of central authority. The Renaissance revived the ancient classical learning with its engaging emphasis on the refined and intellectual enjoyments of this life. Certain mechanical inventions were introduced, partly from abroad, which—all unintentionally—loosened up ideas and ways of living: gunpowder, which eliminated the armored knight and so helped to destroy feudalism; the mariner's compass, which made distant ocean sailing feasible; the printing press, which spread ideas to the common people, making democracy (said Carlyle) inevitable. Accordingly, there came new opportunities in business and trade which increasingly set the guilds aside and showed ever greater possibilities for individually created wealth (as opposed to merely inherited wealth). The discovery of America, moreover, stirred the imagination of men and set new business ventures going. In many parts of Europe the Protestant Revolt pushed aside the priest and the old faith, giving to the individual direct and personally responsible access to his God. It thus brought into existence the vernacular Bible and, in the more Protestant regions, elementary vernacular schools to teach reading to all. These various movements led *toward* individual freedom as opposed to authoritarian control, freedom of conscience, of thought, of speech, with—ultimately—individual political action. Science, working from another angle, as we saw in Chapter II, increasingly moved men in the same direction. The eighteenth century Enlightenment with its wide acceptance of Deism helped to break the power of entrenched theology in Protestant and Catholic countries alike and worked in other ways against the older established order. Popular power grew. The divine right of kings was in effect set aside. Democracy began its modern career under the banner of liberty and inalienable rights. The American and French revolutions exalted this individual freedom, giving ultimate authority to the voters to set up any government they might deem wise. And finally, the economic theory of laissez-faire advocated for trade and business complete freedom from governmental oversight or regulation.

Discussion of the question of democracy, the right of the people to govern, we postpone to a later chapter. It is the development of individualism* that here concerns us. Under the title of the "police power" theory of government, laissez-faire was widely acclaimed and accepted in the mid-nineteenth century. Herbert Spencer was a chief proponent, especially of the extreme form. In general this position would restrict governmental action to two functions: one to protect the individual's right to life, personal liberty, and property; the other, to enforce contracts freely made. In the extreme form advocated by Spencer, there was to be no governmental regulation of business, no tariffs, no public support or control of education, no milk inspection, no compulsory vaccination, no national post office, and even no government system of money. (152: Pt. III) While many advocated a "police power" theory, few went to Spencer's extreme. However, as if to support the extreme doctrine of individualism, there arose a theory of ethics based, so it seems to us now, on plain selfishness.

Alexander Pope (1688–1744) in his *Essay on Man* put God behind the point of view, and thought it was all for the best anyhow:

> Thus God and Nature link'd the gen'ral frame
> And bade Self-Love and Social be the same.—3d Ep., 1. 317

Adam Smith (1723–1790) in his deservedly famous *Wealth of Nations* (1776) thus defended the effect of selfish aims without defending the selfishness:

> Every individual necessarily labors to render the annual revenue of society as great as he can. . . . led by an invisible hand which was no part of his intention (148: Bk. IV, ch. 2).

A tract of the Society for the Promotion of Christian Knowledge defended the same outlook in these words:

> It is curious to observe how, through the wise and beneficent arrangements of Providence, men thus do the greatest service to the public when they are thinking of nothing but their own gain (qtd. in 95:17).

* There was a time when doubt existed as to whether a different and more favorable meaning of the term *individualism* might not prevail; namely, that each individual is to be respected as a person, and that all institutions, as the Sabbath for instance, were made for man, not man for them. This more favorable sense of the term seems to have yielded definitely to the meaning here implied.

Jeremy Bentham (1748–1832), in many respects a great social reformer, accepted selfishness as an essential feature of man's nature, saying specifically:

> Man, from the very constitution of his nature, prefers his own happiness to that of all other sensitive beings put together (12:X, 80).

It may at first glance seem a bit far-fetched to name the atomism of Newtonian science as one support of the social doctrine of individualism, but the analogy is striking and the connection more than probable. The evident success of natural science had very great influence on thought. The recognized scientific procedure was to analyze any phenomenon down to its ultimate elements–society, for example, into human individuals; study these as distinct and separate entities (social atoms); then in this light to understand the original phenomenon. It seems reasonably certain that "scientific" psychology was until the 1920's strongly influenced by Newtonian atomism; and the influence remains even to the present. Although natural science has now for several decades given up its belief in the ultimate character of Newtonian physical atoms, the atomistic theory lives on outside of natural science "long after its brains have been knocked out." Almost as if to illustrate the doctrine of social atomism, John Stuart Mill (1806–1873) is quoted as using the following words:

> Human beings in society have no properties but those which are derived from, and may be resolved into, the laws of individual men.

It would, it appears, be difficult to assert atomistic individualism in any clearer terms. What we have been calling the inherent social nature of man seems here explicitly denied.

CONCRETE MEANING OF THE TERM "SOCIETY"

Our various studies thus far of man in society lead easily to the general notion that men do engage in many associations, that these overlap both as to membership and in practical bearing, and that society consists of a large group of people joined thus together in many overlapping and interacting associations. To give greater concreteness to this general conception, take Mr. John Smith as a specific instance; let us study the various association groups with which he is connected to see how these constitute as far as they go the concrete society of which he is a member. Then by multiplying Mr. John Smith to take in more and more individuals at all their varying social levels and with all their associated relationships, we get a practical conception of what the term *society* does in fact mean.

First of all Mr. Smith grew up in a family. His father was a Methodist minister and accordingly traveled all over his state. His mother and father had grown up in the same small village; so Mr. Smith has many relatives on both sides now living in that village.

Also Mr. John Smith is married; and he and his wife have three children, nine, twelve, and fifteen years of age, respectively. Mr. Smith owns his own home. His wife and children, with the help of a maid hired one day a week, do all the household work. They deal personally with grocer, butcher, baker, and dry goods stores, etc., etc. The wife grew up in the city where the Smiths now live and she has a goodly number of relatives living in and around the city. Mrs. Smith and her two daughters are sociable and have many friends and acquaintances, of whom most but by no means all live near them in the city. Thus we see another set of associations.

Mr. Smith is a traveling salesman for a hardware house. Covering a considerable region by his business travels he keeps in touch with many boyhood friends made during his father's varied pastorates. This all stands him in good stead with his firm. It is a farming area and his firm sells considerable agricultural machinery to the farmers. Here two sets of associations interact.

Mr. Smith, in accordance with his rearing, is an active member of the Methodist church and teaches a Sunday school class for business men. By these connections Mr. Smith not only makes many friends on his own but the better keeps alive many of the friendships that his father had left. All of this is further grist to his mill as he works for his firm.

Mr. Smith belongs to Rotary and is active in its affairs. This gives him an active set of connections in all of the larger towns; for he takes pains to go to all the local Rotary meetings in the towns he visits.

Mr. and Mrs. Smith belong to the Country Club and Mr. Smith plays golf while Mrs. Smith plays bridge and the children swim in the club pool. Mrs. Smith belongs to various women's clubs. The children go to the public school. Mr. and Mrs. Smith belong to the P.T.A.; she goes regularly and he goes several times a year. Mrs. Smith is rather active in local politics, Mr. Smith more guardedly so.

These are some of the ways in which Mr. Smith, through his various associations, is an active member of society. And each one of all the persons with whom Mr. Smith is associated, Mrs. Smith for example, is likewise associated in all sorts of analogous ways with a host of other persons in their similar associations and these in turn throughout the society. The number of lines interconnecting persons with one another in the whole society are very, very numerous. The number of these connecting lines lessen, however, as divisions of any sort are met—political divisions, national boundaries, church divisions, party divisions, race and immigrant group divisions, differences of wealth, of occupation, of education. Ease of association and communication is thus a factor in binding groups together. Degree of industrial development, with its resulting interdependence of productions and regions, is another factor which serves to integrate a people and the world.

EFFECT OF SOCIETY ON LIFE AND ITS QUALITY

Society then *is* the combined aggregate of all the people associated thus together in all these varied ways. But society is more than a number of associations numerically counted. More significantly, it is what these associations mean and the educative effects they bring. Directly, the associations have meaning to the individual members of society in immediate enrichment of life—through food, clothing, books, human association, and other direct satisfactions. Indirectly, they have meaning by their less immediate contributions of law and order—a fundamental essential to all else—and by the broader economic and cultural opportunities and relationships they offer. And finally, these associations of all kinds have educative effects; in the course of their operation they build Mr. Smith into a more complex and competent man, one with more insight, wider appreciations and expectations, greater ability to manage and to secure what he wants from life.

Consider Mr. Smith and his relations with society in the light of what has just been said. Specifically, how does society affect the content and satisfaction of his life? Much, in every way. Almost everything by way of content or satisfaction comes from his various associations. Three areas can here be distinguished: first (but probably not the most important), all the things that money will directly buy, both material goods and other enjoyments; second, the satisfactions from Mr. Smith's own individual activities and from direct personal contacts as he meets and deals with other people; and, third, those more basic contributions made by the agencies for law and order, by institutions for research, by schools, churches, and other agencies for human betterment. And all of these bring their specific educative effects as suggested above. As to the things that Mr. Smith can buy, if we compare what the typical person in our country can buy with what the typical person in India or China can buy, the advantage lies greatly with this country. The machinery we have and its expert utilization give us a standard of living far in advance of that typically enjoyed in these countries. It is not that Mr. Smith works harder or that he is natively more intelligent than his correlative in those countries; it is this industrial society constructively back of him which, directly and indirectly, gives the Smiths their present standard of living. Without these associations their standard of living would be that of India or China.

As regards the second type of life content, the satisfactions from one's own activities, two observations may be made. One, that a large variety of possible associations (possible lines of work, possible associations for enjoyment) allow Mr. Smith wider choices and so probably greater chances of finding personal satisfactions. A recent emigré to this country stated it as his early outstanding impression that America provides many opportunities; if one line does not work out happily there are many others in which to engage and find satisfaction. A second consideration is that in satisfactions from his own personal associations Mr. Smith stands more nearly on the same basis as the man in India or China, in spite of his more numerous and more complex opportunities. In fact, people can and do argue as to which is more fortunate in this respect. It may be that Mr. Smith suffers in that, as a typical American, he has not yet adjusted himself to the complexity of American life and its rapid and uncertain changes. But comparisons of civilizations aside, it is clear that the actual personal satisfactions in Mr. Smith's life depend very largely on how he and those he deals with get on together. If he and Mrs.

Smith do not get on well together a large part of his life goes sour. If he and his employer do not get on well together, another large part of his life may go sour—with a direct bearing on the amount of money he obtains to use under the first head, the enjoyment of things that he can buy. These family and business relationships are highly strategic. All the rest of Mr. Smith's personal contacts further contribute each its share of personal satisfaction. Thus under the second head, Mr. Smith lives richly or not, partly as he gives satisfactions to the others, partly as they give satisfactions to him, partly as they mutually stimulate each other to greater personal satisfactions.

Third are the contributions from social organizations and social institutions—for example, those which uphold law and order or carry on research. These contributions underlie all else. In these respects Mr. Smith is dependent on what society gives. Even the contribution from material goods depends on existence of law and order, on the research which improves production, on provisions for education of the research worker, the manufacturer, even the machine tender. Research also brings to Mr. Smith and his family better health and longer expectancy of life.

But all of the types of life content above mentioned are dependent, very strategically, on the understanding and appreciation and support of the people who make up the society. What society can give is dependent on what the aggregate of individual men like Mr. Smith think and do. If they and enough others like them believe in law and order and actively uphold it, then all have it—at least on the whole. If the Smith family and enough like them are indifferent to law and order, then none may enjoy it. Like considerations hold, only in lesser degree, as regards research, schools, and other institutions. In all such it is largely what people generally believe and wish that counts. In the degree that a sufficient number of people see the significance of social institutions and services and accept responsibility for upholding them, will the institutions and services operate effectively, or in fact survive. Without this understanding and moral support, social agencies are ineffective and the society is hollow and weak. For example, law and order cannot operate through policemen and courts alone; in a democratic country a law can be enforced only as an active majority of the people support it. A similar consideration applies to health services, support of research, and the like.

But note that financial support is not sufficient. Moral support, acceptance of responsiblity for the common good, more than self-seeking concern, are essential also. This was mentioned above in connection with maintenance of law and order; if each thought only or primarily of his own good there would be no properly operating framework for living.

And note further that negative attention to the common good—refraining from what harms others—does not suffice to make society work well and so give its greatest potential contributions to individuals. A positive attitude of unselfishness (as contrasted with mere self-seeking), of positive intent to serve, is necessary if life and institutions are to go on well. Let us see how this is so.

Mr. Smith's firm, in the degree that it is effective, not only makes money for its owners and their employees; it also serves the needs of the community. In fact, only as it does thus serve, can it prosper. The early individualists said, "Yes, this is an instance of how self-love and social are the same; the firm is concerned solely to make money, but to make money it has to serve." There is a sense and degree in which this is true; but if that is all and if this narrow spirit pervades the whole concern, then that firm will fail alike to make most money and to render best services. If self-seeking is the pattern, if each one thinks only or primarily of his own welfare, of what he makes out of it; if no manager finds self-expression in serving both firm and customers; if Mr. Smith and his fellow salesmen think only of the salary they are making and do not identify themselves both with the firm's good name and with the real interests of the customers; then in that degree will the firm fail to serve its customers and in the end itself. In other words, unselfishness, at least to the degree of taking interest in what one is doing and of *desire to serve*, is in the long run essential to the effective working of social institutions and of society and so to the good life.

What meaning has this for education? As regards informal education, the more deeply proper insights and attitudes are rooted in the older generation and the more wisely they guide the young, the more hope there is for that society. For the necessary attitudes and responsibilities can in general take effective root in the oncoming generation only as the young learn them from the old. A society, a family, which values acceptance of responsibility for the common good, will teach this to its young.

As regards formal education, the building of insight and constructive attitudes is, broadly considered, the main social task of the schools—schools of all levels and kinds. The school has the positive social duty to help the young people (i) to see how we are all tied together, the welfare of each being dependent sooner or later on the welfare of all; (ii) to believe in and support the common good; (iii) to see how common social institutions serve us all and to understand the contribution of enough instances to get from them the feeling of their common service of all; (iv) to see that selfishness defeats the effort to live well together; and (v) to accept responsibility for making our social institutions serve all as well as possible —responsibility in particular for the institutions we are personally connected with, but also the wider responsibility for the total network of institutions that serve us all. We can have truly effective society only as these dispositions enter into the individual to make him socially minded and socially disposed. As MacIver so well said:

> Society is in us, in each of us, in some degree in all, in the highest degree in the greatest of us (106:70).

As we put together these various considerations we build, each one for himself, both our generalized conception of what the term *society* means and our degree of an understanding attitude to make society function effectively.

INSTITUTIONS, COMMUNICATION, AND THE BUILDING OF MIND

A further word is necessary here to show how society permits the exchange of ideas and what this means for the good life. H. G. Wells, writing with others, said (italics supplied):

> All political and social institutions, all matters of human relationship, are dependent upon the means by which mind reacts upon mind and life upon life, that is to say, *upon the intensity, rapidity and reach of mental and physical communication* (10:CXXIII:108).

The human mind is, in a true sense, a product of communication.*

* This does not mean, as we shall later see the Alexandrian theory of education implying, that all we are and know we get by acquiring the formulations already made by others.

First of all, men think because they have first talked. As John Dewey says:

> Social communication is not an effect of [prior] soliloquy. If we had not talked with others and they with us, we should not talk to and with ourselves (45:170).

In connection with this statement, Dewey further says that "language is the record that perpetuates occurrences and [so] renders them amenable to public consideration." (50:20)

The discussion on the self-other origin of selfhood in Chapter III outlined the part that communication plays in helping to build the self. The quotations from Wells and Dewey take up, so to say, from that point. The mind is the cumulative and integrated aggregate of all one's specific thought learnings—learnings of meanings, attitudes, ideas, distinctions, and relationships. The "public consideration," in Dewey's quotation, is the process in which mind meets mind as they face some common ("public") matter. In such meetings mind gets stimulation from mind and besides, perhaps more important, it gets checking. Also, common social needs give motivation for the "public consideration" of situations and common problems. Written language allows the mutual stimulation and checking to take place at a distance. The better the means of communication (other things being equal), the more frequent and more effective the stimulation and the checking, and the more effective the building of mind. If only we could succeed with communication, with real com-munication, the effect would be startling. On this Dewey is very emphatic:

> Given a social medium in whose institutions the available knowledge, ideas, and art of humanity were incarnate, and the average individual would rise to undreamed of heights of social and political intelligence (49:69*f*.).

INDIVIDUALIZATION AND SOCIALIZATION

Do these two processes of becoming more individual and becoming more social hinder each other, or do they, on the contrary, mutually support each other?

The conception of the individual as a social atom—capable of entering into social relations but, as John Stuart Mill seemed to imply, remaining still the same atom as before—would seem to allow only a minor kind of socialization. So also would Schopenhauer's position that "society is a collection of hedgehogs drawn together for the sake of warmth." It may be, as Dealey and Ward said (34:1), that "man is not *naturally* a social being," but their further statement that "human association is the result of the perceived advantage which it yields" probably overstresses the conscious choosing in the matter, as if social atomism were the necessary basic principle. All of the foregoing would seem to imply a belief that individualization and socialization are contradictory.

It appears, however, from study of the subject, better to say that the child is born a-moral and possibly a-social, and that potential in him at birth are many possible characters, some perhaps with stronger predispositions to assert themselves than others. Which one of these characters the adult will show is the result of the aggregate succession of choices as heredity (or, more exactly, interactive development up to that stage) and environment mutually interact. The eminent biologist, H. S. Jennings, has spoken thus against any forefixing of adult character at birth:

> The characteristics of the [human] adult are no more present in the germ cells than are those of an automobile in the metallic ores out of which it is ultimately manufactured (94:28).

Let us consider, then, the conception of individuality, what it does mean and how it is developed. The following appear to be the characteristics which together constitute individuality: First is the idea of uniqueness; no two individualities are just alike. In a way that is what the word means. The difference which gives this man his individuality is, however, not so much the result of endowment, or even of favorable environment taken alone, as it is the use the individual has made of himself and his opportunities. Individuality, in the better sense at any rate, must somehow build itself and run itself. Morever, the true individual has a recognizable pattern, his choices follow consistently to build up such a pattern. But true individuality will not result without social interaction. The richer the cultural environment, the more likely will there be rich individuality.

From these considerations it is easy to believe that a person of individuality, because of that fact, lives more ardently. This is partly because he has specific interests and partly because he accepts these more definitely, has digested things more thoughtfully. Bacon says:

> The more good things we are interested in, the more ardently we live.

Of the second of the two contrasted terms, *socialization*, Giddings says this means "the attempt to adapt ourselves to one another." This, however, is too atomistic, as if the individual simply yields and is not remade in the process of socialization. MacIver is profounder when he defined socialization as "the process in which a being strikes deeper root in society, in which his social relations grow more complex and more extensive, in which he finds fulfillment of his life in and through increase and development of his relations with his fellows." (106:214*f*.) This implies, though it seems better to make it explicit, that the individual as he becomes more and more social undergoes a corresponding change in his very being. Sociality enters increasingly into the warp and woof of his thinking, his feeling, his valuing, his consequent behaving; he is a different being. As we saw earlier from MacIver, society is actually in us; and being in us it remakes us. In the degree that society is thus in many of us, in that degree do men qualitatively enjoy society. Actual social relations accepted as such by the individual mold him to fit them and their demands, change him into more of a social being than he had been before.

Now as to whether growth in socialization thwarts or supports growth of individuality, we may begin by accepting the fundamental democratic doctrine as stated in the words of William James:

> Surely the individual, the person in the singular number, is the more fundamental phenomenon, and the social institution, of whatever grade, is but secondary and ministerial (85:102).

Those who advocated the atomistic outlook—objected to above—were probably feeling for what James has here said. In fact, life and value can be centered and located only in human individuals. The arrangements of society exist that these human individuals may live better than otherwise they would. As Whitehead has said:

> The worth of any social system depends on the value experience it promotes among individual human beings. . . . A community life is a mode of eliciting values for the people concerned (10:CLXIII:315).

As to the question whether growth in socialization thwarts or supports growth in individuality, J. Mark Baldwin (1861–1934) gives a more explicit answer:

> The individual's normal growth lands him in essential solidarity with his fellows, while on the other hand the exercise of his social duties and privileges advances his highest and purest individuality (11:16).

MacIver speaks to the same effect:

> The first and greatest of all the laws of community . . . *socialization and individualization are the two sides of a single process* (106:214).

To get MacIver's thesis in its true and full sense we need to recall from Chapter III that man rises above the brutes primarily by achieving selfhood or personality and this only by living with others who have already achieved it; and from Chapter IV that freedom is not absolute, that "no man has a right to all his rights," that liberty must be limited by justice, which itself is the equilibrium of freedoms. We must accordingly understand that the desirable individual and the desirable society are defined with mutual regard to each other. To live well men must live together; those institutions then are good which best promote this living well together. But in order that institutions may work best, men must so think and feel and act that the institutions do work well, that is, men must be socially disposed and so act; for institutions are nothing but men working appropriately together. The good individual then is one who cooperates best with other individuals to make life best for all. The good society is one which so works as to bring about the individual cooperations which promote the good life for all. Socialization and individualization do thus bring each other mutually into an ever-higher degree of being and action.

CHAPTER VIII. *Morality: A Social Necessity*

PREVIOUS chapters have by anticipation already treated various phases of this topic. The discussions on government and on rights (Chapter IV) and on the validity of their demands for obedience come close to the essence of the problem of morality. The Egyptian acceptance of the moral obligation to respect personality wherever found (Chapter VI) similarly approaches the essence of the present problem, but from another angle. Consideration of various interrelations of the individual and society (Chapter VII) have also prepared for this chapter. We now attack the problem explicitly in order the better to see just what is meant by morality and wherein it is a social necessity.

THE MEANING OF MORALITY

An approach from anthropology and history will help us to see the natural continuity of morality with the rest of life. Primitive men faced the problems of life, we believe, on a "trial-and-error" basis, and on this basis selected slowly and gradually their ways of meeting their urgent social needs. Their selected ways of behaving, reduced thus to "habit, routine, and skill," were what Sumner calls *folkways.* These the young learned "by tradition, imitation, and authority." In time, the folkways were further developed to take care of truth and right and the public welfare as these then appeared to the men of the tribe. In this, a higher level than mere folkways was reached, namely, folkways imbued with ethical bearing. These Sumner calles *mores* (borrowing the Latin word for this purpose). In connection with mores there arose *taboos* to express the common feeling that some things were simply *not to be done.* Mores and taboos thus "contain judgments as to societal welfare" and so are meant to promote the common good (154:2–28).

Morality belongs on the next higher level above Sumner's mores; but before we can consider properly the inner and more exact meaning of morality, certain prior conceptions useful in the discussion must be examined. The discussion of self-consciousness in Chapter III gives a point of departure. When a child has so far developed that he can not only do various things, but knows that he can do them, he then can, we say, *act intentionally*. He can mean to do what he does and know it. He is now ready for the next advance, to understand that these acts of his are part of the public world in which he and others live together. And, accordingly, his elders begin to tell him that he *must not* do this and he *must* do that. In other words they are beginning to hold him *accountable* for what he does, accountable for his conscious and intentional acts. When a child has lived in this stage of accountability long enough to learn to control himself along the lines for which he is held to account, when he will thus make himself do, at least measurably, what is expected of him, he has entered the next higher stage of responsibility. He begins now to hold himself responsible for doing what, according to his elders, he *ought* to do. If this growing child is fortunate in his home guidance he will, in this last-named stage, build a *conscience* as the correlative of his sense of responsibility. By *conscience* we mean the tendency of a person to hold himself consciously responsible for doing or not doing certain specified things thus accepted as *right* or *wrong*. To act properly with regard to a recognized *right* or *wrong* becomes a *duty*. To each such *duty* belongs a feeling of *oughtness*. Conscience is the active feeling of *ought* in connection with a recognized *duty*.

Returning now to consideration of the meaning and authority of morality, it appears that in the development of morality there are two successive stages, in both the historical and the personal (individual) development. In the first stage, the morality is imposed on the individual, typically in his youth, by the group, as we have just seen. In the second stage, though the individual is of course always influenced by his culture as interpreted by his fellows, he now acts on his own; he is now in a true sense the author of his morality, author in the sense that he recognizes moral situations for himself, perhaps creatively senses new moral distinctions and obligations, and at any rate accepts personal moral responsibility for his decisions and acts in such cases.

As regards the first stage of morality, whenever the group about an individual holds him actively responsible for any act of his that might affect others adversely, then a question of morality has arisen. The group thinks that he *ought* to see and accept certain types of behavior as *duties*, thinks that he *ought* to do these things, thinks that something is wrong with his *moral insight* and *conscience* if he does not so feel and act. This we may say is *morality* from the *external* and public point of view. In a static society or culture group where custom rules, the young typically grow up accepting what custom thus demands. In such a society, conflict between individual and custom will be rare and seldom acute. Many people even in the modern world remain for the most part in this first stage of morality as conformity to group custom.

By contrast, the second stage of morality is in a true sense both an individual responsibility and an individual achievement. Without the critical thinking first given to the world by the Greeks, this type of creative morality would, it appears, be rare indeed. Now, however, it should be the normal achievement of all more sensitive and more critical minded individuals. The Swiss scholar, Jean Piaget, tells us (135:275*ff*.) that in his country at the typical age of six by far the majority of boys deem it right to obey parents or others in authority, but by the age of twelve the same ones demand that something they have come to call fairness or equality of treatment or the like shall control. This marks the transition from imposed morality to personal morality, the beginning, we may say, of moral wisdom; but there should be more than this. It appears that with our own young people a more serious questioning frequently arises in later adolescence. Youth begin then to go about more and to mingle, perhaps in college, with people of different minds. One may thus be led to compare and to question the more fundamental positions he had grown up accepting on authority from parents and community. Out of this questioning, if the young person is fortunately situated, there can, and should, come a maturing character critically conscious of its moral obligations.

It thus appears that conscience and a sense of ought begin as the internal demand for obedience to recognized external authority. These attitudes based at the beginning on external authority may, and should, go on developing until they reach the point of personal recognition of the inherent reasons for counting some things as right and others as wrong. Probably for most people most of the time an undifferentiated combination of both types of obedience holds—partly obedience to external authority, to what others demand, but partly obedience to personally seen reasons for doing such things. But the more consistently and the better one can and will judge for himself in such matters, the higher the type of character. For one's character is built by one's cumulative choice in the conflict of good and evil.

But to return to the original question, what does morality mean? What is it driving at? What is its purpose or function in human affairs? The words *ought*, *duty*, and *conscience* have been used as if they are meant to support *right* and oppose *wrong*. But people have differing conceptions of what is right and wrong. What conduct is right? And how can we find out in a particular case what is right and what is wrong? And where does morality enter? What, after all, is morality?

In the attempt to define morality, several constituent ideas must be considered—*individual good*, *public good*, *right vs. wrong*, *justice*. A simple actual case will give us a start here. Some years ago in New York City certain persons in a third-story back room were startled at hearing a rifle shot near at hand; they were more startled to find that a bullet had imbedded itself in the wall opposite their open window, and still more startled when the incident was repeated time after time. The police were called. On investigation there was found in the opposite third-story back a young man with a rifle, who readily admitted that he had been practicing with his rifle, shooting at a target he had hung from the sash of his open window. He had no intention, he said, of hurting anybody. The man was taken to court and there told that the law holds everyone responsible for foreseeing the probable consequences of his acts and then acting accordingly.

Clearly one's individual interest or other good cannot be allowed to jeopardize the good of others. Right and wrong therein get at least a partial definition, as does justice. Clearly too the consequences of an act constitute a central factor in determining whether it is moral. We saw above that the development of morality began in primitive life with the group judgment that certain acts—murder, stealing, lying, for example—affect adversely the lives of others, and this to such degree that these acts must be forbidden. This argument gives us the essence of the whole discussion.

In keeping with this E. L. Thorndike (1874–1949) has justly stated the essential basis on which we judge some acts as *good* and therefore *right* and others as *bad* and therefore *wrong:*

> Things are not good and bad for no reason. Better and worse, worthy and harmful, right and wrong, have meaning only in reference to conscious beings whose lives can be made more satisfying or more bearable (159:9).

But there is a further respect to consider. We are now less content than formerly to conceive morality in a merely negative fashion, as consisting only of things *not to do*. Suppose I live in a small village with no fire department; if my neighbor's house catches fire, I must join with others to help as best I can either to put the fire out or to save the neighbor's goods. To be sure, it is not easy to state just how far this positive morality should go. Suppose my neighbor's field needs plowing, shall I leave off my plowing to help him? I helped when his house was afire, shall I help now with his plowing? In general the answer is no. The fire was an emergency, but not so with the plowing. I have my fields to plow, he has his. But it might be that illness strikes my neighbor just when the need for plowing has arisen. It may then be the duty of all the neighbors, in this emergency, to join together to take care of the sick man's plowing. But emergency is far from the sole grounds for positive morality. Many matters concern us all together; clearly each one is morally obligated to do his "fair share" in supporting law and order, in supporting public health, public schools, public parks—in a word, in supporting the common good.

Possibly a formal conclusion regarding morality can be drawn by bringing in at this point the conception of the life good to live (which we are to consider more fully in Chapter XI). It begins to appear that any statement regarding morality or any specific effort to apply morals begins by assuming some guiding definition of the life good to live here and now. Each primitive people in drawing up its code of morals, however informally this was done, had their conception of the good life which their code was, in origin, meant to promote. Succeeding civilizations have developed finer insight and accordingly have changed their conception of the good life and modified their codes to fit; but each time any one person or any group has tried to apply moral obligation on a basis other than mere tradition or mere authority, there has been implied a content of the good life to support and promote. *Conscious morality thus becomes the settled conscious obligation and will so to act as to promote and foster the good life in all persons affected by one's conduct, and to do this as well as possible, all things considered: negatively, not to hurt or lessen the good life for any; positively, to foster and promote the good life in all persons affected to the fullest degree that wisdom and justice demand and/or approve.* Wisdom and justice would, for example, demand the help of all for fires where there are no regular fire companies, but, to the contrary, would demand that we not interpose and interfere where fire companies are adequate. Similarly wisdom and justice would rule out plowing for a neighbor under the ordinary conditions of farm life. But wisdom and justice would probably approve more individual concern for law and order than most ordinary citizens give, and, in like measure, more for most other instances of the common good.

Practical morality will thus accept for itself the concept that, though people will differ as to what is right and wrong, *each individual is under positive obligation (i) to make every reasonable effort to find out what is the right of each particular situation and (ii) to live up honestly to the best he thus has found as right. So to live and act is moral; failure thus to live at any point is wrong and immoral.*

It may make the discussion clearer to repeat some of the same essential argument just given from a slightly different angle. A recent writer proposed to study in a work of fiction a group of people living in a socially and morally "pure" state, that is, one in which the people studied had no economic or other social worries whatever. As he saw it, they were up against nothing "extraneous"; they had "only the problem of their own souls and the long look ahead in eternity." A more artificial and unreal moral state it would be difficult, if not impossible, to imagine. And it would seem equally impossible to draw any lessons from such study for use in our world. The thing about life that sets its moral problem is exactly life's problems and "worries" of all sorts—how men can and do impinge upon each other for good or ill; how they live in ways that do—or do not—bring the good life as *reasonably* best for all; what to do so that the net result shall be the best life feasible to get; and what attitudes to take in connection with getting it.

In our own day these social worries give us more and more complex problems than man ever faced before; so that a conscious and critical morality is now more needed than ever before. Primitive man reduced his few recurring conflicts to established mores. A higher stage reduced these to written codes. But the more complex and shifting a civilization, the more is the "active spirit" of morality needed rather than the letter of a code. The "spirit" can be more discerning and discriminating, and can take far more into account. So we find, particularly in our day and time, that conscience needs the considerations of wisdom and justice to determine just where the duty of any particular situation lies. And what it must judge by is the respective consequences of the several alternatives before it as found by thoughtful study.

Several types of moral problems accordingly present themselves to conscience. A student whose proper work would take his full time has friends in the city who urge him to join them in various exciting amusements. His conflict is internal. His conscience recalls that his work really requires his full time; he has saved up his money to take this professional course; his future depends on how well he does the work. On the other hand, his friends are urgent, and what they offer is very inviting; they tell him that he must not dry up into a stick, that this itself will hurt his future. Here are two alternative possibilities. If he is wise, he will ask himself seriously (i) what are the respective consequences of the two proposed courses and (ii) which set of consequences is, in *the long run,* the one to choose. With both of these questions he must keep present inclination in the background; in the first question, it has, as inclination, no place whatever in determining the facts; in the second, it must take no more than its due place in the "long run" view. For the latter he must ask such questions as, What will I think when I get back home to my life work? Which present choice will I then approve? What would the wisest and best of my long-time friends now advise? In fact, it would probably be wise for him to consult some of these long-time friends before he decides. The probabilities are that the student knows that he should for the most part stick to his work. If so, the difficulty is with his backbone. Does he have the character to do what he knows he ought to do? Possibly, his real problem is building a character to follow the right.

This student's professor might have a different type of problem. His study might lead him to a conclusion on a social-moral problem opposed to that held by the ruling spirits of his institution—officers, staff, and trustees. He is greatly troubled. On the one hand, the long-run view tells him, much as it told Socrates, that he must say what he honestly believes so that the merits of the case can be heard and appraised, if not by his institution, then at any rate by the larger world outside or perhaps only by a wiser generation yet to come. On the other hand, he will probably suffer at close range, perhaps lose some of his friends and much of the influence that so far has advanced him. Possibly he will feel compelled to resign his present position and face the world on an unpopular platform. This, if he were alone in the world, he would not so much mind, but he has a family to support and children to educate. It is for him a truly difficult problem. As with the student, so with the professor, he must ask (i) as to the respective consequences of the alternatives before him and (ii) which, on the highest level of conscience and right, he should choose. Facing a like situation, Socrates chose to drink the hemlock, and the intelligent conscience of the world has never ceased to approve.

In each of the cases of moral deliberation above analyzed, the effort was to find a line of conduct most adequate to take care of all the values at stake in the situation. Each proposal considered was weighed against the others to find the proposal which of all could best promise to fill this desired aim. When the doubt as to what to do has been resolved and the decision made, it follows *morally* that, in the degree to which the decision is clear and the process of deciding trustworthy, it is the individual's *duty* to follow the decision thus made; he is under *moral obligation* to carry out this decision, to do this thing; he *ought* to do it. His *conscience*, if properly active, will accept the decision and demand that he act accordingly. It should also be added that when a satisfactory decision has thus been made, the chosen line of conduct becomes, so far as the one deciding it can determine, " the *right* thing to do in that situation," and the other rejected proposals would now be *wrong* to act upon. Before the decision is made, each proposal stands as a candidate for choice as the right course to follow; afterwards each one is right or wrong according as it was or was not chosen as promising best to care for all the values involved.

The main point here is to note that moral problems arise, as was seen in the case of the dangerous rifle practice, in the natural setting of ordinary life. There is nothing mysterious or transcendental or supernatural in the wish of people to be free from such danger as this thoughtless man was bringing about. There is similarly nothing unnatural or extraordinary in the law's holding each person responsible for the natural consequences of his acts. It is, on the contrary, but natural for people to demand that others so act as not to damage them. It is further but natural that a thoughtful person, as the student or the professor above cited, should at times find himself in doubt as what he ought to do. And if one is in doubt, the process of deliberation seems certainly the best way known to man for finding out what is best to do. In other words, the whole process of morality as so far discussed is continuous with the ordinary natural life process as we all know it and live it. It involves study to find out the right, but there is nothing mysterious about it.

To this discussion on the meaning of morality there may properly be added the definition of ethics. As morality is based on conscious choice conducted in the light of consciously adopted principles, so is ethics, as the next higher step, the effort to apply the severest criticism to the principles proposed for use in morality. And this criticism can go forward adequately only as part of an inclusive system of philosophy. Ethics thus deals specifically "with the principles governing ideal human character and with the ideal ends of human action." (168:556)

In this way folkways, mores, morals, and ethics form a scale of successively higher and more critical study of the bearing of conduct on the quality of living.

CONSEQUENCES AS THE BASIS OF RIGHT AND WRONG

In everything thus far said about morals, the emphasis has been placed on consequences, on making decisions in the light of probable consequences as seen in advance of the act. Because some may be troubled by the apparent conflict of this emphasis on consequences with what they had previously thought, it seems wise to consider some questions that commonly arise in connection.

1. Does not a morality based on consequences tend to reduce itself to the problem of expediency, which in its turn is precisely a denial of moral quality?

The answer is no. The term "expediency" as used in posing this question is intended to imply a narrow conception of the good, perhaps no more than skillfully schemed personal advantage to the doer, and in any case shortness of view if not actual immediacy. The conclusion of our whole discussion stresses the reverse of any such expediency: it is the good of all concerned that must control, with the doer counting only as one among the "all concerned" and with special advantage to him expressly denied. In other words, the long-run good of all concerned is the decisive factor—the long-run good as opposed to the merely immediate good, and the good of all concerned as opposed to the apparent good simply of the doer himself.

What this questioner may have meant to uphold is stated in the appealing but easily misleading words of Tennyson:

> Because right is right, to follow right
> Were wisdom in the scorn of consequence.—*Œnone*

The easy, perhaps necessary, implication of these words is that the right thing to do in any situation is somehow fixed absolutely and that man can know it for certain. But the life man actually faces is not like that. It often proves highly problematic. It typically develops in novel fashion. Each situation that presents itself has in it not only old, but also new elements. Which, if any, past conclusions apply, one can tell only by careful study. Moreover, new and more adequate insights are possible. To find what to do may call for much good thinking. The "right" of any particular situation can become known only after weighing the respective sets of probable consequences to be expected from the several possible ways of dealing with the situation. When such a study has been made and a clear decision reached, then only can one know "the right" of that situation; and this knowledge is of course subject then, as always, to human limitations. After we have thus found "the right" as best we can, we can go along with Tennyson—we must live up to "the right" thus found and this in scorn of any hindering consequence. But the right we are then obeying was got precisely from a study of all the probable consequences, including generally some consequences that opposed "the right" view as reached by our study. It is these opposing consequences we must now scorn.

2. So far the discussion on morality has stressed consequences, the consequences of the act of behavior. Does this mean that motive and attitude play no part in determining the moral quality of an act?

Rightly understood, motive and attitude play an essential part in moral quality. To be sure, the total actual consequences do determine the effect of the act on the other persons involved, and the doer must choose and direct his act accordingly. But the motive and attitude of the doer, plus of course his insight, will, generally speaking, determine *how* he will study, his *intent* in so doing, and the *spirit* with which he finally acts; and all these (including the consequences of *what* he does) taken together determine the moral quality of his act. Moreover, as we shall later consider in Part II of this book, the motive of any act, plus the attitude in the beginning of the study, the attitude in the evaluation, and the attitude in carrying out the decision mainly determine the educative effect of the act on the doer.

How motive and attitude largely determine the content, the intent, and the spirit of an act is easy to see. Recall the three constituents of a moral act as previously discussed: (i) the habit of acting after thinking—as careful and critical thinking as the particular situation properly demands; (ii) the honest search for the line of conduct which promises the truest good, the best available good of all affected, not simply one's own private personal good; and (iii) the habit and will to act up to the truest good that search has found. Reflection directly shows that in the degree to which one has the prior moral motive and attitude to do the right (whatever honest search may later show this to be), will this prior moral motive and attitude pervade the steps just named and guide them toward a moral decision and act. It will in (i) help one to take the necessary care in thinking; it will in (ii) stimulate the doer in his search to do his honest best; it will in (iii) spur the doer to live up to the best value found. In these ways do moral motive and attitude tend to bring about the effective moral act.

3. Some will ask, as they consider the two preceding answers, "But is it not the very essence of morality that it is commanded by supernatural authority? How can the human process described above, with all its possibilities of error, ever give the compelling

force, the supreme sense of duty and obligation which must constitute the essence of the moral ought?"

Suppose for the sake of argument we grant for the moment—but only for the moment—the contention that morality, in order to summon the necessary and compelling sense of ought, has to be authoritatively commanded; have we thereby abolished the human factor? How do I know without my own study of the confronting situation which command applies to this particular case? And is it not inevitable that I may be mistaken? And can a specified command always be applied absolutely?

To face the problem squarely, take one of the most acceptable of general moral commands and see what would happen if it were taken absolutely. Take for example, "Thou shall not kill." Does this hold absolutely? Many people in India are ready to say, "Yes, we must not kill anything." And if we question them further we see they really mean it—we are not to kill snakes, mosquitoes, beef cattle, any more than men. Most other people we know would refuse not to kill snakes, mosquitoes, or beef cattle; but killing men, all would agree, stands clearly on a different basis. But does the rule apply absolutely to men? Among the Hebrews, whence came this particular wording, there were other commands which carried the explicit penalty: "He shall surely be put to death." In most countries of the world, capital punishment is still to be found; also there may be war, and certainly there is the right of self-defense. So that even this command is not absolute. To fix absolute commands is to commit us to an impossible regime of denial of adaptation to circumstances.

In keeping with this we can better understand the position of Durant Drake (1878–1933) that "authoritarian morality is blindfolded morality. Not being founded upon a study of the consequences of conduct, it is not open to correction by the sight of disastrous results." (57:9) There can be no comparative judgments reached when absolutes are involved. Thus one of the finest spirits in modern history could use these words:

> It were better for sun and moon to drop from heaven, for the earth to fail, and for all the many millions who are upon it to die of starvation in extremest agony, than that one soul should commit one venial sin, should tell one wilful untruth, though it harmed no one, or steal one poor farthing without excuse (qtd. in 82:47).

The demand for absolute commands may be placed in a wider setting. Consider again the earlier discussion on folkways, mores, morals, and ethics, and the scale of moral development which civilization has been developing. Study of this scale and its historic development shows that in earlier days specific codes were more acceptable than later. Another way of saying the same thing we saw with the quotation on Piaget's boys: at first mere obedience sufficed, later principles of fairness and justice were demanded. Is it not a higher type of morality when men understand and follow the *why* of their moral conduct? Is it not a higher type of character that is built on understanding the *why* of the moral demand and on the correlative *love* of that better way? And is it not a higher and finer moral character which includes responsibility for its own decisions? In fact, the more we think about it, the less sure we feel that *mere obedience* really falls properly under the head of conscious morality.

That civilization outgrows certain ideas and develops others becomes quite apparent from historic study. That an earlier day failed to see morals as a natural and essential part of social life can be seen in the three following quotations. The topic there under discussion (but not here) was personal immortality; these quotations state the implications as seen by their author:

> Were there no future life, morality would cease. Man's only destiny would be to provide for himself the enjoyments of this life, irrespective of the means applied.
>
> Were there no future life, there would be no reason why man should be harassed by conscience. His only rational endeavor would be to avoid detection and escape the punishment threatened by law.
>
> Were there no future life, no motive whatever would induce us to practice virtue. The only restraint on vice and crime would be the fear of temporal loss or punishment.

In accordance with our previous discussions it is both reasonable and natural for people as they live together to feel and accept the need for adjusting themselves and their conduct mutually to one another that life may go on more satisfactorily to all concerned. At first these mutually satisfactory ways are worked out rather by trial and error than by deliberation. Later as a critical civilization develops, these moral customs themselves become objects of criticism, as Socrates especially showed. This criticism thus carries the customary morality beyond the stage of obedience to external commands into the higher stage of deliberative morality. Here people ask as to the *how* and *why* of moral obligation; and the clear answer is a morality inherently and inexorably demanded by the highest conception of human living. This seems the reply to the three quotations cited and the sufficient answer tc the third question.

4. At this point some professedly "modern-minded" person might say something like this: I reject practically your whole discussion of morality. To me, pleasure and my own personal happiness --only infrequently collaborating with that of others—are all I deem worth a hoot. That I am selfish, yes, and so are most other men if you get really to the heart of the matter. And, more, I have yet to find and know intimately any man worth his salt who does not think of himself first and foremost. The man who thinks of others before he thinks of himself may become a Grand Master of the Elks, a Socialist of parts, or the star guest of honor at public banquets, but he will never become a great or successful artist, statesman, or even clergyman.

We must thank this man for making his position so clear. He has shown us—not only for himself, but, sad to say, for many others—how one may so build his character that he does think first and foremost, and almost exclusively, of his own personal pleasure and happiness. No one has ever doubted that some people, even many, are like that; but, fortunately, most are not. This man has shown us one sad reason why public life is no better than it is, why politics is so often dirty, why corruption is so widespread. He himself may be financially honest, but he accepts no personal responsibility for the common good; and his lack of responsibility helps to promote the same lack in others.

But this man is a social and moral sponge. He lives well (as he defines it) because others provide the moral foundations of society, the law and order, the security, which he enjoys. If everybody accepted this selfish outlook and lived up—or rather down—to it, life would be, not livable, but deplorable. This man would himself soon find that he could not live as he now does. Thieves and assassins would surround him. No one could feel secure. His "pleasure and personal happiness" would largely vanish.

The real question regarding this man is not the merit of his position; that is indefensible. Everything so far said contradicts him. The real question is how did he get that way. What kind of home life started such an attitude in him? What community or school influences confirmed his bad start and built such an abiding character? This, however, is not the time to enter upon the problem of education thus raised—that comes later; but we can follow up this frank portrayal by a consideration of several related topics.

STANDARDS AND PRINCIPLES; HOW MADE AND HOW USED

Because the use of morality depends on standards and principles of action, it is well for us to see how these are made and used.

Each normal person as he goes through life gradually builds more or less definite standards and principles by means of which he judges others and directs his own conduct. The housewife has her standards for a bed properly made or a floor properly swept or the baby properly cared for. Each farmer has his standards regarding plowing, feeding his cows, how the hired man should work, how much help to expect from his wife and from each of his children who vary in age. It is the part of wisdom to give thought to such standards that they may be properly made. This is particularly true in moral matters, for so much turns on the standards actually used. How then are standards made and how should they be used?

A standard to live by is an instance of cumulative learning. In a way, each specific standard is compounded of all one's previous experiences and conclusions along that line. Take, for example, the case of a teacher who builds a standard of proper human relations with children. Her own upbringing may have included harshness and scolding. While at the time she resented this, still she may have accepted it as the way of a mother with her children. Later, at her teachers' college, watching the practice school teachers deal kindly and considerately with children, she began to question her mother's ways as old-fashioned and wrong. But when she first began teaching, she found herself at times falling back on her mother's ways. However, with more experience and further study at summer school of the psychology of human relations, mental hygiene, and an ethical philosophy of education, she tried harder to live up to her ideals. She watched the effects on children, compared her efforts with those of other teachers, and gradually built, simultaneously, a clearly defined standard of proper human relations and a firm faith in its effectiveness.

Thus does anyone build such a standard. From a particular experience of effort to find the right thing to do the individual learns how that effort turned out: he did certain things in a certain way, and certain results followed. The next time he faces that kind of situation, he will, if wise, recall what he did last time and how it turned out; and out of that experience he will have a clearer view of what is right to do. Again, after this second experience is over, he looks back and sees certain things done with certain results following. If he is wise—uses proper critical thinking—he will put these two experiences with their results together. In certain respects the two were alike, in other respects different. These results of likeness and difference will recur again and again; and the likenesses, being put together, form the essence of the standard or generalization as to what to do along that line; the differences give the variations to suit different situations. The human mind evolved out of goal-seeking efforts through the ages and accordingly is built essentially on the goal-seeking basis of effort. So here the mind naturally, perhaps inevitably, puts together its successive experience results at searching for the right into a cumulative learning whole to form a standard of conduct to serve further goal-seeking efforts. The more critical the thinking at every point, the more trustworthy is the result.

In similar cumulative manner does the individual build ideals. By comparing varied experiences of better and worse, he builds creatively a conception of still better. Thus is formed an ideal, perhaps too high to realize at present, but still something to hope for and work for. By contrast, a standard of conduct is a realizable ideal.

In all of this cumulative learning the results will be better if they are subjected to critical thinking as they develop, and then rebuilt as criticism may show necessary. Desirably, as one grows up, thoughtful examination and critical thinking will increasingly accompany and direct everything that is done.

One concluding remark on building moral character. Life presents many problematic situations, where men are in doubt as to what to do. In each such situation we are morally obligated to consider the possible alternatives. Many are the possibilities here of going wrong: In the first place, we may fail to sense that a given situation is doubtful, and so fail to take the best possible course of action; or we may fail in a doubtful case to do a good job of thinking, and so again we may fail to act properly; or we may let an undue regard for some person, possibly for one's self, wrongly influence the decision; and even if we decide rightly we may fail to live up to the best we see. In these various ways we may go morally wrong, and so build that much of a wrong moral character. *We must then know that the problem of morality is potential in every life situation; and that the way we face each such situation determines the moral character we build. For good or ill, each act and each decision leaves its moral effect on character.*

SELFISHNESS: THE NARROW VS. THE BROAD SELF

Some people, misled by misconceived words, say that all people are by psychological necessity selfish in all they do. All conduct, these say, originates in the self and is therefore selfish. Such reasoning shows a willingness to determine the meaning of the words *a priori* and not by induction from actual usage; and, as with all other *a priori* effects, the practice is likely to be misleading. An inductive study both of conduct and of words will show the error committed.

How are self and conduct related? What does "selfish" really mean? Suppose a mother is so selfish as to let her sick child suffer while she plays bridge. Every right feeling mother will condemn such heartless conduct. The true mother counts her child and its welfare as the dearest part of herself. The selfish mother and the true mother each acts out of herself, there is no other way to act; but the two selves are morally different. The selfish mother, we say, has a narrow self, like the selfish man quoted a few pages back, restricted to her own being and its pleasures narrowly conceived; the true mother has a broad self, a self broad enough to take the child inside herself. The selfish bridge-playing mother and the child-loving mother each gets pleasure from what she does. It is not the fact of getting pleasure that convicts one of selfishness, but rather the quality of the behavior. When anyone, for the sake of personal gratification or advantage, disregards the rights or feelings of other people, that person is guilty of selfishness. Selfishness is obedience to the call of a narrow self in the face of the just demands of a broader self.

A further word can be said about the term *selfish.* Consider the suffix *-ish.* One of its recognized uses carries a derogatory implication. Contrast "womanish" with "womanly" or "mannish" with "manly." The Oxford English Dictionary gives a long list of terms thus made objectionable: apish, babyish, brutish, mulish, prudish, swinish. In each case the *-ish* carries disapproval. And it is the same with self-*ish.* All conduct does grow inevitably out of the self; but the term *selfishness* is used to indicate disapproval both of the conduct and the kind of self out of which such conduct comes.

It may be added that simply to seek pleasure in and of itself indicates generally, if not always, a self with few or no worthy interests. To have strong and worthy interests and to pursue them effectively brings real and worthy pleasure. The more one thinks of the worthy interest and wishes it for what makes it worthy, the finer the character. And the finer the character, the less thought is given to the pleasure aspect that may be expected. The truly moral character then seeks the line of conduct that promises best for all concerned, with next to no thought—even if that much—to the pleasure this will bring him.*

CONSCIENCE

Because such diverse statements have been made about conscience in connection with moral conduct, it must be considered here.

Many have spoken as if conscience were infallible, giving one voice to all men everywhere. Rousseau (1712–1778) said, though hardly expressing a view in keeping with other positions held by him:

> Whatever God wishes a man to do he does not cause it to be told him by another man, but he says it to him himself, he writes it in the depths of his heart (141:193).

* We can only have the highest happiness, such as goes with being a great man, by having wide thoughts and much feeling for the rest of the world as well as ourselves; and this sort of happiness often brings so much pain with it that we can only tell it from pain by being what we would choose before everything else, because our souls see it as good (60:Epilogue).

Lord Byron (1788–1824) said:

Whatever creed be taught or land be trod,
Man's conscience is the oracle of God.—*The Island*, Canto i, st. 6.

And Immanuel Kant said explicitly that "conscience is not an acquisition" and that "an erring conscience is a chimera." Even so modern-minded a man as Felix Adler (1851–1933) said that "it is only necessary to hold the rule of right-doing before a man, and if it be really right, he will accept it," adding that "the appeal to conscience is direct and the response of conscience is immediate." (128:I, 600) A current churchman is even more explicit. Speaking of man's "divinely implanted conscience," he says that this "dwells in every normal person, quite independent of domestic or social conditioning" and that it speaks thus authoritatively against "blasphemy, murder, unchastity, and stealing." (137:XXXII, no. 191:28)

As against these, Montaigne (1533–1592) remarks very wisely: "The laws of conscience which we pretend to be derived from nature, proceed from custom." (112:I:150) And Alexander Pope said in the same strain: "Our consciences are like our watches. None go just alike, yet each believes his own." John Locke spoke to the same effect: "Conscience . . . is nothing else but our own Opinion or Judgment of the moral Rectitude or Pravity of our own actions." (103:I:ii:8) A later British writer, Thomas Fowler (1832–1904), expresses the modern idea more precisely in saying: "In any tenable sense of the term, conscience stands simply for the aggregate of our moral opinion reinforced by the moral sanctions of self-approbation and self-disapprobation." (67:29) But Durant Drake, previously quoted, still better states the best current opinion: "Conscience is not a faculty which gives all normal men identical guidance. On the contrary, the consciences of different men differ to an extraordinary degree; and it is clear that this internal moral sense is the *product*, rather than the *source*, of our moral standards." (57:17) He might have added that it is not simply the *contents* (decisions) of the several consciences that differ according to the differing environment each has had and the individual's reaction thereto, but also the *kinds* of conscience differ for the same reasons. One kind will accept obedience to external commands, while the more highly developed will seek the morals inherently demanded by the seen merits of moral situations.

One final word may be added. Belief in conscience as an infallible source of moral standards began before the study of comparative religions and modern anthropology. To the modern-minded man who knows anthropology such a position is impossible; it is rather a deduction from an *a priori* position than an induction reached from a study of the pertinent facts. Durant Drake seems incontestably right: Conscience is the "*product*," not the "*source*," of our moral standards.

THE AUTHORITY OF MORALS

Why morality has, and must have, authority is easily stated: We live better with morals than without them—that is alike the reason for having them and the reason for granting them authority to control both individual and group conduct. As soon as we place morals among the institutions of a civilization—as indeed we must—the discussions in Chapter IV on the right of institutions to be and to control apply at once to morals. Life goes on best in the long run for all concerned under a regime of appropriate institutions, specifically so under a regime of proper morals.

CONCLUSION: MORALITY A SOCIAL NECESSITY

From all the foregoing discussions two abiding problems remain, each forever difficult: the one, what constitutes under any given set of conditions the precise content of a proper morality; the other, how to get the best resulting answer accepted for use. But some things appear no longer open to doubt: (i) certain attitudes and conduct in preference to their opposites do make an appreciable difference in the lives affected; (ii) both attitudes and appropriate conduct can be so studied and advocated as to spread their use; (iii) acceptance of personal obligation in connection with these is an essential part of their efficacy; (iv) the difference to society between the acceptance or rejection of morality so defined is so great as to make such morality a social necessity.

CHAPTER IX. *Respect for Personality*

THIS chapter fits most intimately with the three preceding. In fact the four chapters present four separate phases of one and the same thesis—that associated living, organized properly and directed in the right spirit, adds significantly to the resulting quality of individual living. An earlier chapter (IV) had already laid the foundation for this thesis by showing the necessary service of institutions. Chapter VI on culture showed how human personality, selfhood itself, with its resulting possibilities of a higher quality of living, depends on the functioning of culture as "the funded capital of civilization." Chapter VII discussed our growing insight into the fact that society, if well managed, helps men live together more richly. Chapter VIII showed how the moral attitude of man to man is essential to any satisfactory social or individual life; and that man has the moral obligation to make the common life go well for all. Now the present chapter repeats this theme of Chapter VIII from another angle: that a proper respect for human personality both develops that personality and gives it opportunity to express itself in fuller living.

THE PECULIAR SIGNIFICANCE OF PERSONALITY

What is there about personality that makes it so important? Suppose a lamb and its sheep mother had self-consciousness, and so understood the lamb's fattening for slaughter as do we. Is it not at once evident that under such circumstances to slaughter the lamb would become an intolerable cruelty, a cruelty so great that we could not permit it? What self-consciousness, if he had it, would thus do for the lamb—allow him to see meanings and feel implications in what he sees, be aware how he is involved—all of that self-consciousness does for man. We saw in Chapter III that man's selfhood, which gives him self-consciousness, also gives him the possibility of both giving and demanding moral treatment. Selfhood and personality thus mean awareness of one's self in relation to others; awareness of past, present, and future, and consequently the conception of one's self as an abiding entity; the ability to feel hope or fear or pleasure along with meanings seen; the ability to act as conscious cause, to plan and execute plans; the ability to accept responsibility for what one does, to develop a conscience, and to act with conscious morality. In connection with all of this each person normally develops the specifically human trait of self-respect and along with it the possibility of a like regard for others.

In the light of all the foregoing, active and effective respect for personality has rich positive meaning: it means such an attitude towards others and such resulting dealings with them as permit each person, in the degree of his development, to feel enjoyment in his own self-respect; to learn increasingly to use his own mind; to exercise responsible self-direction; to develop (responsibly) his own individuality; to share effectively with others in directing the common life; and in general to enjoy freedom to live his own life as to him shall seem good, consistent, of course, with a like freedom for others.

We saw in Chapter VI that the Egyptians made the great advance of recognizing the right of human personality to equal respect irrespective of social status. The Hebrews thus expressed the same thing: "Ye shall not respect persons in judgment: but ye shall hear the small as well as the great." (Deut. 1:17) In the same connection, though much later, Immanuel Kant used the words so often quoted: "So act as to treat humanity, whether in thine own person or in that of any other, in every case as an end withal, never as means only." (97:56)

This use of the world *end* is perhaps not so common as certainly to carry its meaning. If we contrast "man as *means* only" with "man as *end*," we shall come close to Kant's intent. When we so treat another that he too can set up ends and live and develop himself as above advocated, then we are treating him as an end in himself. When we treat him as means merely, using him for our ends with little or no concern for his own ends or his right to self-development, we are denying him the fullest opportunity, possibly any opportunity at all, at the kind of living and development he would choose for himself. Plato said that a slave is one who takes his purposes from another (his master). A modern writer has declared the evil of slavery to be that in it one person (the master) attempts to set bounds for the development of the personality of others (the slaves). In fact one way of defining slavery would be to say that it is a regime which condemns certain persons and their offspring after them to be used as means merely. A thoroughly moral society would demand that all be treated as ends and that all social institutions be intended and so managed as to promote the development of all. In general, exploitation of others is present in the degree that they are used merely as means; it is such use of others as denies them the opportunity to live consistently as ends; it denies them the life we would wish for ourselves.

We may thus far conclude that the definition of respect for personality means, negatively, to refuse to engage in any personal exploitation or discrimination, racially or otherwise; and, positively, to respect the feelings and values of others as fully as "the equilibrium we call justice" will allow and to encourage and promote on the same basis the fullest development of each person, his ability to think for himself, his self-direction, his full and equal share in governing—in a word, to grant to others on the basis of equality and justice the same rights and privileges that we, at our best, wish for ourselves. What has just been said is specifically applicable to the unfair treatment only too commonly meted out in this country to certain minority groups.

PRACTICAL RESPECT FOR PERSONALITY

Some will say that it is impossible to respect all people, the drug addict, for example. Can we respect his personality? If yes, how? Shall we out of respect to him give him at his will as much of the drug as his infirmity craves? The answer to the last question is no. Respect for him means that we start where he is, respect his feelings and needs whenever we can justly do so, but at the same time do all we can to build up his better self into normal self-control. Just what this means for curing the addict's weakness for drugs, the experts must tell us. Possibly we shall be told to lessen gradually the amount of the drug he is allowed to have, while meantime we increasingly help him back into normally satisfying life. We will work at this until his normal physiology is restored and his better self is in adequate control.

How shall we respect the personality of a criminal? Some will say we cannot respect his criminality and therefore cannot respect his personality at all, that he does not deserve it. But again we must, so far as we reasonably can, try to bring a better self into control. Again we begin with what he is; but we try to get the best of the present self operating and on this as a basis cultivate step by step a growing better self until an effectively better self is in control. This educative or psychiatric approach must start where the man now is, with his present tastes and interests. These will cover a range from low to high. We get going the highest we can; and if we are successful, this will build a somewhat higher range. The most promising of this higher range we appeal to in its turn; and so go up, step by step, as high as we can. We start where the criminal now is, but we treat him with reference to the best he can become.

The same thing holds for respecting the personality of a delinquent youth. We cannot respect his acts of delinquency, but we must respect him as a person still having possibilities for good. We deal with him in kindly fashion, and, so far as we honestly can, we speak from his point of view, from ground that he and we hold in common; for we shall thus have more effective appeal to his better self. We strive to get him actively at work, self-actively at work, upon the most worthy interest and activity that will grip him. As he works at this, we shall if necessary help him to succeed, for sense of failure may turn him back to his old bad ways. We wish him not only to succeed on the new basis but to feel that he did it; and so we try to lead him step by step to rebuild the effective control of his own best self to normally proper standards. At each stage we treat him as he is, working on the highest available aspect of his best self, and always with reference to the best that he can become.

How shall a teacher respect the personality of a "naughty" child? Treatment will of course differ according to the age of the child and according to the depth of hold the "naughtiness" has on him. Consider the case of a young child—not severe enough to demand the services of a psychiatrist. The teacher will inwardly disapprove of the child's "naughtiness"; but to stress this in voice or manner may do more harm than good. The teacher wishes, for one thing, to increase her influence with the child, not lessen it. Probably, with a young child, the best treatment is to distract attention from the present case of "naughtiness" by getting some good activity going which enlists the vigorous interest of the child. If this activity can be shared with others, so much the better. One cause of naughtiness is to feel that one is not taken into account by others; one cure is to feel one's self included actively by those who count. If the teacher can herself get into the activity, at least by pointedly sympathetic interest, this too will help. Three things can thus follow: (i) the child is less tempted to naughtiness, and is working constructively (and so building up a constructive self-control); (ii) the child is building up respected relations with others who count (and so building up his regard for their good opinion; (iii) the teacher has somewhat improved her relations with the child (and so has increased her influence with him). If this sort of thing be consistently continued, these three lines of good effect accumulate increasingly to lessen the probability of relapses, more positively to build wise self-control in the child himself.

Every step here taken began where the child found himself, and treated him with respect to what he might become, namely, a character in which his higher and better self is in more effective control. This is effective respect for the potential personality of the once naughty child. The analogous treatment of course holds for any age.

If we look again at this general procedure, we see that it will fit also the normal child, giving a pattern for the daily treatment of even the finest and most promising youth we know. He must grow; his present outlook and equipment are inadequate for the demands that lie ahead. He, too, has a range of interests. Some of these have in them more promise of growth than others. We try then to get going an interest which in maximum degree promises both growth and present active interest. As he works at this we try to guide him toward maximum growth in desirable traits, skills, knowledge, ideals, standards, acting on thinking, and self-control. If the growth is to be real and effective, each step in advance must be internally accepted by the youth himself. Otherwise his own self will not be growing. The same principle holds here, then, as with the others, to treat each one as he now is but always with reference to the more adequately self-directing person he may become.

Does the foregoing discussion mean that a person's mere wish suffices to determine which of his personalities is to be respected? Suppose two people encourage each other in degrading living, are they properly respecting each other's personality? The answer is a clear no. It is the best potential self that is to be respected. We may perhaps have to approach this goal by steps; but even so, it is the best possible self that must at each stage determine what steps we take with any person in any situation.

Respect for personality means, then, to help each to grow by his own active efforts into the best that in him lies, specifically to help him to make, of his own volition, choices toward ever better ends. This applies to all persons everywhere, to any person-to-person dealings of any sort. To foster and encourage the best now in each one and do this in such a way as to lead to the best result possible for him to develop—such respect for personality is the most sacred thing known among men.

FREEDOM AND RESPECT FOR PERSONALITY

Hegel went so far as to say that "the History of the world is none other than the progress of the consciousness of Freedom." (74:19) Certainly freedom is so intimately related to respect for personality that the mutual bearing of the two must be considered. And study of the problem soon shows two kinds or degrees of freedom to be considered, freedom to act (freedom of external constraint), and freedom from ignorance and prejudice (freedom of the highest self to control one's choices).

1. *Freedom to Act.* This is the most obvious of all freedoms. In the degree that society unjustly restricts this freedom, it refuses to respect personality. Alfred North Whitehead says, "Freedom of action is a primary human need." (171:84) If one is to live in any full sense, if he is to be himself and act accordingly, he must have freedom to act. Denial of such freedom or limitation upon it (save as demanded by justice to others) is by so much a denial of the right to live, to be one's self, and by so much a denial of respect for one's personality.

What does it mean to be free to act? Thomas Hobbes has quaintly stated it thus: Anyone is free if "in those things which by his strength and wit he is able to do, [he] is not hindered to do what he has a will to." (78:II, ch. XXI) The modern-minded may perhaps prefer a more familiar sounding statement by John Stuart Mill: "Liberty consists in doing what one desires"; or perhaps a longer statement by Dorothy Fosdick:

> So liberty [freedom of action] is held to be endangered or denied when some outside influence prevents the doing of what one desires to do, feels able to do, and has otherwise available means of doing (66:5).

Clearly freedom to act is not unlimited; otherwise other personalities will not be respected. Eighteenth-century individualism tended to assert unlimited freedom; now we know better. We saw with Shotwell in Chapter IV that freedom is at bottom both a social and an ethical matter, being specifically "the equilibrium we call justice." Walter Lippman said, "There is no freedom in mere freedom." (102:326) Norman Angell said, "When all demand complete freedom, none has any." (123: Mar. 1, 1942) So that respect for personality demands definitely that freedom be limited by justice to all.

2. *Freedom to Be One's Best Self.* This freedom John Dewey defines as "the release of capacity from whatever hems it in." (52:207*f*.) The more fully and effectively one realizes in his actual living the best that lies potential in him, the more he lives; the freer he is to make choices which truly serve, the freer to be and to act his best self; the more, accordingly, will others respect his personality. We have said that what gives man his manifold superiority over the beasts is, at bottom, that he knows what he is about and can exercise consequent control. If we join the freedom to be one's best self with the conscious self-control imposed by justice for all, we have that kind and phase of freedom called "freedom of conscience." In this we see a peculiar respect for personality: respect for the efforts of the individual to conclude regarding the demands of duty as he sees it without being either coerced or hindered, by government or otherwise. "Freedom of conscience" is accordingly one of the basic freedoms; exercised thoughtfully it becomes an instance of the highest freedom of action, the internal freedom of autonomous and responsible personality.

What was just said cuts even deeper than was stated. In this highest kind of freedom of action we not only see what appears to be the highest instance of respect for personality; we gain, besides, new insight into why we must respect personality and, still further, we see how to assign greatness. We value highest that personality which in deciding what to do shows at once the greatest insight into life's problems, the greatest refinement of distinctions pertinently made, the most inclusive and best ordered view of what is at issue; and along with these must go the strongest disposition to use this insight to improve living. All men have potential in them more or less of these high qualities. Because the human personality has such potentialities we respect personality wherever found; but it is the degree of these high qualities actually manifest in conscious action that determines greatness. "These," as Christopher Marlowe said, "are the men that all the world admires."

EDUCATION AND RESPECT FOR PERSONALITY

The discussion just given leads almost inevitably to the problem of education as the means for attaining the freedom to be one's best self. Education must aim at developing in the individual the best possible insight into life's problems as they successively present themselves before him; at helping him to make ever finer distinctions in what he does, to take more and more considerations ever better into account, and finally to bring the best social-moral attitudes to bear on each decision as made and enacted. For the only proper aim of education is fullness of living through fully developed character. We know from our own observation that "one man may live more in a day than another in twenty"; or as Philip James Bailey said: "He lives most who thinks most—feels the noblest—acts the best." (*Festus*, v)*

Education as here understood includes all the factors that effect learning, not only in school but in all of life. For, as we shall later consider, we learn only and exactly what we live; we learn what we accept as our way of living, and we learn it in the degree we live it. Education is thus the cumulative effect of all one's successive learnings. In Part II of this book we shall consider how, psycholog-

* Philip James Bailey, *Festus*. Reproduced by permission of E. P. Dutton & Co., Inc., New York; and Routledge & Kegan Paul Ltd., London.

ically, such an educative process best goes on. Here the concern is to consider what education should aim at in terms of respect for personality, and to see how respect for personality demands such education.

The education sought is one designed (i) to develop in the individual both practical knowledge and attitudes, knowledge of the things that count most significantly in life as it can be lived; (ii) to add richness to life here and now and an increasing richness from now on; (iii) to develop positive control over one's thoughts and acts; and (iv) to foster the attitude of justice for others that all may live happily together. Such an education will seek to prevent and remove prejudice; for prejudice is exactly the practice of acting before judging and therefore of acting blindly. In one word, such an education seeks to build the behaving character, the all-round effective character which seeks fullness of living for one's self and so manifests a deservedly fuller respect for the personality of others. In this double sense education exists to respect personality, and so to realize the finest and best potential in each person.

EDUCATION VS. INDOCTRINATION

The education thus far discussed is an education designed to free the whole personality of the learner for the fullest living, for the best and most independent exercise of all his powers, for the control of his own destiny. This alone we have counted true respect for the personality. It was further brought out that without such development the individual is not free in perhaps the most important sense, that true and effective freedom depends thus as much on inner growth, on the ability to use the mind effectively, as on the absence of external restraint. In fact, it might be said that a condition of inner slavery is the worst kind of slavery; such an individual has no wish to change his status, he even fights against his true freedom. To aid the individual, then, to the fullest use of his powers, to fullest intelligent and responsible self-direction and effectiveness, is to give the greatest possible respect to his personality.

But teachers have not always thus sought to respect the personalities of those studying under them; many today still act otherwise. In other words, teachers have too often cared more for the subject-matter they teach or the cause they represent than for human personality. In the early days of the Protestant Revolt, for example, both sides alike competed for proselytes, each side struggling to get control of as many youth as they could in the effort to fasten their respective doctrines upon the minds and hearts of the young under their care. It was only at a later date, under the democratic teaching of respect for personality, that men grew to the point of questioning such partisan indoctrination.

The term *indoctrination* just used demands a word of explanation. The word means, literally, implanting doctrines. When such implanting on an uncritical basis was the common practice of the school, and indeed one of its principal aims, to indoctrinate and to teach came to be but diverse ways of describing the same process. The term *indoctrination* then carried no derogatory implication, and this was until recently its recognized meaning and status. The Oxford English Dictionary (this part published about 1900) recognized no other meaning. But with the development of democracy and the coming of modern rapid change, it was increasingly felt that education could no longer be content with inducing uncritical belief, but must instead develop responsible thinking on the part of all as a necessary preparation for democratic living and citizenship and an unpredictable future. In this way the term *indoctrination* has been increasingly restricted to its derogatory implication of an improper inducing of uncritical belief.

There are, to be sure, some who still believe it right for parents and teachers to implant their own doctrines in the young under their care so that these doctrines will remain fixed beyond the possibility of later question or revision. These people accordingly use the term *indoctrination* with a favorable implication. Also, curiously enough, during the late war the American Navy adapted the term *indoctrination* to mean "instruction in the fundamentals of military discipline, naval customs, and usage." Naturally this interpretation carries no derogatory implication. And this naval use of the term has since been extended to other areas. So that the term is currently used in several different senses, the one here followed being, however, the more usual meaning in educational writing.*

That democracy must refuse and reject indoctrination in this prejudice-building sense would seem beyond question. Where

* A fuller consideration of this meaning of this term is given in Rivlin and Schueler's *Encyclopedia of Modern Education* (1943), p. 393.

competent opinion differs as to what to believe, for parents and teachers to take advantage of the child's ignorance and docility to fasten in him beyond recall their own chosen views is to enslave this child to those who thus teach him. Democracy and a proper respect for the child's personality must reject such enslavement as partisan exploitation of the individual's right to be educated to do his own thinking and make his own decisions.

This modern attitude of condemning such indoctrination is not limited to the present day. Dryden spoke definitely in 1687:

> By education most have been mis-led;
> So they believe, because they so were bred.
> The priest confirms what the nursery began,
> And thus the child imposes on the man.—*Hind and Panther*,
> pt. iii, 1. 389.

And further, at the 1807 dedication of Milton (Mass.) Academy, Rev. Thomas Thacher said: "A Preceptor has no right to inculcate his peculiar sentiments in theology on the mind of the pupil." (qtd. in 16:239) And Bronson Alcott is quoted as saying: "The true teacher defends his pupils against his own personal influence." (168:728) Professor Raphael Demos of Harvard has recently said: "We *mould* material things into the pattern of human ends. But we do not *mould* human beings, and do not wish to do so. That way lies indoctrination, propaganda, the worst tyranny of all because it is tyranny over the human mind." (8:XV:99)

Various questions, however, properly arise in connection with what has just been said.

1. The child's education cannot wait until he is mature enough to think for himself. We have to begin from the first. Does this not force indoctrination upon us?

Possibly some indoctrination is thus inevitable with younger children, but even in these cases the ultimate intent should be to the contrary. For example, we will work as best we can to build the habit of truthfulness in the young child, and we must begin this before he can understand why lying is a bad social practice. But as soon as we can and as fast as we can we lead him to see the social reasons for truthfulness. The practice of honesty in the form of not stealing can be taught on a basis of understanding why earlier than truth-telling; for the child can easily understand how he would feel if someone should take his toys. In all cases where habits are desirable, we teach the habit even though the why has to come later. Even if there is controversy as to what is right, the parent or teacher will still teach his own best insight as to the proper habit. As soon as possible, however, the child, now grown older, should be helped to get a reliable understanding of what is socially and morally involved, so that he may be intelligent in his moral conduct. Ultimately, when adolescence has well advanced, the youth should be encouraged to review critically both his habits and the earlier accepted why of those habits and attitudes. He does this in order that he may now make both habit and reason really his own. Previously, he had learned them as a child, when he thought as a child. Now he must rethink them, to make them his own or to reject them or revise them on his mature level. If he does not do this, he will be living henceforth enslaved to his childish ideas.

2. A decade or two ago there was positive demand that the schools actively help build a new social-economic order. If this means that teachers should plan such an order and then by specific indoctrination raise up a new generation committed to the new order so planned, we cannot accept this program. Teachers as such have no proper or exclusive commission to plan such an order; and any attempt by indoctrination of the young to create such an order would of itself be a clear denial of the democratic process.

It does, however, seem a specific duty of the school to recognize that the existing social order demands a certain amount of continual remaking, and that the school accordingly has a correlative duty to have the young study, suitably to their age, the strengths and weaknesses of our civilization. And no custom or institution, however cherished, can claim exemption from such study and criticism. This means the free and untrammeled study of all pertinent controversial issues; but in such study the teacher's aim must be the upbuilding of the students to make thoughtful choices, not the winning of them to his side of a partisan controversy. "If any teacher, by the way in which he teaches, either wilfully or carelessly permits some bias or prejudice of his own, or even the inappropriate expression of his reasoned convictions, persistently to mar the process of fair-minded study on the part of those studying under him, he is to that extent damaging those students and in that same degree is manifesting his unfitness to teach." (116:8)

3. While agreeing that indoctrination in other matters is wrong, some still feel that the case for democracy is different; for it we should indoctrinate. They claim (i) that, democracy being fundamental to our way of living, we should run no risk regarding it, but indoctrinate all in it from earliest childhood. They point further to the facts (ii) that our democracy is now threatened from without as never before and (iii), sad to say, that some of our own people do not even now fully accept democracy. From these considerations, they say, indoctrination of all is demanded.

To such a proposal the reply seems to be to agree to the three facts and assert that the conclusion does not follow. To teach democracy in undemocratic fashion, in a way to foster uncritical acceptance, would seem an odd way of fostering democracy. To indoctrinate a belief in democracy without including the reasons for democracy, and without building ability to think critically about it, is to make blindfolded adherents of democracy. Such people would not know the why of their practices or dogmas and consequently could not be trusted to apply the doctrines intelligently. When they grow up into active citizenship they might be easily induced, for example, to forbid the study of controversial issues in school. They might forbid the critical study of democratic doctrines and so prevent wise adaptation of these doctrines to new conditions that arise. In one word, such indoctrination would make blind dogmatists of democracy, quite unfit to carry on the democratic process in a changing civilization. That way lies fanaticism.

The conclusion of the whole matter, it appears, is that democracy and ethics must at bottom respect the personality of all concerned, to develop each as best possible toward more effective use of his mind and toward intelligent and responsible free play of intelligence. On this we must stand. Such respect for personality is indeed the most sacred thing among men.

CHAPTER X. *Democracy*

DEMOCRACY, both as a term and as a conception, shows through the ages many historic changes of meaning and scope. Originally the term meant a kind of government, government by the citizens generally as opposed to government by a king or an oligarchy. Henceforth the individual citizen would enjoy freedom from an arbitrary control by a king, and instead would himself share in determining the management of law and order. At the founding of our own nation it was the freedom aspect that was perhaps most active—freedom from the rule of Great Britain.

In our day the meaning of democracy, while thus taking its start in government, is increasingly widened beyond government to indicate a way of life, a quality of associated living based on active respect for human personality, and this along all the lines that consistently go to make up desirable living. In this sense democracy becomes, practically, the effort to run society on the basis of ethics and respect for human personality. And this growth in the meaning and application of democracy is still actively in process in the world today.

The development of the meaning of democracy beyond the area of actual government has, it appears, grown out of a more extended consideration of the proper aim of democratic government, namely, to ensure to each individual the fair and equal chance to live fully as a conscious and self-directing person. Such an emphasis naturally carries the aim of democracy beyond those areas of life in which the compulsions of government are suitable into certain wider areas where compulsion is too crude to be effective, where instead the inner attitude of moral obligation must be our reliance. It is with this stress on inner attitude that democracy reaches beyond mere government and becomes instead a way of life.

The term *democracy* is thus used in two senses. On the one hand, it indicates a kind of government, a government of the people. On the other hand, it means a way of life, a kind and quality of associated living in which sensitive moral principles assert the right to control individual and group conduct. It is worthy of note, however, that in either sense democracy involves control, the control of both individual and group conduct for the good of all affected. In the first sense, the control is by the coercion of government; in the second sense, the control is internal, the demand of intelligence and conscience upon the individual himself to obey and serve the varied calls of a social morality. It may be added that neither control is to repress any proper individuality, but always to allow expression of individuality as effectively as possible in all relationships.

As part of an inductive study of the developing meaning of democracy, it may help at this point to review briefly the history of its development with culminating reference to our own country. Recognition of the varying opinions and attitudes along the way will help to build a more adequate conception of democracy and perhaps in some measure help to anticipate difficulties of the future. In general, this historic review will, as above suggested, reveal an increasing regard for human personality wherever found.

HISTORIC DEVELOPMENT OF THE CONCEPTION OF DEMOCRACY

So far as appears, the term *democracy*, and probably the idea, arose in Athens in the fifth century B.C. This early effort had the advantage of a small city-state as a setting and, in considerable measure, of equality among the voting citizens. Nevertheless, it did not succeed too well, and by the time of Aristotle, a century later, the term, but not the essential idea, had fallen into disrepute. This bad name has hurtfully reappeared through succeeding centuries, coming especially to the fore in the seventeenth and eighteenth centuries when modern democracy was struggling to be born in Europe and America. Thus Bishop Joseph Hall said in 1614: "Nothing . . . can be more disorderlie, than the confusion of your

Democracie, or popular state." (70:732) And Governor John Winthrop of Massachusetts wrote: "A Democratie is, among most civill nations, accounted the meanest & worst of all formes of Governm't: . . . & Historyes doe recorde, that it hath been allwayes of least continuance & fullest of troubles." (175:II:430)

Looking back now upon Athens, the slavery of perhaps half the population was to our present way of thinking a clear denial of democracy; but as the world was then constituted, slavery seemed natural if not inevitable. Aristotle, following the current Greek practice and thought, divided men into two diverse groups according to native ability, "natural slaves" on the one hand and "natural rulers or natural masters" on the other—an unwarranted distinction that has survived, at least in degree, even to our own day.* But the Greek term *democracy*, meaning government by the people, has also survived; and it is, outside the influence of the U.S.S.R., increasingly accepted to mean government by all the people, not simply by certain privileged ones, as was formerly the practice even in our own country. At the adoption of the Constitution suffrage was limited to property holders amounting in number to about one fifth of all male whites above twenty-one. This excluded, of course, women and slaves. It may be added in passing that though the Greeks originated democracy, their political genius failed when it came to conceiving the principle of representation, which makes possible a large democratic state or an effective union of states. Success in achieving representative government belongs to Great Britain with its Parliament; success at forming a federal union of legally equal states with elected representation had to await the formation of our own Federal Union.

About the time of the Athenian democracy, Rome was a city-state governed by a Senate chosen at the first from the patrician families of the city. The word *republic* was their word for this kind of government as opposed to a kingdom. In later years this term was used in our own country to mean a government by chosen representatives, with perhaps a restricted electorate. Such a government, as we shall see in a moment, represented the position of those

* On the other hand, it must be kept in mind that these same Greeks developed a way of life which has profoundly influenced our present best conception of the life good to live. This enters most constructively into modern democracy considered as a way of life.

opposed to democracy at the founding of our American government under the Constitution of 1787.

During the Middle Ages, feudalism established itself strongly within the European ruins of the Roman Empire. This was of course the exact antithesis of democracy. In the universities, however, in the south of Europe there was a considerable element of democratic control by the students themselves, and by the end of the Middle Ages there had developed a very considerable attitude moving toward free inquiry. A legal maxim that originated in these days sounds much like modern democracy: *Quod omnes tangit, ab omnibus approbetur* (What affects all, should be approved by all; or, if it affects all, it should be passed on by all). But on the whole the individual, as we saw in Chapter VII, was rather straitly controlled during the Middle Ages by the authorities above him.

Following the Middle Ages, various factors, some of which we further discussed in Chapter VII, operated to break down feudalism and move toward a world in which the individual as such had larger sway, even in the end to the establishment of modern democracies. The invention of gunpowder served in time to eliminate from effective warfare the armored knight, who, in a way, had been the keystone of the feudal arch. Then the rise of cities based on widespread trade built a new economic regime founded on exchange and money payment. As gunpowder eliminated knighthood, so this new trade regime built up a prosperous middle class independent of feudal control. About this same time the Renaissance came as a great intellectual movement growing out of the revival of ancient classical secularism. This tended, though with a rather backward look, to establish human reasoning as the court of last resort; but this reasoning, it must be kept in mind, was still from principles already fixed, that is, *a priori* rather than inductive.

The modern scientific movement a little later established inductive reasoning, at first as the chief basis, and later as the only basis, for reaching dependable conclusions in the physical sciences. This movement soon had profound influence on man's estimate of his own powers, showing what man could do with his own natural resources. We now see this growth of inductive science as the most significant single factor to make the modern world modern. The invention of printing and the Protestant Revolt were, along with modern science, highly significant influences to give effective social place to individual thought and decision, thus increasing respect for the individual as such. These various movements in a very true sense led to the coming of modern democracy.

The Dutch Republic, which first established modern freedom of thought, arose largely out of the Protestant revolt against Spanish rule. The English Revolutions of 1642 and 1688 broke the "divine right" of kings and put the English king under the rule of Parliament, which is now under the ultimate rule of the people. Following especially the Renaissance and the development of science came the Enlightenment, whose motto, Kant said, was *sapere aude* (dare to reason, dare to trust reason, dare to use your own understanding). This meant, to those who most fully accepted it, reliance solely on human intelligence, without recourse to any supernatural help or authority.

This Enlightenment movement, especially in its influence from Great Britain, had very extensive acceptance in our country about the time of our Revolution. The language of the Declaration of Independence is the language of the Enlightenment: "the Laws of Nature and of Nature's God, . . . we hold these truths to be self-evident, . . . all men are created equal, . . . and endowed by their Creator with certain unalienable Rights, . . . Life, Liberty, and the pursuit of Happiness, . . . to secure these rights Governments are instituted among Men, . . . deriving their just powers from the consent of the governed, . . . whenever any form of Government becomes destructive of these ends, it is the Right of the People to alter or to abolish it, . . . appealing to the Supreme Judge of the world for the rectitude of our intentions, . . . with a firm reliance on the protection of Divine Providence." As regards these two closing phrases, it must be understood that the men of Enlightenment, many of them called Deists as opposed to the theism of orthodox theology, tended, as above suggested, to reject supernatural revelation along with its theology, but contended that a study of nature and natural phenomena disclosed "laws of Nature," a natural morality, and a "God of Nature." To this God of Nature they could refer as "the supreme Judge of the world" and as "Divine Providence." Such a general position, it seems, can properly be ascribed to Jefferson, Adams, and Franklin, who principally drafted the Declaration.

While these various movements were changing the public attitude, especially of northwest Europe, from medieval authoritarianism to a strong individualistic trend, the New World was discovered and its settlement begun. Especially in the British Colonies, this transplanted life favored a fresh start. New conditions of living demanded—and effected—changes in ways of living and, eventually, new attitudes. New opportunities stirred the imagination. Many settlers—for example, the Pilgrims, Puritans, Quakers, Scotch-Irish, French Huguenots, and various German sects—came to get religious freedom. On the receding frontier, lands were always cheap, and after the very first the returns fairly sure. A traveler to Long Island in 1670 exclaimed that "if there be any terrestrial happiness to be had by people of all ranks, especially of an inferior rank, it must certainly be here: here anyone may furnish himself with land, and live rent free." And he went on to say: "you may travel . . . hundreds of miles . . . and never hear the least complaint for want, nor hear any ask you for a farthing." And he concluded: "If there be any terrestial Canaan, 'tis surely here, where the Land floweth with milk and honey." (37:19–21)*

The equality brought by these abundant opportunities worked mightily in itself to produce the American doctrine of democracy. Alexis De Tocqueville (1805–1859), that discerning student of American life, recognized this equality of opportunity as highly significant: "The more I advanced in the study of American society, the more I perceived that the equality of conditions is the fundamental fact from which all others seem to be derived." (38:I, 3) The frontier gave not only this equality; it gave in comparable strength that other characteristic noted earlier of the beginning American democracy—love of liberty, independence, aversion to external control. While at the time of the Revolution there was serious division

* As regards the new conditions of living in the British colonies and the changes of attitude thus produced, Thomas Jefferson writing in 1796 from France used these strong words:

> If all the sovereigns of Europe were to set themselves to work to emancipate the minds of their subjects from their present ignorance and prejudices, and that as zealously as they now endeavor the contrary, a thousand years would not place them on the high ground on which our common people are now setting out. Ours could not have been so fairly placed under the control of the common sense of the people, had they not been separated from their parent stock, and kept from contamination . . . by the intervention of so wide an ocean. To know the worth of this, one must see the want of it here. (Letter to George Wythe, August 13, 1786.)

near the coast as between the Whig and Loyalist, on the actual frontier the great majority were for independence. Later the same frontier effect favored Jefferson, and still later Andrew Jackson.

But this American democracy gained its dominance only against definite opposition. Our colonial period showed many strongly entrenched remnants of the earlier feudalism; and the beginning period of the republic showed strong aristocratic attitudes among many of the patriot leaders. Early colonial laws gave certain distinctions of dress to upper-class people and denied them to the lower classes. The old deeds often include the terms *gentleman* and *yeoman,* using these to indicate higher and lower social distinctions. At Yale until 1767 students were listed in the order of the social standing of their families.* Some 1768 regulations at Princeton are quite interesting in regard to institutional superiority and inferiority:

> Every scholar [student] shall keep his hat off about ten rods to the president and about five to the tutors.
>
> And if called or spoken to by him [by a superior], if within hearing, shall *give* direct pertinent answer, concluding with "SIR" (80:55*f*.).

This distinction between the privileged and the masses was strong and active in the more conservative among the founding fathers. Alexander Hamilton well stated his position on this subject in terms at least suggestive of Aristotle:

> All communities divide themselves into the few and the many. The first are the rich and the well born, the other the mass of the people. . . . The people are turbulent and changing; they seldom judge or determine right. Give, therefore, to the first class a distinct, permanent share in the government. They will check the unsteadiness of the second, and as they cannot receive any advantage by a change they, therefore, will ever maintain good government (123:*Bk. Rev.,* Sept. 17, 1939).

Roger Sherman, Elbridge Gerry, Gouverneur Morris, John Jay, all prominent as "founding fathers," are quoted as opposing anything like democracy. John Adams, in spite of his strong advocacy of independence, gave this opinion of democracy:

* The same (until 1772) has been asserted of Harvard, but also questioned. See *American Antiquarian Society:* Franklin B. Dexter (7: new series IX:34–59, Oct. 1893) and S. E. Morison (7:XLII:371–431, Oct. 1932).

Remember, democracy never lasts long. It soon wastes, exhausts, and murders itself. There never was a democracy yet that did not commit suicide (3:VI:484).

Fisher Ames, a very strong Federalist, was even more emphatic, as the *Dictionary of National Biography* shows. And Martha Washington, finding a hand smudge on the wall after one of her husband's conferences, is reported to have said to George: "You must have had some of your dirty democrats here today." (qtd. in 149:IV:306)

As we look back on the early days of our country, it seems clear that it was, as remarked at the time, a "republic," not a democracy, that the Constitution of 1787 intended to establish. Not all people were to share equally in final authority. The elaborate system of "checks and balances" was in part intended to limit the power of the populace. The device of a Senate as a highly privileged upper house, elected (at first) not by the people directly but by the state legislatures, the extended term of office for the Senators (longer than that of the President and three times as long as that of the Representatives), the continuity of the Senate (only one third going out at a time), its check on Presidential appointments, its two thirds consent necessary for ratification of treaties, the (intended) method of electing the President (not by the people directly but through electors), the strict separation of the three functions of government—all these, it seems fair to assert, were measures intended to keep the power of government within the hands of the privileged few.

But the events of history willed otherwise. The vast domain of public lands, the equality and independence of the frontier-educated people, distance from Europe, the unwisdom of the Federalists, the fortunate leadership of Thomas Jefferson, the variety of Protestant sects—all these things concurred to make our country in time accept democracy as its way of life. It must be confessed that too often our people have been slow to see, and unwilling to accept, what their professed democratic faith inherently demands. It took three quarters of a century to eradicate slavery, even though Jefferson said regarding it: "I tremble for my country when I reflect that God is just." (90: Query XVIII, Manners) And similarly it took another half century to recognize that democracy means equality of treatment also for women. And we are not yet ready to apply a consistent democracy either to women or to certain minorities in our midst.

DEMOCRACY AS RESPECT FOR PERSONALITY

Having seen somewhat of the history of American democracy, let us dig deeper and ask about the development of its fundamental theory.

First, what is the essence of democracy? What way of conceiving it best reaches the heart of the matter, best shows how to appraise our own democracy and to further it? An earlier day would probably have answered that "the essence" of democracy is freedom, freedom of the individual to decide and act on his own. Certainly such freedom is essential to any decent democracy; but it may show a truer regard for all the factors involved to say that respect for personality comes first, with freedom (limited by equality, and thus defining justice) following as necessary to implement any true respect for personality.

The preceding chapter discussed respect for personality in some detail. Here we may say of it that it stems from the inside of the self and speaks in behalf of others. Knowing how we feel in the enjoyment of self-respect and satisfying life, we wish the like for others. This is our respect for them: it is kin answering to kin.

The term *personality* means, at bottom, a being who is self-conscious (feels, has concerns, strives to realize his concerns—and knows all this). The higher the type of person, the more he acts knowing what he does, the more widely sensitive he is, the more thoughtfully he makes his decisions in the light of foreseen consequences, and the more he accepts responsibility for what he does. Such a person acts freely (lives fully and effectively, is a self-determining agent) and, acting freely, enjoys life.

If personality means doing and feeling of this sort, to respect personality in others means to wish for and strive to foster such opportunity for them. Respect for personality is the Golden Rule applied in these more personal aspects of life: what I thus enjoy I wish others to have.

The past two centuries show in many respects an appreciable advance in sensitivity to man as such, to his personal feelings, and in determination to make the world a better place in which to live. Treatment of criminals, of the insane, of the unfortunate, of youth, is immensely more considerate than was true two centuries ago.

RESPECT FOR PERSONALITY: ABOLITION OF CHILD LABOR

One especial advance in respect for personality is seen in the treatment of child labor. To a degree that now seems incredible the beginning of the Industrial Revolution found a lack of regard alike for youth and for the underprivileged. In the children of the poor these two were combined. In 1808 the Baltimore (Maryland) Cotton Manufactury advertised for "a number of boys and girls from eight to twelve years of age," offering "constant employment and encouraging wages"; and expressed the hope that "citizens having a knowledge of families, having children destitute of employment, will do an act of *public benefit*, by directing them to the institution." (6:CCXXXVI:83, Nov. 1944. Italics supplied) In 1832 it appeared that two fifths of all persons employed in the New England factories were between seven and sixteen years of age; while the hours of labor were never less than ten, seldom less than twelve, and often fourteen or fifteen and even more. Even 1900 saw less than a dozen states in this country seriously attempting to limit the labor of children in mills, mines, factories, or stores (62:III:414, 418). In this particular regard, conditions are now much better. Today few or no children work in our cotton factories and none at such hours.

GROWTH OF RESPECT FOR PERSONALITY; THE BETTER STATUS OF AMERICAN LABOR

The developing better treatment of labor is a definite phase of the historic growth of regard for personality in America. We saw earlier in this chapter how roseate appeared life in America to the 1670 traveler. It was out of such that "the American dream" arose to beckon many from older lands. And as long as agriculture sufficed and abundant Western lands were available for settlement, the dream could be realized. Horace Greeley said: "Go West, young man, and grow up with the country." Abraham Lincoln in 1860 thus stated the three stages in such "growing up" as he had watched the process:

> We . . . wish . . . the humblest man an equal chance to get rich with anybody else. When one starts poor, as most do . . . he may look forward and hope to be a hired laborer this year and the next, work for himself afterwards, and finally to hire men to work for him. This is the true system (101:VI:67*f.*).

However, the time came in the history of our country when there were no more free lands for frontier settlement. And at the same time industrialization was pushing agriculture into a subordinate position.

It is out of this situation of increasing industrialization that our "labor" problems have arisen. To work in a factory was soon seen to be very different from working as a hired man on the typical old-time farm. For one thing the hired laborer on such a farm could hope, following Lincoln's formula, to save his wages and in time own and manage his own farm; no such hope, or anything like it, confronted a factory hand. Once a factory hand always a a factory hand, seemed nearer the truth. And the effect of this difference was far-reaching. A flexible social scale had hitherto seemed characteristic of American life; merit and industry would carry one perceptibly up the scale. Instead of this the factory, as at first managed, seemed to bring into the social group a basis of abiding cleavage: on the one side those who either now or in hopeful prospect could "own" their own business and become "independent," even wealthy; on the other side, those who could not hope to "own," but must work forever under orders. And, perhaps worse, the "mill hands" and their families lived in those early days, typically, in "mill villages," shut off actually from the rest of the people, and even more shut off in their own deep feelings. Adverse external control seemed inevitable. As W. P. Montague expressed it, in a "thoroughly industrialized [capitalistic] society, those who control the machines have absolute mastery of those who must find work at the machines or starve." (84:XLV: 147, Jan. 1935)

During the earlier days of the Industrial Revolution, as suggested above, the personality of the worker seemed to count for little.

There was little or nothing the mill workers could legally do if they found their wages or working conditions unsatisfactory. In England up to 1824 actual laws forbade unionization and strikes, while in America court decisions counted all such moves to be "unlawful conspiracies" against the owners. So that in that earlier period the statement of John Stuart Mill (1806–1873) held true for both countries, that "the majority of laborers have as little choice of opportunity as could exist in any system short of slavery."

Opposition to unionization and strikes has been greatly modified within the past fifty years. Laws have been passed to protect labor against various wrong practices of management, especially against resort to court injunctions. But among a large number of our people there still survive many of the old feelings that labor unions and strikes are inherently wrong.

Under Theodore Roosevelt (1858–1919) and Woodrow Wilson (1856–1924) the cause of labor made advances. During World War I, under the influence perhaps of Woodrow Wilson and the very liberal Kerensky revolution in Russia, there arose about the beginning of 1918 what the writer feels to have been the most pronounced and widespread spirit of liberalism that he has yet observed in this country. It was, we may suppose, under the influence of this spirit that Nicholas Murray Butler, speaking before the Commercial Club in St. Louis, February 16, 1918, took a position very different from that commonly held at the time by his political associates:

> Production for use or for enjoyment [must be put] in the place of production for mere profit. Production for profit alone is plainly an inhuman undertaking; it can and does close its eyes to human exploitation, to human suffering, and to human want. . . .
>
> Perhaps no one could have predicted that the war [World War I] would have gone far toward putting this larger and finer and more democratic view of production in place of that which has prevailed for more than a century, yet that is precisely what is happening (123: Feb. 17, 1918).

Alas, the close of that war brought a pronounced moral slump. "Production for profit alone" regained much if not all of its former exclusive hold on owners and management, there to stay until the great depression of the 'thirties shifted the scene. Under the depression and a new political outlook, "labor" then went forward as never before. And World War II crowded upon the departing depression to carry labor's status still further forward.

Now after World War II the problem of the relation of democracy with industrial affairs takes on an importance hardly second to the problems of peace and the One World. Our war production experience shows beyond a doubt that, given adequate incentive and adequate direction, we can produce plenty for all our people—and even to spare for other countries. But how to effect, democratically, this adequate production and fair distribution is something we have not yet worked out.

While for a long period the main question seemed to be that of securing just rights for the workers, now with the present great strength of labor organizations the issue has in growing measure shifted. In serious industrial disputes where some essential public service is involved, the rest of the population may suffer. So that latterly the problem of the unlimited right to strike is being seriously questioned. Many are holding that government civil servants have no right to strike, and some laws have been passed to carry the idea into effect. Not a few are disposed to hold that when any industrial strike so stops essential social processes as to threaten public welfare and safety, that strike is morally wrong and should be prohibited by law. Opponents of such laws insist that in all such proposals the democratic liberty of the individual is at stake.

Thus does democracy find itself challenged to deal with the complex of serious conflicts in our contemporary industrial life. New institutional forms have to be devised for the fuller safeguarding of respect for personality wherever found.

DEMOCRACY AS A WAY OF LIFE

Now that we have examined various phases of the historic growth of the spirit of democracy we are ready to ask in conclusion about the fundamental spirit which should animate democracy and how it should work itself out in essential institutional arrangements.

The spirit of democracy as a way of life we have already seen as the moral obligation to respect personality as such. In what follows this principle of respect for personality is accepted as the focal essence of the democratic way of life, its ruling conception, its aim—in a word, the criterion by which to judge whether any proposed measure is or is not consistent with the spirit of democracy. This can be restated as the effort to run society in all its relations on the basis of ethics. But as we saw in Chapter VIII, the content of ethics is determined by the way that differing types of behavior work themselves out in life. We wish here to inquire further regarding the ways in which ethical regard for human personality needs to be worked out, so that the dignity of the individual as such may be respected and each one may have adequate opportunity, on a basis of equality, to make of himself the best that in him lies.

What, then, are the characteristics that must prevail as recognized principles of the good life, as attitudes in individuals, and as institutional arrangements, in order that the spirit of democracy as just stated may win out? In answer, six fundamental principles present themselves:

1. "*Sovereignty of the Living Individual.*" These striking words are from William James and point directly to the heart of democracy, to the human individual as the unit of judgment and responsible action. It is this individual who alone lives; all social institutions and arrangements exist to express and serve him. And they derive their just powers from the consent of these individual citizens. The historic phrase "freedom of conscience"* repeats the same idea from another angle, denying what the totalitarian states have always affirmed, that the individual gains his freedom—his "inner freedom," some called it—by merging his individuality with the state. A democracy follows majority rule; but the individual always holds to his individuality, his freedom of conscience, and—as we shall see in a moment—exercises his freedom of speech to persuade the majority, if he can, to his point of view.

But this sovereignty of the individual, essential though it be, is still not absolute, and cannot be; for, as quoted earlier from Norman Angell, "when all demand complete freedom, none has any." This leads naturally to a second principle.

* It was in accordance with this freedom of conscience that our people decided that our government shall not create any establishment of religion.

George Mason said in the (1776) *Virginia Declaration of Rights:*

> Religion, or the duty which we owe our Creator, and the manner of discharging it, can be directed only by reason and conviction, not by force or violence, and therefore all men are equally entitled to the free exercise of religion according to the dictates of conscience.

2. *The Principle of Equality: "Equal Rights for All."* The principle of equality precisely limits the principle of liberty, limits the freedom of the sovereign individual to those acts which, at least, do not hurt others. The quotation is from Jefferson and is but a variant and explanation of the Declaration doctrine that "all men are created equal."

This doctrine, together with the further Declaration doctrine that "governments derive their just powers from the consent of the governed," suffices to establish the right of universal suffrage, the right preservative of all rights.

Perhaps the most personally cherished of all democratic rights is the right to grow and thrive, so that each may be given a fair chance in comparison with others to make of himself and his life the best that in him lies. In connection with this statement democracy will further demand (i) that the "fair" chance be made as nearly an *equal* chance as is possible without doing more harm than good and (ii) that the individual, again as far as feasible, be the judge of what he will become.

It may be well to say a passing word about the possibility suggested in the preceding paragraph, that equality may be so used as to do more harm than good. In various preceding chapters we have considered the principle therein implied that rights are not to be taken as absolute. In Chapter VIII we saw that to hold rights as absolute leads only to fanaticism. More concretely, we saw just above that the right of individual freedom is not to be regarded as an absolute; and now we see the same thing concerning the principle of equality. A specific illustration may show the concrete content of this rejection of absolute equality. Consider our family system; children cannot have absolute equality of opportunity so long as they stay with their unequal parents in their unequal homes. To demand absolute equality of opportunity would mean that we must take children away from their unequal families and bring them up, say, in public institutions, where all could be treated equally. But experience shows that children do not thrive as well in institutions as they do in reasonably good families. To treat them with absolute equality would both destroy the family and hurt most of the children.

This conclusion thus corroborates the preceding conclusions that principles of thought and act are not to be applied as absolutes. We work always for the best result we can achieve, using each principle involved as an hypothesis, and out of all the principles involved we seek that program which promises best.

It was in accordance with this fundamental principle of equality of opportunity that Jefferson, after Independence, attacked the system of aristocracy intrenched in Virginia by abolishing land-holding in fee-tail and primogeniture, and in another area the established church. These various reforms eventually spread to all the other states where they did not already hold, while the Constitution of 1787 forbade any titles of nobility. We might add that the quotation given in the wording of Principle 2 is but part of the whole as Jefferson wrote it—"Equal rights for all; special privileges for none."

In these various ways was the feudal system of hereditary privileges largely abolished in our country. The word largely as here used refers to the fact that under the social and economic conditions prevailing today the children of the well-to-do still have a decided advantage over the children of the least well-to-do, advantage as regards health, home care, education, and economic opportunity.

How to effect in these respects a greater equality of opportunity and still maintain the desirable separate family system and the other desirable features of individual freedom, initiative, and responsibility hitherto associated with the American dream—that is one of our unsolved problems which the democracy of the future cannot ignore.

One of the worst features of this social heredity evil is the educative effect on its beneficiaries. Too frequently those enjoying these special privileges build the attitude of willing exploitation, a willingness to hold the less privileged to lower living standards in order that the more privileged may live the better. It is easy for us to look abroad and see this evil attitude in the aristocratic circles of Europe and Asia, and so seeing, to agree with Lord Acton that "all power corrupts and absolute power corrupts absolutely." But we must clear the beam from our own eyes. E. A. Ross, with America mainly in mind, seems to agree fairly well with Lord Acton:

> *The will to exploit lasts as long as the power to exploit* [italics in original]. Exploiters never tire of exploitation. A kept class never loses its taste for consuming the fruits of other men's toil. Nor does it ever give up exploitation out of conviction of sin. Its manner of life becomes completely adjusted to its parasitism and it never fails to develop moral standards, theories and ideals which chime with the economic basis of its life (139:152).

3. *Rights Imply Duties.* This principle follows directly as a corollary from the principle of "equal rights for all"; but it must be stated explicitly. For me actually to enjoy any specific right, other people involved must feel the obligation to treat me in accordance with that right. My right implies their duty. And analogously, in order that anyone of them may enjoy his right, I—if I am involved—have the like duty to him.

Thus again we see that we are all members one of another. No individual can of right consider simply his own direct good and no more. He must also consider the well-being of others.

4. *Cooperative Effort for the Common Good.* This, in a way, is an extension of the preceding principle. Since each individual enjoys the common good, each is involved in supporting the common good.

The only alternative is selfishness—that I be allowed to enjoy the common good without being obliged to carry my fair share of the burden of supporting that common good. Without law and order, for example, all suffer, and the like holds for all other arrangements and institutions found necessary for the common development and expression of human personality.

It was with Principle 3 in mind that Walt Whitman gave expression to the following "sign of democracy": "By God! I will accept nothing which all cannot have their counterpart of on the same terms." (174:53) And in the light of Principle 4 John Dewey said:

> If democracy has a moral and ideal meaning, it is that a social return be demanded of all and that opportunity for development of distinctive capacities be afforded all (44:142).

In the early days of our country, with domestic agriculture our main economy and a wide ocean on either side to protect us, we could live, it seemed, each family for itself. These two last-named principles had then small appeal. Now, however, in the modern world, inherently interrelated by division of labor and beset by threats from depression at home and by danger of war from abroad, there comes a stronger need to consider and support the common good. It is now abidingly true that "we must indeed all hang together, or most assuredly we shall all hang separately."

5. *Faith in the Free Play of Intelligence: Discussion and Persuasion, not Force or Violence.* In a true sense, everybody has always used his intelligence as best he could in the pursuit of his own purposes as he has understood them. So it was with those of ancient days who cast lots or studied entrails or sought advice from the oracle; it was their intelligence, such as it was, that directed their steps. But something quite different from their use of intelligence is meant in this fifth principle, and this in two essential respects.

First, the best known way of using intelligence so far found is the method of modern science. John Dewey says, regarding this, that "intelligence after millions of years of errancy has found itself as method" (49:93); and elsewhere: "Mankind now has in its possession a new method, that of cooperative and experimental science." (49:83) Still further he observes: "One of the only two articles that remain in my creed of life is that the future of our civilization depends upon the widening spread and deepening hold of the scientific habit of mind"; and he states finally that "intelligent action is the sole ultimate resource of mankind in every field whatsoever." (51:252) It is not necessary to argue here in behalf of this method of intelligence; its use has been sufficiently implied if not explicitly affirmed in many previous discussions. In fact, it may be called the cornerstone of modern effort, whether individual and private or social and public.

Second, in explaining the "free play of intelligence" certain quotations may help. John Milton called this "free play" "the liberty to know, to utter, and to argue freely according to conscience," and he counted this "above all liberties." (110:128) In keeping with this viewpoint, Thomas Jefferson said that "reason and free inquiry are the only effectual agents against error." Mr. Justice Holmes in quite modern terms said (250 U.S. 630) that "the best test of truth is the power of thought to get itself accepted in the competition of the market." W. A. Shimer wrote in the *American Scholar:* "Only by absolute freedom to think and speak can man dare hope for a permanently better world." (8:IV:260, Summer 1935). Mr. Justice Holmes again, but from a slightly different angle, advocated free thought—"not free thought for those who agree with us, but freedom for the thought we hate." Clearly it was true freedom of thought that he meant to uphold. The Universal Declaration of Human Rights by the United Nations thus summed up in its Article 19 the question of personal rights: "Everyone has the right to freedom of opinion and expression; this right includes freedom to hold opinions without interference and to seek, receive and impart information and ideas through any media and regardless of frontiers." Without such possibilities the free play of intelligence would be meaningless; practically there could be no basis of hope that the better way would win out over the worse, in a word there would be no effective freedom to act wisely.

These rights exist, then, not only for the individual so that he may speak his own mind, but also for the public so that individuals may have the greatest likelihood of hearing what others think. As Mr. Justice Brandeis said, "Public discussion is a political duty." It is clear that discussion and persuasion as opposed to force and violence constitute the very essence of the democratic process at work among citizens—the only method consistent and appropriate to democracy for determining public policy or changing private opinion.

Other social philosophies both of past and present have taken the opposite position. The most definite one of these, the dictatorship (under whatever name pursued, at times even that of professed democracy), makes up its own mind on its own terms, builds an acquiescent attitude in its people by the biased propaganda of its controlled press and radio, then issues its orders and enforces these by threats and violence. Right now in various parts of the world we see press and radio sending out propaganda under orders while secret police threaten with every kind of ill treatment any who resist—arrest in the night with no assigned charge, secret incarceration regarding which relatives can learn nothing (if they dare to try), trial before a biased court. Ultimately, either an incredible confession of guilt or open conviction on forged testimony dooms the victim to disappearance involving death or unknown punishment.

How different all this is from true democracy—no arrest except on open charge, right of immediate appeal on *habeas corpus*, every right to speak one's true mind on any subject (except to libel), effective right with other citizens to secret ballot to fix public policies.

This contrast shows what democracy offers.

There was a time when in even the most civilized countries of Christendom religious persecutions darkened life for the independent minded. The rulers of those peoples had small confidence in the method of free intelligence. Now, fortunately, in the more democratic countries we can, along with Samuel Butler (1612–1680), smile in amusement at those earlier days when men sought to

> prove their doctrine orthodox
> By apostolic blows and knocks.—*Hudibras:* pt. i, C I, 1. 197

Whitehead thus states what most of us have now come to believe: "The progressive societies are those which most decisively have trusted themselves to . . . the way of persuasion." (171:109) He says further that "the worth of men consists in their liability to persuasion." (171:105) The acceptance of this principle has clearly brought us beyond democracy as government into democracy as a way of life.

In various preceding discussions, a position has been taken against holding to absolute ideas. It is worthy of further note here that true discussion is incompatible with absolutes. Entrance upon true and honest discussion implies the mutual possibility of being persuaded by new insight gained through the discussion. And further, since discussion and persuasion constitute the democratic way of effecting changes in men's attitudes, we can conclude that in the degree to which citizens hold their ideas as absolute, as beyond possible reach by new insight, they shut themselves off as regards these ideas and their influence from discussion and democracy.

It may be well at this point to add a word about majority rule. Many, with democratic government in mind, will carelessly say that to decide matters by majority vote is the very essence of democracy, and further that there are no limitations to such rule. Both statements we must reject. If it were feasible, democratic decisions should be made by consensus, all agreeing. Practically, this is not often feasible and majority rule is the easiest way out. But there can be such a thing as tyranny of the majority. To guard against this, wisely made constitutions include such safeguards as trial by jury, *habeas corpus*, "due process of law," by which the courts protect the individual against possible tyranny of police or law-makers or despotic governors.

6. *Freedom of Discussion.* In a true sense, this follows as an immediate corollary from the preceding; but the matter is so important as to demand a place of its own. Specifically, democracy demands that each be free to think for himself—this is the chief dignity of man—and free likewise to argue his belief before others. These considerations, involving precisely the democratic process at work, mean freedom of speech, of press, and of assembly.

Without these freedoms the preceding fifth principle would be meaningless; practically there could be no basis of hope that the better way would win out over the worse; in a word, there would be no effective freedom to act wisely. These rights exist, then, not so much for the individual in order that he may speak his own mind, as for the public so that individuals may hear even against their will what others think. As Mr. Justice Brandeis said, "Public discussion is a political duty."

Certain pertinent quotations will close the discussion on the theory of democracy. What an unknown author said of civilization we may affirm of democracy, that it "consists in teaching men to govern themselves by letting them do it." William Jennings Bryan said: "The people have a right to make their own mistakes." More constructive was Alexander Meiklejohn: "The art of democracy is the art of thinking independently together." (71:CLXI: 474*f*.) Charles W. Morris showed true discernment in his statement that "democracy is the acceptance of the method of science and the attitude of morality in the conduct of human affairs." (68:VI:152) Ralph Barton Perry thus states his inclusive conception:

> The ideal polity must be that in which the happiness of citizens is the end, and their enlightened consent the seat of sovereignty; or that form of society in which men rule themselves by discussion, persuasion, and agreement for the sake of their common and maximum happiness (1:II:207).

CHAPTER XI. *The Life Good to Live*

For those at home in the study of philosophy a different title, *The Good Life,* would probably have been preferable to the title here given. But so strong is the connotation of the word *good* in our historic American attitude that such a wording would have misled many to expect a discussion of the morally good life. Morality has a clear and proper part in the good life, as we shall later consider; but it is no definition of "the good life" in its full meaning. The word *good* in this phrase means the consummatory good, good to the consumer for its intended purpose; as a good apple is one good to eat; or good music is music good to hear. So the good life as here discussed is the life good to live, good for living purposes, a life that answers well to the various content demands of actual living, qualitatively considered.

Seneca long ago suggested a beginning toward the line of thought we here pursue in saying that merely to live is not the goal we seek, but to live well (*Non enim vivere bonum est, sed bene vivere . . .*). And a modern, Philip James Bailey (1816–1902), previously quoted, gave this closer content to the same thought:

> We live in deeds, not years; in thoughts, not breaths;
> In feeling, not figures on a dial.
> We should count time by heart throbs. He lives most
> Who thinks most—feels the noblest—acts the best.—*Festus*, v.*

Such a conception of the good life, in the degree that it is given a reliable content, becomes a most useful standard and criterion for defining the content and end at which morality, democracy, and

* Philip James Bailey, *Festus.* Reproduced by permission of E. P. Dutton & Co., Inc., New York; and Routledge & Kegan Paul Ltd., London.

education should respectively aim. Moral obligation is the obligation so to live and act as to bring the good life as well as possible to all concerned; democracy is the effort to run society on the basis of bringing the good life to all people, in part at least, by letting them manage it; education, conceived in any proper sense, should have as its aim to lead the young—and all the rest of us—to learn and to live *the life good to live.* How this is true for morality and democracy we have already seen in preceding chapters; how it is true for education will appear later.

VALUES: THEIR PSYCHOLOGICAL BASES

Earlier we saw that out of the interaction of organism and environment comes the stirring to action which constitutes behavior; that the inner aspect of such a stirring we call a want, and that the external outworking of the want we call the effort to get what is wanted. In this general setting we can locate the diverse types of psychological satisfaction which constitute the good life, five of which are here considered.

1. *The satisfaction of getting and enjoying what we want, with the added fact that the stronger the want is felt, the greater is the resulting satisfaction.* This type of satisfaction is so common and so well recognized that no special comment is needed. We can call it briefly *the satisfaction of wants.*

2. *The satisfaction from effort, from devising and using means in the pursuit of a desired end or aim.* This type of satisfaction stands in contrast with the satisfaction of wants (1). There the satisfaction came from the *end*, from enjoying the end attained; here the satisfaction comes from the *means* used, from the actual process of devising and using promising means. The more we are interested in any end or aim, the more will we be interested in the means to attain that end. This derived interest in the means will vary according to the closeness of connection between means and end; the more promising and necessary the connection is felt to be, the stronger will the interest in the aim extend itself to the means.

Many have insisted that the satisfactions from effort (2) are both greater and nobler than the satisfactions of wants (1). Shakespeare thus aligns himself, regarding degree of enjoyment, on the side of satisfaction from effort:

All things that are
Are with more spirit chased than enjoyed.—*Merchant of Venice*, act ii, sc. 6.

Walter Bagehot (1826–1877) holds that "the great thing in life is to find that there is no fun like work." Bertrand Russell states his attitude toward effort in these words: "Desire, activity, purpose are essential to a tolerable life; and a millennium, tho' it may be a joy in prospect, would be intolerable if it were actually achieved." (143:138) William James used these stirring words in connection with this subject:

> Wherever a process of life communicates an eagerness to him who lives it, there the life becomes genuinely significant. Sometimes the eagerness is more knit up with the motor activities, sometimes with the perceptions, sometimes with the imagination, sometimes with reflective thought. But, wherever it is found, there is the zest, the tingle, the excitement of reality; and there *is* 'importance' in the only real and positive sense in which importance ever anywhere can be (88:234).

One chief factor in the joy of effort is the presence of the self as a cause. To a child, as Thorndike points out, "merely hearing the toot of a horn is a feeble joy compared to blowing it." In an earlier day when psychologists made much of instincts in man, "pleasure at being a cause" was included in the list, so widespread is this source of satisfaction. And of course one usual constituent of this pleasure is that others recognize me as the cause of what I do.

3. *When an enterprise grows under effort, additional satisfaction is produced.* This is the principle of "leading on" (later to be discussed), according to which some activities engaged in open up new prospects and possibilities. On this point John Dewey says: "The emotional accompaniment of the progressive growth of a course of action, a continual movement of expansion and achievement, is happiness." (48:35) Dewey has here put his finger on important considerations. For one's effort to succeed so well as to yield a new aim to pursue combines, so to say, the satisfaction of success, the personal satisfaction that I did it, and the added value of a new interest. A life so lived does bring happiness.

4. *Variety increases satisfaction.* That variety can add to the satisfaction of life seems indisputable. Various writers in the past, however, have overstated the case. John Gay (1685–1732) thus asserted that "variety's the source of joy below." To say "the source" is too strong. Dr. Johnson sided with Gay: "The great source of pleasure is variety." Cowper was even stronger:

> Variety's the very spice of life
> That gives it all its flavour.—*The Task*, bk. ii, 1. 606

Soberer consideration would perhaps suggest that variety is not so much a new or original source of satisfaction as recognition of the fact that one kind of activity tends, if continued too long, to pall. Change to something new is thus welcome, especially if the new is satisfying on its own account. It is further true that variety offers new sources of possibility.

5. *The satisfaction from living up to one's own personally held standards.* This satisfaction depends of course on having standards and on the degree of devotion given to them. The more clearly the standard is defined, the higher its type, and the greater one's devotion to this higher type, the greater and the finer quality will be the satisfaction from living up to the standard. There are alternative ways of stating this principle, such as "living up to one's ideals," "obeying conscience," "doing one's best." Regarding "doing one's best," J. H. Muirhead (1855–1940) said in his *Ethics* (113:45): "An artisan or an artist or a writer who does not 'do his best' is not only an inferior workman, but a bad man." Regarding standards Ortega y Gasset (1883–   ) said in his *Revolt of the Masses:* "There is no culture where there are no standards to which our fellow-men can have recourse. There is no culture where there are no principles [standards] of legality to which to appeal." (129:79). From this point of view civilization itself depends on this source of satisfaction for its higher quality. Clearly, the finer the character of an individual the surer and finer will be the quality of his satisfaction from living up to his standards; and the greater the proportion of such individuals the higher the civilization.

It seems fair to conclude that concern for the highest feasible standards with determination to live up to these constitute the best single criterion we have for judging the quality of a civilization.

CONSTITUENTS OF THE GOOD LIFE

Having examined certain psychological sources of life's satisfactions, we here consider some of the more important areas of life in which these satisfactions or, perhaps better, life's values are especially to be found. Clearly such lists will differ from writer to writer.

1. *Physical Health.* The value of bodily health and vigor no modern-minded person would deny. The lack of it is a positive and painful annoyance, and therein everything else is also hurt. Moreover, healthy appetites add definitely to the joy of living.

An interesting conflict in this area presents itself as between Herbert Spencer (1820–1903) and Aristotle. Spencer put the preservation of the body and its health first and highest on his list of educational values, highest because to him it underlies all else (151:42). Aristotle, from perhaps the same facts, draws exactly the opposite conclusion. To him the body exists to realize, make possible and actual, the mind or soul; the former is therefore subordinate to the latter. We can, it appears, resolve the apparent conflict by seeking such physical health and vigor as allows the other constituents of the good life their best chance to come into vigorous being. Bodily appetites thus would not be allowed to assert themselves to the hurt of other and higher values.

2. *Mental Wholeness, the Well-Adjusted Personality.* If a motor car is to run well, its internal arrangements must be in good working order, in good mutual adjustment. So it is with man; if he is to live effectively and enjoy the good life, his internal arrangements, his attitudes and habits, must be in good mutual adjustment. Specifically, both emotion and habit must always be ready to obey one's reason. Otherwise, the individual is enslaved; he does not control his emotion and habit, but they him. For example, the man who gets angry on slight provocation is a nuisance to himself and to all about him. He should, but does not, control his anger; it controls him. One who suffers an inferiority complex will not try, even where he could really succeed. A child suffering from insecurity will live and behave in a way to reduce his own quality of living and that of others about him.

As history goes, this particular life value has been but recently differentiated. Herbert Spencer, for example, who meant in his

Education (1848) to survey the whole range of life, makes no reference to it. It was Sigmund Freud (1856–1939) who first gave this conception effective definition. If there be any one single value which is essential to all else of the good life this seems to be it.

Nevertheless, this prime value is too often disregarded. We often see school life and curriculum so set up and so managed that otherwise normal pupils become maladjusted because normal satisfactions are denied them and demands are made which they cannot meet. Thus children, with "lowered thresholds" to maladjustment, have their tendencies ignored or even augmented. Such treatment is immoral, sinful in the highest degree. And it is worse because the younger and the less capable are most likely to suffer, and the bad effects often trouble them all the rest of their lives. The saying of Jesus against causing hurt to "one of these little ones" seems quite applicable here.

3. *Satisfying Personal Relationships.* Everyone feels the presence or absence of this source of satisfaction throughout conscious life. In fact, there is experimental evidence that the newborn infant shows effects almost at once if he is "not wanted," even though he is in those early days not able to *know* consciously what the trouble is. Lack of affection and sympathetic treatment is said to bring obvious signs of insecurity and unhappiness within a few weeks from birth. The maladjustment of personality discussed in the preceding section usually develops from unsatisfying personal relations beginning in early childhood.

The lack which the infant feels without knowing why and which young children feel with beginning awareness, more mature people–beginning especially in adolescence–feel only too consciously. Not to get on pleasantly with other members of the family, not to be acceptable to other children, not to find congenial companionship among one's fellows in school or college or business, not to be happy in marriage–these are the more usual instances known among us of unsatisfying personal relations.

Since few things cut deeper than unsatisfying personal relations, few things bring more abiding pleasure than satisfying personal relations. While this source of happiness or unhappiness has been present with man from the beginning, it seems probably true that we have made more progress in understanding the matter within the past two generations than in all preceding history. Education has a peculiar duty here to make effective use of this growing knowledge, both in its own treatment of the young and in its education for all living.

4. *The Chance to Choose as a Responsible Self*. No animal other than man can choose in any full sense; and "choice," as Dewey says, is "the most characteristic activity of a self." (54:316) Not to be allowed to choose freely, to choose for one's self, makes one a slave. Not to learn to choose thoughtfully and responsibly is to be enslaved to ineffectiveness, to be unfitted for decent living either as an individual or in the group. As was earlier discussed, choice implies acting in the light of expected consequences. In facing, then, a particular situation one chooses first an aim or goal because of its promise to meet the felt need and then selects the means because of their promise to secure the goal or end. And if, now, this choosing be thoughtfully done, the self by what it learns from such successive choices is continually rebuilding and enriching itself and its living. Especially is this true of choices which one accepts responsibility for supporting. The process of choosing just described, if carefully and critically done, is pre-eminently the way to build responsible character, on the one hand, and a criticized philosophy of life on the other hand.

To foster such critical and responsible pupil choosing becomes then pre-eminently the rule for good teaching. If there be any educational kingdom of God, this is it. If those we teach really seek this first, they have the best possible chance at all other desirable outcomes.

5. *Meaningful Work* (*vs. a Life of Leisure*). As Bagehot said above, "There is no fun like work." He meant, of course, work which grips the individual, work for ends which the individual feels important. It is in connection with this that satisfaction from means especially comes—satisfaction from devising or using means to an end we truly desire. This is not to deny the possibility of drudgery nor that life is often too full of it. Drudgery is work which one must do without identifying one's self with it, without seeing and accepting its justification; it is effort without heart, without interest. Many employed persons so work. The work here upheld is purposeful activity with which one does identify himself. We can in this sense thoroughly applaud Carlyle's statement: "Blessed is he who has found his work"; but not so thoroughly the conclusion of the

sentence: "let him ask no other blessedness." (22: bk. iii, ch. 11)

6. *The Chance to Create.* To feel one's self actually creating is one of the highest and keenest of joys. Few other possibilities of life seem so satisfying. In creating, one can forget himself in what he is doing, can identify himself with something that in the truest sense is his own. Thomas Lovell Beddoes (1803–1849) said in his *Death's Jest Book:*

> I have a bit of FIAT in my soul
> And can myself create my little world

On the other hand, to have one's work prescribed for one by others, especially to be compelled to work or live mechanically, with no chance to devise or create—this is to live meanly. Even ordinary men, given the chance, can create. It thus becomes the moral duty of society so to contrive and order its institutions that every one may have the chance to work and live both thoughtfully and creatively, at least in reasonable measure. If this can be done then each can enjoy both his work and his life.

One type of creation, that of nicety of distinctions, is perhaps limited to the more thoughtful. To make new and finer distinctions is a true act of creation and as such satisfying in itself. Then to feel, and so enjoy, the new distinction is an additional satisfaction. If the distinction is well made, it will bring to the creator personal progress in his line of endeavor and may, in addition, add to the culture and so bring objective approval.

7. "*Leading on.*" It was earlier pointed out that some activities open up new vistas, new possibilities to follow up, with possibly a new disposition to realize the new insights. We saw also how a growing and developing experience can carry its own unique value. Said Wordsworth:

> Effort, and expectation, and desire,
> And something ever more about to be.—*Prelude*

To use this principle effectively, distinction must be made between true and deceptive leading on. The deceptive kind takes on many forms. An old Chinese story tells of the quarrel of a merchant with a buyer over an inferior coin offered. They came to blows. Friends on both sides joined the fight, eventually including the whole village. In the end lives were lost and every house in the village burned. This activity did "lead on" powerfully in one sense, but soon resulted in a loss to all involved and by so much a lessening of further possibilities of action. Moreover, during the exciting process the bad feelings engendered acted to reduce the quality of living. Lesser activities than fighting and war show the same deceptive loss in life's desirable activity—gambling for example, any dissipation, in fact any sufficiently bad or unwise use of time, money, or effort. Such activities may seem to lead on for a while, but the end is loss and failure.

Rightly understood, this principle may be said to restate the end and aim of all moral behavior and even of living and civilization itself: to find and embody in institutional life and its supporting attitudes those ways of behaving which open up new possibilities in both content and richness of life, which lead on so consistently and so widely as to promise increasing good life to all.

8. *Range of Interests.* Francis Bacon said succinctly that "the more good things we are interested in, the more ardently do we live." And in general his statement is probably true. But it is possible for one so unduly to disperse his interests as in the end to accomplish little. It is also true that a man may make a great contribution to civilization by concentrating interest, thought, and effort mainly on one line of activity. The effect of this on his personal life may or may not be good. Charles Darwin felt toward the close of his life that he had so greatly restricted his interests as to hurt the quality of his living. Also, many do so restrict their interests and thought as to hurt even their chosen work by failure to allow helpful outside ideas to enter into their thinking. Many more fail of their duty to their fellow men by failing to think broadly enough about the bearing of their work on the lives of others. Employers in the earlier history of the Industrial Revolution distinctly so failed. Probably now the largest number of failures in this area are those who disregard the larger interest of the public good, selfishly finding sufficient to satisfy them in personal and other close interests.

In the main, then, it seems that Bacon was right, only as with all general principles we must watch the boundaries of their application. Possibly the principle of "leading on" just discussed furnishes the guiding corrective.

9. *The Esthetic.* That art can and does, if given the chance, ele-

vate life, give it richness of quality in high degree, has, by general consent, been demonstrated through the ages.

I. A. Richards speaks as follows: "In the arts we find the record, in the only form in which these things can be recorded, of the experiences which have seemed worth *having* to the most sensitive and discriminating persons." (138:33) Whitehead speaks more precisely: "Great art is the arrangement of the environment so as to provide for the soul vivid, but transient, values. . . . But . . . great art is more than a transient refreshment. It is something which adds to the permanent richness of the soul's self-attainment. . . . It transforms the soul into the permanent realization of values extending beyond its former self." (173:283) Walter Pater seems to see only the transient values: "Art comes to you professing frankly to give nothing but the highest quality to your moments as they pass, and simply for those moments' sake." (131:252) But perhaps some other words of Pater's give us his deeper insight into the esthetic experience: "Not the fruit of experience, but the experience itself, is the end." (131:249) Dewey gives us more of the process: "To feel the meaning of what one is doing and to rejoice in that meaning, to unite in one concurrent fact the unfolding of the inner emotional life and the ordered development of material external conditions—that is art." (43:17)

10. *Music*. Logically, music is part of the preceding constituent of the good life; but it seems better to give it a place of its own. None would deny music an important place in the good life except those who fear to enhance life on earth. But even of those looking forward to another life most would agree with the Reverend Rowland Hill that there appears no reason "why the devil should have all the good tunes." The praise of music by Addison (1672–1719) is probably stronger than most would accept

Music, the greatest good that mortals know,
And all of heaven we have below.—*Songs for St. Cecilia's Day:* st. 3.

It is possible, however, that he based his statement on a literal interpretation of Revelation.

While there is more to music than singing, most of us would agree with William Boyd's statement in 1582:

Since singing is so good a thing
I wish all men would learn to sing.

Most of us think that music very readily and very obviously shows its own unique value. We are accordingly puzzled and troubled to read a 1933 statement attributed to the Soviet Russian composer, Dmitri Shostakovich, that "music should be regarded not as an esthetic expression, but as an utterance of economic truth." (123: Oct. 6, 1946)

11. *An Adequate Social Life Process.* The elements of the good life so far considered have been rather individual than social; but the human individual is, as we have seen, inherently dependent on his social environment and his relations with it. The modern individual will live but a poor and thwarted life unless his surrounding society furnishes him both stimulating climate and institutions to call out his finer and better possibilities, and meanwhile protect him in this better and finer life. There seems abundant evidence that for most people only a democratic and moral society can supply these necessary conditions for the good life as here conceived. Only such a society can develop and express the necessary aggregate of personal traits.

We accordingly judge any civilization in two related ways: first, how well the aggregate of institutional arrangements calls out, makes possible, and protects the good life; second, how well these arrangements educate the members of the society actually to live the personal qualities of such an associated life.

12. *Religion.* For the purposes immediately at hand it seems better to avoid consideration of the supernatural and restrict the present discussion to the part religion can play in life as we know it. We may then define religion as the spirit with which one holds one's supreme value—the value in terms of which one values all else—plus the outworking of this attitude appropriately in life. Perhaps for a discussion of the good life it is better to consider that religion is a unifying of one's self and one's life on the basis of some supreme and inclusive outlook and consequent program of action.

Thus defined we actually find many diverse religions among men today, not all of them worthy. For many, making money appears to be such an unworthy religion; though they may not avow it, many do appear to put this first in life and to evaluate everything else in terms of it. Again, Bertrand Russell stated in 1917 that "devotion to the nation is perhaps the deepest and most widespread religion of the present age." (143:116) Many inhabitants of the

U.S.S.R.–and some elsewhere–hold Marxism and the program of the Communist Party as their religion.

We have defined religion as one's supreme devotion to his highest values, to the values in terms of which he evaluates all else. What bearing on the good life has religion as thus defined? The answer apparently demanded by the foregoing discussion is that the overarching concern of each individual should be that all people shall have and enjoy the fullest and finest life possible. Whatever other elements in religion one may cherish in addition, this much and this kind of religion should be his highest concern; it should be the supreme value in terms of which he values and orders all else, including other elements in his religion. Personal attitudes and institutional arrangements should be made to carry this aim into effect.

What has just been said concerns the aim of life. When we consider the problem of means and ask what security it can give, certain words of John Dewey seem highly pertinent:

> There are a steadily increasing number of persons who find security in *methods* of inquiry, of observation, experiment, of forming and following working hypotheses. Such persons are not unsettled by the upsetting of any particular belief, because they retain security of procedure. They can say, borrowing language from another context, though this method slay my most cherished belief, yet will I trust it. . . . In this . . . fundamental they rest in intellectual and emotional peace. (40:457)

One lesson from Dewey's penetrating statement is to recall the earlier consideration of faith, and note its place in this present discussion as helping to give a sense of security. Life on any large scale faces inherent uncertainty, with the development of events always precarious. In many situations the decisive factor is the degree of intelligent effort. This, then, is the place and function of faith, that a man see clearly what basis there is for hope and by his resolved will make the most of that hope through determined effort. Such a faith furnishes an effective attitude for life's efforts. We conclude, therefore, from the whole present discussion that some inclusive philosophy of life is necessary to give the needed faith to life as a whole; and that this kind of faith becomes thus a necessary part of any adequate religion.

RELATION OF MORAL GOODNESS TO THE GOOD LIFE

It was stated at the beginning of this chapter that moral goodness, though a necessary factor in the effectively good life, was not to be taken as defining the good life. To repeat what was there stated, it is not moral good which defines the good life; on the contrary, it is the life-good-to-live which both defines the content of moral goodness and gives the logical reason for moral obligation. This argument was anticipated in Chapters VII–X, but that was before the conception of the life-good-to-live had been discussed.

We saw in Chapter IV that the fundamental reason for having *institutions* and for *obeying* them is that we *live better* with them than without them. We saw in Chapter VIII that morality belongs among the necessary institutions of any decent civilization; and further, that conscious morality means the settled obligation so to act as to promote the life-good-to-live in all affected by one's acts. If now to these considerations we add the discussions of the present chapter on the life-good-to-live, we see clearly (i) that the life-good-to-live is the end and aim of all our institutional arrangements, including specifically such principles as honesty, truthfulness, and respect for law and order; and (ii) that the *effective* working of our aggregate of institutional arrangements logically requires moral obligation as an active factor in the life process, both individual and social.

It is in this way that the concrete content of the life-good-to-live, as this content is inductively determined, both defines the content of social-moral obligation and at the same time gives the logical basis for upholding moral obligation. But objective logical defense of morality is one thing, and personal acceptance of moral obligation to obey it is quite different. From what source, then, must we expect the powerful ought of adequate moral obligation?

This matter was discussed at some length in Chapter VIII. What follows is in part a condensation of that discussion, in part a restatement from a slightly different angle. To the question as to the nature and source of moral obligation, there are two answers: one logical and theoretical, the other practical and psychological.

As for the logical and theoretical answer, conceive and consider three societies all alike except in one regard: one society (*Sy*) in which all the people say *yes* to accepting moral obligation and treat one another accordingly; a second society (*Sn*) in which all the people say *no* to any moral obligation and accordingly treat one another immorally, as inclination may at any time suggest; and third, a society (*Syn*) in which the practice is mixed, a dominant majority say *yes* and so act, while a small minority seek to profit from the morality of the others but themselves refuse to act morally, refuse to contribute their fair share of behavior for the common good. Which of these three societies has, logically, the best hope of living well? Is there any possible doubt that *Sy* has the best chance, while *Sn* has the least, and that *Syn* will live well in the degree that it approximates *Sy?* If anyone is in any doubt, let him ask whether it would help matters in this country if people lied or stole or killed more often than they do. Any decent consideration of these questions carries the logical or theoretical answer in favor of adopting a regime of moral behavior and accordingly of moral obligation.

But in practical life mere logic carries small weight with the very young or with any undisciplined character. In other words, it takes personal characters specifically built to fit *Sy* if we are practically to realize *Sy* in our civilization. Of course what we actually have is *Syn*, and the proportion of liars and thieves and murderers in it hurts the rest of us in three different ways: first, by the positive damage from their lying, stealing, and murdering; second, by their failure to help support law and order and morality, including importantly the bad educative effect of their evil conduct on others; and third, by the costs these entail by way of police service, courts, jails, and all their upkeep. What we need, then, is better education in home, school, and community to build the needed characters. This we shall discuss in later chapters.

We conclude that moral goodness is an essential part of the life good to live; that both content and aim of moral goodness get their definition from the constituents of the life-good-to-live as these are discovered by inductive study of the life process; and that moral obligation is validated by the way it works when tried as over against the observed effects of failure to make it work.

Perhaps the most characteristic feature of the philosophy of life thus far presented has been its insistence that life is to be counted worth living on its own terms, that properly we may, and even should, seek to express and enjoy life as a positive good. A second characteristic is the belief that the quality of life can be improved by proper study and effort and by consequent appropriate individual cultivation; and a third that the good life of each individual is inseparably bound up with a like, but not identical, good life of all others. From this last we have derived the positive obligation—by definition called moral—that each one control his own life and its development and expression so as to make the best possible realization of his own life and that of others affected. The will to act must not yield to uncriticized impulse, either to subordinate one's greater good to mere present pleasure or to choose one's selfish advantage to the hurt of others. The highest and the finest good one can find out by searching must be put into actual practice; to be moral, one must live up to the best he knows. Further, it is by study of effects on living that we learn what sort of life is good when it is lived; and from study we learn accordingly the kind of personal character to foster and the social arrangements and attitudes to approve.

As opposed to the position just stated, some, perhaps influenced by teachings of former ages or by disappointments of the present life, are disposed to question whether life is after all a good to be sought and enjoyed. But mankind seems on the whole to be moving away from such negative attitudes toward a more positive view, one akin to the position sketched above. Possibly this change of attitude comes in part from man's increasing control over nature. Modern science increasingly brings within the reach of man the necessaries, the comforts, and enjoyments of life; so that the general process of current living less inclines men to seek escape from life. Samuel Butler (1835–1902) is quoted as saying that "all animals except man know that the object of life is to enjoy it." William James calls for a positive attitude: "Believe that life is worth living and your belief will help create the fact." (89:62) This seems the healthy minded answer. The words of A. E. Haydon give us a still more positive injunction:

> Once more the trial must be made to realize the dream, to distill out of this little piece of cosmic stuff and this tiny stretch of time a strain of music, thrilling, glorious and beautiful (130:XII).

CHAPTER XII. *The Problem of Progress*

THE term *progress* as here used is of course social progress, the progressive improvement of civilization. The history of thought shows few problems to which successive ages have given more diverse answers than to that of progress. Essential matters do not change. What can progress mean? Is progress possible? Along what lines? Is net progress, the improvement of civilization as a whole, possible? How get more of net progress?

Apparently, the earliest answer found among men was that the best had already been; the Golden Age lay in the remote past. James Russell Lowell said that from the days of the first grandfather everybody has remembered a golden age behind him. The sophisticate answer of classical Greece, as we saw in Chapter v, was that reality, important and essential things, do not change, that there is no new thing under the sun. Later, with the Enlightenment, men first conceived progress as they saw inventions change life before their very eyes. Then for a while optimism reigned: progress is "inevitable"; "progress is not an accident, but a necessity"; progress is the law of life, man will become perfect. Still later doubt and discouragement came: civilization is a disease, man is not capable of progress; progress and perfectibility are but a dream. The present, and apparently wiser, view is that progress, though not written in the nature of things, is still possible; but to attain it requires constant and persistent effort.

The formal discussion may well begin by distinguishing several pertinent terms. *Change* is the most general of these, implying alteration of the item under consideration, either in part or in whole, but without implication as to whether the change is for better or for worse. *Process* is a succession of related changes by which the original is changed into something different, but again without implication as to better or worse. *Development* is a process, with some implication that the character of the end result was implicit in the original state. *Evolution* is a process in which each succeeding stage is determined as to character by what precedes and surrounds it, but in such way that, unlike development, the result is significantly different in character from the original. *Progress* (in general) is a process moving toward an approved end (approved by the user of the term). *Social progress*, the subject of this chapter, is evolution toward an improved state of society, so that life therein is made better.

HISTORIC PERSPECTIVE

The nineteenth century was so in love with the idea of progress, had such faith in achieving it, and transmitted so much of this idea and faith to the twentieth century, that it comes as a surprise to most to learn that the idea of progress was not fully conceived before the eighteenth century. Indeed, most of preceding thought, whether Greek or Hebraic-Christian, took a quite opposed position.

The Greeks, who furnished the foundation for much of our thinking, looked back in their earlier writings to a mythical Golden Age when men lived much as did their gods, without labor or pains. Later Greek thought, carried on into the Roman Empire, tended to look on history as an endless series of cycles, each with its successive beginning, growth to culmination, degeneration, and chaos followed by a new beginning. With such an outlook many during the decline of the Empire accepted resignation as the wise attitude. The Stoic Emperor Marcus Aurelius (A.D. 121–180) expressed his explicit conviction (quoted at greater length in Chapter v) of no-progress and his resignation thereto in these words:

> The men who come after us shall see no new thing, and they who lived before us saw nothing more than we.*

The Hebrews, from whom the Western world got much of its religious outlook, also had a kind of past golden age, the Garden of

* A quite similar thought and attitude was expressed, probably around 200 B.C., by the cosmopolitan-minded author of Ecclesiastes: "The thing that hath been, it is that which shall be . . . and there is no new thing under the sun" (Ecclesiastes 1:9).

Eden, in which Adam and Eve lived innocently and pleasantly until by sinning they lost their innocence and happiness. Later, after the Hebrews lost their independence as a nation, they looked forward to an earthly Messiah who would re-establish their national state in power. The Christians in their turn accepted the Garden of Eden and Adam and Eve. The Messiah, however, they took not as an earthly restorer of power but (at least after the beginning years) as the ruler of a future state in another world. True, the term *millennium* (thousand years) of Revelation has been taken by many to refer literally to a thousand years of rule by Christ on earth. So that the very word *millennium* has come to mean an ideal state of good government and great happiness in all ways.

By exploring further these various opinions as to change and progress held prior to modern times, we can understand better, first, why the idea of progress was so long coming, and second, by what steps it did come.

In the first place, to look back on the past as in any sense a period favored of history tended by so much to shut out any thought of progress through current effort. The same effect would also follow from the notion of inevitable recurring cycles, against which effort would likewise be worthless. Similarly would Plato's idea that essential things do not change militate against any idea of progressive improvement of civilization. Also the belief that man is naturally depraved, mentally and morally, and therefore unable of himself either to wish effectively or to plan constructively, would, so long as this belief prevailed, exactly deny the primary basis for effecting progress. The correlatives of this low opinion of man, that all truth must come authoritatively from above, that history is not so much the work of man as it is of supernatural intervention and that this world exists primarily as preparation for the world to come—these correlatives but repeat man's impotence and altogether emphasize a philosophy of life which does not encourage the idea of possible progress here on earth.

During the Renaissance the backward look upon a golden age took on a peculiar but powerful new aspect. The leaders in this new movement were, in effect if not by profession, largely secular in their outlook: man as such could achieve, he had done so. But classical Greece and Rome had set such high standards of excellence that current man could do no better than admire and imitate; to equal was quite impossible.

It was in sum such varied considerations as these that opposed the idea of progress and held back the coming of that conception until the eighteenth century. The original classical attitude was fairly clear that history shows inevitable degeneration and decay. This view got also a certain support from the basic doctrine of both Plato and Aristotle, written more or less explicitly into both early and later theology, that truth and nobility belong solely to the changeless and that change is either trivial or evil or (with Aristotle) strictly limited. The succeeding Middle Ages held, generally speaking, that history is not the work of man, that to the contrary man is depraved and impotent and his history is but a succession of divine interventions and revelations.

Gradually, however, a change came in this prevailing outlook; and man's stock rose. While the early Renaissance had glorified the backward look, man's knowledge of history grew and the later Renaissance began to take on a new and quite different view. Man as he was now known could achieve. Rabelais (1494?–1553) made Gargantua say: "I am of the opinion that neither in the time of Plato nor of Cicero nor of Papinian [the great Roman jurist, who died 212] were there such facilities for study as now one sees." And Peter Ramus (1515–1572) went even further: "In one century we have seen greater progress in men and works of learning than our ancestors saw in the whole course of the preceding fourteen centuries." If we compare this statement with that of Marcus Aurelius quoted above we can see how far the idea of progress had meanwhile advanced. Bodin (1530–1596) added to the growth of the idea of progress by pointing out the essential factor in the origin of progress: "History depends largely on the will of men." And he listed certain achievements of his period which he counted equal or superior to any among the ancients, among these the invention of the mariner's compass (which he said makes, as it were, the whole world into a single state for travel and commerce); the invention of gunpowder, itself more significant for warfare than any achievement of the ancients; and finally the invention of printing. This alone, he said, could be set against anything the ancients had achieved.

But the most significant factor was yet to be heralded—modern science, the great new instrument of the will of man. Francis Bacon (1561–1626), while himself no practical scientist, was able to state the case for science—and so for progress—in a new and strong light. The end and purpose of knowledge, he asserted, is not, as Aristotle seemed to think, the satisfaction which comes from contemplating it, but rather the benefits that come from using it—"the endowment of human life with new inventions and riches." In a word, knowledge is power, it exists to further the reign of man over nature. To those who worshiped antiquity as superior to the present, Bacon gave answer: *Antiquitas seculi, iuventus mundi* ("the period of antiquity was the youth of the world").*

However, it was Descartes, so Bury thinks,† who more than anyone else wrote "the Declaration of Independence of Man." And this he did by leading men to accept (i) the supremacy of scientific reason and (ii) the rule of natural law. These two principles of modern science, Bury thinks, gave, as it were, the world to man, gave it to him to conquer if he could, but with the full assurance that there would be no outside interference. It was to be man *vs.* nature or, more exactly, man in nature working to control nature to his own chosen ends.

Following this as effect in the literary-philosophical realm, though a century later, came the Enlightenment (*Aufklärung*) with its assertion that man now dared to follow his own understanding independently of all else. As we saw earlier, Kant gave to this movement its motto: *Sapere aude*, "Dare to think for yourself." On these principles was built the modern doctrine of progress.

But it was the eighteenth century which first achieved a measurably clear conception of progress. Abbe de Saint-Pierre (1658–

* Pascal (1623–1662) later elaborated this idea as follows:

> Those whom we call the ancients were really those who lived in the youth of the world. As we have added the experience of the ages between us and them to what they knew, it is in ourselves that is to be found that antiquity which we venerate in others (quoted 62:XII, 497).

John Locke (1632–1704) thus expressed himself as to what he counted important:

> He that takes away reason to make room for revelation puts out the eye of both (quoted in 18:133).

† See J. B. Bury, *The Idea of Progress* (New York, Macmillan, 1932), *passim.* His discussion has proved useful in what is found here.

1743) published in 1737 his *Observations on the Continuous Progress of Universal Reason.* At present, he said, the human race is apparently not more than seven or eight thousand years old and is therefore only "in the infancy of human reason" compared with what may be expected in the long-time future. "Here we have," says Bury, "for the first time, expressed in definite terms, the vista of an immensely long progressive life in front of humanity. Civilization is only in its infancy." (19:136*f.*) The theory of human progress can of course be tested only by the facts of history. And, as might be expected, we find a new outlook on history being built in the eighteenth century to fit the growing conception of progress. Montesquieu, Voltaire, and Turgot together began a new vision of man's history.

Montesquieu (1689–1755) said explicitly: "There are general causes, moral or physical, which operate in every monarchy [nation], to raise it, maintain it, or overthrow it; all that occurs is subject to these causes." This statement, Bury says, "excludes Fortune, it also dispenses with Providence, design, and final causes." Montesquieu's *Spirit of Laws* may well claim to be the parent work of modern social science. Voltaire had less optimism than many regarding the future, but he insisted on a universal reason implanted in man which "subsists despite all passions which make war on it, despite all tyrants who would drown it in blood, despite the impostors who would destroy it by superstition." Turgot (1727–1781) had a plan, never realized, to study history in the light of the idea of progress, a history whose course would be a strict sequence of particular cause and effect relationships "which bind the state of the world [at any given moment] to all that has preceded it." For Turgot the idea of progress based on cause and effect was an organizing conception to give unity and meaning to history.

One aspect of the theory of progress had to await the failure of the effort in the French Revolution to wipe out the past and start civilization afresh. Until this failure had been digested, few if any had seen adequately the place played in associated life by the culture, the social inheritance. After the Revolution this came to be understood, and in terms of this we can now define progress as such accumulation and improvement of the culture as brings a more adequate civilization.

OPTIMISM REGARDING PROGRESS

The idea that mankind can accumulate wisdom for the individual to use was so fascinating as to lead to what we now consider an undue hope of perfectibility. Condorcet (1743–1794) voiced this hope perhaps most clearly of all the eighteenth-century writers. He counted that the actual facts of history show no limit to be "set to the perfecting of the powers of man . . . that the progress of this perfectibility, henceforth independent of any power that might wish to stop it, has no other limit than the duration of the globe upon which nature has placed us" (31:I, 19); and the thought was so inspiriting to him that he thus bursts forth:

> What a picture of the human race, freed from its chains, removed from the empire of chance as from that of the enemies of its progress, and advancing with a firm and sure step on the pathway of truth, of virtue, and of happiness (31:II, 99).

Thomas Jefferson was perhaps a little more guarded:

> And it cannot but be, that each generation, succeeding to the knowledge acquired by all those that preceded it, adding to it their own acquisitions and discoveries, and handing the mass down for successive and constant accumulation, must advance the knowledge and well-being of mankind, not infinitely, but indefinitely (Rockfish Gap Report).

It was the nineteenth century, however, that gave the strongest statement to the notion of inevitable progress. The Industrial Revolution had meanwhile come in strength in Great Britain, and scientific technology was beginning its triumphal march. Macaulay wrote in 1835: "The history of England is emphatically the history of progress." Herbert Spencer (1820–1903) thus spoke, most strongly of all, in 1850:

> Progress . . . is not an accident, but a necessity. . . . It is a part of nature. . . . As surely as there is any efficacy in educational culture, or any meaning to such terms as habit, custom, practice; so surely must the human faculties be molded into complete fitness for the social state; so surely must the things we call evil and immorality disappear: so surely must man become perfect (152:80).

In much the same spirit Robert Browning (1812–1889) wrote in 1835:

Progress is
The law of life, man is not
Man as yet—*Paracelsus*, Pt. v.

and again, but more discerningly, in 1864:

Progress, man's distinctive mark alone,
Not God's, and not the beasts': God is, they are,
Man partly is and wholly hopes to be—*Death in the Desert*, 1. 586.

Darwin's *Origin of Species* (1859), along with its wide influence otherwise, taught men better how to study the problem of progress and so disclosed the great complexity of the problem. John Fiske in his *Outlines of Cosmic Philosophy* (1874), had advanced definitely beyond Spencer's inevitability of progress: "Far from being necessary and universal, progress has been in eminent degree contingent and partial." And John Morley still later (1905) said:

> To think of progress as a certainty . . . is a kind of fatalism—radiant, confident, and infinitely hopeful, yet fatalism still, and like fatalism in all its other forms, inevitably dangerous to the effective sense of individual responsibility (58:29:7*f*.).

Huxley (1825–1895) saw things in a different light from his contemporary, Herbert Spencer: "Social progress means the checking of the cosmic process at every step and the substitution for it of another which may be called the ethical process." (19:345) A little later we shall wish to consider whether this dichotomy between the cosmic and the ethical process is a proper one; but a further statement of Huxley's has been, at least in a measure, cruelly verified in recent years: "I know of no study which is so saddening as that of the evolution of humanity as set forth in the annals of history. . . . Man is a brute, only more intelligent than the brutes." (19:344)

OPPOSITION TO THE IDEA OF PROGRESS

The merely reactionary point of view was well expressed some two centuries ago by an unnamed Britisher: "When it is not necessary to change, it is necessary not to change." But others, more discerning, have spoken specifically against the popular faith in progress. William Butler Yeats (1865–1939) spoke of "this slow dying of men's hearts which we call progress." (qtd. in 163:142) George Bernard Shaw (1856–1950) has said, with a touch of tongue in cheek: "Civilization is a disease produced by the practice of building societies with rotten materials. . . . We must, therefore, frankly give up the notion that man as he exists is capable of net progress." (qtd. in 163:136*f*.) This idea of "net progress" is one we shall in a moment consider more closely. More in keeping with the attitude of the Middle Ages are two final quotations. Gladstone, in his debate with Huxley on evolution, said: "Upon the grounds of what is called evolution God is relieved of the labour of creation, and in the name of unchangeable laws is discharged from governing the world." (qtd. in 18:180) A great churchman thus spoke further in the same vein: "Our race's progress and perfectibility is a dream, because revelation contradicts it" and "it would be a gain to this country [Great Britain] were it vastly more superstitious, more bigoted, more gloomy, more fierce in its religion than at present it shows itself to be." (qtd. in 18:240)

PROBLEMS INVOLVED IN THE CONCEPTION OF PROGRESS

So controversial is this particular area of thought that in treating it we must walk warily. The effort here will be to state the more important issues and see what can be said regarding each.

1. What is the goal of social progress? Various thinkers have offered single-item formulas. Hegel, for example, said that "progress is growth in freedom." Much can be said in favor of this particular formula, but when we consider how complex a matter is human life in society, we begin to doubt any one formula. Dewey's definition of progress as "increase of present meaning," fruitful as it is, is not all-inclusive. In fact Dewey, in connection with his proposed categorical imperative, "so act as to increase the meaning of present experience," would dispose of all simple formulas by saying that his imperative, "like everything absolute, is sterile." And he concludes: "Till men give up the search for a general formula for progress, they will not know where to look to find it." (46:283)

But we do mean something when we speak of social progress. Is there some end or goal in terms of which to evaluate progress? If so, how shall we conceive such a goal? And how state it?

An answer to this question was implicitly given in Chapter XI in the discussion on the good life. The goal is such an improved culture as gives a better life. If civilization is conceived as progressing, the end or goal of that progress is an even better life in the highest possible degree for all. This statement leads at once to a second issue.

2. What should be the character or content of this "ever better life" which is to define progress? The basis for an answer has already been given, especially in the chapter on the good life and in Chapters VIII, IX, and X, which deal respectively with morality, respect for personality, and democracy. From these discussions we are ready to affirm that the progress we wish is such a culture and such a civilization (the living of the culture) as promises the continued elevation of life in content and quality for all concerned.

3. What has been achieved to date? Can we point to specific lines or areas in which progress has surely been made?

Noting that the question restricts itself to progress along specific lines, an emphatic answer of yes can be returned. There are many specific lines along which progress in improving the culture has undoubtedly been made. Since man began his career with no more culture than the other animals can show, the presence of actual human culture is, in itself, Exhibit A of progress achieved. Certainly few, if any, would prefer life with nothing of culture in it. And the nearer to the present (since say 1600), the more numerous the lines of progress and the more inclusive and more rapid has been this progress. This is, of course, not to underwrite all modern change as progress. The application of modern science to the study of nature has brought the most obvious advances and of these the advances in technology are most obvious; but, as we shall consider in a moment, this is by no means all. As some specific lines of progress the following may be named:

(i) Of all specific areas of modern progress the most obvious area is scientific technology. Aristotle said, almost as if anticipating modern technology and its effect on civilization: "If we could make the shuttle weave and the plectrum touch the lyre without a hand to guide, chief workmen would not want laborers nor master slaves." In a more modern vein a Chinese scientist writing in the *Scientific Monthly* said that agricultural production in China costs more than ten times as many man-hours of work as in the United

States. (146:LVIII:170) In the sense of both Aristotle and this scientist progress has been demonstrably achieved. Our scientific technology does things for man in ever greater degree. It begins to appear that so far as any process is simply repetitive we can expect in time to make a machine to carry the process. Nor is this all; for as Whitehead reminds us: "The greatest invention of the 19th century was the invention of the method of invention." (173:136) This does in fact add a new dimension to man's control over nature.

(ii) Among specific technological inventions few, if any, are more spectacular than those of transportation and communication. In transportation Napoleon had little or no advantage over Julius Caesar; horses were no faster, and roads little if any better. Since Napoleon we have invented the railroad, the motor car, the airplane, and now the jet plane which will travel faster than sound. Improvement in communication is, if possible, even more striking. In this respect, also, Napoleon had no superiority over Caesar. But since Napoleon we have acquired the telegraph, the ocean cable, the telephone, the radio, and the various sound-repeating devices. Words can now be repeated at will and heard all but instantaneously around the world.

(iii) The matter of preventing and curing disease shows special demonstrable advances. The germ theory of disease, first clearly seen by Louis Pasteur (1822–1895), has revolutionized the study and practice of medicine. Yellow fever has been banished from our country and from most of the world. Malaria can be controlled if only we will; surgery has been revolutionized. The average length of life has been greatly extended. For holders of Metropolitan Life Insurance policies the average life span has increased from 34 years in the period 1879–89 to 67.8 years in 1949.

(iv) Following these specific and demonstrable instances of progress have come certain evident changes of attitude. It is fairly clear that in comparison with the prevailing attitude of the Middle Ages we have a much greater faith in human intelligence. All the foregoing advances contribute to this. Dewey words it thus: "Intelligent action is the sole ultimate resource of mankind in every field whatsoever." (51:252) Lancelot Hogben (1895–) put it in these words: "The exercise of the human reason is an indispensable condition of social progress and the maintenance of human welfare." (79:1) This attitude shows itself especially in modern times as faith in inductive study rather than, as formerly, in *a priori* and deductive study. Along with this greater faith in human reason and free play of intelligence has come freedom of speech and freedom of press discussed in Chapter x. Unless men are free to learn and free to confer, progress will be limited to the lines approved by the limiting authorities. Bury said, as if in support of Hegel's formula on freedom:

> If the history of civilization has any lesson to teach it is this: there is one supreme condition of mental and moral progress which is completely within the power of man himself to secure, and that is perfect liberty of thought and discussion. The establishment of this liberty may be considered the most valuable achievement of modern civilization, and as a condition of social progress it should be deemed fundamental (18:239).

And further, as if to answer in advance any present-day defense of the "iron curtain," he added: "The consideration of permanent utility on which it [free discussion] rests must outweigh any calculations of present advantage which from time to time might be thought to demand its violation." (18:239)

Another significant change of attitude is that change itself is now no longer considered a trivial or a wrong matter; "change" is no longer associated in the mind with "decay" as the old hymn had it, voicing a common attitude:

> Change and decay in all around I see

Rev. Dr. A. C. McGiffert, a great religious leader (1861–1933), voiced the modern view: "Growth and change belong to the very essence of reality." (105:295) One of the greatest intellectual tasks of modern times—a task as yet far from complete—is to rethink and restate our fundamental conceptions in terms of this inherent change as opposed to the old Platonic notion that important ideas neither change nor contemplate change.

One result from all the foregoing is a wider disposition in men to question and study, each man for himself. This is one of the encouraging signs of more recent years. Two centuries ago the proportion of men who read and studied was very small and of women much smaller still. The proportion is still too small, but in comparison it is now very much greater. Even the recent depression, library statistics show, much increased the number of those who consciously study. If we could get our schools to stress the study of life's current problems instead of emphasizing formal subject matter, the number who study after leaving school would probably be appreciably increased.

The last change of attitude here to be noted is still so subtle that few other than students of history know it. This is the disposition to locate value in life itself. We have previously quoted Ruskin as voicing this in his statement, "There is no wealth but life." Although a growing number now accept this, we have not yet learned, as we saw in the preceding chapter, how to study adequately the problem of what constitutes real richness of life. In a later chapter we shall consider many disquieting instances of the failure of our American civilization to solve this problem of the true richness of life.

4. What is "cultural lag"? What bearing has it on the problem of progress?

Because progress along different lines comes at different rates, it often happens that advance along a given line brings the need for corresponding (or correlative) changes elsewhere. Until the needed new cultural arrangements are created, we have the state of affairs that Ogburn calls "cultural lag." (127:200*f*., 280) Thus, when motor cars first became so numerous as to cause traffic congestion, and before traffic lights and special traffic policemen were provided, there existed a definite cultural lag. Now the great increase in cars has in many places brought, in spite of lights and policemen, unmanageable congestions, and we have again an unmet need, a new cultural lag. Let it be noted, then, for its bearing on further argument, that a cultural lag is a positive lack at one point caused by a cultural advance at another point. To be sure, not every advance causes such a cultural lag, but this result is frequent.

Certain very significant cultural lags are by some not recognized as such, and so last longer as cultural lags than they should. An example is the discriminatory treatment of minorities in our midst by certain people. Among these are some who profess to be Christians and as such profess to accept the Golden Rule as binding on all, and some who profess democracy with the Declaration of Independence principle of equal rights for all to "life, liberty and the pursuit of happiness." Another cultural lag, which many have great difficulty in recognizing as such, arises from failure to sense the need for a newer and more adequate type of education; developments in psychology and human sensitivity now strongly demand it. Of this we shall have much more to say in Part II.

As to the bearing of cultural lag on the problem of progress, perhaps the first question to arise is how to get rid of the lags. Specifically, (i) How can a people awaken themselves to such a sense of the new need as will result in proper efforts to remedy the evil? and (ii) How devise the needed new arrangements? These two questions taken together come very close to restating the abiding problem of improving the civilization we have. One promising answer is to improve our conscious education so as to bring up a new generation more sensitive to social issues and more disposed both to study social problems and then to live up to the most promising leads thus found. Discussion of how to improve education we postpone to Part II. Devising the needed new institutional forms and arrangements calls exactly for the application of the method of intelligence, the free play of interested and informed intelligence upon the confronting task.

A second bearing of the fact of cultural lag on progress is perhaps more serious, a problem which crucially concerns any continued increase of progress. With our greatly increasing rate of change, we are—so it appears—accumulating an ever-increasing body of unsolved cultural lags. The question then arises whether these unsolved cultural lags may not so accumulate in number and cruciality as not only to stop, or at least greatly thwart, progress, but even to threaten civilization itself. To this question an answer of yes seems at least theoretically possible. We do face that danger. In the degree that any large group—for example, any specific civilization as Toynbee defines it*—becomes so discouraged by the multiplicity or the severity of its unsolved problems as to lose courage and cease trying, will progress in that group probably slow down to the great hurt of that civilization. What we used to call "the Dark Ages" in western Europe seems a case in point. Certainly the creative mind went into a relative eclipse in those hundreds of years. The "resignation" of the Stoic Marcus Aurelius noticed above appears to be an accompaniment of this widespread loss of courage. It is not difficult to see in the state of mind of Europe and America for the past two or

* Arnold J. Toynbee, *A Study of History* (London and New York, Oxford University Press, 1946).

three decades some loss of courage. Many are discouraged, the tasks ahead seem too great. But we must never forget Toynbee's warning that a civilization disintegrates when it fails to respond actively to its confronting difficulty.

This particular situation of current discouragement we discussed earlier in terms of loss of faith. To fit this present decline of faith into its proper setting we have to see it as part of a larger whole We have previously discussed how, in the Middle Ages and more especially in the earlier Reformation, man had little or no faith in himself because he was regarded as naturally depraved. The Second Helvetic Confession (1566), for example, said explicitly that man is "unable to do or even think any good whatever." While many factors were at work to change this attitude, probably the most influential of these was modern science. The success of science gave to man a new and strong faith in human effort. Increasing numbers, particularly among the intelligentsia, came to believe that the most reliable thought and control resource available to man had come through science and by man's own unaided efforts.

Naturally, not all accept in equal degree such faith in man. The scientists probably feel it in greatest degree. If then we put these at the high end of the scale of man's faith in himself, we would find at the other, the low end, two quite diverse groups. One of these would be those among us who are most ignorant generally of all such matters; the other group at the bottom would be those who, from their ideology, distrust science and oppose its teaching. In between the high and low extremes would come the great mass of our people, each one taking his place on the scale according to his degree of this faith. As the older ones die, the younger ones tend to move up the scale. This we may say was the general picture of our civilization up to 1914.

But when in more recent years the great depression followed hard upon World War I, and World War II hard upon the depression, man's power of control began to seem less than had been thought. Many, especially those in the lower half of the scale, accordingly lowered their faith in man and so moved farther down the scale. Then those who had all the while resented and fought this faith of man in himself came more strongly forward to claim that their position was at length seen to be justified, that we must now acknowledge the impotence of men to think for themselves or to govern themselves, that instead of men thinking for themselves the external authority of some dictator or dogma must lay down the law to govern men's thoughts and acts. Hitler's rise to power was an instance of such external authority, but by no means the only one. Meanwhile those who still maintained their same faith of man in man gave as answer to their opponents that when we see all these matters in their larger setting, the most reasonable conclusion appears to be simply that life is more complex than had formerly appeared, that the task of managing is more difficult than our earlier successes had led us to expect, and that we must accordingly put forth more thought and effort than so far we have done.

But it must be emphasized that to retain one's faith in man and in the free play of intelligence is the exact opposite of shutting one's mind to disagreeable problems. To the contrary, the more disagreeable the situation, the more reason for man to face it. Refusal to try is plain moral cowardice. Acting on thinking and the free play of intelligence seem the surest rule that man can lay down for use in life. We must try. That is our hope. We must not let the cumulative aggregate of cultural lags conquer our will to effort.

5. What is meant by net social progress, or general social progress? Has mankind ever achieved it?

Net or general social progress implies a comparison as to relative quality between two periods of living, with the judgment that the later perior is *on the whole* superior in net good living to the earlier.

Has mankind ever achieved such net or general social progress? Most of us believe yes; most of us, if asked to judge between the life of the primitive Eskimo and that of, say, Periclean Athens or Elizabethan England, would not hesitate to decide against the Eskimo. And if the Eskimos should hold out for theirs, most of us would say it was because they know no other life, they have no adequate basis of judging. Furthermore, many, and probably most, would say that modern Western civilization, even with great problems and lacks, is preferable *for most people* to any primitive or even Middle Age civilization as lived then by *most people.*

However, proof in matters of value can be very difficult to obtain, and so it seems here. Probably we shall have to conclude that final proof on this particular issue is at present, if not forever, impossible; there are too many factors involved.

But this does not mean that we are helpless to bring about progress, at least along specific lines. If men will set themselves to work at the problem, they can find phases and aspects of our current civilization that need bettering. A number of these aspects, some very important, can even now be definitely bettered. If the wisest and best will then help the rest of us attack the problem, we can improve the general quality of living over what it would otherwise be—certainly in detail, possibly on the whole.

CONCLUSION

The practical problem of effecting progress is exactly the age-old problem, stated in other words, of improving our civilization itself. It is at bottom the problem of life, of making life as good as we can for all, of putting life (if we believe in democracy) on a basis of equality of rights and opportunity for all. This would mean making life in comparison better for all than it now is, with promise of continued improvement in the future.

Government was instituted among men to do its part toward making life good to live. Morality works to the same end. It began with formal codes but grew through the development of ethics and religion to stress the internal attitude and what that could do, through appropriate behavior, to enhance life. Art, music, and literature early established themselves as ways of giving life a higher spiritual quality. Philosophy works at the problem of life, to find or build the most inclusive and consistent outlook possible on the good life, and also to build higher spiritual quality. Education takes up the process with the young to make the best of philosophy—so far as educators and the surrounding community see and accept it—live effectively in ever better self-directing characters in the rising generation.

The problem of progress becomes thus exactly the practical problem of getting all these forces so to work together as to make life ever better for all concerned.

CHAPTER XIII. *Philosophy of Thinking: Modern vs. Classical Role; Body-Mind Relationship; Ethical Freedom; Predeterminism*

To the modern mind, the limited role formerly allowed by philosophers to thinking is quite surprising. To us, thinking is essentially active and creative, playing perhaps the dominating role to determine the character and content of life and civilization. In a word, to us thinking is primarily for *control*, not as formerly for intellectual *contemplation*. But besides this specific difference in attitude toward thinking, deep conflicts have otherwise arisen even in modern times as to the nature and function of thinking. This chapter will consider certain questions in the area which seem most to concern education.

THE CHANGING ROLE OF THINKING

To see how thinking is man's primary resource for exercising control over his living, consider again briefly the analysis brought from biology as sketched in Chapter II. When something in the environment or within the person himself *stirs* him to act, he finds himself *involved in a situation*. In the degree that he is stirred he feels a *want* and accordingly strives to *control* the situation if possible, that is, to make it so come out as to meet his want. Typically he sets up a *goal* or aim, the attainment of which will presumably satisfy the want. In order to attain his goal, and so satisfy his want, he takes steps (devises means and uses them) which promise to secure his aim and goal. In the degree that he succeeds in these *efforts* he is said to exercise control over the situation.

All of this seems so natural to us of the modern mind (once we see that the terminology used is simply describing what we have already known and done) that we are astonished to find Aristotle limiting this kind of goal-seeking behavior to slaves and artisans and therefore considering it degrading.

To the classical Greeks a cultivated gentleman of leisure more appropriately used his mind not to effect changes in affairs, but instead to understand and enjoy the finer distinctions and thought relations which the cultivated mind alone could see and appreciate. It was in keeping with the same idea that Aristotle denied to his God any wants or even interest in human affairs; for to want, or even feel interest, is by so much to *lack* and therefore to be imperfect. So that according to Aristotle God spent his time thinking only on thought; and this thinking could thus be nothing more than contemplation. Socrates seems to have had something like this in mind when he said:

> I think that to want nothing is to resemble the gods, and that to want as little as possible is to make the nearest approach to the gods; that the Divine nature is perfection, and that to be nearest to the Divine nature is to be nearest to perfection (Xenophon, *Memorabilia:* I:vi, 10).

As opposed to this classical contemplative role of thinking, biological evolution seems to show that thinking came into existence to help meet actual situations; and so it remains principally to this day, even though some among us, especially those much influenced by the older attitudes, object to such a statement. If the situation at hand is familiar and simple, little thinking is required; if the situation is complex and/or unfamiliar, creative thinking must devise the means to use. In choosing appropriate steps to attain the goal, for example, such thinking is essential. In facing many practical problems, consideration of the "means-consequence" relationship is necessary; or, in other words, before deciding to use any *means*, one must consider what *consequences* will follow its use. And on the basis of the contrasted promising leads, one chooses the means to use. In such an effort ignorance hurts by failing to furnish the knowledge needed for the effort. Lack of effective intelligence results in failure to do the kind of thinking needed. Bad logic results in failure to test adequately the steps proposed to be taken. Personality maladjustment may hurt the process in a number of ways, most generally perhaps by weighting some emotional factor to a degree that better thinking would not approve.

In the history of the changing role assigned to thinking, three problems are so outstanding in their bearing on the philosophy of behavior, and consequently on education, as to demand special attention here. The first of the three is the body-mind problem, whether body and mind are so different in character as to be unable to interact. The second is the problem of causation and ethical freedom, whether in the relation of causation to thinking the common scientific "law of causation" so controls thinking as to deny personal responsibility. The third is the problem of cosmic determinism or predeterminism, whether the "law of causation" is so inclusive as to foreordain the whole future in every detail from the very beginning of the universe.

THE BODY-MIND INTERACTION PROBLEM

Those who have not studied the history of philosophy may wonder why space should here be given to what seems a highly artificial problem, whether by thinking and willing I can or cannot raise my arm. They will wonder more to learn that the history of thought probably knows no problem which, in its many ramifications, has received more attention.

As to the interaction of mind and body, scientists tended from Descartes (1596–1650) until William James (1842–1910), and to a lesser degree even later, to hold that mind only mirrors what it sees; that is, that mind (thinking) is somehow too immaterial (too spiritual) a thing to move the material body which it inhabits and so is unable to affect observable phenomena. Mind could, to be sure, see and study and learn—that much self-respect demanded—but for thinking to move the body and so effect observable results—no, impossible!

Can thinking move a physical object? Of course, I cannot sit still and just by thinking and willing make a chair move across the floor. But most will say, "Surely by thinking and willing I can make my body get up and move the chair." It is true that most among us do now so believe and apparently the common run of people have always so believed; but for some two hundred and fifty years, beginning about the middle of the seventeenth century, a large proportion of the best students of the problem doubted that "the mind" could make "the body" move.

In fact, up to a half century ago many leading psychologists held a doctrine called "psycho-physical parallelism," in which the human mind and body parallel each other's processes without either affecting the other. E. B. Titchener (1867–1927), a prominent psychologist in his day, thus wrote in 1896:

> Especially must we be careful to avoid, as psychologists, the popular view that bodily states are the *causes* of mental, and mental states the *causes* of bodily: that a ray of light is the cause of the sensation of light, or an impulse the cause of a physical movement (162:343).

It was Descartes who gave this problem to the world, adapting, it appears, certain older ideas to his purpose. He defined mind as "thinking substance" and body as "extended substance" (matter), and said that two such different substances could not affect each other. It may seem strange to us, but such was Descartes' influence that the leading thinkers who followed accepted this doctrine.

The question then arose as to how to explain the fact that one's mind does appear to control, in part at least, the movements of the body. And three contradictory answers, all accepting Descartes' doctrine that mind and body cannot interact, were returned as follows: (i) mind and body, like two perfect clocks, run two separate and parallel courses (or histories); neither affects the other but they fit precisely together (the "psycho-physical parallelism" above mentioned); (ii) there is really no such thing as mind, but only body; and body so acts as to do the things we call mind ; (iii) there is really no such thing as body, but mind only; and mind so acts as to make us think (mistakenly) that there is body.

It was Leibnitz (1646–1716), one of the greatest thinkers of his day, who proposed the idea of the two perfect clocks. One clock, so to say, ran the mind and the other ran the body. Neither affected the other; but when mind thought or willed a certain hand movement, the body—keeping perfect time with the mind—made the appropriate movement, not because the mind had willed it but because the body was so wound up. This sounded too artificial to many subsequent thinkers and we find such a man as Thomas Hobbes (1588–1679) taking the second of the three positions, that body alone exists, it doing the things mind has been supposed to do; and later Berkeley (1685–1753) and Hegel (1770–1831), among others, denied any existence to body or matter as such and counted all existence to be mental in character. Whitehead (1861–1947), who rejected the Cartesian dualism and along with it all three of the positions given above, asserts that "modern philosophy has been ruined" by the failure to deal more effectively with this body-mind problem (173:79).

The most satisfactory approach to this problem of "interaction" seems to be to study the situation inductively. Do we find that thinking plays any part in action? No one can doubt the observed fact that what we do is affected by what we think, that thinking is, in the degree it is good thinking, the key to wise action. Even those who have tried by deduction from their *a priori* theories to deny the influence of thought on action have themselves all the time acted as if thinking does affect action; for they have persistently tried to do good thinking in order the surer to present a reasoned position, and they have published their thoughts (a material process) in order to impress others with the results of their thinking.

If any feel that the answer just suggested to this old body-mind question disposes too easily of so hoary a problem, let him ask further about the Cartesian dualism. Specifically, let him examine the conception of substance, and particularly of "thinking substance." What did Descartes really know about such? What does substance mean, in any final or metaphysical sense? And how did Descartes find out about such a substance? Is not "thinking substance" a mere assumption like the ether which physicists used to postulate—but now reject—as the basis for the wave (undulatory) theory of light? In the light of later study Lord Salisbury (1830–1903) said that all we know about the ether is that "it is the nominative case of the verb to undulate."*

And, similarly, all we actually know about "thinking substance" is that thinking and behavior do take place. And when we study the situations in which thinking is allowed to play its full part, do we

* We could just as well have asked about material substance. What seems solid was first analyzed into a congeries of molecules so moving as to create the illusion of a solid substance; and each molecule similarly analyzed into a pattern of moving atoms. And, still further, the atom has with recent years been analyzed into electrons and protons and now neutrons, so that energy appears at one moment as a solid and next as a wave motion with nothing to wave. If anything is left to the original notion of material substance, it is very difficult to say what it is.

not find that thinking normally and typically results in action guided by the thinking? And is it not generally admitted among practical people—farmer, housewife, mechanic, engineer, statesman—that the better the thinking, the better, on the whole, is the resultant action? Which, then, do we really know more about: the nature of substance, or the observed effect of thinking on action? In one final word, if we refuse to make the unwarranted assumption of "substances," we have no problem to solve. We can then, as we should, study inductively the normal effect of thinking on action and from this study learn how better to think for the guiding of action.

Thus the more we study the actual place of thinking in conscious effort, the clearer do we see that thinking, in its effect on one's bodily movement, is beyond any sort of question a positive factor in effecting desired changes, and this whether the affair be great or small, whether it be material primarily or social or ethical. In other words, we must reject the separation of mind and body as an artificial assumption, not valid in practice. Metaphysics must fit the facts of life, rather than have facts fit a metaphysics made prior to and in disregard of the facts.

ETHICAL FREEDOM AND THE "LAW OF CAUSATION"

Under older ways of thinking, the first two words of this title might better have been written "Free Will," but of that more later. What is here meant is, perhaps more precisely, the relation of "causation" to moral responsibility, to man's freedom to act ethically. In Chapter II, as will be recalled, it was brought forward as the fundamental belief of scientists expressed in the "law of causation" (i) that each event is determined by the action of preceding "causes"; (ii) that these prior determining causes fix exactly what the resulting effect shall be; and (iii) that like causes always produce like effects.* Now if the "law of causation" holds for human conduct, it would appear, at least at first thought, that man's conduct is also "caused" by the pertinent preceding events; and if so, it might

* To be sure, the "Heisenberg principle" has for many, perhaps for most, introduced a doubt as to causation in the case of microphysics; but, even so, scientists in general still hold to the "law of causation," certainly in larger matters.

seem that he is not really free to choose his acts. Specifically, then, we ask here whether the "law of causation" holds for man's mental and moral processes as truly as for material things. And if so, what becomes of "free will" and moral responsibility?

In a true sense, this is but another aspect of the preceding problem. We concluded there that one's thinking, working through the body, can be a real factor in effecting observable and even material changes. Here the setting is different. Many persons, especially those brought up to use the term *free will*, become troubled at any proposal to make man's mental and moral life continuous with the rest of nature, and specifically shrink from any proposal to bring his mental and moral processes under the rule of the "law of causation."

Two variant aspects of the problem must be considered: (i) Wherein and how is man free to act in a way not true, say, of a brick or of a candle moth? (ii) If the "law of causation" holds for man's mental and moral processes, wherein is man, after all, different from brick or moth?

Let us discuss first wherein and how man is free as a brick or a moth is not. What do we mean by such freedom in man?

As for a brick, clearly its history is determined from without in a sense and degree not true of a man. Left to itself a brick does nothing, makes no effort, performs no action; it will "stay put," as we say, forever. In contrast, man does not simply take whatever comes. He is stirred to act according as he feels either threat to his welfare or hope of good to be attained. He then makes an effort according to the need he feels, the meaning he sees. This we observe every day and all the time. And, as we saw above, this goal-seeking behavior is typically directed, more or less intelligently, by thinking.

The moth, in contrast with the brick, illustrates one definite human trait, that of acting on stimulus. When the moth sees the candle flame, she too, is stirred and flies toward the flame, even into it. If the first burning does not kill her, she will, as soon as she sees the flame again, once more fly toward it; and again and again, until she finally loses her wings or is devoured in the flame. In a word, the moth, while capable of being stirred to action, is unable to learn. The first burning teaches her nothing. Man, on the contrary, learns by his mishaps what not to do. Man thus not only reacts positively, as the moth does but the brick does not; in addition man learns from his experiences, as the moth does not. By learning and thinking man thus accumulates practical wisdom, so that he now can behave more intelligently. He may perhaps avoid next time the evils he experienced this time. He can now better choose his goals and means, and perhaps take steps next time to avoid a repetition of this time's misfortune. This fact is abundantly illustrated both in the history of man's life on earth and in the personal experience of individual man. In these respects at least does man differ from both brick and moth. And precisely in this difference lies man's peculiar freedom, a freedom denied to brick or moth; he has freedom not only to act, but so to profit by the successive results of action as to be able to plan and realize a happier life. He can criticize his own wants and then so organize his resources as to live the better criticized life. He can better avoid evils which otherwise would come, and he can more surely attain the values resulting from his criticism. It is this kind of freedom which is not only peculiar to man, but is best found in the highest type of man.

The second line of inquiry repeats the first question, but from a different angle: Does the "law of causation" hold for man's mental and spiritual activities? And if so, wherein, after all, is man different from brick or moth? Are not the details of his life history, being fixed by the "law of causation," as definitely, though differently, determined as those of either brick or moth? How, then, can we say that man has any special freedom? And what becomes of any supposed moral responsibility?

The discussion to follow is, as it must be, more psychological than philosophical, but the answer itself seems clear. "Causation" is not necessarily, or even generally, of the "billiard-ball" kind it was once counted to be. "Causation" as a process varies according to the kind of phenomenon under consideration. Specifically, "causation" is the combined effect of all the factors that enter into an event to determine what it shall be. When the question under discussion is how billiard balls affect each other, the pertinent factors are such matters as the size, weight, motion, and elasticity of the balls involved. When a moral decision is being considered, it is the influence of thought on thought and feeling, and of these on decision. The result is caused precisely by the interaction of such factors. For example, when a man faces a situation of moral doubt, he will, to the degree of the appropriate intelligence and character he has built, study the situation to see what is involved; he will then try to find or construct a program of action which promises, better than any alternative he has found, to take care of all that seems at stake. When a program promising to do this has been found, the man's moral character, if effective, will accept this program and proceed to put it into effect.

In such a thoughtful decision and act, we see the answer to our problem. On the one hand, such a decision is a true and effective case of causation. Granted the person with his intelligence and his character, out of this intelligence, by searching, will come the insight used and followed at the moment of decision. This insight and this particular character as they come thus together, each being what it is at the time, will uniquely determine the decision. And this resulting decision, granted the circumstances, is as inevitably caused–determined at the time, not *predetermined*–as is true of the action of brick or moth.

But, on the other hand, for the man fortunate enough to have developed previously the needed intelligence and character, there is true freedom of the kind discussed above; specifically there is, for present purposes, freedom of the kind needed to discharge moral responsibility. Such a man is free to study the situation and come of himself to his own decision as to what he should do. Being able thus to study and learn, he is free to act intelligently, as intelligently as his thinking and choosing will allow. Freedom thus to act intelligently, and so responsibly, when a situation of moral doubt arises is the only kind of moral freedom we wish or need. As he is able to decide and act with knowledge of consequences and in the light of them, the rest of us will hold him to account for what he does; and he, knowing this, can and should accept the obligation to act according to the best that he can find and see. So to study and act as well as one can with proper regard for foreseen consequences–this is by definition to act with moral responsibility.

We find, then, the "law of causation," "freedom to think" (freedom to study and decide accordingly), and "moral responsibility" all present in one and the same instance of honest search and decision and act. "Causation" is not only not opposed to desirable personal freedom and moral responsibility; but it is in fact an essential ingredient of the dependable character necessary for such.

This last statement may so surprise those who use the phrase *freedom of will* that a further word seems necessary. The term *causation* or *law of causation* assumes regularity in human conduct as truly as in the material world of physics, and without this dependable regularity the term *character* would lose its meaning of dependability. There would otherwise be literally no telling what a man would do. No one else could depend on him and he could not depend on himself. The word *learn* also would cease to have dependable meaning; for it too could not be depended upon to build character; no one then could learn from his experience. Accountability and responsibility would alike lapse. Prudence and morality would cease to have meaning. The assumption of dependable "causation" underlies both. The "law of causation" both makes man free to be himself and determines that he act in accordance with himself.

The term *freedom of will* used above has now largely lost its former acceptance because of two considerations. One is that psychologists no longer accept "the will" as a separate faculty to decide what one shall do. Rather is the process of willing the action of the whole organism. To ask whether "the will" is free is accordingly to use an out-of-date term, now no longer acceptable. But further, aside from the use of an outmoded term, the term *freedom of will* is itself unacceptable because it is ambiguous. It may mean, in fact it does seem to mean for those who use it, that "the will" acts independently of "causation"; and this, as we have just seen, cannot be accepted without destroying the dependability of character and of nature, which would mean in turn to destroy both prudence and moral responsibility. It is from these various considerations that the phrase "freedom of will" is now avoided by careful thinkers.*

One further phase of the problem of freedom—of moral and practical freedom alike—may well be noted at this point for the sake of its later usefulness. The kind of moral freedom we have just considered assumes actual situations—situations, that is, where some

* F. H. Bradley (1846–1924), a very acute thinker of the past generation, said:

> Free-will means Non-determinism. The will is not determined to act by anything *else;* and, further, it is not determined to act by anything *at all* . . . Freedom [of this kind] means *chance;* you are free, because there is no reason which will account for your particular acts, because no one in the world, not even yourself, can possibly say what you will, or will not, do next. You are 'accountable,' in short, because you are a wholly 'unaccountable' creature. (14:10*f.*)

outcome portends (either threatens or beckons) in such a manner that the person who is acting feels called upon to try to bring about desired results, which, without his effort, would not come to pass. Responsibility—whether as fact or attitude and whether moral or merely prudential—thus contemplates a plastic situation where the outcomes are not as yet fixed but are contingent upon the appropriate efforts of the person who feels responsibility. It is this sort of undetermined future, with its as yet contingent outcomes, to which attention is here directed as a fundamental assumption of any and all responsibility.

PREDETERMINISM

If the "law of causation" holds universally, does it not follow that the whole future has in fact already been determined and this in every detail? If so, is not moral freedom, after all, a delusion? We thus come to the third of the three questions raised at the outset, that of "cosmic determinism" or predeterminism.

This doctrine of predeterminism was formulated, it appears, by the Stoics and accepted by many theologians and pre-Einstein scientists. Against this William James described our universe as, in his own salty words, "a universe with the lid off," that is, a universe still actually in the making, a universe developing in such a way that man, by his thoughtful efforts, can help to determine, at least within limits, what shall come to pass.

Of course common sense, concerned chiefly with immediately practical affairs, has always rejected predeterminism—at least in immediate matters. The most primitive tribesmen (outside the tropics) never doubted that they had to put forth efforts, or there would be no food to eat; similarly every modern housewife knows that if she, or someone else, does not get dinner, the family will go hungry. That is, in all matters close enough at hand for practical judgment to rule, no one has doubted that effort does really count in effecting outcomes; and few or none have doubted that, on the whole and on the average, the better the thinking the surer we can count on the hoped-for outcome.

But it seemed different with the future of great affairs. Here men sought by signs to foretell the outcomes of battles and other important occasions. In this way, it appears, there arose a belief in fate, that certain weighty events, such as the death of a king or the outcome of a battle, had been inexorably foreordained and must come to pass exactly at the preappointed time *irrespective of whatever efforts might be made to hasten it or to avert it, or whatever natural events might meanwhile intervene.* Some way, somehow, fate would bring this predestined event to pass.

Just how such foreordainment was brought about seems now not clear. Greek mythology designated three goddesses to manage the matter, and these seemed to effect it quite arbitrarily; but once fixed, the fated outcome, they thought, bound both men and gods. In a time when causation was little understood and little regarded, such a doctrine of fate could be believed. Now, however, we see that a theory of fate, which fixes events in advance despite whatever actions may intervene, runs exactly counter to all common sense and all science in that it denies every accepted theory of causation.

Later the Stoics and various religious groups extended the doctrine of fate to include all events in history, large or small. Thus Marcus Aurelius says:

> Whatever may happen [to] thee was prepared for thee from all eternity, and the complex series of causes from time everlasting intertwined the threads of thy destiny with the incidence of this chance (109:X, 5).

And the *Rubaiyat* gives as the old Moslem doctrine:

> Yea, the first Morning of Creation wrote
> What the Last Dawn of Reckoning shall read.
> 1st version, st. 53.

Still later Newtonian science took much the same view. We thus find Laplace (1749–1827) saying:

> Given for one instant an intelligence which could comprehend all the forces by which nature is animated . . . it would embrace in the same formula the movements of the greatest bodies of the universe and those of the lightest atom; . . . nothing would be uncertain and the future, as the past, would be present to its eyes (98:3*f*.).

This doctrine of Laplace, that by inclusive causation all natural events—past, present, and future—have already been pre-established, we call "cosmic determinism" or "predeterminism" (thus distinguishing it from "particular determinism," according to which each event is caused precisely as it occurs, uniquely determined by its own set of conditioning events).

When scientists accepted cosmic determinism—and most of them once did, in theory—they did so on an argument that ran like this:

> Each event is caused, and this has always been so everywhere.
> Whatever is caused is thereby determined to be just that and nothing else.
> Therefore all events, past, present, and future, were fixed as soon as the universe was started off.

It might be thought that the scientists who believed in cosmic determinism and the theologians who believe in all-inclusive predestination were in exact agreement as to the resulting state of affairs, even if they differed as to how things became thus foreordained. But this was not so. The believers in predestination usually included also the possibility of miracles which set aside the ordinary order of nature, as, for example, when Joshua commanded the sun and the moon to stand still. This, if it were admitted, would be to disregard for the time the law of causation or to set it aside, which would go against the scientific principle. On this point scientist and theologian would be squarely opposed.

But this dispute between scientist and theologian is not our concern here. What does concern us is the bearing of the doctrine of cosmic determinism on man and his behavior. We saw a few pages back that responsibility, whether as fact or attitude, assumes and must assume a contingent situation, a situation where the outcome is considered to depend on what the responsible person does. If that reasoning was correct, then "cosmic determinism" denies the essential condition for either the existence or the acceptance of responsibility. The very notion of responsibility would become meaningless. So much for the answer that logic returns as to the bearing of predeterminism on responsibility.

But in behavior it is human acceptance, not logic as such, that affects action. What is the bearing of predeterminism in our present world, where the cultural life has been built on acceptance of responsibility as a proper obligation? Suppose a man comes to believe that everything is already fixed in advance, that what is to happen is already somehow written down; will this not make a practical difference in his sense of responsibility? Will not some men, at any rate, ask themselves why they should worry when the result is already fixed? Why labor and sweat at all? In fact, is not the very foundation of effort an active belief that effort does count, a belief that effort, properly directed, will produce results which—without the effort—would not come about? In other words, is it not true that belief does affect conduct? And is it not equally true that in the long run belief along any particular line tends to follow recognized logic? Are we not then forced to conclude that predeterminism, in the degree accepted, would tend to destroy faith in either the necessity or wisdom of effort?

The same question can be considered from a slightly different angle. Suppose a man holds to two doctrines that seem to contradict each other—one tells him the result is already fixed, the other tells him that the result is not yet fixed but depends on him and his effort; will he not in such case suffer confusion? And if many people together suffer this confusion, will they not so influence each other as to increase the confusion?

The more we think about it, the more we see that all conscious and intentional human conduct depends on the active belief that *effort counts*, that the outcome actually depends on what we do. There is involved here not only the prudential conduct of ordinary affairs—though that would suffice to justify the discussion. Equally involved is responsible moral conduct, with the need to build personal moral responsibility for the consequences of one's acts. The essence of moral responsibility is acceptance of personal responsibility for consequences and therefore of personal responsibility to make the outcome the best that can be effected. Any doctrine that lessens the sense of such responsibility destroys the very essence and strength of moral character. Still further, any doctrine that distracts attention from the positive effects of what one does or does not do, distracts attention by so much from one's duty to others, from one's duty positively to make this a better world.

Because this question of predeterminism (or cosmic determinism) is so important and at the same time so complex, it seems wise to sum up the matter by presenting in detail a number of different considerations for rejecting the doctrine. We cannot accept the dictum that the "law of causation" fixed all events at the beginning of the world once and for all. The five arguments as given are largely parallel, but partly overlapping. They may vary in the strength of their appeal to each reader, but the aggregate, it is believed, will suffice to refute the doctrine of cosmic determinism.

1. *The Argument from Common Sense.* No matter what theory of fate, predestination, or predeterminism one may hold, everyone in simple, everyday, close-at-hand affairs acts on the theory that what he wishes he must seek, that effort is necessary and does (within limits) affect the outcome. If there is any one principle on which all mankind acts and always has acted, this is it. And all the food gathered, all the clothes made, all the houses erected—everything, in fact, that man has to show as the result of planning and contriving—appears as evidence that effort does count, that acting on thinking does justify itself.

And the argument seems strengthened when we take into account the quality of thought and effort. The better we plan, the better the results. The more consistently we carry out the plans, the better the results. The more creative new thinking we do, the more do the results show it. The principle of effort seems justified by its fruits.

Those who attack the argument just given do so on the basis stated by Alexander Pope in his *Essay on Man:*

> Heaven from all creatures hides the book of Fate,
> All but the page prescrib'd, their present state—Ep. I, 1.77

These go on to say that the effort put forth is as truly part of the foreordainment as is the outcome, and fixed in advance along with all the rest is the feeling of worry, the felt need to put forth effort, the sense of responsibility for results.

To this the opponents of predeterminism reply that if all the present is but the unrolling of what was fixed at the beginning, the argument proves too much. Acceptance of such predeterminism would take away all meaning from effort and deny any sense of responsibility. In short, *it would explain away the whole behavior situation on which life is based, including even the wish to argue the question. Against such notions common sense does and must rebel. If anything is real, it is that effort counts.*

2. *The Argument from the Logic of Science.* This is, in a way, an extension of the preceding argument.

The argument in favor of cosmic determinism is based on the scientific "law of causation." This, in its turn, is an inductive conclusion based upon uniformities observed by scientists in their experiments and scientific observations. Now each such scientific enterprise carries with it the assumption that if the scientist will think creatively enough in making his hypotheses and will devise his experiment or observation suitably, then the results will properly test his hypotheses. In other words, he, like the man of affairs in argument (1), assumes that his thought and his effort will actually affect results and are proper and necessary thereto.

All of which is to say that the conclusion to accept cosmic determinism is based on procedures which assume, actually and inherently, the opposite of predeterminism, namely that effort really affects outcomes. The proponent of predeterminism thus attempts to prove his doctrine by assuming throughout that his doctrine is not true. Such a logical contradiction invalidates the conclusion.

3. *The Argument from the Psychology of Behavior.* This is simply to reaffirm and apply several preceding discussions. We saw under (2) above that "causation" is not only consistent with desirable personal freedom and moral responsibility, but is in fact, by its essential part in building dependable character, necessary to the actual existence and effective working of such freedom and responsibility. We saw further that the actual exercise of this freedom and responsibility requires a plastic and contingent situation, one in which effort can effect true results, can make real changes. Putting these two together we conclude that, on the one hand, determinism (causation as such, not predeterminism) does not interfere with the essential life process of free and responsible effort; but, on the other hand, that predeterminism exactly negates and denies the plasticity and contingency needed for the life process as we know it and value it.

In support of the conclusion just reached, we can quote the following from Edwin G. Conklin:

> Such freedom is not uncaused activity, but freedom from the mechanical responses [as of brick or moth] to external or instinctive stimuli, through the intervention of internal stimuli due to experience [learning] and intelligence . . . [thus] the beginnings of rational life, social obligations, and moral responsibility. . . . (32:337).
>
> All that is meant by that term [determinism] in science and in actual life is that every effect is the resultant of antecedent causes

> and that identical causes yield identical results. *Determinism does not mean pre-determinism* [italics supplied]: the one finds every effect to be due to a long chain of preceding causes, the other attributes every effect to a single original cause; the one is scientific naturalism, the other is fatalism (32:334).*

4. *The Argument from the Existence and Need of Morals.* This has already been anticipated in several of the foregoing discussions; but it seems worthwhile to restate it more explicitly here.

Man had common sense and morals before he had science. The need for moral conduct in human relations has been universally recognized by tribes and other groups of men in every age and time. And there never was a time—since World War II and the atomic bomb—when man more seriously needed proper conduct relations among men and nations.

If, then, we most seriously need social-moral conduct, always have needed it, and always will; if we have a choice of accepting or denying a theory which, if accepted, will confuse and obstruct moral behavior and will even deny to morality the plasticity and contingency in human affairs necessary to its very existence; and if at the same time this theory of predeterminism is increasingly denied by competent scientists—if all these things are true, we seem authorized, at least until further argument is adduced, to refuse to accept the hypothesis of predeterminism; and this for the double reason that it is as yet unproved and that it denies any effective status to the essential social institution of morality.

5. *The Argument from an Infinite Universe.* If, for the moment, we imagine a universe composed of a finite number of discrete physical objects, the laws of mechanics (so it appears) would fix the future movements of each of these objects forever. While we could not with our present knowledge of mathematics always foretell what these several movements would be, we cannot doubt that they would be fixed forever and precisely. This is to say that in a universe composed of a finite number of discrete physical objects, the principle of inclusive cosmic determinism does hold. In such a universe "the first morning" would "write what the last dawn of reckoning will read."

But our universe is not of that kind. It is in its details infinite. Sup-

* Edwin G. Conklin: *Heredity and Environment.* Copyright 1929 by Princeton University Press, Princeton, N.J., and used by their permission.

pose that within our infinite universe we choose for study a finite number of discrete physical objects in such a way that we can apply our known mechanics and mathematics; can we then foretell the future movements of these chosen objects? The answer is no, we cannot foretell these movements with certainty; for we cannot tell when from outside these chosen bodies, from somewhere else within our infinite universe, there might come another body, a wandering star or a big enough comet, to upset the otherwise known movements of the selected finite system. And this would be true no matter how large or how small a finite system we choose to consider.

This is no denial of determinism (particular determinism, that is), of the "law of causation." On the contrary, it is precisely the acceptance of the latter. But it is to deny predeterminism, for in an *infinite* universe whether the outside body will or will not influence events remains uncertain up to the last moment of the determination of any event chosen for consideration. In other words, that particular event is finally determined only as it actually happens, but not in advance of the happening. This must be true of an infinite universe. To be sure, looking backwards, we may be able to say of a particular event that it was predetermined from a long, specific, previous period of time because we can now see that no wandering object did in fact interfere later. But this proves nothing if we look ahead. For looking ahead, we always face the uncertainty of what an infinite universe may supply. In one final word, we can in our infinite world accept determinism without accepting predeterminism.

CHAPTER XIV. *Conclusion of Part I: Major Unsolved Problem Areas*

THE effort here is to present seven problem areas which stand out from the discussions thus far as highly important but still unsolved. No attempt is here made to solve the problems involved. There is good reason to believe that certain of these, the problem of abolishing war, for example, can be solved and in time laid aside as settled. Others are abiding obligations, as, for example, building a philosophy of life, on which men will and should forever work.

These seven problem areas are presented here at the close of Part I, partly to direct attention to their strategic importance, partly to give direction to the study of education, which is to constitute the theme of Part II. It need not surprise us that these outstanding and strategic areas overlap and interact. That is the way with life.

1. ONE WORLD: WAR; INTERNATIONAL RESPONSIBILITY

That modern technology has made One World of all the peoples of the earth is perhaps the clearest lesson from our two world wars. As against this, nationalism still constitutes what many are calling the greatest religion of the modern age. In this conflict of nation with nation we have the greatest single current threat to proper living. The fact of One World coupled with the suicidal threat from atomic warfare furnishes an argument stronger than any ever before known that the separate nations must yield enough of their national sovereignty to abolish both war and the threat of war. Until this is done, none can feel safe. Meanwhile, the attitudes and expenditures required for satisfactory military preparedness seriously thwart many possible steps toward better living.

But world-mindedness must do more than abolish war. It must besides take effective care, first, of certain troublesome matters of international relations, such as trade, air-routes, postal service, disease germs, narcotics, intercultural relations, and the like; and second, of certain matters of concern to humanity wherever found, such as an adequate standard of living for all, human rights, minority problems, international good will, dependent peoples.

We now have the United Nations. Where its structure is adequate, we must make it work. Where its structure is inadequate, we must strengthen it till it does work. With One World now so patent a fact, such national sovereignty as interferes becomes a menacing anachronism. How to do what is necessary and how get the will to do it—these together constitute the first of the resulting great problems. To help build a more active and intelligent citizenship interest in this One World problem becomes a major task of our schools.

2. WHAT SYSTEM OF ECONOMY?

Taking all the world together, four distinct systems of economics are found, with various combinations of the four: (i) free private enterprise (no governmental regulation); (ii) regulated private enterprise; (iii) communism; (iv) state socialism. Our country remains the chief exponent of private enterprise, but it has also the other three systems: *regulated private enterprise*, principally found in the railroads and other public utilities and wherever health is involved in the sale of products; *communism* (useful services furnished by the government free of charge) found principally in public roads and free public schools, but also in our police system, certain river-and-harbor services, board-of-health services, and the like; *state socialism*, principally seen in the post office (which is the greatest single business enterprise in the country), toll bridges, various municipal public utilities.

At the moment in Europe, state socialism seems to be gaining. Great Britain is entering upon it in greatly increased degree, as are also the Scandinavian countries. The U.S.S.R. stresses state socialism both at home and in its satellites. Great Britain, however, in its advocacy of state socialism differs significantly from Russia in two respects: first, in having a background of free enterprise which still largely holds, and, second, in insisting strongly upon the individual rights which we of this country associate with democracy—parliamentary government, free ballot ("two-party" system), free speech, *habeas corpus*, and trial by jury, none of which Russia has.

For our country the problem is not which of the four different economic systems we shall have, but what proportion of the four we shall have. It seems probable that the growth of technological industry in our country, together with the increasing size of business corporations, will in various ways bring the governmental factor more and more into the economic realm, certainly to regulate relations in the labor-management area, possibly to guarantee jobs under emergency conditions, probably to work for a more equitable division of the national income and thus insure a more equal standard of living. But the problem remains how much and what proportion of these four systems of economy to use; and how far and wherein government can and should get into the picture in order to preserve effective freedom for the individual.

That government will maintain an interest in economic affairs seems certain. Modern industry makes us all dependent on the adequate working of our economic system. We saw in World War II that the government can, if it really tries, take over the economic system and make it work. If another depression comes, the people will, in great probability, not sit idly by waiting for the depression to depart. They will demand governmental action and they will get it. A danger more real than such governmental action is the threat of selfish interests wishing special favors from the government. We already see this at work; and the danger will probably increase, since the possibilities for such selfishness are very inviting. The question is whether enough people will bestir themselves to force the government to proper action for the common good. On this point the history of our tariff bills is most discouraging. The Smoot-Hawley bill of 1930, for instance, which so hurt the rest of the world as greatly to increase the great depression for us and them, was enacted against the outspoken opposition of practically all the experts on the subject in our country. We face the like danger in this whole economic area so long as our citizens are no more intelligently concerned with what government does. On this specific point our high schools and colleges should consciously seek to build a more intelligent and dynamic citizenship.

3. THE INDIVIDUAL IN MODERN INDUSTRIAL SOCIETY

The lot of the individual in our present society is not all that it should be. Democracy demands concern on this point. Political independence is pretty well assured to the individual, except for the anachronistic denial of this to Negroes in some of the former slave-holding states. But economic independence is not so assured. During the colonial and early national years of our country there was a long period when economic independence was the typical characteristic. Slaves excepted, each healthy individual could expect to own his own farm—either where he grew up or farther west where opportunity and land were both abundant. And on the then (nearly) self-sufficient farm the family was independent.

That type of independence, however, has gone. Free lands are no longer available, agriculture demands increasing capitalization, and the farm is no longer self-sufficient. The city and modern industry have put most workers on a payroll. These workers are now dependent on finding a job and on market conditions for the sale of their labor. As previously quoted, "the industrial revolution has substituted unemployment for famine as the nightmare of mankind." But even if the worker has a permanent job and can live on what he earns, he is still not really independent, that is, he is not an independent personality. Except for the few at the top, the worker neither purposes nor plans nor judges; he does what he is told and another judges him. And for many the work is, and apparently must be, monotonous.

When these various factors are put together a dark picture appears: uncertainty as to a job, with no certainty, accordingly, of a living either for self or family; for most who have jobs, monotony of work with little or no self-direction in what they are doing; the necessity of following orders almost exclusively; almost no possibility of creativeness. When life under these conditions is contrasted with the relative security and creative independence of the nearly self-sufficient farm of a century ago, we have to admit that, though the successful worker now works less and has more to spend and the net production per capita of population is much greater, life has lost a quality which is very important. Independence and self-respect and contentment have decreased; restlessness, craving for excitement, and a feeling of not counting have multiplied. If these tendencies continue to increase, trouble can easily come.

There is yet another phase of this problem. Labor has had to unite in order to get a fair wage and fairer conditions of work. Management, as we have seen, was at first strongly opposed to unions; so that antagonism grew. To labor, strikes then seemed the necessary resource. But a strike is a kind of lesser warfare with much of the evil, on a smaller scale, that goes with warfare. Moreover, under modern conditions, some strikes threaten the common good. Democracy accordingly becomes involved. Peaceful and orderly measures must, if possible, be devised to settle labor-management problems in a way to secure and preserve the essential values for all concerned. In a word, the labor-management problem constitutes at present perhaps the most serious domestic problem of our land. If we cannot learn better how to manage in this area, the future is dark.

There are still other serious problems facing the individual. Life under conditions of modern interdependence presents so many problems that government becomes increasingly complex. Citizenship becomes a greater task. But so far little provision has been made for the serious study of social problems by ordinary citizens. If the individual citizen does not somehow wake up and give more thought to social problems than hitherto, the future of our civilization is not bright. School and college are not doing their duty here, and adult education has scarcely made a beginning.

From still another angle, not all is good. Our complex civilization demands broader vision, with thinking and action on a bigger scale than was formerly true when life was so largely restricted to home and neighborhood. In a word, the social-moral demands are greater than formerly, but the conditions for shaping the appropriate moral attitudes are less favorable. Remoteness of contact interferes. As people deal with corporations, they tend not to feel moral demands as keenly as when they deal with individuals; and similarly when people deal with individuals whom they do not personally know, they tend less to feel moral demands than when they are dealing with people they know well. In comparison with the situation when most people seldom saw a person they did not know, present urban and industrial conditions are much less favorable for forming adequate moral attitudes. The need is greater, but conditions are less favorable. This is a further serious aspect of the problem under consideration.

4. DEMOCRACY AND THE SOCIAL SCALE

Because our government, unlike traditional Europe, has refused from the first to have anything to do with titles of nobility, many here have carelessly concluded that we have nothing like a social scale in this country. However, the facts to the contrary are clear. Not only does a social scale exist, but it plays so prominent a part in life as to constitute one of our most serious unsolved problems.

To see that such a scale does exist among us, consider the facts implied by the phrase "standing in the community." Those families which possess the characteristics and/or assets generally approved will "stand well" or "stand high" in the community. Those families which exhibit characteristics generally disapproved will have "low standing" in the community. Students of the subject recognize three main divisions on the scale: lower class, middle class, and upper class, with each of these often subdivided further into upper and lower. An ambitious upper-middle-class mother would rather see her daughter married to a lower-upper-class boy than to one from the lower-middle class, since such a union would better fit her aspirations. She might hesitate to approve marriage with an upper-upper-class man, lest his family look down on the new daughter-in-law and refuse to associate with her family. The same mother might be troubled if people knew that the daughter were about to marry into an upper-lower-class family, and would feel "disgraced" if she were to marry into a lower-lower-class family. That an actual social scale does exist in practically every community in every part of our country seems too true, worse in its effects in some communities than in others, to be sure, but still nearly everywhere present.

However, because an undemocratic social scale does now exist is of itself no sufficient argument that it must exist, certainly not with its present very hurtful features. But it may be asked properly whether some sort or degree of social scale is not to be expected in a free society. Is it not probable that every intelligent and discriminating citizenship, as it faces the inevitable individual and family differences to be found in any modern community, will so judge these differences as thereby to constitute a *de facto* social scale? Certainly any modern civilization will have, in varying degree among its people and as an inevitable part of its culture, ideals at which to aim, ideals of moral behavior, ideals of cultivation and refinement, ideals of education, ideals of manners—these along with more "mundane" desires for wealth and recognition. Certainly, too, there will appear among the people of any community differences as to the degree in which these ideals and wishes are attained, differences due, it seems beyond question, in great measure to past and present environmental factors, in lesser degree to innate individual differences.

But because some degree of social scale seems probable is no reason why we should accept the evils in the present scale. In fact, any decent conception of democracy will most seriously demand the elimination, or at least the great diminution, of the existing evils. Three lines of these evils must be attacked without further delay: (i) the denial of equal rights to individuals now low in the scale; (ii) discrimination against certain minority groups and the attempt to fasten all of one group to a predetermined position in the scale; and (iii) the tendency of present limitations of the lowest stratum to be perpetuated by social inheritance—to the hurt not only of this stratum but of society as a whole. These will be considered in order.

As to the first named evil, democracy holds as a fundamental ideal that each individual be judged and accepted on his personal merits. The feudal system denied just this, as does a caste system wherever found. In either a feudal or a caste system, family and birth determine one's typical vocational work and the kind of social status enjoyed. As the father, so the son. While our country has no legalized social heredity system, still hereditary wealth and hereditary poverty (if pronounced enough) tend to perpetuate themselves; the result is too often almost a caste determination of probable vocational status and social acceptance. Take any large city with its surrounding suburban areas. It is possible in connection with such a city to name one or more residential sections in which the children (except those of a servant family) will almost certainly live out their days in the upper half of the socio-economic scale; analogously there are other sections in which the large majority will live out their days in the lower half.

There are various other respects in which the scale brings similar undemocratic results. Real-estate dealers reckon that the coming of lower-class families into a community where they had not hitherto been will be likely to lower land values of the neighborhood. Accordingly, various suburban residence centers have (illegally, according to recent Supreme Court decisions) arranged exclusion provisions in the land deeds to keep out "undesirable" families. Public school districts have had their boundary lines similarly drawn to exclude the "undesirables," and "segregate" these together. Many private schools have come into existence in order to make sure that "undesirable" commingling will not take place. It appears probable that the quotas found in various privately controlled colleges and universities have originated from like motives. College fraternities and sororities flourish largely on exploitation of the social-scale idea, and high-school fraternities even more so.

To deal with these evils is by no means easy, because they are supported by strongly entrenched attitudes. Schools must then cooperate with socially-minded groups and organizations to foster the greatest possible application of the Golden Rule. But until we can attack successfully the second and third of the three evils here under consideration, our efforts on the first will probably have but limited success.

Second, the evils just described reach their worst degree in connection with the treatment of minority groups. Large numbers of our people speak openly against certain minority groups in our midst. These upholders of discrimination defend the existing social scale and demand that these minorities be kept "in their place," at the bottom of the scale. And often there is resort to violence and lynch law to keep them so.

When we study the matter, we find that the discriminations are largely explained by the prior existence and tradition of the social scale and its acceptance as proper and desirable by those who profit by it. Those with high status on the scale wish to retain their superiority and so oppose infiltration by those counted inferior. Those who themselves feel least secure as regarding higher rating on the scale are most inclined to assert a place for themselves by pushing the minority members down. Many who have felt the sting of inferiority as judged on the scale "take it out" (scapegoat fashion) on others. In other words, the evils of the scale increase the evils of the scale.

And the evils here are not limited to effects in our own country. Abroad, at a time when world leadership in behalf of democracy should be ours, this treatment of our minorities brings wonder and distrust. The world asks in amazement how we can speak so loudly in behalf of democracy and yet fall so far short of decent democracy in our treatment of Negroes and other minorities in our population. During the last war, Japan took advantage of each outrage against Negroes here to show the Indonesians and other Asiatics what to expect from us. Also certain Asiatics resent our discriminating laws forbidding them to become citizens here. The U.S.S.R., which long ago abolished racial discrimination within its borders, points the finger of scorn at us that we pretend to uphold the doctrine of equality, yet so flagrantly refuse it to non-whites.

This second evil demands the most serious efforts of all thoughtful people. Education of both young and old is apparently the key. The young must be the especial object of school effort, to build consideration for others, to cultivate friendly relations among all groups, to show the unscientific character of the prejudices. But the school working alone cannot succeed against family and community antagonisms. Parent-teacher organizations must cooperate with the school efforts, and citizen groups must enlist community support. The task is difficult, but urgent and insistent.

The third of the three evils is at once the most serious, the most strategic, and the least recognized. It is the tendency of the socio-economic scale to make permanent, through the factor of *social* heredity, both the economic and the social-moral evils which especially characterize the lowest stratum of the scale. Along with this, characterizing the economically privileged, are found, too often, attitudes of selfish disdain of the less fortunate and indifference to the evils that these experience. It seems likely that these evil attitudes among the privileged are to a degree in process of elimination; but the hereditary effects of upbringing in the lowest stratum are clear, definite, and at present strongly in evidence. Though native ability is pretty evenly distributed in children born up and down the social scale (with perhaps a slight theoretic disadvantage at the bottom), family influence works differently. In the upper *half*, family influence appears, on the whole, to be a positive factor in developing potentialities, but in the lowest stratum it definitely thwarts the development of the best. The two factors of family poverty and inferior rearing of children seem clearly matters of social heredity, and the hurt thus done to the rising generation at the bottom of the scale is so serious that government and social effort must intervene.

As matters stand, disease and crime and inferior home influence characterize the lowest stratum of the scale and so condition the lives of children born into this group that to leave this problem to the working of conditions now in control would probably fix poverty and inferior rearing practically as a caste feature of the lower part of the scale. This would be to the serious hurt of these people as individuals and a definite and flagrant violation by society of respect for their personality. Moreover, thus to leave these unfortunate ones in their present inferior condition is not only injurious to them, it is also injurious to society at large. The poor and ignorant and depraved who fill our slums and form our poorest tenant groups are, largely because of their unfortunate *social* heredity, a drag on society. Because they are poor they fail to support the common commerce, they do not pay their proportion of taxes. Their crimes compel a very large expenditure of public funds. Their health record is the worst of all. And for the most part these things need not be. The amelioration if not the removal of this evil by proper economic arrangements, by better education, by intelligent social planning—this is the task which the future must accept.

It was suggested above that we shall probably always have some sort of a social scale even after the evils just discussed have either been eliminated or at least greatly reduced. It may be added that until economic opportunity is fairly available to all, no one can tell what social contribution can come from those now condemned to inferiority or worse. It is essential that the new scale be as democratic in character as we know how to make it. Two characteristics of the new scale we must demand—(i) that the scale be flexible and (ii) that position on the scale depend on real merit. The scale must be flexible to recognize individual merit, not rigid to allow only for what the family has done in the past. And the merit to be recognized must be of a fine and elevating quality of living and behaving, certainly not of wealth alone or ostentation. Society must accept responsibility for the kind of scale it accepts; specifically it must accept responsibility for true equality of opportunity as against the deleterious influence of family poverty and poor parental cultivation. Only in the degree that we can make "the good life" available to all on equal terms can we hope to eliminate the evils of the present social scale.

5. QUALITY OF PERSONAL LIVING

Various aspects of this problem have already been considered, especially in the discussion of the good life. The treatment here given is brief, but this brevity must not be taken to imply lack of importance of the problem; for in its bearing on the good life actually effected, this is certainly one of our most serious unsolved problems.

Probably the greatest single factor to affect the quality of one's living is the spirit one brings to life's activities, the zest one feels for life. As a basis for this zest, physical health is crucial; for if health is bad and pain racks, satisfaction is definitely lessened. Similarly, if personality adjustment is bad, there is no stable hope for rich living; life is the poorer for the individual himself and for all others whom he touches. Also, if work time and other conditions are such that one comes to his leisure-time activities so wearied or distraught or irritated as to have no taste for the finer things, then again life is much the poorer.

This last point takes us back to the discussion of the surrounding institutional life. It may well be, as we have previously considered in Chapter XI, that an inadequate and self-defeating popular taste comes from our monotonous industrialization. One wonders whether certain "popular" music has not found its vogue simply because its followers are too tired and emotionally starved to enjoy better. Factory work and the monotonous work of the business office can, it appears, have the effect of unfitting one for anything except an escape, a forgetting, a losing of one's self in wild excitement. Many who turn to drink in the evening seem thus led. It is a real problem which we cannot ignore. It may be that our civilization itself is herein in question. Better machines to take care of the more monotonous tasks may be one answer; a wider participation in decision-making both as to the work itself and as to conditions of work may well be another and very important measure.

But in the meantime, while we are working to make surrounding conditions right, there remains the problem of rearing our people to truer and fuller personal richness of living. At bottom this is a problem for education: how to arouse and cultivate worth-while interests and how to lead the interests so aroused to their potentially richer content both in the way of creativeness and of appreciation. Any full answer belongs elsewhere, but a hint here may help. Concrete effecting is often a great awakener. A cynical city teacher was induced to engage in metal working. She hadn't known she could do it. Now she knew better; she could see the result herself, and others could see it. Something woke up within. She tried the idea of arousing a love of creating in her children; they woke up also. Thenceforth she was a different person. Schools can do the like for nearly all pupils, and thus in time help materially to bring a new quality to the life of our nation.

Meanwhile we can work on parents; bring them together in the evening to hammer brass, paint pictures, write and act in plays, engage in group discussion on live issues—to engage in any worthwhile activities which encourage creativeness and deeper appreciations and understanding. These, we hope, will be but the beginnings of further original work. Our task is to bring into our country more of the open mind, more of the imaginative spirit, more of the appreciation of the finer things that others are doing. In a true sense all else of life comes together to function uniquely in the creative quality of personal living.

6. THE CONTINUANCE AND DEVELOPMENT OF OUR CIVILIZATION

The two phases of this topic could, of course, be treated separately. The development phase, for example, might have been treated at the end of Chapter XII on progress. But these two phases of development and continuance are more closelv connected than might at first appear. From Toynbee's study* it seems a fair con-

* Arnold J. Toynbee, *A Study of History* (Oxford University Press, 1946).

clusion, as previously suggested, that the only successful way to continue a civilization is to go forward. To refuse to go forward is to refuse to face problems as they arise, and this means practically certain disintegration. In any event it seems wise to include the present compound topic in the list of major problem areas.

From one angle, the actual continuance of our present civilization is the most basic of our major problems. For unless our civilization continues, we obviously have no basis either of hope or of effort for attacking the rest. It is of course conceivable that this civilization may fall and in its place arise a higher and finer type of civilization; but to act now on such an hypothesis seems, at least to the present writer, to be gambling away a present solid fact for the hazy hope of attaining a dream. We must, it would seem, take the continuance of the changing civilization we now have as the safest, if not the sole possible, *pou sto* from which to attack the other problems.

Of the factors which affect the continuance of a civilization, one seems basic: the presence of a social spirit sufficiently dynamic to bring the available cultural resources persistently and creatively to bear upon critical problems as they arise. One outstanding instance in American history of this dynamic social spirit was the creation of the Constitution of 1787. An instance of outstanding failure was the refusal of our country to join with others at the close of World War I to make the League of Nations work. Now after World War II we are at last ready for a united One World effort, but the present world situation seems almost insuperably more difficult than after World War I; and it took the worst war in history to persuade our people to accept what good judgment and a proper dynamic social spirit should have seen at the first.

This dynamic social spirit in its turn depends, it seems, on the continued presence and operation of three concurrent factors: (i) the effective working of law and order sufficient to allow (ii) the needed creative study of difficult situations as these arise; and (iii) the intelligent willingness of an effective majority to fashion new institutional arrangements in the light of this creative study. It was the difficulty attending this third factor which nearly defeated the 1787 Constitution and did prevent our joining the League of Nations.

Granting effective law and order, the actual working of the dynamic social spirit usually turns on the presence of adequate leadership. If difficult social problems came only one at a time, so that indefinite time could be given to each problem as it arises, the matter of leadership might be less crucial. But life is emphatically not like that. Usually a difficulty must be taken in time or it will get indefinitely worse, and meanwhile other problems arise to complicate the situation. Under such conditions democratic leadership on the part of a few can render effective service by making the necessary study in advance of the many and then by helping the many, through discussion, to see and accept the wisdom of making the needed changes. Thus in the post-Revolutionary period a relatively small group, having sensed the fundamental inadequacy of the Articles of Confederation, studied what to do, called the Constitutional Convention of 1787, and in that Convention did remarkably creative work. Practically the same group, once the Constitution was drafted, persuaded the people to adopt it. Lincoln led effectively throughout the Civil War. Woodrow Wilson led the Versailles Conference to found the League of Nations, but could not persuade the American Senate to ratify the necessary treaty. When Great Britain faced the darkest days of World War II, Winston Churchill proved a great and effective leader. Leadership of the quality and on the scale of these instances we call statesmanship. Such leadership is essential to the effective working of any great society.

But the needed democratic leadership is not limited to the work of statesmen, not even to the work of statesmen plus the recognized lesser leaders. The people themselves must exhibit leadership in the way of forward-looking outlook and thinking, and unless the society is pervaded by such qualities, the greater statesmanship has small chance either to develop or to operate. The shared search that we call discussion calls for and permits—even demands—a true but simpler type of leadership. In any effective discussion what one proposes stimulates others to further thinking, perhaps to add, perhaps to criticize, perhaps to amplify. The most creatively minded will probably advance the best ideas, but even the humblest may know of bearings missed by the more intelligent. In such a discussion whoever helps at any point to carry forward the effort or otherwise to make the process more effective is therein leading the group to a better decision. In this way is democratic leadership possible to all, and effective statesmanship made more probable.*

The difficulties that stand in the way of effective attention to the problems of a civilization thus lie mainly (i) in the inadequacy of the existent social spirit and (ii) in the inadequacy of leadership. Modern society works on so great a scale and its problems are so complex that the typical citizen is tempted to give all but exclusive attention to his own affairs. Only as the citizen can see the bearing of the larger social problems on his more personal interests can we hope, in the usual case, to get him to consider public questions. The matter is made even more difficult by the necessity for the holder of public office to get himself re-elected. In his search for votes he caters only too often to voters' prejudices. Really statesman-like views thus appear to the typical politician to be too hazardous to risk. His campaign discussion is accordingly so inadequate that the voters often fail to see the true merits of the matter at issue. Unless, then, we can somehow get a larger proportion of our voters to be more intelligently interested in matters of public concern, the future welfare of our civilization is not bright. While selfish pressure groups are very active, intelligent and unselfish citizenship is too much lacking.

It thus seems clear that the continuance of any civilization depends on the quality of that civilization, whether enough of its people have sufficient insight and public spirit to give the needed study to its problems and then enough wise unselfishness to unite in implementing the resulting new insight.

These considerations bring us finally to the matter of quality of citizenship. It is certainly true that all the various parts and aspects of a society concur in building the actual citizenship of that society. The actual citizenship of this generation thus builds the citizenship of the rising generation. So from every angle the crux of our problem, the continuance and development of our civilization, seems to depend on developing better citizenship—more sensitive, more intelligent, more unselfish—and more active individual citizens, able and disposed to work together for the common good.

* For a further discussion of the point see the author's *Education and the Social Crisis* (Kappa Delta Pi Lecture No. 4, New York, Liveright, 1932), pp. 33–41.

Upon this as a basis the needed social spirit stands or falls. Only as such citizenship is available can discerning leadership get its needed support; in fact, only as such citizenship is alert and active, can society hope to bring forth the needed leadership.

7. A DYNAMIC PHILOSOPHY OF LIFE

By a dynamic philosophy of life is here meant an outlook on life sufficiently forward-looking, intelligent, and unified to permit and encourage active and consistent effort. If such an outlook is lacking, effort will be weak, and varied efforts will tend to hinder each other. Such a philosophy is needed by each individual, by each nation, and now by the One World. The outlook of the nation will, to be sure, include far more of diversity than the individual can acceptably use; and the world will probably show greater diversity than the nation.

One aspect of such a philosophy will, however, concern alike the individual, the nation, and the One World—the ability and disposition to confer. In fact the supreme consideration between contending persons or groups is not whether they come with like or opposed views or wishes, but whether they can meet in conference so as actually to confer, whether in such efforts their minds can actually meet. This we may say is the great issue now before the United Nations. The world is really one, but it has at present no sufficiently unified outlook. We are all tied together, but our conflicting aims, values, and outlooks prevent us from conferring together effectively. We are tied together but we do not live as One World. This issue of real communication becomes thus an initial test of the world's ability to live as One World, and this may—from the danger of atomic warfare—mean a test of its ability to live at all. The need, then, appears supreme to build at least enough of a common world philosophy to allow effective world communication.

Implicit in the foregoing is a necessity always present when contending parties come together to settle their disputes: namely, that neither party shall come with absolutes in mind on the matters at issue, absolutes, that is, which prevent free consideration of new suggestions on their merit. If either side says to itself, "We know and we know that we know," then that side has to that extent cut itself off from true conferring. For these words mean that, on the points at issue, that side is inflexible, on those points it does not mean to hear the other side with any possibility of taking what is heard into conferring account. The will to confer means the will to hear and take account of what is said on its merits so as to reach a fresh conclusion in the light of all data then known, including the new material brought forward by the opposite side. In a word, true conferring assumes in advance at least the possibility of changing one's mind. Whoever comes to a conference not thus open-minded and flexible makes only a pretense at con-ferring; his mind and his deeds are inconsistent; he is not acting honestly. He says he will confer; he means not to confer. But conferring, as we saw earlier, is the essence of the democratic process. Who cannot or will not confer, in that degree rejects democracy.

Not only does the One World need a common working philosophy, the like need holds also for the nation. Within each country the various segments of life and attitude must be able to confer through a meeting of minds, to communicate regarding their differences and their common problems; otherwise that nation has within itself the same impasse that we have just seen as regards the One World.

This need for conferring within the nation calls in question, as we shall further see in Part II, the practice found in certain of our cities of having three school systems, a public school system, a private school system, and a parochial school system. Any group shut off generation after generation from the rest is in danger of building attitudes which militate against conferring across the divisional lines corresponding to these school separations. The labor-management problem, for example, has almost surely been made more difficult by segregated schools for the better-to-do. In the degree that any nation is cut up into groups which live separately from the rest, will that nation have difficulty in making up its mind on certain of its essential social problems. Such a nation is likely to act inconsistently with itself, and almost certainly not in consistency with democratic equality for all concerned. Those groups which are more selfish and more effective politically will act selfishly with regard to the rest; and this holds true on whatever basis of difference that the group is formed. The real welfare of a nation depends on the degree in which it can effect a working philosophy in the whole nation on the more strategic aspects of life. Within this area will be enough lesser differences to keep thought alive and active.

As was earlier suggested, the individual needs a far closer and more unified philosophy of life than does the One World or even a single nation. This need for the individual to effect a personal working philosophy concerns both his social and his individual welfare. He is socially a good citizen in the degree that he has a thoughtful and consistent outlook on life based on an intelligently informed concern for the common good. Only thus can he be an effective citizen. Individually, such a working philosophy is the necessary basis for a happy, effective, individual life. One who has no thoughtful, consistent outlook on life gets in his own way and troubles his own mind. Without concern for the common good he soon runs similarly into conflict.

To ask how to build such a philosophy is much like asking how to grow up effectively; and the statement carries a helpful suggestion. Every child, just because he is a child, builds a child's outlook on life. No matter how careful and thoughtful his parents may be, he cannot at his age see what they see at their age; he thinks as a child, he understands as a child. This means that at some time toward the close of adolescence each one should think through for himself what he had previously taken for granted, either on tradition or on faith or at best with childlike insight. This rethinking is best done in connection with discussions led by a sympathetic and critical adult, one who knows how to question and guide without so interposing his thinking as to prevent the young person from himself facing the real problems and coming to his own conclusions in the light of the various views men have held and/or do hold on each such problem. The writer well recalls what reading Darwin's *Origin of Species* did for him in his eighteenth year. He missed, however, discussion with competent others.

It seems a fair conclusion that our future is dark unless we can help a majority of our young people thus to reconsider their traditional outlook and remake these into personal possessions held on individually seen merit. The growing complexity of modern life offers so many new and urgent problems that unless we can bring up a citizenship flexible minded and better able to think independently than thus far has been true, the world is in for trouble.

These seven great problem areas we may count as a special message sent by Part I to Part II. They are not sent, however, for Part

II to solve; that is not its work. The resulting problems belong directly in and to life as such, and so must be solved, if at all, in life itself. The hope in sending these from Part I to Part II is that the latter, with them and their like in mind, will so help to educate the rising generation that it will be better able and more disposed than it would otherwise be to deal effectively with such problems.

PART 2

Philosophy of the Educative Process

CHAPTER XV. *A Theory of Education to Implement Part I: A Preliminary Statement*

PART I ended with a sobering list of unsolved problems now facing the world. It would be wrong to expect school education to accept direct responsibility for solving these problems; but it is the duty of the school to help rear the young to be ready as far as possible in both attitude and ability to face the problems of their civilization. To do this will require a different and more effective school than has thus far prevailed.

Especially essential for implementing Part I is a new and more adequate philosophy of the educative process, one designed to fit alike the observed facts regarding learning and the philosophy of life developed in Part I. This new outlook, largely developed within the past hundred years, holds that thinking, and accordingly education, is for behavior, for active service in individual and social life, and not, as formerly conceived, primarily for refined and abstracted enjoyment; that intelligence put to use is man's chief reliance for meeting life's problems. It also counts that as change is an essential factor in individual life and in institutional development, we thus face continual novelty and must learn to carry on life accordingly; that institutions exist to serve humanity and must therefore be changed as new needs arise for the human beings concerned. It further holds that as the human being and his living are essentially social in nature, the individual cannot, from considerations of either safety, morality, or happiness, be simply self-centered; that accordingly morality based in actual effects in human living is a social necessity and that democracy must be seen not simply as a form of government, but even more fundamentally as a way of life, a way devoted especially to respect for personality and consequently to equality of opportunity for all to develop their potentialities and live as free men; that the conception of the life-good-to-live not only demands for its realization the democratic way of life but is at the same time crucial to the content both of morality and of democracy.

This new outlook must remake both the aims and procedures of education. As to aim, because thinking and education must be for behavior, education must adopt character building as its fundamental goal. By character is here meant not simply moral character, though that is a proper part, but inclusive character—all of one's ways of thinking, feeling, and acting with reference to one's self and others and the world. If character is to be the inclusive aim, education cannot as heretofore be exclusively intellectual, or even primarily so. No longer should students in high school or college be evaluated simply as to their knowledge, however full or exact; the real concern should be behavior—character and behavior. Knowledge, to be sure, is a highly essential part of the effective character, but it is not sufficient; it is not true that to know what to do suffices to bring about the right behavior. Education then must aim at the whole personality, the all-round inclusive character. In this character, thinking and feeling—disposition to think and to act on thinking, attitudes to dispose thinking and acting to constructive ends—must suffuse and interpenetrate each other and together penetrate all conscious action. Only thus can all the available resources of the human organism be called forth and educated cooperatively together. Only on such terms can we expect the really effective character.

What kind of character should we aim at? What traits should we seek? And how shall we develop those traits? The character we want is implied, almost stated, in the philosophy set out just above: it must use intelligence, be socially and morally disposed, be effective. It must be well balanced, honest, reasoning and reasonable, socially effective, creative, self-reliant, persistent (in accordance with reason), concerned for the well-being of its fellows. Because we live in a democracy, this character must be able to discuss and decide intelligently, able and disposed to cooperate with others in shared enterprises and for the common good, disposed to make group living such as to foster the well-being and growth of all. So much for some of the most obviously needed traits.

How are these traits to be developed? The full answer to this must wait until we have considered the learning process. That, too, emphasizes behavior: we learn as we behave, behave inwardly as well as outwardly. And this means that the school must be a place of living what is to be learned; for each one learns what he really and truly lives. In one word, our philosophy of education will turn out to be the correlative of our philosophy of life. The kind of civilization we at bottom wish, that kind must our children *live*, live at home, live in school, live all their conscious life.

The school, then, must aim to exemplify the finest attainable quality of living. For the pupils and students will learn what they live. If their living is poor, of low quality, they will then build low quality characters. If we wish pupils to grow in intelligent self-determination, then their school living must include both the possibility and encouragement of intelligent self-determination. If we wish pupils to build high ideals, then we as teachers must work with them as skillfully as we can to help them gradually build good working ideals; if we wish them to build self-direction, then we must leave, under guidance, as much self-direction to the group as they can manage. In such ways should school aims on the one hand, and school procedures and methods on the other, follow and exemplify—and accordingly implement—the chosen philosophy of life which was developed in Part I.

CHAPTER XVI. *The Old (Alexandrian) Conception of Education vs. the New*

As a means to consideration of the type of education we need, let us see what the situation is at present. Twentieth century education increasingly shows, especially in this country, two warring trends. One tends to follow what it calls the "humanistic" tradition handed down from the past; the other, as was discussed in the preceding chapter, seeks new paths apparently demanded alike by a closer study of the psychology of learning and by the philosophy developed in Part I. The present chapter will aim at bringing out the distinctive differences between these two trends. For reasons immediately to be given, the old is here called the Alexandrian outlook.

THE ALEXANDRIAN CONCEPTION OF EDUCATION

After the death of Alexander the Great (323 B.C.) the Ptolemies ruled Egypt for some three hundred years. Almost from the first, they set out consciously to make Alexandria the intellectual capital of the world. They founded the greatest library of ancient days, ultimately including in it the personal library of Aristotle and many original official copies of the Athenian dramatists. They founded also what we may call a scientific university, which brought forth creatively the Ptolemaic system of astronomy to rule the world of thought for fourteen hundred years and the Euclidean geometry still taught without a rival (at its level) throughout all civilized lands.

But when these educational statesmen came to philosophy and literature, the situation was different. Here they could not hope even to equal what the Greeks, centering at Athens, had already written in the matchless classics of their fruitful era. So they decided, as second best, to found a school to teach these classics—the first school in the Western world built simply to teach the content of the written word.

When a century or two later the Romans conquered this eastern region they brought back with them to Rome this idea of a school to teach the written word and set it to work to teach the more intellectual of the Romans the written wisdom of the Greeks. In time, schools built for the young on this idea supplanted the prior type of Roman education, and schools of the new (Alexandrian) type spread from Rome throughout the empire. Later, when Christianity had formulated an authoritarian written creed, the same type of school was used to teach the written doctrine.

During the Middle Ages, Latin remained the common literary language of all western Europe; and schools survived to teach in the same Alexandrian way either a secular or a religious written content, or combination of both. With the Revival of Learning, the Alexandrian conception of education was continued, this time to teach the secular beauty and wisdom of the ancient classics, now found anew and cherished afresh.

The schools of the Protestant Reformation continued the same type of school, stressing specifically their new religious outlook. Thus the Classis of Amsterdam in 1636 adopted regulations for the schoolmaster going out to the Dutch colonies: "He is also to implant the fundamental principles of the true Christian Religion and salvation, by means of catechizing." (120:97*f*.) It was schools of this same type of teaching that were brought to all the thirteen colonies.

In these ways the Alexandrian type of education for acquiring the content of the written word became universal throughout Christendom. Education in the school sense came to mean learning the contents of books, with what this could offer—this and this only. And the believers in this type of school had great faith in such memorizing. These Dutch Protestants, as we saw just above, explicitly expected that "catechizing" would "implant the fundamental principles of the Christian Religion and salvation." So deeply and widely did this kind of education take hold that today most people, both the better educated and the less, find it difficult to conceive of any other kind of education for school or college. This traditional outlook seems at present strongest with those who stand closest in interest to the older type of humanistic learning. But even our psychologists, or many of them, write as if the acquisition of the formulated content of books or lectures—probably the way they were taught in school—constitutes the whole of school education. For these, the words *study* and *learn* get their definition, for school purposes, from Alexandria. Note how the announcement of a course in a 1946 state university summer school exactly illustrates this:

> HOW TO STUDY.—The major emphasis is upon the acquisition of skill in reading and organizing assignments, and techniques for writing term papers and examinations. Special attention will be given to teachers who wish to train high school students in methods of study.

A more adequate conception of education, as we saw in the preceding chapter and shall in a moment further consider, must contemplate the whole being of the learner; for it is now well recognized that in any significant instance of behavior the organism acts as a whole. But the Alexandrian kind of education practically reduces man to intellect only, and further reduces this intellect largely to memory. Chancellor Hutchins, who in one of his phases very clearly represents the older conception, says explicitly: "If education is rightly understood, it will be understood as the cultivation of the intellect." (81:67) And elsewhere, speaking of the ideal curriculum for the four year [junior] college, he says: "We have excluded body building and character building." (81:77) And still further, as if to clinch the idea, he says that "the arts central in education are grammar, rhetoric, logic, and mathematics." (123: Jan. 31, 1937)

Mark Van Doren, another strong Alexandrian, asserts: "Elementary education can do nothing better for a child than store his memory with things deserving to be there. He will be grateful for them when he grows up, even if he kicks now." (167:94)

We can be grateful that this Van Doren quotation states so clearly three outstanding weaknesses of the Alexandrian position: first, that a child is not to be counted as living now, in any full sense, but only later; second, that rote memory is the main, if not the sole, educational resource to be taken account of; third, that if only we can effect Alexandrian learning, we can disregard other accompanying kinds of learning, such as the attitudes being built in the child by his "kicking against" the teacher now, kicking against this Alexandrian type of learning so alien to the pupil's life, and probably also kicking against school as a place where such boring things go on. It is probable that the consistent Alexandrian (including many a psychologist) has paid no attention to the resentful thoughts and feelings of the non-verbally-minded child bored by the memory gems. But such attendant or concomitant responses give rise to very important kinds of learning, some helpful and some hurtful, out of which are built conceptions, attitudes, ideals, standards, and the like. The concomitant kinds of learning (later to be discussed in detail) probably influence the life of the pupil more than what chances to remain with him of the distasteful lessons against which he kicks. It is further probable that the modern Alexandrian has given little thought to the democratic doctrine that children are people and that childhood should not be used merely as means to fuller adulthood. Along with this age-old depreciation of childhood went that other age-old doctrine (later to be discussed) that "the rod and reproof give wisdom," that "foolishness is bound up in the heart of a child," but that "the rod of correction will drive it far from him."

A reliance on memory, in the cold-storage sense, has been quite characteristic of the Alexandrian outlook from the early days until now. Plutarch, writing in the second century A.D., said explicitly: "We must most of all exercise and keep in constant employment the memory of children; for that is, as it were, the storehouse of all learning . . . nothing doth so beget or nourish learning as memory." (111:319) Dean Colet (d. 1519), who first brought the Renaissance learning to England, wrote a grammar, the preface of which—addressed to "all lytel chyldren"—bids them commend this book "dylygently vnto your memoryes." An American teacher of our own time showed the same faith in memory when she said to her children: "To-morrow you are to read from p. 72 to 98. Now read every word, because that is the only way you are going to learn." (77:XXII:174)

If one wishes a criterion easy to apply for telling whether any school or college or system of teaching is Alexandrian, the criterion can be found in the way in which that institution or school system judges success of learning. If the primary test of success is passing a written examination, and if cramming or other specific memorizing will materially help in passing the examination, that kind of teaching is Alexandrian. A British headmaster now living complained that "most headmasters [in Great Britain] are compelled to devote all available time to subjects which have an examination value and to organize the teaching to meet examination requirements." (117:XV:31) And a New York State district superintendent said as late as 1946: "The Regents' exam. is the best possible measure of teacher efficiency." (122:XXXIII:553) This Britisher was justly condemning the overruling examination in vogue in his country. This New York official testified eloquently to his own blindness, a blindness which too often results from the Regents' examination system in New York State.

With this brief consideration of the Alexandrian outlook we can now ask more specifically as to its lacks in comparison with a more adequate type of education.

CERTAIN DEFICIENCIES IN THE OLD EDUCATION

It is of course true that there are many opinions regarding a desirable type of education. Many of these, perhaps most at the present time, represent, in varying degrees, efforts to hold on to the old conception as above discussed. In order to see more clearly the shortages of the old (Alexandrian) outlook, let us state some of the requirements for a better type and examine the old in terms of these. What is presented here is offered especially in the light of the preceding chapter and of the earlier discussions on democracy, morality, the good life, and the changing world.

With these ends in mind and using the earlier discussions of this and the preceding chapter, we can lay down at least three characteristics essential, it appears, to any system of education that can be approved:

1. *Education must primarily seek character and behavior, all-round character of a kind to lead to proper behavior.* An essential aspect of this character, underlying in fact all the rest, is the well-adjusted personality. With this and beyond this we wish a vigorous and effective character which (as previously discussed) acts after thinking and out of warm human values, which feels and acts with appropriate reference to self and others and the world.

This stress on personality, character, and behavior must begin in early infancy; for, as was implied in the preceding chapter and will later be discussed in detail, each act, each feeling, each thought, from the beginning leaves its effect. Also, no person, and no part of his life, is ever to be treated merely as means to the ends of some other person or period of life. Instead, each is to be counted as having its own dignity and worth. Only thus can we respect personality or build it adequately.

2. *Learning, the key constituent of education, must be understood in behavioral terms.* It is to be measured in terms of its tendency so to stay with one as to re-enter appropriately into further experience and behavior.

In order for anything to be thus genuinely learned, that thing must first be lived; that is, it must enter functionally, in its own true character, into an actual life situation, a situation which the learner himself feels he is living. We learn what we live; we learn it as we accept it to live by, and we learn it in the degree we accept it. Memorizing for the purpose of passing an examination is in itself a very mild degree of living; so mild that the resulting learning often fails to get back effectively into life.

3. *The concomitant learnings, especially as accumulated through successive experiences, must be taken fully into account in all guided or directed learning.* These learnings are often, probably generally, more significant for character and life than is the intellectual knowledge that alone, perhaps, was meanwhile being sought.

We are now ready to see the inadequacy of the Alexandrian position. Its aim is the acquisition of formulated statements of knowledge assigned in books or given in lectures. Its method is to memorize the written formulation. But neither that aim nor that method nor both together will suffice to build adequate character, nor will these taken by themselves even tend significantly toward the building of such character. From them the essential of character building is absent, namely, behaving in a life situation. It is the learner's active responding to such a situation that alone brings learning of a kind likely to function in life.

To the foregoing weaknesses of the Alexandrian school must be added the further weakness of ignoring concomitant learnings. It seems to us impossible that intelligent teachers could overlook the attitudes and other cumulative learnings their pupils were all the time building. It is, however, significant that these learnings come whether the teacher knows about them or not. In fact, this kind of learning thrives—to the bad—most completely on being ignored. The wise modern teacher sets up concomitants among his most cherished aims; for out of the heart are the issues of life. These things the Alexandrian teacher tragically overlooked—and yet overlooks.

Consider now the classroom procedure as the modernized "Alexandrian" teacher wished it to be: single seats screwed down in straight rows, each pupil in his seat, no two pupils conferring in any way and consequently no possible cooperation except against the teacher's wish. The only desired *behavior* of any sort was study to master the assigned lesson or recitation and offer courteous obedience to the teacher. Specifically, there was no responsibility in this Alexandrian system except to study (and learn) and obey, no initiative on the pupil's part save in getting the lesson and in reciting, no necessity in such arrangements to connect what was learned in school with life (other than in study and reciting). It would be hard to conceive a situation, except solitary confinement, worse adapted to character building. Fortunately "extra-curricular" activities were contrived which did encourage character building; but these were, as the descriptive term explicitly states, *outside* of the curriculum, outside of the learning program provided by the school.

The aridity of the pre-Pestalozzian program seems today incredible, aridity of a kind that naturally built bad concomitants. The Boston Latin School of 1773, as good probably as any in the colonies, taught nothing but Latin and Greek except that, in the fifth of its six years, English was present as the translation of Caesar. There was no mathematics. In fact, Brinsley wrote earlier (1612) that boys ready for the university often could not read the page numbers of their books. Before Comenius (1592–1670), the rule was to begin the Latin grammar in Latin with no pretense of teaching the meaning of the Latin words in which the grammar was written.

Since Pestalozzi (1746–1827), the elementary schools, under his leadership and with later developments, have been increasingly rescued from this Alexandrian aridity and put more nearly upon a basis of current living. However, much yet remains to be done to put the elementary schools of our country on the most adequate basis now known. As for the secondary school and the college, these are still bound, in the main, to Alexandria. Even the best efforts at "general education" still leave unchanged, in most colleges, the

Alexandrian essence of mere knowledge-getting. In such practice, passing examinations is still the test; and cramming (last-minute memorizing so it won't be forgotten in examination) is still all too prevalent.

As suggested above, it is probably not fair to blame all the harshness of pre-Pestalozzian school method on the Alexandrian theory; but much of the blame belongs right there. That theory accepted quite willingly a very inadequate psychology of learning and discipline. This was, to be sure, supported by the surrounding hardness of heart toward children and a frequent belief in innate total depravity. Certainly the harshness began at an early period and lasted long. Alcuin said, "It is the scourge that teaches children the ornaments of wisdom and to accustom themselves to good manners." (qtd. in 56:149) "Letters go in with blood" was an old proverb used to defend school whippings for the youngest (64:77*f.*). Dr. Johnson said: "My schoolmaster beat me most unmercifully, else I had done nothing." (35:I, 533) Oliver Goldsmith stated: "Whatever pains a master may take to make learning agreeable to his pupil, he may depend it will at first be extremely unpleasant." (35:I, 532*f.*) Horace Mann reports that a typical Boston school of 1844 had 400 children and used an average of 65 whippings a day (21:20). A writer of 1851 restated the Alexandrian position with the bad psychology which in good measure explains the whippings: "The business of a teacher . . . is strictly that of a conveyor of knowledge—moral and intellectual—to a yet unoccupied and growing mind." (108:65) The first sentence of the typical English grammar used in this country until 1880 will easily explain the aversion of youth to such learning: "The four parts of grammar are orthography, etymology, syntax, and prosody." No child reading this sentence for the first time could possibly get any real idea of its meaning. It is in the light of these Alexandrian school procedures, still too prevalent in American education, that we can understand the attitude of the boys reported in the following news item: According to the 1939 report of the New York City Missing Persons' Bureau 90 per cent of the 3,620 boys who ran away from home did so because they were "sick and tired of school."

As to the present working of the Alexandrian system consider some more modern facts and comments. Dr. Francis T. Spaulding (until recently New York State Commissioner of Education) found in his 1936–38 study of the high schools of New York State that in spite of the books read in school, the graduates read few or no serious books afterwards. He further found that the longer pupils attended high school the less disposed were they to public service (150:25, 28). A librarian stated (1935) at an association of fellow librarians: "No institution does as much to destroy the love of reading as does the average high school" by the manner "in which [it crams] the classics" down the throats of the pupils (76: Oct. 26, 1935). Floyd Dell (1887–) said: "The book, as a center of our educational process, must be demoted: It is a good servant, but a bad master." (36:46) Lancelot Hogben in his *Retreat from Reason* (79:12) sums up his criticism against "the present content and outlook of humanistic education" by saying that in it "knowledge is encouraged as a means of more knowledge instead of being a means to action." He elsewhere says (*ibid.*, p. 10) that the pitiable predilection of the rising generation "for action without thought is the legitimate offspring of thought divorced from action." Herbert Matthews, the well-known *New York Times* foreign correspondent, says in his autobiography: "As far as I am concerned knowledge gained through living in and with events and pondering upon their meaning is the only knowledge that has any value."(123: Aug. 25, 1946) Lessing (1729–1781) long ago said: "Books may make me learned but they will not make me a man." Tagore (1861–1941) observed: "We rob the child of his earth to teach him geography, of language to teach him grammar." (155:143) An anonymous writer has described the lecture system as "a process by which words are mysteriously transferred from lecture notes of the professor to the notebook of the student without passing through the mind of either." W. H. Auden is quoted as saying that "a professor is one who talks in someone else's sleep." (qtd. in 144: Apr. 27, 1940)

Bernard Shaw, on being asked permission to have part of one of his plays included in a volume for use in the secondary school, replied in these characteristic words: "No. I lay my eternal curse on whomsoever shall now or any time hereafter make school books of my works, and make me hated as Shakespeare is hated. My plays were not designed as instruments of torture." (123: *Bk. Rev.*, Jan. 6, 1946).

By contrast with the foregoing we may note the findings from the Eight Year Study of thirty experimental high schools.* Graduates of these high schools were studied after they had graduated from four-year colleges. When the thirty schools were arranged in order of their desirable variation from the ordinary (Alexandrian) high schools, the college graduates from the six schools who varied least from the ordinary showed no especial variation from their paired opposites of the ordinary schools; the college graduates from the six schools that varied most from what we are here calling the Alexandrian pattern showed "consistently higher academic averages and more academic honors . . . clear cut superiority in the intellectual intangibles of curiosity and drive, willingness and ability to think logically and objectively, and active and vital interest in the world about them. They are more frequently concerned with democratic values and the importance of assuming their share of responsibility for the general welfare. They are more often cooperative, tolerant, and self-directing, and less often purely personal or selfish in orientation." (23:173*f.*)

THE EDUCATIONAL SITUATION IN OUR COUNTRY TODAY

Though the past thirty-odd years have seen a widespread advance in acceptance of more adequate educational ideas, the advance has been uneven. The preschool and the primary grades have shown by far the greatest advance. Here the new has practically no conscious opposition. But in the upper elementary school, in the secondary school, and in the college there appears definite opposition, increasing as we advance to higher age levels. The opposition comes largely from the entrenched past, remnants of former attitudes dominant at different times and of different life philosophies. Some of these remnants are socio-economic, nostalgic longings for aristocratic status, fears of a consistent, all-inclusive democracy. This manifests itself especially in anti-group prejudices, with consistent opposition to an education to elevate the out-group youth. Other remnants come from the theological past, a distrust of "human nature" especially in children and youth; on the one hand, a distrust of intelligence lest spiritual values suffer if indoctrination be denied;

* Progressive Educ. Assn., Commission on the Relation of School and College, Adventure in American Education, v. 1–5 (New York, Harper's, 1942).

on the other, a positive wish to train to specific beliefs, with the demand for a school so to train. Other remnants are from the former reign of the classical tradition, one aspect of which has been well stated by Irwin Edman, who refers to culture, in one of its senses, as "a combination of elegance and nostalgia, of preciousness and disdain." In this sense it is "an elegant escape into beautiful anachronisms." (144: June 29, 1935). It is, however, but fair to say that many upholders of the classical tradition see in it—mistakenly, it would surely seem—the principal remaining support of the liberal outlook. A better grounded attitude is the fear lest vocational and other material interests crowd out broader and finer interests in more human affairs. As an opposition attitude to the new this carries more weight with the college bred than it deserves; the newer education can take better care of the finer and broader interests than can the Alexandrian outlook, though Alexandria does not believe this.

There are many other left-overs from the past that prevent consideration of the educational problem on its merits. Many still believe that any *difficult* study "trains the mind"; but as commonly used *difficult* turns out to mean what the pupil or student finds repellent and requires compulsion to make him work at it. An analog of this attitude is the fear of interest expressed by Mr. Dooley: "It makes no difference what a boy studies so long as he doesn't like it." This attitude is still so common and so strong that caricatures of the doctrine of interest are readily and widely accepted. Along with these goes the age-old belief in the efficacy of punishment. This is so easy a method to apply and, following irritation and anger, so natural to use that it is possibly the most deeply entrenched of all educational superstitions, especially—but not at all exclusively—in the lower reaches of the socio-economic scale.

The chief conscious opposition to the new seems to appear in the professors of the liberal arts college and in the high school teachers whom these influence. Two beliefs under-lie and motivate this attitude of opposition, a belief in the efficacy of the Alexandrian outlook and a belief that research—"graduate school" research—represents the proper aim of higher education. Of course these two beliefs do not necessarily look in the same direction, and few holders stress them equally; but together they have for a generation dominated the typical liberal arts college. The university "graduate school" requires knowledge as a prerequisite to research, but its heart lies in its research aim. This "graduate school" is the only recognized institution for preparing college teachers; and the Ph.D. degree, for which research is the crowning essential, is an all but necessary requisite for appointment to the liberal arts college faculty. The typical professor in the liberal arts college brings from this graduate school its emphasis on research as the ultimate aim of education. As a result each typical college department arranges its "major" work to prepare its graduates for graduate school research. Everything (typically) leads up to this end—and this in spite of the known facts that only a minority of college graduates go on to such research and that preparation for research is no adequate preparation for effective American citizenship. Any college student expecting to teach in the high school will "major" in a college department so organized and run on the research aim. He is typically indoctrinated with this idea as the outlook that should guide him in his high school teaching: he is to prepare his high school students in his subject with the idea that, when they go to college, they will major in that same subject and perhaps, if they really succeed, go on to the graduate school for research in that same subject.

Such a high school teacher, thus taught in college, will think that education consists in learning subjects, his major subject especially. If school authorities with a better educational outlook wish high school teachers to stress character and personality as the dominant aim of secondary education, this indoctrinated subject-matter teacher, recollecting his college professor, will oppose such a proposal as a lowering of scholarship standards. Indeed, if, while this high school teacher was getting his liberal arts college preparation to teach, his professor of education had sought a strong commitment to the character-building educational program, his subject-matter major professor would probably have opposed the idea as a departure from established ideals and not worthy of serious consideration.

It is this situation, supported by deep-rooted custom, that prevents the secondary school from following the free play of intelligence as it faces its educational task. The graduate school typically mis-prepares college teachers for their work; and they in turn similarly mis-prepare high school teachers for their work. To break this vicious circle is the greatest single task that faces American education today.

Later chapters will go into closer detail on certain matters here sketched. This chapter is simply to introduce the Alexandrian term and conception in a way to show its essential difference from the newer outlook and procedures.

CHAPTER XVII. *A Modern Theory of Learning*

CHAPTER XV gave an outline sketch of a general theory of education designed to implement the philosophy of life developed in Part I of this book. As the central feature of that theory of education, this chapter now develops a conception of learning believed to be strategic in its possibilities for implementing that philosophy of life. In brief, the proposal here made is (i) to choose from the whole range of factually supported theories of learning that one which best answers to the social and moral demands of the accepted philosophy and (ii) to make this theory the basis of the teacher-learning process in school and out. In this effort, it is particularly desired to strive for the highest type of living as constituting alike the means and the end of the educative endeavor, the highest type of living as judged by the positions taken in Part I on respect for personality, morality, democracy, and the life-good-to-live.

This is a different aim from that ordinarily set up by psychologists. They are naturally more concerned to develop the science of psychology as such than to develop the subject of education. Thus when they undertake in educational psychology to deal with educational problems, they often assume outmoded and now inadequate conceptions of education which prevailed when they went to school. In at least three respects the treatment of learning here given differs significantly from what is ordinarily found.

1. It is the learning of self-conscious humans that here concerns us, not learning of lower animals. Many psychologists base their study of learning on experiments with rats or guinea pigs, expecting —it appears—that these presumably simpler instances of learning will give insight into the essential nature of the learning process wherever found. But these lower animals lack both selfhood and

all the higher type of life which selfhood alone permits; specifically, they lack the ability to set up purposes, to watch themselves work, and to profit consciously by experience. But in man all of these experiences are typical, and because of them he lives on a human (higher-than-animal) plane. We should, for these reasons, if for no other, expect the learning of humans to differ essentially from that of the lower animals.

This statement, however, is not to deny validity to the study of animal learning. We can never tell in advance what useful suggestions may come from related study. But it does seem clear that lower-animal learning will never show what most concerns us—the learning behavior of man at his self-conscious best.

2. The human learning which most concerns us here is that which promises the most for man, not the least. Many psychologists, led, probably unconsciously, by Newtonian atomism, have sought to explain conscious action by reducing it to less-than-conscious elements, such as neuron-synapse action, conditioned reflexes, or mere trial-and-error learning. The educator cannot ignore the low end of the scale of human behavior, but still less can he live down there. He must take account of the whole person and in particular must work for the higher possibilities of the learner. As suggested above, no theory can disregard the pertinent facts; but it need not therefore restrict itself to the lowest type of behavior. Stress will here be given to conscious action and its development. Many psychologists, unduly influenced by the old theory that children cannot even begin at the development of responsible self-direction, have sought psychological processes, leading to little more than obedience and routine habits and skills. There is, to be sure, a proper place for obedience and habit and skill, but primarily as the servants of such higher traits as initiative, creativity, cooperation, and moral responsibility. We wish, therefore, and shall seek a theory of learning which especially develops these higher traits.

3. Still further, the effort here will be made to find a theory of learning which does not, as does the older outlook, use the child's present simply as means to some distant future, a future as yet unforeseen by the child and indeed unpredictable for him by the adult. The older educational outlook originally held that the child's mind is, in the language then customary, a *tabula rasa*, a clean slate; it counted that education is properly a writing on this slate, the

storing of the child's "memory with things deserving to be there"; for which they said, "he will be grateful . . . when he grows up, even if he kicks now." Here, by contrast with all such ideas, a learning theory will be sought which sees the child from birth as a behaving, feeling human being and which, by respecting and utilizing the child's present status, helps to bring about continuous growth in and from his properly guided current living. In this living (as will later be discussed) what is learned now will be used *now* to help remake the present living into more effective living—living consequently a step further along in meaning and accordingly a step higher in quality.

This emphasis on the child's present is not to deny a proper regard for the future. Such regard is, as we saw in Chapter IX, one of the two demands of ethics; but we wish this regard for the broader and distant view to be developed from within—which means gradually—and not imposed from without, as the older education customarily tried to do, with serious dangers as we shall presently see. In other words, just as we must oppose using any human simply as means, so must we oppose using the present life of persons simply as means and not also as end in itself.

The problem resulting from the wish to meet these democratic and ethical demands of learning has, then, as was earlier suggested, two parts: (i) to find or construct a theory of learning which, on the one hand, answers scientifically to the observed facts of life and learning and (ii) so to use this theory as to meet the express demands of higher human living for reasoning, initiative, creativity, responsibility, cooperation, and the like. No lesser theory of learning can be acceptable.

SUGGESTIONS FROM BIOLOGY

How will a theory of learning to fit the personality demands stated above differ from the ordinary theory of learning long dominant in Western education? It may be that further consideration of biology—*building on what was discussed in Chapter II*—will help to make this contrast clearer and at the same time furnish reasons for preferring the new to the old.

The common or conventional theory, hereinafter called "learning theory A" (or type A for short), has the following characteristics:

(i) it is primarily a theory for learning from books; (ii) it thus consists typically of learning the words or statements of others; (iii) it expects the learning to come in a situation abstracted from life and so (typically) to center around a content of little or no present meaning to the learner; (iv) it expects the learning to be got mainly, if not solely, by repetition; and (v) it counts that the learning will be applied generally, if not always, in an experience different from that in which the learning takes place, usually appreciably later.

By contrast the theory here proposed, called herein "learning theory B" (type B), shows the following characteristics: it holds (i) that behaving is typically an essential part of the learning process; (ii) that the learning goes forward best, if not solely, in a situation of concrete personal living; (iii) that the learning comes from behaving, not from mere repetition of words, as with type A; (iv) that the first application of the learning comes, normally, within the experience in which the learning takes place, in fact that the learning comes typically in order to carry on this experience. As a corollary it is here maintained that the best learning under type A really came chiefly when it operated *not* as A–learning in an abstracted situation, to be applied later in life–but when it operated as B(iv), that is, when the content was in fact used to carry on some experience. Study of the biological evolution of man may help us to contrast and evaluate these two learning theories.

It is a recognized principle of evolution that "acquired characters," learned instances of behavior, are not transmitted by birth from parent to child. Evolution does not proceed that way. The theory of evolution does, however, hold that the more useful any organic functioning is for survival, the more surely will a variation in the direction of its better functioning win out in the struggle for existence and so more surely will it be transmitted. For example, ability to learn is highly important to survival; thus increased ability to learn means greater chance of survival and so greater chance of being transmitted.

Two illustrations may thus help at this point. Note how they both illustrate the B type of learning.

Consider first an instance of animal activity prolonged enough and complex enough for an early stage of the activity or experience to enter through the process of learning as a significant factor in a later stage of that same activity or experience. Let us say that a tiger threatens a deer, but at a distance sufficiently great for the deer's superior running ability to get her safely away. Will the deer actually get away? Yes, if she starts in time and runs thereafter for a sufficient length of time. But she will run long enough only if the original impulse (or that reinforced by the tiger's further threats) remains in action sufficiently long after the tiger has been left behind to get the deer fully out of danger. Now the fact that the original impulse to run remains with the deer after the tiger is out of sight gives us, fairly considered, a case of learning; for it is a responding after the original stimulus has ceased to act as an external fact.

A second illustration from human experience will perhaps make the fact of learning more obvious. I wish to talk with a man over the phone. I give the switchboard girl the man's number, and she calls him. Here an interval–short, to be sure–follows between the time the girl hears the number and her use of the number. (Whether the girl first called the number and then wrote it on her report slip or whether she first wrote it and then called the man matters not; in either case, a short but real interval intervened.) That she acted after she heard shows that she learned (remembered) what she heard and then acted on memory (learning). (And the better type of operator keeps in mind the whole incident of the call sufficiently to make sure the call does go through.)

Four questions now confront us: (i) Just exactly what do we mean by learning? (ii) Is type B really an instance of learning? (iii) Is type B so important biologically that evolution would seize upon it, as asserted above, to fix it, as truly as type A, in the species? (iv) Is not type B really the main source of learning used in mature life? Let us take these in order.

1. Just what do we mean by learning? The definition here chosen is this: Learning is the tendency of any part or phase of what one has lived so to remain with the learner as to come back pertinently into further experience. When such a tendency has been set up, learning has to that extent been effected. To accept anything less of a definition of learning than to expect it to tend so to remain and come back relevantly into experience seems indefensible. If "learning" does not do this, why should it be called learning?

But this definition, the result of many years of study by the author of the problem of learning, is, like every other statement, justified only if it fits the observed facts. How well it does so fit the facts will, it is hoped, become clearer as the discussion continues. In addition, it should be noted, this definition will, as is obvious, fit equally both theory A and theory B.

Various other questions about this definition call for consideration. Just when anything has been *lived* is one such question. But all such points we now postpone to later discussions.

2. Is type B—learning in order to carry on the present experience—really an instance of learning as just defined? The answer is yes. The deer lived the threat of the tiger so vividly that it stayed with her after the tiger had dropped out of sight; she accordingly kept on running until a safe distance had intervened. The girl lived the telephone number when she heard it, she took it in both as a bare number and in its life setting, that is, in the setting of her work; and having thus lived its coming, it stayed with her until she used it. The question of degree of learning enters here. The girl next day probably could not recall the number without looking it up. But even so, it had not entirely gone, for when I called again, she *recognized* it as the same number I had previously used.

We can go on to say that in any complex experience, the earlier stages will ordinarily so stay on with one as to enter pertinently into the later stages, thus giving a connecting unity between earlier and later stages and thereby making the successive happenings into one continuous experience. The point for us here is that the earlier stages actually pervade the later stages and that this fact is essential to the character of the later stages. Without this pervasive effect of learning, the successive happenings would be only physically determined and so would be essentially different from what the pervasive learning makes them. Here is sixteen-year-old Sally talking over the phone with her best friend Mary. Sally learned at the opening of the conversation that it was Mary at the other end; and this consciousness enters into the whole content of the conversation to give it a Sally-Mary character essentially different from a Sally-John conversation and even more markedly different from a Sally-Father conversation.

We conclude, then, that type B certainly is true learning, and that its presence in experience is essential to the very existence of human experience as such.

3. Is type B learning so important biologically that evolution would seize upon it to fix it as an abiding feature in the life of the species? The answer is yes. The importance seen just above would suffice to bring about this effect. Even in subhuman organisms the unity of a life episode is fixed by and in the type B of learning, working, of course, at the same time alongside other kinds of learning from previous experiences. It seems probable that at least some of the deer's fear of the tiger is the result of such previous learning. What happens *now* in *this* activity to give unity to *this* episode or *this* experience is, however, largely the fact of its own B type learnings.

4. Is not type B the principal source of the learning used by the typical adult in life? It is clear that in each life experience this adult learns some things directly in and through this very experience as he works at it to make it go. This learning is of course type B. But the adult in this experience also uses many kinds of learning that have come to him in the past. It is this past learning that we wish to study further. How were these past items learned? Were they learned by the type A process as outlined in the original definition of type A? Or were most of them learned by the type B process? To answer this question consider four possible sources of the past learnings used in this experience: (i) those learned before the adult left school or college, but learned entirely outside of school or college; (ii) those learned in school or college; (iii) those learned since leaving school or college, but learned in and through life; (iv) those learned since leaving school or college, but learned by type A school learning procedures. It is clear that the learning under (i) and (iii) is type B learning and that the learning under (ii) and (iv) is type A learning. Which pair gives the greater aggregate? Is it not highly probable that the ordinary nonscholarly adult's learning of (iv) kind are very, very few in number, and also that a large proportion of the original (ii) kind have been forgotten? And is it not probable that for any typical adult, (i) and (iii) are largest in number? Is not the answer that type B is the principal source of learning used by the typical adult?

To return now to the bearing of biology on the question of learning, it is generally believed that man has not developed biologically in any significant manner or degree since he became *Homo sapiens;* culturally, yes—greatly so; biologically as regards mind, no, not so far as we can tell. If this be accepted, then man's present capacity to learn was developed during the long period which ended with the coming of *Homo sapiens*. As we contrast theory A with theory B, it becomes clear that B stands closer to man as a behaving organism, and that A came into existence only after *Homo sapiens* had invented writing. As between the two, then, theory B is the only one that certainly appears in the biological evolution of man. Man thus naturally behaves according to B; A belongs solely to cultural development.

This ends our consideration of suggestions from biological evolution of behavior. Its principal suggestion has been to show what the B type of learning is, how it evolved, and somewhat of how it works—works within the experience in which it originates and thereafter as may be needed. Put with this now the discussion of Chapter II, where we see what we here call type B learning at work in more detail in any instance of actual experience. The two together constitute the framework for the consideration of education throughout this book.

In the discussion of question (ii) above it was brought out that the earlier stages of any experience *pervade* the subsequent parts of that experience. That is the result seen here. This conception of B type learning, learning to carry on and improve living, will pervade practically all the remaining discussions of this book. It will prove the key element to unlock many of the problems to be considered later.

ADDITIONAL CONCEPTIONS STRATEGIC IN LEARNING

Though the conception of B type learning just discussed furnishes the basic frame of reference for the rest of the book, certain additional and supplementary conceptions should be considered.

1. *The Transitive Verb "to Live" and the Place of Acceptance Therein.* In the definition of learning given above, the verb *to live* played an essential part, implying, if not asserting, that for one to *learn* anything, he must first *live* that thing. This transitive use of the verb to live is so unfamiliar that a word of explanation may be helpful. To *live* anything, as *to live* a feeling or a thought or a bodily movement, belongs grammatically in the same class with singing a song, dancing a waltz, or fighting a battle. In each such case the

object of the verb does nothing more than repeat, perhaps more explicitly, the actual content of the verb.

Specifically, what does it mean to say that if I wish my pupil to learn anything, such as a thought or a feeling or a movement, the pupil has to *live* that thought or that feeling or that movement? Suppose as principal of a high school in a fair-sized village, I set as one of my aims or goals that my pupils shall, if I can effect it, learn (acquire, build, develop, each in himself) a spirit of public service to the village.There are really two questions here: (i) What does it mean in such a case to *learn* a thought or a feeling or a movement? (ii) What does it mean to *live* that thought of feeling or movement?

Taking the first question, we can at once name some things which the verb *learn* does *not* mean in this case. It does not mean that any pupil who can get an A on a written examination on the subject has therein learned (achieved) the desired spirit of service. A written examination might disclose *knowledge* (so far as words prove knowledge) *about* such a spirit, but a pupil might have full knowledge *about* the spirit and not have (or feel) the spirit itself. Learning a spirit certainly means more than learning knowledge *about* it. Nor could ability and willingness to say a pledge of allegiance to such a spirit tell us that the pupil had got (learned) the spirit. No, a pupil has not *learned* this desired spirit until he has so got the spirit in him that he will of himself, as opportunity may open, really work for the public good of the community. Learning means, in this case, to build (acquire, develop) the habit, the attitude and the interest of so working; it means so to build this habit and attitude that others can rely on him, when occasion demands, to work this way both outwardly and inwardly. This is what learning means in such a case.

The second question is now more easily answered: What does it mean to *live* such a spirit so as to learn it? The answer is more easily given in words than realized in fact. If my pupils are to live this spirit, they must have the opportunity to respond, and must in fact so respond, with that spirit to some life situations. This means, in practice, the opportunity to embark on some challenging efforts in behalf of, say, some village needs; but, as already implied, opportunity alone does not suffice.

And here comes in *acceptance*, the second essential. As the pupils of a class thus work in behalf of a specific village need, some will enter more wholeheartedly than others into the physical effort and into the wish to help; others will be lukewarm; and a few will perhaps inwardly rebel. These represent different degrees of acceptance, some full acceptance, some but slight, a few negative. And each actual experience of each individual student carries its degree of acceptance; it is an inevitable part of actual life. Acceptance in some degree, positive or negative, is always present in the living then going on; each person, whatever the enterprise, feels his degree of acceptance of that thing at that time under those conditions. *Degree of acceptance of any part of an experience means degree of living that part of the experience.*

We are now ready to state the B type law of learning: *We learn what we live, we learn each item we live as we accept it, and we learn it in the degree we accept it.*

Those pupils who were inwardly rejecting what the class was working at were learning negatively, learning *not to do* that thing. Those who in their hearts accepted it positively were learning *to do* that thing, they were building the positive spirit, and they built it in the degree they accepted it.

It may be well for certain future purposes to restate this law of learning also as follows:

We learn our responses, only our responses, and all our responses; we learn each as we accept it to live by, and we learn it in the degree we accept it.

How this statement of the principle follows from the other statement is easy to see. Life, we may say, consists of (i) happenings, occurrences that affect us, and (ii) our responses thereto in terms of doing, thinking, feeling, or the like. But consider these happenings further. Do I respond to the happening as it actually and objectively took place—"as God sees it," so to say? Or do I respond to it as I understand it, as I take it to be? The more we think about it, the clearer it becomes that I respond to the happening as I see and feel it; I respond to the character which I ascribe to the happening. We may then distinguish three things: (i) the happening, objectively considered; (ii) the happening as I accept it; and (iii) my response to the happening as I understand and accept it. That I may mistake the happening is quite possible; but if so, the clearer does it become that I respond not to the objective happening, but to my mistaken sizing up of it.

What I live, then, is not (i) but (ii), my (possibly) mistaken sizing up, and (iii) my response thereto. But (ii) is my response (mistaken though it may be) to (i), the actual objective happening. As my response, it gives my version of (i). The only part of (i), the true happening, that gets into my life is (ii) which is my understanding of (i). So always do I live exactly (ii) and (iii), each of which is a response of mine. So I live my responses. But we learn what we live, so we learn our responses, each as we accept it.

2. *Degrees of Learning*. That we learn some things better than others everybody knows. Some things drop out almost as soon as they are over; others we can neither forget nor ignore even if we try. We can then say that one thing has been *better* or *more strongly* learned than another, if it *stays longer* with one to come back into further experience and/or if it has a *stronger tendency* thus to come back into experience.

What is it that makes one thing better learned than another? A full discussion would be long and complex. For our purposes it suffices to name three principal factors. That we learn what we live gives us a starting point; the following gives an illustration: We read in the paper many items of news. Do we remember all and take each equally into account in life from then on? No. Some we size up as unimportant to us and so think no more about them; some we learn strongly, could never forget—as that a dear friend has died or that an opportunity we have long wished for is now open; some we learn weakly, perhaps never to recall them ourselves but still to recognize them if someone refers to them; some we never afterward recall.

(1) We learn any particular item in the degree that we live it, in the degree we count it important to us, in the degree we accept it in our hearts for use in life.

To see the basis of the next principle, try to memorize the following three sets of five syllables each, and see which you have learned best: (i) niz, taf, hig, div, vag; (ii) dog, sin, her, all, big; (iii) the big dog bit her. The three sets are equally long, but differ greatly as to meaning. Hence the second factor in learning:

(2) Other things being equal, we learn any particular item in

the degree that it has meaning to us, has meaning in terms of what we already know.

Again, we all know from personal experience that names, faces, numbers, and other items of experience once learned tend to drop out of recall unless they are kept alive, so to say, by use. We may then add a third principle:

(3) Other things being equal, items of experience are recallable in the degree of the frequency and recency of their use.

3. *Cumulative Learning.* Some things we learn in full strength all at once. When I got a telegram telling me that my long-time friend had passed away, I did not need repeated messages on successive days to strengthen the learning; the first one sufficed. But my regard for my friend had not come to me thus all at once. It was growing all the years I had known him. Each experience we lived through together contributed its added increment of insight into his character and to my regard for his worth. My feeling for him stands forth as a clear instance of cumulative learning. So likewise is it with our standards, our ideas, our principles of action, as we have previously seen. Each is an instance of cumulative learning.

4. *Simultaneous or Concomitant Learning.* In any significant experience the human organism acts as an organized whole; thought and feeling, internal glandular secretion, heart and nerve—all act together. Each experience is thus a complex of many interacting parts and aspects. Any similar experience will repeat in some measure certain of the same thoughts or feelings or movements. Suppose now a series of related experiences, such as my successive experiences with my friend just discussed; the related *thoughts* of the successive experiences I had with him, and so of him, were accumulated and organized into my insight into his character. Similarly the *related* feelings of the successive experiences were accumulated and organized into my *attitude* of regard for him.

In this way every school child, in addition to the arithmetic or history or geography which the old type of school sets him to learn, is thinking and feeling and concluding about the teacher, about school, about himself, about the subject. And these successive thoughts about the teacher are being collected to build the cumulative learning we call the child's conception of the teacher, what the child would expect of the teacher, under this, that, or the other condition. Similarly is the child building his attitude toward school as a place to like, or to dislike and leave as soon as possible; toward school work as interesting or the reverse; toward each subject studied and each kind of work taken up; toward each child in the room. In particular is each child building his conception and attitude with reference to himself in relation to the other persons and things about him, a feeling of security in school life or of insecurity, of confidence in himself or, on the contrary, an inferiority complex. A certain child whose eyesight was defective but didn't know it lost confidence in himself and in the people about him when he couldn't see what they said they saw.

Such cumulative learnings are always in process, many going on simultaneously all the active living time of each normal person. As curious as it may seem to us now, the teacher of the past was in effect ignorant of this cumulative simultaneous or concomitant learning. The modern-minded teacher is well aware that out of these cumulative learnings—conceptions, attitudes, ideals, standards, habits, skills, and the like—is the child's character all the time being formed. Even William James seems not to have considered these concomitant learnings, but if we include in the quotation given below the words added in brackets, we have an excellent statement of the accumulated result of all one's learnings:

> We are spinning our own fates, good or evil, and never to be undone. Every smallest stroke of virtue or vice [every accompanying thought or feeling] leaves its never-so-little scar. The drunken Rip Van Winkle, in Jefferson's play, excuses himself for every fresh dereliction by saying, "I won't count this time!" Well, he may not count it, and a kind Heaven may not count it; but it is being counted none the less. Down among his nerve-cells and fibers the molecules are counting it, registering and storing it up to be used against him when the next temptation comes. Nothing we ever do is, in strict scientific literalness, wiped out (88:77*f.*).*

A close and significant relationship exists between the social and moral demands mentioned at the beginning of this chapter and the conceptions of learning just discussed—that we learn what we live, what we accept, the fact of simultaneous or concomitant learnings, and the cumulative nature of learning. This relationship will appear increasingly important in the remainder of this book.

* *Talks to Teachers,* copyright 1899 by Henry Holt and Company, Inc., New York, and used by their permission.

CHAPTER XVIII. *Purpose: Its Place in Life and Learning*

PURPOSE, like true thinking, is "man's distinctive mark alone." Only those can truly purpose who have achieved selfhood—are self-conscious, know what they are about, and can accordingly plan consciously, choosing goals to satisfy the wants they feel and devising means to effect the goals.

From the critical or philosophic view of life, purposing represents a good in itself—to purpose and to realize one's purposes in reasonable degree is to live as a free person. Besides, in purposing lies the possibility of untold richness in human living, both in the process itself, as just stated, and through its results. The social situation which fosters the setting up and the realizing of purposes therein respects personality, it allows the person to choose and to effect (if he can) what he wants and enjoys—what to him seems worth-while, what to him adds to life and makes it nearer to his heart's desire. To be respected by being allowed thus to purpose is to enjoy that freedom which is the peculiar characteristic of democracy. Says Shotwell, "Democracy is freedom in action." (83: No. 350:267) Whitehead says, "The essence of freedom is the practicability of purpose." (171:84) And Dewey comments: "We are free in the degree in which we act knowing what we are about." (51:250)

To grant the right and encourage the opportunity to exercise purpose is, as indicated above, effectively to respect personality. For the school to respect the personality of the child, and thus to encourage democracy and develop its supporting traits, is one crucial difference between the new and the old philosophy of education. The new stresses purposeful activity; the old ignored and denied it. To make purposeful activity the typical unit of school procedure is at one and the same time to respect the learner's personality, to uphold democracy, and to cultivate the traits necessary for democracy: self-respect, self-direction, initiative, acting on thinking, self-criticism, persistence. To choose one's purposes, with due regard to all the values affected, is to give meaning, richness, moral quality, and satisfyingness to life. It is around such conscious purposing that the defensible life is built.

The fact that the active presence of purpose in the learner effectively helps the learning process is the complementary reason for making purposeful activity the unit element of the learning process. This, too, is one crucial difference between the new and the old theory of education. The old was glad to have the child feel a strong purpose to learn the assigned lesson; but it had no notion of allowing any prior or alternative choice or purposing on his part. The new makes child purposing, conducted under teacher guidance, its key to effective learning. This will be discussed in detail later in this chapter.

UTILIZING OUR ORGANIC RESOURCES

William James has a famous statement on tapping our latent resources which will help to orient our discussion:

> Few men live at their maximum of energy . . . a man who energizes below his normal maximum fails by just so much to profit by his chance at life . . . a nation filled with such men is inferior to a nation run at higher pressure. . . .
>
> As a rule men habitually use only a small part of the powers which they actually possess and which they might use under appropriate conditions. . . .
>
> We are all to some degree oppressed, unfree. We don't come to our own. It is there, but we don't get at it (86:7, 8, 11, 24).

The factor which most significantly serves to tap these otherwise latent resources is purpose. Everyone knows that absence of purpose or weakness of purpose operates to reduce the amount of energy and determination put into an enterprise. To see better how these things are true, let us turn once more to the biological theory of behavior as discussed in Chapter II and elsewhere. Here we find certain age-old biologic devices for tapping latent organic resources.

One organic device for yielding effective behavior is the fact, previously noted, that the organism acts as a unitary whole. This means that all the various parts of the behaving organism cooperate, part with part, to serve the needs of the organism. A second and more striking device for tapping latent energy is the coordination of resources called *set* and *readiness*. A description of how these two actually tap energy will probably furnish the best available means for defining these two terms.

Who has not seen a cat intent on catching some, to us unseen, object of prey, perhaps a bird, perhaps a chipmunk? We can tell at once and beyond a doubt what the cat is about. She is creeping stealthily forward, her body hugging the ground, her eyes fixed on her prey. There can be no doubt that she is deeply intent on catching some manageable live creature. Every muscle and every nerve seems involved—all she has and can use are at high tension; even her tail tells the story as it switches nervously from side to side. When she approaches closer, she gets perceptibly ready to spring. When she springs, she is perceptibly ready to seize. The cat has other types of set to fit other characteristic demands of life. Suppose, for example, a fierce dog should threaten the cat. She would at once take on a defensive set with its appropriate readinesses. And the posture for this defensive set, apparent in all parts of the cat, would be as unmistakable and as appropriate as that for stalking.

We say of a cat thus stirred and thus acting that she is *set*, organically set, upon stalking and catching her prey or upon defending herself from the dog. And we further say that at each stage of action in the developing drama the pertinent nerves and muscles get appropriately *ready* for the next needed action. In *set* the whole organism is characteristically keyed to act, all parts cooperating in appropriately high degree. And as each new stage of action approaches, the organism gets specifically ready for that coming phase of action. *Readiness* means the especially high tension in all those precise nerves and muscles which will be called into play to carry out that next particular action. *Set* and *readiness* are then phases of the organism's acting as a whole. They are special biologic devices for securing immediate and adequate effectiveness of action.

There is, as we saw in Chapter II, yet another organic resource for increasing the effectiveness of effort, namely, emotion. In a true sense this is always present in set and readiness, but as a specific organic factor it calls for separate attention. We all know how it feels to be stirred by a situation, and we know further that the more strongly we are stirred, the more strongly we feel. This feeling, which we call emotion, clearly serves to call forth greater vigor of action. George Eliot, for example, speaks of "a sensation of strength, inspired by mighty emotion." We must, however, understand that emotion is not a *thing* which comes to enter the organism; it is merely a name with which to describe a particular functioning of the organism. There are of course different degrees of such emotional stirring varying from the mild degree, seen in ordinary cases of interest, to high degrees. In certain cases, which we ordinarily call passion, one may be, as in anger, so intent on the particular matter faced as unwisely to neglect or ignore other involvements—probably with corresponding regrets the next day. In the extreme degree emotion may be so great as to paralyze action and the person "goes to pieces" or is "paralyzed with fear" or is "scared stiff" or "scared to death."

It appears that the physiological basis of this emotional stirring is an internal glandular secretion into the blood stream. That adrenalin thus prepares one for actual physical fighting, even to making the blood from a wound coagulate and so tend to stop bleeding, is one of the interesting survivals from the life of the past. "Second wind" is another such survival which nowadays is perhaps most useful to the long-distance runner. But other occasions of life make good use of other aspects of glandular, emotional stirring.

The term *interest* affords another instance of the working of set and readiness, one which particularly concerns us in education. A later chapter will be devoted entirely to the problem of interest. Here we simply point out two bearings of the doctrine of interest on the present discussion. First, an abiding interest in any matter is precisely an abiding tendency toward set and readiness with regard to that matter. Second, the readiness accompanying interest means a higher degree of sensitivity to anything that promises a significant bearing on the object of interest. These two facts make for higher efficiency: a person interested along a given line will, as occasion offers, pursue that interest actively in the degree of the interest felt; he will, further, in the degree of his interest, be keyed to sense anything that promises to affect significantly the welfare or upbuilding of that interest.

Here is Betsy getting ready for her high school graduation dance. Her mother has promised her a new dress for the occasion if—with mother's help—she will make it. There need be no doubt as to which shop windows catch Betsy's eye and draw her attentive study when she goes downtown; or that a new copy of *Vogue* will be the first magazine she sees if she goes to the bookstore. It should also be pointed out, for future application, that while interest brings positive readiness for anything that promises to foster or promote the interest, it as truly brings unreadiness for any line of action which thwarts or threatens the interest. When Betsy gets home with the new *Vogue*, she will be distinctly unready to lay it down to help set the table for dinner. This particular manifestation of unreadiness will of course require moral control; but the combined long-run effect of such readiness and unreadiness possibilities is to make for efficiency, as we shall see in a moment.

PURPOSE: MAN'S ALONE; ITS RELATIONS WITH INTEREST AND SET AND READINESS

It was suggested above that purpose, found in man but not in the lower animals, is founded on set and readiness which man shares with the brute world. To see how this is true it is necessary to note the relation of purposing to interest and of interest to set and readiness.

A purpose is an intent, accepted after more or less of consideration, to attain a specific aim. The mother, referred to just above, probably had at least two purposes in mind when she promised Betsy the dress for the dance. One purpose was to put her daughter on an equal standing with the other girls of the class; another was to give Betsy an engaging chance to practice sewing. Each purpose clearly grew out of a long-felt interest on the part of the mother. Betsy on her part felt a strong purpose to succeed with the dress, because she wanted a pretty dress and because she wanted to succeed with her undertaking. In the degree that the girl had a strong purpose did she feel set and readiness active within her for making the dress. In other words, a purpose, in the degree it is felt as such, becomes a set, with its accompanying readinesses and unreadinesses as discussed above.

In purposing, man shows at once his kinship with the lower animals and his superiority to them. He is one of them in that in purpose he feels set and readiness and so can profit through these, as can the lower animals, by tapping energies otherwise not available. He is, however, superior to them in that, by the use of intelligence, he can choose what purposes he will pursue and how and for how long. In other words, through the conscious choice of his purpose he can in high degree control his sets rather than be controlled by them.

Let us say that when Betsy looks at shop windows her heart goes out exuberantly to an entrancing but highly complicated dress. "That's exactly what I want, that's my dream dress!" she says to her mother. Mother, more experienced, points out that the dress would be very difficult to make, less likely to turn out well at the hands of a beginner. But Betsy is "set" toward this particular dress and dislikes to give up the idea. However, as she thinks more about the risks she decides to abandon the "dream dress" for the present and to take instead a pattern she can better manage.

We see, then, that since purposes are consciously chosen, intelligence may be taken in, so to say, on the ground floor. The determination felt in purpose need not, as with the lower animals, be merely blind impulse. The purpose, having been chosen consciously, can be changed or given up altogether as further insight or later developments may demand. In particular, study can enter to change the plans as developing results may show the need for change.

Man cannot, of course, control all his sets. Man is an animal and as such has his animal wants. Hunger, if not appeased, will in time grow imperious. Man cannot by his will alone cause it to cease. But man's intelligence rightly put to work can control the cause of hunger; he can abolish famine.

PURPOSE PERMITS MORE EFFECTIVE ACTION

Thus all the services that set and readiness can render are equally available to purpose, with conscious control added. Set means persistence; but in purpose, persistence can be directed by intelligence. Set also brings readiness and unreadiness, with all that they can d efficiency; but in purpose these need not be obeyed can be directed intelligently so as the more surely to iency. Readiness to see suggestive leads is one part of ; intelligence should operate to decide which suggestions to take and which to reject. Unreadiness tends to reject distracting invitations and suggestions, but here again intelligence must go along to give the practical decision.

All of this means that purpose, in the degree that it is present and felt, permits a higher degree of efficiency of action than otherwise would be possible; but it also means that desirable results will be effected in the degree that purposes are critically chosen and intelligently directed.

PURPOSE BRINGS STRONGER LEARNING

The heading of the preceding section says that purpose *permits* more efficient action, and the wording was accurate. Purpose permits, but does not insure, efficient action; for purposes may be unwisely chosen and/or unintelligently directed. But the present heading asserts, without qualification, that purpose *brings* stronger learning; and so it does. The learning which follows purpose may be a mistaken learning, but it will be a stronger learning in the degree of the strength of the purpose. That this is so is easy to see.

We saw in Chapter XVII that we learn any particular item in the degree that we count it important for us or in the degree that we accept it in our hearts. The presence of purpose favorably affects both of these factors and so constitutes the basis of stronger learning. What we purpose to do has in that degree importance for us; so that purpose, in the degree that it is present and carried out in action, will bring stronger learning than the same things done with less purpose. It is this "done with less purpose" which explains so much of inefficient learning of our schools and colleges; so much of the study is done with but small purpose, with little or no sense of importance to the learner beyond the coming examination.

Betsy's younger sister Jill did not like sewing. Every effort made to persuade her in that direction had failed. But when she decided to decorate her room along modern lines, that was different. Now she had a purpose of her own. She started not only with this purpose but also with some conceptions of modern art, of color, line, design, got in part from her art class in school and in part from an admiring inspection of a friend's home. She studied her room, made plans, consulted the department store decorating expert, revised her plans, went to work vigorously with hammer, paints, even the sewing machine. The room turned out well—quite well for a sixteen-year-old—and Jill regaled all who came to see it with an account of each choice, just why she preferred these particular colors in preference to ones which would look "awful" for her type of room—these particular bookcases instead of ones with "choppy lines." In fact, every innocent bystander was taken behind the scenes as to all her choices.

Purposeful activity paid dividends here in various ways. The learning went on more easily, of course, because of Jill's purpose, set, readiness. But, in addition, because the purpose was her own it was rooted in some ideas meaningful and important to her, it was interrelated with matters already known, it already had a background of inner resources to draw on. But note also another point: When Jill at many points made careful choices as to what to do she studied and explored more or less widely the various possibilities—all the significant alternatives in the way of colors, bookcases, etc., were weighed against each other. In the degree that she chose carefully she knew more of the whole area than she did before (what colors are suited to which situations, even though not to her room), and learned vastly more than if she had done the work mechanically or someone had directed her to do exactly this right and proper thing. Even the possibilities rejected probably brought usefully related learnings, by reason of being considered and judged useful under other conditions.

The closing point in the preceding paragraph is worthy of further examination to bring out more clearly the point there made. We saw in Chapter XVII, in the discussion on degrees of learning, that the more a new item is interrelated with matters already known, the easier and stronger will be the resulting learning. Purposeful activity exactly utilizes this principle and in two ways. When one chooses critically, the end or aim emerges, typically, from a choice among rivals. All the significant rivals are weighed each against the others, with reference both to what is at stake and to the promise of each rival candidate to do what is needed. This involves a study of the field and a relating of each rival to the pertinent factors in the situation, with the resulting final choice and decision that one of the competing candidates will make the best showing. What is chosen is in fact selected because of its favorable relations. Intelligent choice thus relates new and old in a causal relationship. Few kinds of learning are better kept in mind or more easily recalled when needed than matters thus causally related; and even the possibilities rejected may well have brought usefully related learnings, at least by reason of being considered and possibly also by being accepted as useful under different conditions.

The process of choosing an *end* or purpose is thus one way in which purposeful activity brings learning by giving increase of seen relationships among the factors considered. The choice of *means* for attaining a purpose repeats exactly the same process, only among a different set of factors. All of these related learnings from both purpose and the means for attaining the purpose are peculiarly useful in that they give *causal* relationships among factors likely to be pertinent to other activities in the given area. And, besides, they are likely to be well learned, for, as suggested above, causal relationships are perhaps most easily learned and most readily recalled.

THORNDIKE'S LAWS OF LEARNING

It may be of interest to see how Thorndike's laws of Readiness, Exercise, and Effect are all included (at least in part) in the principle of acceptance counted basic in this book, and how, used in this way, they avoid the logical difficulty that some find in the law of Effect.

Suppose—to illustrate a high degree of purpose—that Betsy greatly likes the pattern she has chosen, so that making the dress is to her a wholehearted, purposeful activity. She sets to work with great interest and all goes well up to a certain point; then she does not know how to put in the somewhat intricate sleeves. Her mother studies the pattern but she too does not know, so together they call in a neighbor who is an expert. She shows what to do so clearly that Betsy gets the idea fully.

Because of her high interest in making the dress, this temporary threat to success made Betsy more eager to learn just how to do this difficult part. So that when she did really see, she was greatly relieved and accepted the convincing idea joyfully. Her acceptance (i) was so great that she learned the particular procedure then and there for all time, we may say. Next she put the idea to work, she did the job herself with her own hands. Doing it, we may say, implemented the idea, gave it greater clearness and reality than it had had before; the actual doing reinforced, as it were, the acceptance of what had hitherto been idea only. This reinforced acceptance (ii) strengthened the learning. Then, when the difficult part was really done, and done successfully, she looked at it with pleasure and showed it to others. Her satisfaction at achieved success (iii) corroborated and so again reinforced the original acceptance and the intermediate reinforcement in a way to strengthen still further the original learning.

In the three places marked above (i), (ii), and (iii) we have, respectively, at work the three Thorndike laws of (i) Readiness, (ii) Exercise, and (iii) Effect. In (i) the girl was in a high state of readiness for the idea if only she could see it. Her acceptance was greater and the resulting learning stronger because of this readiness. In (ii) where the girl actually carried the idea into operation, the carrying out was Thorndike's Exercise, and it did by exercise (actual doing) reinforce the idea and strengthen its previous acceptance, so bringing increase of learning. In (iii) the fact that the idea worked, that it really succeeded, brought further corroboration to the two acceptances previously made. This increased the satisfaction and accordingly brought increased learning. This greater learning from the satisfaction of success is Thorndike's Effect. Certain critics of Thorndike have objected that what he called the satisfaction from success seemed to follow only after the doing was over and gone and therefore could bring learning only by *ex post facto* action, so to say, which seems unscientific. Whatever validity might otherwise be accorded this criticism of Thorndike's position, the objection does not apply to the factor of corroboration and its consequent increased acceptance and so still stronger learning as herein discussed. When we learn what we accept, as is herein proposed, satisfaction and consequent acceptance come not merely at the end but at many stages throughout the experience. Each instance of such acceptance brings its quota of learning.

The "acceptance," it should be noted, may operate negatively as well as positively. Suppose when Betsy basted and tried on the dress, she found the idea she had accepted so joyfully at (i) and reinforced at (ii) did not at (iii) really work, was in fact so clear a failure with this kind of dress that the idea had to be discarded. She would still have learned the idea, but only for use with some other kind of dress. Now she learned *not* to use it on this dress. What at (iii) above we called corroboration with its stronger learning of the idea, both as idea and the *doing* of it that way, we now call rejection (the negative of corroboration). The idea as learned at (i) and reinforced at (ii) remains with the girl as a plan of action, but from (iii) as a plan not to use in this situation. This distinction is for many situations of vital importance.

PURPOSE AND CONCOMITANT LEARNING

How does the presence of purpose affect the building of concomitant learning? Two questions are here involved, and they call for different discussions. One is the effect of strength of purpose on strength of resulting concomitant learning. The second question relates to such concomitants as attitudes, where the direction of the attitude is as important as its strength, in fact generally more important: how does purpose affect the resulting attitude to determine whether it will be a like or a dislike, a favorable attitude or an antagonistic one?

Suppose we find that Betsy first applied for help from a neighbor who refused to help, saying rather crustily that the girl had no business to attempt what she couldn't do and then expect her neighbors to do the hard part. This neighbor thwarted Betsy's purpose, while the other neighbor helped good-naturedly. Will Betsy feel the same way toward both? Most certainly not. For the first she will feel annoyance and dislike; for the other, grateful appreciation and stronger liking. The more strongly the girl desired to succeed with the dress, the more strongly she learned the feelings for both neighbors. The fact that one thwarted and the other helped made the feelings learned take opposed directions. The thwarted purpose, other things being equal, brings an unfavorable attitude; the promoted purpose, a favorable attitude; and the stronger the purpose, the stronger are the two opposed attitudes. The conclusion would hold for any factor affecting the attainment of the purpose, and may be stated as follows:

The stronger the purpose, the stronger are the resulting attitudes. As to direction, the purpose tends to build a favorable attitude toward any factor favorable to its cause, and an unfavorable attitude toward anything thwarting its cause.

PURPOSE AND RESPECT FOR PERSONALITY

We discussed earlier how freedom to purpose is the test of actual respect for personality. We wish here to see (i) how purposeful activity successfully pursued tends to build self-respect in the person who is engaged in such activity; further, how a regime of group purposing, properly directed, gives unequaled opportunity to (ii) build respect for the personality of others; and (iii) to develop ability to discover possibilities through shared search and at the same time develop cooperative attitudes and methods of discussing, conferring, making shared decisions on such a give-and-take basis as makes for a proper respect for others. These three points we now consider in order.

1. *Freedom to purpose is essential to building of self-respect. Properly directed it builds not only self-respect, but also ability to choose wisely and to accept responsibility.* To purpose wisely and to pursue purposes appropriately means to choose one's ends and means intelligently and ethically. For pupils thus to accept, under wise teacher guidance, responsibility for their activity and its outcomes will tend, in the degree the work is well done and properly appreciated, to build the following concomitant learnings: greater carefulness in choosing both ends and means; increased thoughtfulness and persistence in pursuing endeavors; better practical judgment in such matters; growth of confidence in ability to succeed and so win justified approval of others. To build these various attitudes is—to that extent—to build a proper respect for oneself as capable within the areas thus conquered and at the same time an increasing acceptance of responsibility for one's acts.

2. *A regime of group purposes wisely and successfully directed gives opportunity for building respect for the personality of others.* In fact it seems probable that nothing can equal such a regime for producing this result. Given a class of pupils mature enough to purpose together and adequate opportunity to form and pursue purposes which to them seem challenging and significant, we can

be reasonably sure that each who enters heartily into the effort will build respect for all the others who join in the effort with like heartiness and deport themselves with reasonable consideration of the rest. And, further, to give youth the chance thus to work together at what they think is worth-while is the best known way of building interest in their work and of evoking their varied powers of thought and action.

Probably the one single factor that most militates against success at such purposeful activity in school is the set demand of the school authorities for acquiring fixed-in-advance subject matter according to a prearranged time table. In the degree that the school is run on this basis is a regime of purposeful activity practically impossible of attainment.

Granted flexibility enough in school requirements, and reasonably sympathetic and wise management on the part of teachers, it is possible to get any typical group of children or youth very happily at work along these lines: (i) choosing ever better projects and activities and experiences to undertake; (ii) planning how to manage and apportioning the work among all the participants; (iii) executing the plans, changing these if developments so direct; and (iv) judging the results, not with intent to apportion praise or blame or even just credit, but to learn how to carry on such an experience better next time and to get from this one experience any suggestions of further things to do.

Care should be taken that individuals are in no sense pitted against each other to win credit or praise, that instead attention and interest are directed to getting the work itself well done, with due appreciation, to be sure, of good work everywhere. In the degree that these conditions are met it is probable that interest in such work will increase, together with interest in successful work of ever finer quality; that mutual appreciation will be built by each one for the others working with him, as persons who can be counted on to do the right thing at the right time. It should be recognized that these results will not necessarily come of themselves, that the teacher will have to work for them. It is also true that there may be some small number who will not successfully fit in with the rest; but the probability is that under wise and sympathetic guidance few will be able to resist the constructive tendencies here outlined.

For teachers planning to shift from the older ways of teaching to the new as here suggested, a word or two of caution seems necessary. Success will not be easy. Many children are entirely unaccustomed to any school procedure except memorizing and reciting. Many have never built any conception of using their own minds in school or of taking responsibility for themselves. Instead, as a result of previous home and school experience, many young people have built antagonisms toward any grown-ups who try to manage them, and many have a like antagonism to anything in the way of school work. The teacher who begins on a program of purposeful activity with such children must expect to advance slowly. Sympathetic insight and patience will be necessary, especially at the first.

3. *Such a regime of group purposing will, under wise guidance, build in the individuals of the group definite ability to work together in a democratic framework of shared study and decision.* They will learn how to get information in many varied ways and devise creative means to their ends; they will build increasing acceptance of responsibility to take others into account; they will also develop real skill in discussing to find out what to think and do. In fact they will develop all these traits to a degree incredible to teachers used only to children made antagonistic and cranky by formal school treatment.

This plan of constructive conferring at purposeful enterprises is our chance to make democracy work. The future will make demands on democracy far harder to meet than in the past. We must make the One World work together; and democracy is the only basis on which this is possible. As discussed earlier we are troubled at present because one side of our split world does not know how to discuss inquiringly and to take due account of the values that others feel. But if we take stock of ourselves we find that few of us know how to discuss questions without getting angry. Still fewer know how to discuss them in a way to get at the real merits of what is at issue, to pool ideas and resources, and to give sincere consideration to the ideas and values of others; and fewer still demand this of themselves and others as the only honest thing to do.

If we are to make democracy work, our schools must remake themselves; and this consciously shared effort at decision and executing is an essential part of the remaking. If we can begin this kind of thing in the lower elementary school and continue it from there to the upper elementary, the high school, and the college, we can greatly improve the social process in our country and ultimately in the world. If labor and management had only learned how to confer honestly on a basis of getting at the best possible solution of their difficulties, we would have been spared many if not most of our industrial quarrels. If our schools worked at this sort of thing sufficiently to build it into the minds and characters of nine tenths of our people, instead of as now probably in no more than one twentieth, we could remake our civilization. With more discerning citizens many of the worst of our newspapers would have to go out of business, and the best could raise their standards still higher. Our political campaigns could and would be conducted on a higher level. Congress would argue more honestly and legislate far more effectively.

It can be done, but not in schools run as they are now commonly run. Practice in the intelligent pursuit of group purposes is our key to the future.

CHAPTER XIX. *Coercion and Learning*

THE discussion of this chapter is restricted rather closely to the psychology of coercion and its resulting learnings. Later we shall consider how education, whether in school or at home, should in the light of this and other pertinent matters decide on its philosophy of discipline.

Because the problem of coercion is complex and in certain of its bearings highly controversial, we must proceed with care. Three distinct aspects of the problem need to be considered: (i) the psychological process of effecting coercion—how a parent or teacher may (if he can) make a child do what he would not do if left to himself or what he refuses to do when asked, perhaps even resisting when coerced; (ii) the process of learning under coercion, including the degree in which a child learns to do (or not to do) the specific thing forced upon him (iii) the problem of the simultaneous learnings accompanying coercion. We take these three in order.

HOW COERCION IS EFFECTED

An illustration or two of the common use of coercion will help to make clear the psychological process involved. Little Mary hears the other girls calling her to come out and play with them. She starts out, but her mother calls to her to come back and put away her toys first. Mary demurs, and her mother says decisively: "You cannot go until you pick up your toys and put them away; you know the rule." Mary reluctantly obeys, choosing the lesser evil of putting away her toys in order to gain her greater wish—to play with the other girls. Or take another instance: a father one

Saturday morning overhears his ten-year-old son John speak of going fishing that morning with the other boys. "Didn't I hear your mother tell you yesterday that she wanted you to help her in the flower garden this morning?" "I forgot," answers John. "You are forgetting entirely too often; I'll have to teach you," says the father. "Now to make you remember hereafter I tell you that you won't go fishing this morning and you will help your mother. Do you understand that?" John does understand; when father speaks that way, he means it, and there will be trouble to pay if John doesn't obey. So John phones the other boys not to expect him, choosing the lesser evil of obedience in preference to the certainly greater evil of the punishment his father would inflict.

Coercion means, of course, being forced to do what one would not of himself wish to do. The coercion may take the form of insistence, pressures which cannot well be avoided, or, as is frequent with parents, the threat of a concrete penalty. Thus a choice of evils is offered—do what is commanded or suffer the penalty. The parent knows that his demand is an evil to the child, but he counts that the penalty will be considered the greater evil so that the child will prefer the lesser evil of doing as commanded. The coercion succeeds—at least in this respect—if, as the parent had expected, the child decides that the lesser evil is to do what is commanded.

But there is always the possibility that this effort at coercion may fail, that the child may choose to suffer the penalty rather than do as commanded. Thus Mary might have refused to pick up her toys even though it meant that she could not go out to play with the other little girls. If so, the toys remain on the floor, and Mary wins (so far) over the mother. Or John might have preferred to go fishing even at the expense of the implied punishment. If so, John wins that first round.

Coercion, then, is no sure affair; though usually the coercer wins in the end, perhaps by increasing the threatened penalty. The writer knew of a case in his youth where a child of about two or three years of age was whipped seven times in succession before he would say "Please." In an earlier day parents were advised to "break the child's will," and begin early. John Robinson, pastor of Plymouth congregation, said: "There is in all children (though not alike) a stubbornness and naturall pride which must in the first place be broken and beaten down." (qtd. in 69:76) John Wesley said:

"Break their will that you may save their souls. . . . Begin this great work before they can run alone, before they can speak plainly, or perhaps speak at all." (170:135)

Not only is coercion not sure, but modern thought prefers to avoid the trying situations which arise when the child will not, or pathologically cannot, yield. Of this more later. As soon as we understand that there is no such entity or faculty as "will," then "breaking the will" takes on a different meaning. The will, in any defensible sense, is character consciously and insistently at work; and character is the organized person. Surely no one, once this is understood, will wish to break the character or beat that down.

We have seen from the foregoing that coercion may fail; we have also seen how (when it succeeds) coercion is effected. The next question is as to the learning effects which follow coercion.

LEARNING UNDER COERCION

Let us first consider the learning that the coercion was meant to teach the coerced person. The mother of the little girl said, "You know the rule." She wanted the child to learn to pick up her toys each time as soon as she had finished playing with them, at any rate before she did anything else. That this is usually a good rule, and that the child should build this rule into a working habit, most would agree. The question is as to the efficacy of coercion, all things considered, to teach this habit—and, as we shall presently consider, not at the same time teach undesirable concomitants. But here the question is the efficacy of coercion to build the desired habit, for example in Mary and in John of the illustrations used above. There was a time when practically all school learning took place under coercion, with punishment for failure immediately implied. How does that coercive way of teaching compare with ways of teaching not based on coercion?

We have already seen that always the child learns what he lives, *learns each response* as he sees it and feels it and *accepts* it to live by, and that he learns this response *in the degree that he accepts it*. The three italicized terms and phrases are the crucial ones for us in our consideration of the problem here before us. Each distinct case stands, of course, on its own merits. But two questions must be taken into account. First is the question of just *what* the learner accepts when he acts under compulsion: whether he accepts the course of action in his heart as the thing to do, compelled or no; or whether he accepts it to do only when mother or father is watching or will find out; or whether he so rejects inwardly what is commanded that he is learning *not to do* it whenever he is free to act on his own. Second is the question of *degree* of acceptance. This of course interacts with the *what* just discussed. The *what* tells the content of what is being learned, whether *to do* (and when) or *not to do;* the *degree* tells how strongly this is learned.

What did Mary and John learn? If Mary accepts in her heart that she should always put away her toys (including this time) she is probably learning what the parent wished learned; but we do know that as long as the child acts only under compulsion, she is not accepting very strongly what she does. She is then but slightly learning so to act. But take John. What was he learning? We do not know unless we know what he was thinking and feeling. If he said to himself, "Father is right, I did forget; I didn't mean to and I won't next time," then he is learning in the direction of what the father sought. But suppose John says to himself, "They always think up something for me to do. I don't see why I always have to do something here at home just when the other boys are going off. Next time I'll manage to get out of sight before they stop me." If he thinks this way, as he probably does in view of the father's attitude, he is learning in the opposite direction, learning *not to do* what the father sought. In this second case, John probably was learning *to do* what was required from him only when mother or father was watching, not because he accepted it for himself. It was wiser, more prudential, under the given circumstances so to act. How strongly he was learning so to act would depend on how prudential it seemed to him. To learn to do only when watched and to learn *not to do* represent only different degrees of rejection. John may or may not show openly what he is in his heart learning, but nonetheless in his heart he may be rejecting what is requested of him and so learning definitely *not to do* what the coercion was meant to teach.

Because parents are frequently concerned primarily with only outward behavior and not with the building of inner acceptance and attitudes, many young people learn their morals only to show to parents or to teacher or before other adults who might "tell on them." And such learning carries on into adult life. Thus many men behave one way at home and a quite different way when they go off to the distant city. Or to take another example, a man was recently heard to say: "I never go inside a church. When I was a boy, I had to go every time the bell rang. And I learned *not* to go to church."

We find, then, that as regards the habit and attitude expected from coercion, the result depends on the child's attitude, what he feels and accepts at the time or as he later thinks it over. At best there may result a weak learning in the direction desired by parent or teacher; at worst, there may be a strong learning *not to do* what the parent or teacher had meant to teach. Best results will come when teacher and parent recognize that it is the inner attitude which is strategic and devise their procedures to secure this.

As to learning spelling or grammar and the like under coercion, the argument is essentially the same, but conditions are somewhat different. Most assigned lessons run the risk of being felt as coercion, especially in the degree that they have little meaning or life relevance to the pupil. If a child does accept (see and feel in his heart) that the lesson is pertinent and necessary to him, he will learn it willingly and fruitfully. Or again—but not so fruitfully—some pupils may in a sense like to learn the assignment to show that they know it and so increase their standing in the eyes of others—other pupils or teacher and parents. In both cases strength of learning will depend on the circumstances; it will vary in proportion to the desire to learn and the effort accordingly put forth; and both of these depend on how the item at hand fits into life *as the learner sees it.* And here also coercion may build a distaste for learning and a resistance to all efforts in that direction. It all depends on the responses aroused in the learner and his acceptance of these. As a rule coercion, especially with the young, cuts off rather than increases favorable *internal* urge and so is a poor means of effecting learning.

It may be well to notice the case of such things as music, where many say that at first they had to be made both to take lessons and to practice, but the longer they worked at it the more they liked it; and now they are grateful that their parents did so coerce them into study and practice. This may well be so. One factor at work here was not so likely to enter significantly in the preceding discussion —that of definite musical ability and the satisfaction which comes to the learner when this ability is realized. But the factors otherwise remain the same. Ability or not, in the degree the person does not feel (accept in his heart) that learning the skill is desirable, the accomplishment will be less and the satisfaction from it less or negligible. If native ability is weak and chance of accomplishment accordingly less, then acceptance and satisfaction have less chance of getting in their work. But for the more capable the chance is better that accomplishment achieved will build interest; and this interest means stronger acceptance and so stronger learning. When the child learns that he can play, and so win honest approval by his skill, the whole situation changes. Coercion becomes less necessary. The growing interest and the growing skill mutually bring each other into fuller being and strength. The learner is now pleased at his progress, and may thank his mother that she originally insisted on introducing him to the skill. But the more there is of inner acceptance and satisfaction on the part of the learner himself, the greater the chance of staying with the music long enough to thank the parents who insisted. There have been many cases of children who had sufficient ability, but because of resistances built up and lack of pleasure on their own part have flatly refused to practice or to continue lessons.

We shall later consider at some length how better teaching can accomplish results with very little if any coercion. Building interests is, as we shall see, the key to non-coercive teaching.

CONCOMITANT LEARNINGS ACCOMPANYING COERCION

In the foregoing we have considered how a child may learn to do—though possibly weakly—what he is coerced into doing. But we found that, on the other hand, he may learn, through the building of negative attitudes, *not to do* these things, but to reject them. To see how this comes about let us examine the effect of the concomitant or simultaneous learnings which, as we saw in Chapters XVI and XVII, accompany all conscious experiences.

It was pointed out earlier that the person learns his responses and all his responses, and he learns each *as* it is accepted and *in the degree* it is accepted. We must then ask what responses are likely to follow coercion and how they will be accepted. The answer in each case will depend on the situation. In every case, however, the more coercive a child (or older person) feels a certain treatment to be, the more likely he is to resent it and to have antagonistic thoughts and feelings in connection with it. The more strongly the coercion is felt, the stronger will be the antagonism and resentment, and the more strongly will these be accepted by the person as his ways of thinking and feeling; in other words, the more strongly will they be learned.

Unfortunately, the more unfeeling the parent or teacher, as with the more unwisely conscientious, the more likely is he to indulge in exasperating coercions; and accordingly the more antagonisms are likely to be built. Group workers find that many youth, especially from underprivileged homes, have thus acquired such antagonisms against adults in general that they wish to have as little as possible to do with adults. And from the angle of school education, many youth on leaving high schools given to formal and coercive teaching and management are "through with books."

CONCLUSION

Coercion alone is an extremely doubtful reliance for building positive values, such as the desire to cooperate, a love of reading or of music, or even skill in reading or music. A certain amount of compulsion may, it is true, give a chance for a certain amount of skill to be acquired and even—under fortunate circumstances—for a certain amount of interest to develop. But coercion as a means for developing interest must be recognized as hazardous. The teacher or parent may from certain wider considerations of discipline feel that coercion in a particular case is necessary, but he must understand that internal acceptance is probably not present in the person or persons needing the coercion and that under such circumstances the resulting learning is to that extent not positive. Moreover, coercion, in the degree it is relied on, will likely build antagonistic attitudes, at times very bad attitudes. The use of coercion as a positive aid to teaching is therefore hazardous, even as a beginning measure.

Do we therefore conclude that coercion is never to be used? The answer is no. In certain situations and with certain background matters it seems wise to use compulsion, as for example, with compulsory attendance at school. But even here, if we rely solely on compulsion to make children come to school, we shall not succeed; what goes on in school must commend itself to the learners or legal compulsions will not continue to work. Or again, where certain behavior is necessary because of its effects on the child or on others, it is true that at times, at school or at home, positive coercion may be necessary for the sake of the wider values involved. Even under these circumstances, however, we will be risking our future influence with that child as well as gambling that the attitude built may not have worse effects than the present unsatisfactory behavior. All these factors must be taken into account. The wise person, therefore, will avoid as much as possible the use of coercion. The school management phase of the problem we shall consider later in the chapter on character building.

CHAPTER XX. *Interest: Interest and Learning; Building Interests*

WHY should a philosophy of education concern itself with the question of interest? One answer is immediate and clear: because the quality of life itself is at stake; the factor of interest furnishes the zest of life; without interest life has lost its savor. Bacon was quoted earlier as saying that "the more good things we are interested in, the more ardently we live." Shakespeare says:

> To business that we love, we rise betime
> And go to it with delight.—*Anthony and Cleopatra,*
> Act IV, sc. 4

Rousseau is quoted as saying that "present interest is the grand motive power, the only one which leads with certainty to great results." To have an interest in anything means to have a personal concern with regard to that thing; one has to that extent identified himself with it; he will find himself in pursuing it.

The educator then must have as his guiding aim to help build characters which will feel concern for worthy interests. For this is to enrich the life of the individual and through him of the group. When a pupil feels an interest in an enterprise, his energies and thought are in that degree released. He gives himself to the effort, and success brings pleasure. How to utilize interest in directing the educative process we shall consider in a moment.

THE DOCTRINE OF INTEREST IN THE HISTORY OF AMERICAN EDUCATION

Let us, first, however, go back to a bit of history, in order to see how the conception of interest as a strategic educational resource came into American educational theory. It was the Herbartians who about 1890 brought to America the educational doctrine of interest. As they saw it, the aim of the educative process was character; and for them the conscious aspect of character was the organized aggregate of all one's previous learnings. Biology played little or no part in the thinking of these Herbartians, so that the beginnings of these learnings seem now a bit obscure; but by the time the child started to school a beginning had already been made and was then in fair process. Each succeeding learning step, as the Herbartians saw it, followed a set pattern. Each new step, in order to be learned, had to be taken, through understanding and acceptance, into a body of related learning previously acquired. It was by means of this older aggregate of related learnings that the new was understood and accepted.

This existing (older) body of related learnings—related, that is, to the particular new item which was to be learned—the Herbartians called an "apperceptive mass" (or "perceiving aggregate," the basis on which one noted and sized up and understood the new). As the new was being understood and accepted by the learner, the process of taking it in and fitting it into the existing apperceptive mass not only added this new item to the existing mass, but would, in the course of the process, otherwise modify that mass so as the better to assimilate the new. Thus would a somewhat revised apperceptive mass result from each successive instance of learning.

Learning was the name given to this process by which the old takes in the new to make it part of itself. And this learning would not take place unless the new was closely enough related to the old for the old to be able and willing, as it were, to understand and accept the new and fit it into itself. This readiness and willingness on the part of the old thus to take in the new was what the Herbartians called *interest.* As they saw it, there could be no learning without some prior interest on the part of the old for the new, some "inviting in" of the new, as it were, by the old as needed for its own completion. We can now see how essentially interrelated for the Herbartians were these three terms, *apperceptive mass*, *learning*, and *interest.*

While the term *apperceptive mass* had up to that time no place in the English language, the words *learn* and *interest* had been here all the time. And some American educators were highly suspicious of this new use of these terms; especially were they suspicious of this new doctrine of interest. To say that a child could not learn anything except as there was a prior basis of interest already for that thing would condemn most of the (Alexandrian) teaching then in vogue. It is probable, too, that certain American proponents of the new interest doctrine exaggerated, even distorted, the aspect of "making things interesting." At any rate, it was from this angle of making things interesting that the opponents hit back. These opponents, led by William T. Harris, (1835–1909), said that always to make things interesting was to pamper the child and thus to "spoil" him; that it took effort to make strength grow, that character without effort would be flabby. And these objecting educators made it clear that they proposed to make their pupils put forth effort; if necessary they would coerce them into effort in order, as it were, to save their souls.

So two opposed schools of educational theory faced each other, the school of Interest and the school of Effort. Whether the Herbartian position was fully understood by all the proponents of Interest may, as has been suggested, be doubted; certainly the Effort school did not understand the Herbartian position, and possibly not its own in its fullness.

In 1895 Professor John Dewey in an epoch-making address, *Interest as Related to Will*,* placed the discussion on a new biological basis and cleared the conflict by showing how both sides had agreed on a common educational error; namely, that what is to be learned is to be chosen in advance as admittedly alien to the self of the learner; that the interest group (at least as understood by their opponents), accepted this error and said the thing to do was to make the subject-matter item interesting so that the young would take it in; that the effort group, accepting the same error, said the thing to do was, not to interest the child into learning the subject matter, but to coerce him into it, make him put forth effort to learn it. Professor Dewey proceeded to point out that, in all active behavior, interest and effort are not opposed to each other, but instead are strictly complementary, that the stronger the interest one feels, the greater the effort he will put forth; that, in fact, the interest felt is but the first and inner phase of an ordinary instance

* Published in 1896 by the Herbartian Society. This address was later revised and published under the title *Interest and Effort in Education* (Boston, Houghton, Mifflin and Co., 1913).

of purposeful activity, with effort exactly the outer attempt to effect what the interest wished. So that instead of there being a conflict between interest and effort, both belonged normally and properly together as the inner and outer aspects of one normal on-going activity.

Dewey went still further, and attacked what we have called the Alexandrian position of first choosing subject matter and then teaching it, by the following assertion:

> The genuine principle of interest is the principle of the recognized identity of the fact tc be learned, or the action proposed, with the growing self; that it lies in the direction of the agent's own growth, and is, therefore, imperiously demanded if the agent is to be himself. . . . Genuine interest is the accompaniment of the identification, through action, of the self with some object or idea, because of the necessity of that object or idea for the maintenance of a self-initiated activity (48:7, 14).

The real question thus becomes how to utilize this doctrine of natural interest, which is certainly present as a kind of spring to perpetual motion in all healthy children, so that it may prove constructively educative; we wish to know how to utilize this natural interest so as to get away from the deadening effects of choosing subject matter merely in terms of subject-matter logic and without reference to the child himself; we wish to know how to harness the child's interest to his own good. This cluster of questions will be considered in a moment under the head of building interests and also discussed more fully in later chapters on teaching and curriculum-making.

INTEREST AND LEARNING

It is no exaggeration to say that the doctrine of interest is strategically crucial in the learning theory herein being developed in answer to the philosophical demands of Part I. When William T. Harris opposed the doctrine of interest, as we saw above, he was in a true sense speaking for the older (Alexandrian) psychology of learning. This doctrine of interest is certainly a crucial issue between new and old, and is so felt on both sides. But, more deeply analyzed, the crucial difference is probably a difference in awareness of the significance of interest. From the point of view of the new, to seek interest on the part of the learner is, on the one hand, to respect the learner as a person and at the same time to utilize the biological dynamic in the learning process. Thus to utilize interest in education seems psychologically essential alike to democracy and to the good life.

How interest is related to learning was implicit in the previous discussions on set, readiness and learning, on purpose and learning, and (negatively) on coercion and learning. In the light of those discussions we now attack directly the problems of interest and learning and of building interests.

The word *interest* is commonly used in two senses. In the first sense—as *an* interest—it represents an abiding possibility of set and readiness along a given line; in the second sense the term represents the abiding interest at work, functioning. This is seen of course whenever the abiding interest is stirred to activity. As an example of the first sense, we may say of a certain man that his chief non-vocational interests are golf and first editions; we mean by this that he has an abiding tendency toward golf, to get interested in golf affairs, to give himself interestedly at appropriate times to playing golf; and, on the other score, that he collects first editions of books, is ready at almost any time to hear about new possibilities of finding and possessing yet more first editions. Interest in this sense, as an abiding trait, is sometimes innate—as with the tendency to eat—but more often acquired—as with the interest for golf or for first editions. In this sense, as a trait, it will much of the time be quiet, inactive, merely latent, but still capable of being evoked at suitable times and by suitable stimuli. Also, though latent at most times, it carries always a readiness, a readier sensitivity for anything bearing on golf or first editions, than would be true if the person were not possessed of these interests.

Interest in the second sense, interest reaching out and actively at work, helps learning in exactly the same way as do set and readiness or purpose. Active interest gives a set for working at the object of interest; it therefore gives greater importance to this object and greater readiness to hear about it, to note in any way what promises to foster its welfare. The individual, because of his interest, will then the more readily accept new ideas or new significances or new skills that favor the interest; and thus more readily accepting them, he will more strongly learn them than would be true, other things being equal, of a person not so interested. Everything previously stated to the effect that learning is helped by purpose or by set and readiness holds true then for interest. The importance of this doctrine of interest for an effective educative process is very, very great.

SIGNIFICANCE OF ACQUIRING NEW INTERESTS

As was implied earlier, possibly the most strategic of all kinds of learning is the building of new interests. In adding a new interest the individual has by so much added to life and its content. Life is more fun. The person has found something to grip him, a new concern, a new cause which he now wishes to pursue. He sees and feels in a new way; he has added a new facet to his self; he is more of a person.

In addition the individual has acquired new possibilities of dynamic behavior. When the new interest has sufficiently taken hold, appropriate action may be expected. If new knowledge or new techniques are needed, the interest supplies the drive to go after them.

In these various ways do interests implement the aims and procedures of education. As the aim of the new education is to build character, so are interests the *constituent elements* of character. In other words, the aim of education is to build in the individual interests in the desirable aspects of the life good to live—interests which will make life happier and more meaningful and more constructive for him, interests which will foster a good life for all. That all this is quite different from memorizing the content of assigned lessons in order to pass examinations needs hardly to be mentioned.

What we wish, then, differs from acquiring facts, subject-matter content. These, even though thoroughly learned, function chiefly or only when something else calls them into play. Rather do we wish to build interests—abiding internal centers of dynamic which stay on in the person, which as attitudes reach out for opportunity to get into play, which as abiding concerns activate themselves.

STRENGTHENING INTERESTS: MAKING THEM MORE EFFECTIVE

From the foregoing discussion we conclude that the contribution to life made by an interest will depend both on the quality of the interest (discussed elsewhere) and on its strength. The stronger such an interest is, the more effective will be its part in life. How to strengthen a weak interest becomes, then, an important question. The answer is found in the principles of learning previously discussed. An interest in anything is, psychologically, a way of responding to that thing, a way of responding favorably to what promises to promote it. Since interest, then, is a way of responding, the principles laid down earlier for learning a response hold for learning—upbuilding, strengthening—an interest.

In order to learn anything we have to respond that way, and the more strongly we accept that thing as our way of responding (under those circumstances) the stronger we learn it, and the more it will tend thereafter to assert its place within our life process. If I as teacher wish my pupils to strengthen their interest along any given line—say in courtesy to each other, or in improving the neighborhood, or in constructive discussion, or in reading or in writing letters, or in the proper treatment of the new pupils recently come from a strange land—then I start with their present interest in that thing and get something going along that line. What they undertake must not be too easy, or it won't challenge them; it must not be too hard, or they may get discouraged and cease trying. I will wish them to succeed, for "nothing succeeds like success." I will hope that others will see and approve what they do; for that will help them to accept this enterprise more strongly as a thing to do, as a line of interest to pursue. Also, I will hope, as they work at the enterprise, not only that they will succeed with it but that it will open up, grow under their treatment, that they will see more and other things to do by way of development of it. For that will mean prolonged and beckoning interest in this type of activity. In this way the interest will grow stronger by the reinforcement of other interests which it absorbs into itself.

The foregoing means, for each pupil engaged, that in the degree to which he lives and develops this particular interest, even though it be weak at first, the more it will come to have a definite working place in his life, the more surely he will build that interest as one of his abiding traits. And the richer the possibilities of the interest for growth in content as he proceeds, the greater the probability of its continuing to challenge him.

As one illustration of the development of an interest the writer recalls how as a thirteen-year-old boy in a small village he took over the care of the family's chickens. He had looked forward to this as a sign of growth and responsibility when his older brother should leave for college, but knew very little beyond the mere routine of care. The consequent study of different breeds of fowl to find the one most suitable for all the pertinent conditions gave him an interest along this line which developed in strength and content as he worked at it and lasted for years after he had given up the task itself. As part of this effort he wished, but did not get, some Pekin ducks to experiment with. Over sixty years have passed since then, but a clear remnant of that interest in Pekin ducks still remains. If only someone had capitalized this interest to guide it along further lines the personal development would have been much greater.

A school illustration of the growth of interests and what came from them is given by Ellsworth Collings in his *Experiment with a Project Curriculum.* (28:54–64) In this rural school an intermediate group of pupils, aged nine, ten, and eleven, were stimulated by the illness of two of their mates with typhoid to study why Mr. Smith's family had such frequent cases of typhoid. After some study they concluded that many flies and unscreened windows and doors furnished the explanation. This developed two further interests: whether typhoid was the most prevalent disease of the community, and how to help Mr. Smith combat his flies. The first interest led to a systematic survey of the illnesses in all the homes of the community, with the conclusion that typhoid, while not the most prevalent of all, was the most prevalent of the more serious diseases. The second interest led to a visit to (apparently) the only home of the community that had screens in its doors and windows and then to a report to Mr. Smith with suggestions as to how he could make his own screens at small cost. Some two years later when this school was surveyed in comparison with the surrounding rural schools it was found that the "per cent of parents of [this] district" stricken with disease had decreased 20 per cent while for the other communities the decrease was only 4 per cent. It was further found that now 41 per cent of the homes in the vicinity of this school had screens in doors and windows in comparison with only 6 per cent for homes near other schools.

BUILDING NEW INTERESTS

But how make an interest grow when there is no beginning interest to start with? The fact of indirect or mediated interests is our answer. This opens so many doors that with intelligent insight and wise guidance it can easily lead to almost any significant interest we can reasonably seek.

Each pupil and each class already has an appreciable range of interests. These differ in quality from low to high. Suppose under teacher guidance a better one of these is chosen to pursue. The pupils are already interested along this line, and they chose this as their next activity. As they plan how to pursue this interest, the planning itself—if successfully managed—will increase the present active interest. The planning maps out the various steps necessary for the pursuit of this effort. Now enters the indirect or mediated interest. Suppose these children have decided to put on a play of their own, then each thing felt to be necessary for the success of the play will take on, in good measure, the same interest they feel in the play itself and its success. Suppose the question of spotlights is introduced, then in the degree that the pupils feel spotlights to be necessary for the success of the play will they now take an interest in spotlights.

To be sure, not all pupils will be equally interested in the further study of spotlights. But it is still true that in the degree any pupil is interested in the success of the play and feels spotlights to be a necessary part of the play and its success, in that degree will he feel an interest in spotlights as such even though he never felt it before. How can spotlights help the success of the presentation? How, then, must they be managed? Which one of the class had better see to getting the spotlight arrangements made? And who can best manage the actual spotting? Each of these questions takes on its interest from the original interest in the play, and directs attention to lines never before thought about.

We now see how to begin building an interest in an area where no present interest is felt. The answer is that we cannot start with that interest. We can, however, watch our chances and in time, by wise guidance, get some interesting activity going which will bring in the new and desired line as means to the present interest as end. In other words, the means will take on somewhat of the main interest aimed at. While this interest is thus mediately and indirectly active, we start, as was explained above, by building up this indirect interest into a direct interest that can and will stand on its own feet.

This way of finding the right chance cannot be planned on any precise calendar basis, so that in November in the seventh grade we shall start to build an interest in the United Nations. Interests cannot be built on such a calendar program. True, after some years of experience and observation, we can prophesy that with ten-year-olds in this school we can reasonably expect certain lines of interest to materialize. But we cannot be certain just when (by watching dates) it is best to start, still less can we tell from one set of life conditions (as in this particular school) when to start in another school of widely different conditions.

But if we are reasonably intelligent and persistent, we can hope in time, by proper guidance, to find opportunity to build the more important interests desirable for a good quality of living in our present civilization. That interests can be built around the customary subject-matter areas is obvious—our heritage is rich in such possibilities. But to build interests in these rich potentialities requires procedures quite different from the ordinary memorizing and examination passing. It means to give specific attention as *aim* to finding worth-while areas which *take hold* of the individual, areas which can be fanned into greater appeal and at the same time develop, as the pupil works at them, into richer and more meaningful possibilities.* The writer can give from his own experience a further illustration of interest building. As a graduate student in 1908 he was asked to choose a term paper from a given list of problems. One of the listed problems was the question as to the first school in the American colonies, whether among the Massachusetts Puritans or among the New Netherland Dutch. The fact that the writer had an ancestor among the founding settlers of New Netherland gave him a mild opening interest in this problem.

* It has frequently been charged that the new education is satisfied to let children do anything they like so long as it is interesting to them; even, to cite a common caricature, "to jump out of the window" if it pleases them. But no one living, the author believes, holds that interests—of children or adults—are of equal value, of equal profit to life and living, or that children should do "anything they please," or only "what they please." It is, however, important to note the differences in learning (and living) when learning proceeds on a basis of internal dynamic and when it proceeds on a basis of external "motivation" only.

So he chose this problem and set to work, hoping in a way to prove priority for the Dutch. As he studied the problem, he found data, then recently uncovered, which proved conclusively that the date of 1633 previously claimed for the first Dutch school was wrong, and that 1638 was the proper date. This gave the 1636 Massachusetts school the priority; but that was a small matter in comparison to the credit for correcting the educational historians. The study connected with this grew until there resulted a considerable book on *The Dutch Schools of New Netherland and Colonial New York*, with so great an interest in the topic that now nearly forty years later any slight hint of new or pertinent data on this subject wakens an immediate and insistent response. It is indeed true that interests can be and are built in the lives of every normal person.

CERTAIN PRACTICAL FACTORS AFFECTING INTEREST-BUILDING

School administrators must understand the significance of interest-building for education and life and see to it that regulations are not set up which thwart this primary aim of building interests. For example, requirements of definite fixed-in-advance subject matter to be learned in specified years may make impossible the proper attention to aims other than this subject matter, even the aim of fostering interest in some appealing aspects of the subject matter itself; and if, as frequently happens, the subject matter is difficult or almost impossible to relate to life as children live it, the probability is even greater that the children will build apathy or resistance to it, when they might instead be getting a great deal of the same subject matter pleasantly and effectively by working at interests meaningful to them.

Again, a fixed daily program will in all likelihood prevent the following up of interests, of individuals or groups, while these are "hot," and also prevent trips outside the school which could provide firsthand observation and open up new possibilities of interests.

Or, again, examinations set by others than the teacher may put a premium on conforming to routine requirements and distract attention from the children; or results of such tests used in a way to compare this teacher with others may lead to focus on examination-passing by the children, and so to making a good showing for the teacher herself instead of furthering the growth of the children as their potentialities allow. Against all such administrative ways of managing, the primacy of interest-building must control.

Teachers, too, must always have in mind, as a criterion of their efforts, the interests which are being built by their pupils. They should ask themselves, first, whether any interest in the real sense of abiding dynamic and content of personality is being built; second, as regards interests now present in the pupils, how to guide these appropriately as to direction and strength. They will find it helpful to have in mind a variety of interests appropriate for pupils at this period in their development, in order to help locate suitable ones appealing to these particular pupils and work to get these effectively started. It cannot be too much stressed that active, worthy interests are both the aim and the strategic promise of all else that pupils need. These two aims, then, pretty well sum up a teacher's work: first, to help pupils build progressively the proper interests; and second, to capitalize these interests to procure the other values needed in the all-round education.

CHAPTER XXI. *Philosophy of Educational Method*

WHEREVER competing values are at stake, philosophizing is essential if the choice is to be wise. It is essential, moreover, in the degree that the values at stake are significant for the lives of people. And certainly this is the case as regards educational method, where human beings are being formed—their character, their personality, the quality of their living.

Many so far have not seen that the foregoing is true. Many teachers, for example, have counted that the sole problem of method is how best to teach one's school subject, and that there is no need to philosophize about how to teach physics or Latin. Another group, though not so numerous as formerly, have held that the findings of science constitute the only basis for decisions regarding education; philosophizing has nothing to do with it. Indeed, one extreme member of this group told us some twenty-five years ago that "philosophy is passing—has already all but passed." This man thought Behaviorism would supplant, and so destroy, philosophy; but he bet on the wrong horse.

HOW CHOICE OF METHOD INVOLVES PHILOSOPHIZING: A PRELIMINARY VIEW

As indicated above, whenever competing values are significantly at stake, philosophizing is required. It is contended here that in every teaching-learning situation competing values are involved. To see that this is true let us look at certain considerations arising out of previous discussions and from certain well-known facts of social history.

1. The first consideration has to do with the character building always going on within each child. As pointed out earlier, con-

comitant learnings are an inherent part of every significant life experience, and these accumulate into character traits. The specific character traits built will depend on the kind of responses the learner makes to the life situations he meets. For example, the responses the child makes to those in authority over him are extremely significant. One kind of treatment from parent or teacher will provoke antagonism in the child; another kind will foster servile docility; still another will encourage creative initiative. These varied possibilities are crucial to the problem of method here under consideration.

2. A second consideration follows immediately from what has just been said. There are many ways to run schools and teach children. Each different way of teaching evokes its correlative type of responses in pupils and accordingly fosters its correlative type of concomitant learnings and resulting character traits. The possibility of these different character effects calls for careful choice of method.

3. Still another consideration is the kind of society the school is to prepare for: the democratic or some other kind of society. Different kinds of society—if they are to perpetuate themselves—need different types of education, and each kind of society tends to choose (or devise) a type suited to its ends. A feudalistic class society, for example, will wish to inculcate (literally, *stamp in*) in the young of all classes a reverential conformity to established customs. It will accordingly order all its young to instant obedience, and will employ methods which repress any tendency to variation; and at the same time it will so manage, through its ways of dealing, that the upper and lowers classes will also be learning, respectively, upper and lower class attitudes and manners with respect to each other. As opposed to all such practices, the truly democratic society will seek growth toward self-determination and creative initiative in all, with equal and simultaneous stress on social responsibility and respect for the rights and feelings of others. Thus does one's philosophy of life and society enter inevitably into the management of the teaching process.

THE BROAD PROBLEM OF METHOD

We have seen that methods used in teaching may lead toward or away from desirable character learnings, toward or away from democratic living. How to manage in view of these different possibilities so as to bring about desirable concomitant learnings in the young and so help them to build desirable character traits—that is what is here called the *broad problem of method* to distinguish it from the older *narrow problem of method.* The narrow problem of method is concerned solely with the subject to be taught and how best to manage that restricted type of teaching. The broad problem of method is concerned with the many values at stake—subject-matter values, attitudes and character being built, effects in democratic living, community values, and all other matters inherent in the particular situation. To decide how to deal with a child in the light of these various values does indeed call for philosophizing—weighing the values at stake and searching to find what deeper insight would indicate as the wisest course to follow.

It was stated above that the type of education desired by any society for its young will vary according to the aims, values, philosophy of that society. This applies equally to every society. It is well known that societies differ and that types of education differ. The point to be noted here is that the differences are due to differences in philosophy, differences in what the society values and wishes for itself and so for its young. If the society, for example, desires docility and conformity, traits which all autocrats, all dictators, have sought to develop in the young, it will set up an education accordingly. If the society desires something quite different—for example, thoughtfulness, self-directiveness, personal freedom, free play of intelligence—it will set up a type of education designed to produce these ends.

We saw these differences illustrated in Chapter I in the educational systems of Jefferson and Napoleon. Some further instances from history will now be examined to show in more detail the operation of the philosophy of the society. In some cases the philosophy was more consciously held, in others less so. But, conscious or not, it entered essentially and inevitably into every intentional guiding of the educative process. Intentional guiding of the young always favors one result in preference to others. There is no escape. This is true of every person who follows a conscious aim as he guides the learning process of another person—at any level or under any conditions, whether he be parent, teacher, educational statesman, religious leader, feudal lord, slave holder, despot, führer. Every person, then, who guides others, whether he is aware of it or not, is following some pattern of thinking, is working toward some end result which he believes to be right and proper to prevail in life. And this pattern, when inclusively worked out, fits into, is consistent with—in fact constitutes—a philosophy of life and of society. This is true even though the one who guides may never have formulated the philosophy and may hardly recognize it when it is described to him. Whoever guides educatively inevitably guides, in the degree of his consistency, in conformity with some kind or degree of philosophy of life, of society.

SOME ILLUSTRATIONS FROM HISTORY

The earliest illustrations concern not so much the school as they do education through life, the life of the whole group including the young. The first instances are perhaps the best known in all secular history, Sparta and Athens. Comparison of these two clearly shows how inclusive and fundamentally differing aims embodied in customs and institutions led, educatively, to fundamentally different types of life and character.

For the Spartans the one inclusive all-directing aim was might of arms, and this to two ends: one that they be ready to resist outside aggression, the other that they (the Dorian conquerors), as a conscious minority, should hold under control by force the conquered Perioeci and Helots who far outnumbered them. To effect this aim of might the Spartans were compelled, first, to live as an armed camp, always ready in both mind and might to fight when the need should arise; and, second, to enforce the exact opposite in both respects in the Perioeci and the Helots. To be thus ready in mind and might, all male Spartans, from childhood to the end of the military service age, lived in common barracks, giving practically all thought and effort to this one inclusive concern.

As to the education of their youth, "their chief concern was to make them good subjects, and to teach them to endure pain and conquer in battle." "They had one coat to serve them a year. . . with but little acquaintance of baths and ointments." (Plutarch) Note that even their own Spartan young were to be "subjects," not initiating, creative citizens. They were to lend themselves to militaristic ends, to fit into the military hierarchy. In barrack-life and other training they learned proficiency in arms, endurance, self-sacrifice, ruthlessness in pursuit of Spartan ends. There is no record that they learned anything of thoughtfulness or cultivation of the finer aspects of life.

The Helots were to learn to accept their slave status and to fit into it. To break the spirit of the Helots they were subjected by the Spartans to barbarous cruelty and degradation; they must wear a distinctive dress of sheepskin clothes and dogskin cap, and every year they were whipped to make them remember their servile state. And when their numbers grew threatening, secret bands of Spartans went about with daggers to assassinate the most outstanding of them. On one occasion two thousand Helots, who had fought bravely for Sparta, were encouraged to come forward, ostensibly to receive new liberties but really to be most treacherously murdered.

The two groups, then, Spartans and Helots, were to be educated to different ends, each the correlative of the other and each the correlative of the Spartan philosophy. The Spartans knew clearly what they wanted in the sense of being conscious of their ends. Whether they were *critically* conscious, in the sense of having thoughtfully and critically examined the ends to which their lives were being directed, is another matter. Whether they had so examined their culture it is, at this date, not fruitful to pursue; though the fact of the recurrence of their pattern—of philosophy, values, and, in the large, way of life and procedures—in our day in Nazi Germany and Fascist Italy makes it more than an academic question to ask whether such a life, even though the dominant group wishes it, is sufficiently constructive even for their own ends.

What such treatment made of life for the Helots need not be asked. The question answers itself. But what was the result for Sparta? In the words of the *Chambers Encyclopedia* (1879) the result was "a race of stern, cruel, resolute, rude, and narrow-minded warriors, capable of momentary self-sacrificing patriotism (as in the story of the 300 who fell at Thermopylae), but utterly destitute of the capacity for adopting or appreciating a permanently noble or wise policy." The history of Sparta forces the final question: Must not any culture fail, as Sparta failed, when it tries to found itself on fundamental injustice and, in order to succeed in this, ignores in essence the spiritual possibilities of life? In fact, had not Athens cared for better things, the very memory of Sparta would long since have passed from the earth.

A greater contrast, as to both aim and content of life, could hardly be found between two self-governing civilizations than that between Sparta and Athens. In Sparta, as we have just seen, the dominating aim was strength of arms, both to hold in subjection the Perioeci and the Helots and to protect Sparta against any outer threat of aggression. This single aim dominated Spartan life and defined its content, with the results stated above. The individual life was sacrificed to preparation for war, and the individual himself, as a result, was intellectually and morally maimed.

In Athens the dominating aim, so far as a single phrase may state it, was to effect the rich, free life of the individual. For the first time in history, it seems fair to assert, the state was devised to develop human personality. *Citizens* enjoyed political freedom, social equality, and full opportunity to exercise individual initiative. They also exercised, in high degree, both moral responsibility and moral freedom. The Irish classical scholar Mahaffy (1839–1919) asserts explicitly: "No modern theology has taught higher and purer moral notions than those of Aeschylus and his school, developed afterwards by Plato and Aristotle." In addition, the intellectual development centering in Athens constitutes probably the greatest single creative advance yet achieved by man. An earlier day had achieved language and selfhood, a later day achieved conscious inductive science, but Greece (Athens) achieved the critical mind. It was these people who first in the world strove to live by reason. In esthetics, too, these Greeks led the world, their actual achievement, in the judgment of many, never having been equaled. As a kind of summation we may quote from Pericles (Thucydides), who doubtless meant to contrast Athens with Sparta: " . . . We prefer to meet danger with a light heart but without laborious training. . . . When the hour comes we can be as brave as those who never allow themselves to rest. For we are lovers of the beautiful, yet simple in our tastes, and we cultivate the mind without loss of manliness. . . . The great impediment to action is, in our opinion, not discussion, but the want of that knowledge which is gained by discussion preparatory to action. For we have a peculiar power of thinking before we act and of acting too, whereas other men are courageous from ignorance but hesitate upon reflection."

In accordance with this philosophy of life the education in Athens was totally different from education in Sparta. Athens had a large slave group (at that period this was universally accepted and till many centuries later hardly questioned) and what is here said applies not to total population, but to the Athenian citizen group, in contrast with the Spartan "citizen" group. To the Athenian, the aim of education was, as Plato put it, "to make the child yearn to be a good citizen"; and the aim of the citizen life in Athens was to live the rich life of the free citizen, to live "beautifully" and morally–richly, fully, courteously, constructively, critically. Accordingly, from the first the boy was treated as a person and was helped to build a love of learning and of finding the best way to live. As soon as he was old enough he was encouraged to mingle with adults as they carried on their full and stirring life–in the market place, at the games, at banquets, at the theater–and discussed, inquired, questioned, pursued knowledge, always in as searching and creative a spirit as possible and always with reference to improvement of individual living and group living. The way of life of the Athenians was the expression of their philosophy and their education was the correlative of that philosophy–to build in the young a love of life and of learning, inquiry, search for truth, for more adequate and satisfying ways of living. The Athenians, too, knew clearly what they wanted, they were conscious of the ends they wished to seek; but–in contrast with the Spartans–they examined their ends and values critically, searchingly, unceasingly. If better ends or means could be found they wished to find them.

We are contrasting these two civilizations as the outgrowth of two strongly contrasted types of cultural aims and correlative institutional arrangements. Whitehead was quoted earlier as asserting that "a community life is a mode of eliciting values for the people concerned" and that "the worth of any social system depends on the value experience it promotes among individual human beings." If he had constructed these two sentences to state the results of the contrast that we have here been studying he could hardly have chosen more effective wording. Note in conclusion the very strong statement from Sir Henry Maine (1822–1888) as to the outcome from this Athenian way of living: "Except the blind forces of Nature, nothing moves in this world which is not Greek in its origin." We cannot, of course, agree that nothing has been done creatively since the day of classical Greece, but we must admit that the mode of critical thinking there achieved underlies all later Western thought. And it was Athens, not Sparta, that led. No other nation in history has equaled the intellectual cultivation and achievement of Athenian Greece, or, in all probability, the richness and satisfyingness of living.

If space sufficed, we might next consider the Middle Ages to show how feudal society was by both circumstance and intent designed to fit (educate) each class and distinctive group appropriately and abidingly into its prearranged status; but instead it may be better to use illustrations nearer in time to our current problems.

After the Middle Ages and before the Industrial Revolution, most of Europe was rather clearly divided into two groups, the upper classes who owned the property and the lower classes who did the manual and lesser work. The upper classes managed all public affairs and wished to remain thus in control. To effect this it seemed wise to keep the lower classes ignorant and contented. Bernard Mandeville, writing in England about 1722 against a growing vogue of charity schools for the poor, states clearly this upper class attitude:

> There is no need for any Learning at all for the meanest Ranks of mankind; Their Business is to Labour not to Think; Their Duty is to do what they are commanded, to fill up the most servile Posts, and to perform the lowest Offices and Drudgeries of Life for the conveniency of their Superiors, and common Nature gives them knowledge enough for this purpose. . . .
>
> The more a shepherd, a plowman, or any other peasant, knows of the World . . . the less fit will he be to go through the fatigues and hardships of it with cheerfulness and content. . . .
>
> Men who are to remain and end their days in a laborious, tiresome, and painful station of life, the sooner they are put upon it at first, the more patiently will they submit to it forever after (107:I:216).

Many are the questions raised by this quotation. Only one point, however, here concerns us—that this upper-class spokesman saw the threat to vested privilege arising from what we have called concomitant learning if "the meanest ranks" should through more schooling see more of "the world," more of the easier and happier world of the privileged. Seeing this, they would compare it with their "laborious, tiresome, and painful station of life"; and comparing, they would question the justice of the arrangement; no longer would they submit to their "fatigues and hardships" with "cheerfulness and content." Mandeville was right as to his fears; exactly what he feared and opposed would have happened. Mandeville was not the only one to be apprehensive. Even so fine a man as Dr. Samuel Johnson said toward the close of that same century: "Those born to poverty and drudgery should not be deprived by an improper education of the opiate of ignorance."

And from this same period two further quotations support the same general position, one an old English folk rime, the other from the Church of England prayer book:

> God bless the squire and his relations
> And keep us in our proper stations.

At Confirmation this question was asked, "What is thy duty toward thy neighbour?" These words, among others, follow in answer: "To order myself lowly and reverently to all my betters." In each the intent seems plain to make the underprivileged accept their inferior status by persuading them that God himself sanctioned and approved the existing feudalistic social arrangements.

What sort of education resulted from this outlook, this philosophy? First of all there was still the necessity, as in earlier centuries, to educate upper and lower groups in diverse ways—the one to enjoy higher status and the other to accept lower status, and accordingly to build in each the appropriate attitudes toward themselves, toward each other, and toward life. One type of education, then, for the privileged few, another type for the many. For the few the learning offered was something "precious," chiefly the ancient classics—which now fitted only into the life of the scholar or the gentleman of leisure—plus gentlemanly sports. For the laboring people the aim was, as indicated, to fit them into "their proper stations" of subservience, ignorance, and docility.

The issue in this is not the psychology involved, whether different ways of treating people can build different attitudes—that is clear and beyond question: within limits it can be done. What is at issue is the philosophy of life involved: Is it right to treat people as Mandeville and his group wished? Is it right to degrade the many that the few may live better?

Without being exactly aware of what they did, these selfish upper-class people, in fighting to preserve their special privileges, were in fact fighting off a movement then only feebly beginning, the movement we now call democracy. As a class movement, this was too far off even to consider; but justice and right have unexpected paths of approach. The religious path offered the possibilities of a new day. As James Russell Lowell said, "Puritanism, believing itself quick with the seed of religious liberty, laid, without knowing it, the egg of democracy." (125:C:168, Jan., 1865)

New England Puritanism, as we saw in Chapter x, was far too narrow a base on which to found modern democracy. But the religious movement of which it was part did have a far-reaching effect not only in stressing individual liberty, as Lowell suggests, but also in helping to bring about modern popular education. In order to give the individual soul a more direct approach to his God, Luther and Calvin and Knox advocated teaching everybody to read. So that various parts of Germany (from 1524 onwards), Scotland (from 1616), the Netherlands (from 1568), and New England (from 1647) led the world in universal elementary education. By contrast, England, under stronger class influence, appropriated its first public money for elementary education only in 1832 (after the Reform Bill of that year), but did not really accept the task until 1870 and not fully until 1902. Similarly, France began public education only in 1833 (following the Revolution of 1830). The common attitude, opposed to such changes, was voiced by Emperor Francis of Austria about 1822 that "obedient subjects are more desirable than enlightened citizens." And again in all of this, the essential issue is not a psychological one of whether people can learn obedience and conformity rather than enlightenment. It is instead a philosophic problem of which we *should* wish them to learn, of what from the standpoint of ethics we *should* foster in life.

Were the people of the period conscious of the ends toward which their devices tended? As the quotations indicate, some were very clearly so; they intended exactly what they sought. Many others, however, in this now increasingly complex society, only acquiesced in the customary outlook; they had never thought about differences in values and ends and were not really aware of the ends they were furthering or the effects of the means employed. Thus in all likelihood many fine-spirited people, teachers and others, innocently contributed to evil effects they never dreamed of.

Modern Prussia gives a further most interesting instance of the contrasted uses of conscious education. After the defeat at Jena in 1806 by Napoleon, Prussia determined to take itself in hand. As part of the effort, a deputation of young teachers were sent on Fichte's advice to study under Pestalozzi (1746–1827). At that time Pestalozzi was by all odds the foremost liberal educator in the world, aglow with the idea of helping the lower classes to improve their living. These young Prussians, fired with enthusiasm, came back to establish the new type of school. Acting on Pestalozzi's pattern, they developed schools in which the children were to understand what they were studying, to learn about life around them, and to use their own minds, to learn what they could use in their living. All this was in contrast to practice elsewhere—the customary memorization without understanding, the mere use of words, the verbalization of content with little or no meaning for life. Elementary schools, with teachers' seminaries (normal schools) to match the new point of view, were established to become models for the rest of the world. Our country and France were particularly impressed. Horace Mann (1796–1859) and others made reports on these Prussian schools, both elementary and normal, which greatly influenced educational development in our country.

The result in Prussia of this better type of Volksschule, along with other factors, was an eventual stirring of the people to the liberal Revolution of 1848, at first an apparent success but in the end a failure. When Frederick William IV with his army finally put down the Revolution, he called before him the masters of the teacher seminaries and told them explicitly: "You and you alone are to blame for all the misery which the last year [i.e., the Revolution of 1848] has brought upon Prussia. . . . This sham education, strutting about like a peacock, has always been odious to me." (132:245*f.*) In remaking these normal schools he reduced everything "taught hitherto under the theory of education, didactics, anthropology, or psychology" to simple instruction in "school knowledge." "Christian knowledge" was similarly reduced to "Instruction in the Catechism," which was based on a "compendium fully containing everything the future teacher had to know, word for word." In other words, teachers were thenceforth not to be educated to think, nor were they to educate their pupils to think; for, as the king said, "The man who thinks too much is dangerous." (132:248)

As we reflect upon this Revolution of 1848 and what might have come out of it, the words of Whittier come to mind:

> Of all sad words of tongue or pen
> The saddest are these: 'It might have been.'—*Maud Muller*, st. 53

It is indeed sad to contemplate how near in 1848 a liberal outlook came to controlling Prussia, and how, by comparison, out of that failure and reactionary victory came eventually Bismarck and the Prussian policy of war for national aggrandizement. For from these in the main, it seems fair to assert, resulted the wars of 1864, 1866, 1870, 1914, and 1939.

As for the devitalized elementary schools of Prussia after 1849, Dr. Thomas Alexander reported from his study of them made just before World War I: "I had visited over three hundred classes in the *Volksschulen* in Prussia before I heard a question from a pupil or a request for an explanation of a question which had occurred to him." (5:277) Docility of thinking had been desired and docility of thinking had been achieved. Students of the problem say that the same type of teaching holds largely up to now in the Volksschule. Pupils, parents, and teachers have been trained against thinking for themselves.

During the nineteenth century and largely up to World War I the common type of school in Europe was a class-structured school system of elementary schools leading up to trade schools for the masses, with the secondary school and the university designed for the leaders of society. Following von Humboldt's ideal for the University of Berlin there was in the universities usually a very high degree of freedom of teaching and study, but both the elementary and the secondary schools tended to make docile followers. Acquisition of subject matter on the Alexandrian model was the rule. The vast majority of the population seemed relatively content with the lower caste system provided for them. In the secondary school, attended by a very small per cent of the age population, scholarship standards were high, but the stress was on acquisition, with practically no chance given for creative thinking. E. A. Ross calls such a caste society "pyramidal" and thus explains its choice of this educational system:

> For a pyramidal society . . . the safest and best education is one that wears away the energy of youth in mental gymnastics, directs the glance toward the past, cultivates the memory rather than the reason, gives polish rather than power, encourages acquiescence rather than inquiry, and teaches to versify rather than to think (140:172).

Thus did a feudal outlook control the philosophy of education for most of the Continent until well into the twentieth century; and the end of that control is not yet everywhere in sight.

THE RESULTING EDUCATIONAL METHOD FOR OUR COUNTRY

What meaning has the foregoing for our country? What aims and procedures does the philosophy of our country indicate? Are our present aims and methods suited to our philosophy? How many teachers are critically conscious of the social aims they wish to foster? How many have examined critically their methods and procedures in terms of these aims? One of the most fundamental human theses is that man, by taking thought, can influence life. In other words we can, to appreciable degree, move toward what we fundamentally wish if enough people are sufficiently conscious of their social aims and of the relation between these aims and the methods appropriate to achieve them.

In this country most people believe that democracy constitutes the most promising philosophy of life, that the well-being of the people and the development of people to their fullest potentialities is the aim we wish to promote.

If democracy is to be our choice, then we must decide whether to take as our primary aim for schools the imparting of knowledge, in and of itself, or the building of character of the kind demanded by democratic living—inclusive character, the individual's inclusive tendencies to behavior in personal living and in group living, as a person and as a citizen. This character must be of the kind to make the individual self-directing (rather than ruled from above, as we have seen in the many historic instances); it must be sensitive to the needs of people and of society and to obligation to act on these needs (as opposed to the selfish insensitivity found in many educated people through the ages); it must be informed, intelligent, thoughtful (rather than blind to the surrounding world and incompetent to think about it and cope with it on any intelligent basis). This means, of course, that the individual must have knowledge, much knowledge, but knowledge to be used primarily for better thinking and consequent better acting (not primarily to satisfy a social scale index or for mere personal enjoyment).

As a means of implementing these aims the theory of learning earlier discussed (in Chapter XVII) was adopted: that we learn what we live. This theory of learning makes very specific demands on education, demands for which the older aims for education made no adequate provision. If we wish our pupils to build the kind of character indicated above, they must *live* what they are to learn and so build it into character. Specifically, each trait that is to be learned—such as initiative or self-direction or responsibility or moral self-control or disposition to inquire, to think for one's self—has to be *lived*. Suppose, for example, we wish to develop self-directiveness, initiative, an inquiring mind, as befits democracy (in contrast with the accepting and swallowing which fits authoritarianism); then must the children live accordingly. To teach pupils *not* to question, *not* to take initiative, *not* to engage in self-directiveness, the old school had the perfect answer; it was set up to keep the pupil memorizing subject matter set out for him, memorizing ideas, content, supplied by others; it was set up so that the teacher did all the directing that was done. Those pupils *lived* what *they* were to learn—docility, no initiative. But if we wish pupils to learn democratic traits they must live quite different experiences. This means with regard to developing, say, self-directiveness, initiative, and thinking for one's self, that (i) the learner must have many experiences in which he faces an actual life situation calling for such behavior on his part; that (ii) the learner must feel in his heart that the situation calls for such behavior by him; that (iii) feeling the call, he responds thus self-directively, with initiative and critical-thinking, himself accepting this specific type of response as his way of meeting the situation. As the learner thus lives this instance of democratic life, he will *to that extent* learn to think for himself, use initiative, direct his own behavior responsibly. If he makes this choice often enough, consciously enough, and under sufficiently varied conditions, each time with inner acceptance on his part of the desirability of so acting, he will cumulatively build these traits of responsibility as an integral part of his character. A similar discussion holds for the other desirable traits.

From the considerations just discussed *the school must*, as previously stated, *be conceived as a place of living*, the best living we know how to develop. Whatever we do, those in school will learn what they live. If they live on a poor and meager level, they will learn that meager content and build poor characters accordingly. The school must thus seek to provide the finest and richest living possible at each succeeding stage of the child's life. It was this provision for living which was explicitly denied by the "silent, motionless, memorizing" school in vogue, according to Thorndike, until a generation or so ago. And that school, he thought, "repressed and thwarted and deformed mental growth." (158:187) It was even more the growth along social, moral, and emotional lines that was repressed, thwarted, and deformed, thus denying the all-round efficient growth that we need.

This theory holds most definitely for learning to behave democratically. If democracy is to rule in our society, youth must be learning democracy in preparation; and this means that they must live democracy in home and school and community. This is no call to identify democracy with voting, that the children at home or in school are to vote on questions along with parents and teachers, with the decision going to the majority vote. No, children and youth are immature; some questions are beyond their present range of judgment. If this young child wishes to climb up on a chair, I as parent must decide whether a fall would damage him. If a fall would only pain him and not damage him, I had better let him climb and learn, perhaps by painful experience, how to climb. If, however, the child wishes to climb in and out of an upper window, a fall would be too dangerous to risk; I must stop him. But we who are in control at any stage must provide ample education for initiative and intelligent self-control. At each succeeding stage of development we see that there are areas within which those under our care may exercise self-direction. We accordingly give them opportunity and responsibility in these areas and then help them learn to exercise these wisely. And as quickly as feasible we increase the area of self-direction.

Subsequent chapters will deal with the implementing of this discussion in teaching and curriculum-making. As regards the problem of method, the effect of properly chosen teaching-learning method on the building of constructive, inclusive character for personal and social living—this, it seems fair to assert, more nearly constitutes the essence of the education of the young than any other part or aspect of school work. Gaining knowledge and skills are important, even necessary, but building inclusive character of the kind to live democratically is the crux of it all; this "living and learning method," properly used, does so build character; and it does this far and away better than can any amount of mere knowledge as such. It is character, informed, intelligent character, that counts in behavior; and behavior is what counts in life.

It was with such considerations as the foregoing in mind that the title of this chapter was chosen. Method—in one direction or another—is inherently and inevitably educative, each different type after its kind. We who teach must know this and must accordingly study the character effects of the several possible types of method. Then, in the light of the best philosophy of life we can find or make, we must so manage our school method that, through the character it helps to build, it shall as well as possible realize the finest life we can conceive. How well will the effort succeed? Not perfectly. In so complex a thing as life we never succeed perfectly. We must do the best we can.

CHAPTER XXII. *Teaching: Its Function and Its Proper Procedures*

TEACHING exists to help learning take place, to help proper and effective learning come into active existence. But, as we considered earlier, different kinds of teaching affect the young differently. The different responses thus called forth bring about different kinds and degrees of learning and consequently develop different kinds of character. Teachers must know these things and in the light of them select, from all the differing ways of dealing with the young, those that promise the best possible learning and character effects.

In Part I we recognized certain fundamental ideals demanded by democracy: respect for personality, the life good to live, a morality determined by its social effects. Good teaching will keep these ideals and aims in mind as it evaluates the probable learning effects from the different ways of teaching; for learning effects, as suggested above, must be counted good in the degree that they foster character making for the recognized ideals of life. Similarly in Part II we have discussed the choice of a learning process best suited to bring about the desired type of character and the effect thereon of purpose, interest, and coercion. We also have seen that the significance of concomitant learning for character development is strategic, even crucial. All these factors on the process side good teaching will keep in mind as it chooses procedures for guiding the learning process to the best possible character effects.

In fact, to help guide the teaching process aright is the basic service which this book seeks to perform: so to guide teaching that through its resulting learning the most desirable character may be developed. The specific purpose of the book is thus to help develop a philosophy of education more adequate to the guidance of childhood and youth along the educational road. In this sense, all the preceding discussions of the book focus upon and converge in this and the other succeeding chapters especially devoted to the teaching function. The following chapters will in the main develop other aspects of the teaching process not adequately considered in this chapter.

PRESENT AND FORMER TEACHING CONTRASTED

The aim and process of teaching as now best conceived differ significantly from what formerly prevailed—and, as we have seen, still largely prevail in high school and college. In the older outlook the almost exclusive teaching emphasis was, and is, on imparting knowledge. In the newer outlook the emphasis is on helping to develop desirable, inclusive character and personality, with especial regard to the dynamic quality of such a character. Does the person being taught grow as a total personality? Does he grow, as a result of the teaching, more sensitive to possibilities inherent in life around him so as to seize upon these fruitfully? Does he grow more disposed to take hold effectively to bring things to pass? Is he more persistent in his efforts? Does he meanwhile become practically better informed and wiser about such matters as he works with? Does he become more creative in his approach? Does he grow in the tendency to consider thoughtfully what he does? Has he adequate knowledge from present and past with which so to consider?

And while he is developing these individual dynamic qualities, does he at the same time become more effectively social? Is he growing more sensitive to the rights and feelings of others affected by his acts? Does he, in his social decisions, take more and more ever better into account? Does he increasingly subordinate his mere personal wishes to the proper demands of the wider situation? Does he increasingly subordinate present and merely personal impulses to the long-run good of all? Is he more disposed to work for the common good?

But there is still more to be expected from effective teaching. While these individual and social traits are being developed, is the learner growing more emotionally secure within? Is he developing better internal poise? Is he developing an inclusive outlook on life, with adequate standards and ideals and such breadth of view that he can avoid emotional upsets as he fits his inevitable trials and disappointments into one consistent and defensible life pattern? It is such all-round personality development along with this inclusive outlook upon life that good teaching must seek.

From these considerations it becomes clear that, whatever may be right in specialized education, proper teaching in "general education" must aim first and primarily at character and personality. As John Ruskin said:

> Education does not mean teaching people what they do not know. It means teaching them to behave as they do not [otherwise] behave (142:142).

And it is this emphasis on behaving that this book wishes to uphold. Teaching (in the "general education" sense) must aim at behavior, at behaving according to the fullest meanings of the good life. But between the teaching and its ultimate desired behavior there are—as we saw in the discussions on the learning process—the three intermediate processes of (i) living, (ii) consequent learning, and (iii) consequent character building. One can hope to realize the type of behavior ultimately desired only as the learner develops an appropriate and reliable character. To build this character, the learner has to live the proper content of that character until that content, through the process we call learning, becomes fixed in the structure we call character. Thus teaching, in order to develop the ultimately desirable behavior, must aim directly at helping the growing person to live—live, in his own true life and out of the promptings of his own heart, a content and a quality which, being learned precisely by living it, will build the needed character. Teaching thus aims both immediately and ultimately at living: *immediately* at present actual living and behaving of a quality and content fit to be built as structure into character; mediately at character of a kind that promises the kind of behavior and living *ultimately* desired.

What has just been said is exactly what the older teaching failed either to consider or do. If questioned, that older teaching would probably have answered that learning the proper content will lead to proper behaving. But that older type of learning was a learning *about* behaving, not itself a behaving. That older school did not anywhere within its teaching or learning processes include a living of the things to be learned; it had no place in its procedure for responding with the character traits it extolled, any more than catechism learning includes behaving the religion upheld in the catechism. The practice and behavior provided in the older school was of the mind only; in fact, of memory mainly. The learner emphatically was not expected, in order to learn anything, to behave that way. Behaving as such had no place within that old-time educative process. Its total school procedure not only ignored such behaving, it actually denied and forbade it in school time. Single seats, screwed down in rows, explicit rules against pupil conferring, nothing expected except learning and reciting what the book said —this procedure effectively excludes adequate character-building behavior. On this older view, the necessary behaving was left to chance; the school as school accepted for it no responsibility.

Such necessary behavior was not all that the older school ignored. As we have previously seen, it ignored the fact of many simultaneous or concomitant learnings. Specifically, it ignored the often, apparently usual, antagonistic responses that its coercive assignments provoked in the learners. Until modern procedures began to affect the school processes, a pronounced attitude on the part of pupils and students was opposition to school and teachers. The history of this is long extended. Lucian in the second century A.D. said: "Whom the gods hate they make schoolmasters." Shakespeare told us, as we all know, of the "whining school boy . . . creeping like a snail unwillingly to school." (*As You Like It*, II, vii, 145) John Brinsley, writing about the same time, said of pupils in the Latin grammar schools that the work was so distasteful they "would rather desire to goe to any base trade or drudgery than to be schollers." (16:21) At a later date Henry Adams (1838–1918) said (2:12) that he never knew a boy of his generation to like a [school]master." John Todd, a popular writer on schools in 1854, said that "one of the most useful books" would be one on "college rebellions"; the only difficulty was that it "would be too voluminous." He gives a specific instance of college boys blowing up "five of the outbuildings with ten pounds of powder." (164:247*ff*.) Prime Minister Stanley Baldwin said in 1924 to the London Teachers' Association: "Forty years ago all the king's horses and the king's men would have failed to have drawn me into . . . a company of schoolmasters. . . . I am credibly informed that the children today actually enjoy going to school. . . . You have succeeded in working a miracle which would have been incredible in my younger days." (161: Dec. 6, 1924) Daniel A. Prescott, one of our best current students of the problem, says that "children are sure to protest or to attempt compensatory behavior when a classroom situation frustrates or fails to meet a basic personality need." (136:126) It is out of such situations that bad concomitants are built. These the older school way did much to develop, but nothing consciously to avert or remedy. In fact, its teaching theory ignored the whole matter.

In conclusion as regards old vs. new, the old saw the business of a teacher, in the words of one of them, as that of a conveyor of knowledge to a yet unoccupied mind. The process was authoritarian. Assignments were made under penalty, expressed or implied, for failure to "learn" what was assigned. The test of successful learning was the ability to give back on demand in recitation or examination what had originally been assigned. This Alexandrian procedure, as said above, reduced the human organism to mind, and mind largely to memory. The ultimate trust and hope was that the child would remember until the need should arise and would then act appropriately. Such a procedure ignored the facts (i) that character, which is essential to behavior, is built only by behaving, that if a child is to learn anything and so build it into character, he has to live that way, has to respond that way in behaving; (ii) that the organism acts as a whole so that the child, during all active behavior, learns under all the heads of his responding, with such sideline learnings as habits, attitudes, skills always in process; and (iii) that these sideline learnings are possibly the most significant of all the determinants of character.

THE NEW: TEACHING AS GUIDING

The test of teaching is the learning it begets. Since each pupil learns what he lives and builds that at once into character, the quality of that pupil's living becomes the essential and crucial aim immediately before the teacher. If the child's living is of low quality, that low quality is fixed as an abiding characteristic. Thus, as said above, teaching exists to encourage and develop a good quality of living, living of a quality fit to be built into abiding character.

These words "encourage and develop" are used here advisedly. As has been said, "the quality of mercy is not strained," that is, high quality of response comes not by constraint and punishment; so here, the quality of good and proper and rich living is "not strained." It comes not by constraint or punishment. Parents and teachers cannot force it, cannot force a quality of living that counts for best learning purposes; for each one learns *what he accepts in his own heart* as his way of living; and he learns this, moreover, *as* he accepts it. Coercion can, as has been discussed, be properly used as an emergency measure to prevent outward behavior along a hurtful line; but even this is attended by risks. For any coercion tends to provoke antagonistic thoughts and feelings which, in their turn, tend to be accepted by the one who undergoes and so feels the coercion. It thus remains true that parents and teachers are limited to encouragement and guidance as the principal positive and constructive means of character development.

What a "policy of encouragement" means we saw in part in the chapter on interest and learning, especially in the part on developing interests. How this works in the elementary school and in the common core work in the secondary school is suggested under the following seven heads. In college and secondary school departmental work, a somewhat different discussion would be necessary.

1. The teacher (or parent or group leader) must have as an essential part of his professional equipment what is here called a "map of values." Such a map consists of his hopes, aims, ideals—all the criticized values which he will use as aims in guiding those under his care. Everyone has in fact such a "map," for the most part not consciously organized, but still there to call on as needed. Teachers should aim continually at keeping this aggregate of values alive and growing. Specifically it should include all that the teacher could hope for pupils (or students) to learn so as to make life for them as rich and fine as possible. Along with each such included item should go some notion of how to help pupils or students to live it so as to learn it.

2. We must start where the learner is; for the new can be learned only as the learner already has in mind and heart enough relationship between new and old to make him see, understand, value, and wish (accept) the new. From another angle (saying the same thing in different words) we must enlist the pupil's active interest in what he is to do and learn, else he will lack the set and readiness we have previously seen as necessary to best learning.

We start thus where the learner is, either by seizing upon some promising interest already stirred and active or by stimulating some latent interest. Let it be noted, emphatically, that in teaching at its best we do not first choose subject matter, then ask how to make it interesting. This, as we saw in Chapter xx, is to miss the crucial bearing of interest on learning. In a true sense the point here being made is once again the fundamental difference between the old and the new. The old first chooses its subject matter and then proceeds to teach it, either by sugar-coating it (often thinking that thus "making it interesting" is what the new upholds) or by assigning it under penalty. The new, as we have been saying, starts where the child is so as to capitalize on the child's personally directed activity springing from his real interest.

What is being now discussed concerns primarily the "general education" of the elementary school, the "core" work of the secondary school (elsewhere discussed), and in lesser degree the "general education" of the college. In such work it will be necessary for the teacher, before the term opens, to give most serious thought to planning what is to be done and what will, hopefully, be learned. In this planning the primary stress will be on character and personality development, which will be consciously sought all the time. An essential part of this development will include certain areas of thought and attitude, with their supporting knowledge and skills, as demanded by the good life of the individual and of society. When any of these areas come into the class work will depend upon the specific growth and development of class activities, which cannot be fixed by the calendar; but the wise teacher will all the while be guiding the class work so that the important areas will not be disregarded or unduly postponed.

Each learner has a stock of interests, most of which at any given moment are lying dormant. We can conceive all of these interests arranged on a scale, those promising best for behavior and learning at the top; those that are least promising or promise the worst, at the bottom. The teacher, having in mind the whole class and the promising lines of activity for this age of pupil, may on the first school day have lying around the room specimens of art or craft work or books used or made in previous years, or may start discussion of what the summer vacation yielded, or ask openly for suggestions as to the line of work the class should take up first. A list of resulting suggestions may be written on the board for the pupils to discuss.

3. The next step will be to choose the most promising of these suggestions. The teacher will have in mind (i) possible values to be sought (as found in his own "map" of values); (ii) the more promising lines of activity apparently open to the class; and (iii) some conception of the class interests and aptitudes (as disclosed by its previous record). Pupils and teachers will together consider the several items on the list, the teacher aiming to get from the class as intelligent and responsible discussion as possible. To meet the needs of the situation the activity chosen should (i) rank high in class interest; (ii) be difficult enough to challenge the best efforts of the pupils, but not so difficult as to threaten discouragement; (iii) rank high in promising valuable items on the "map" of values, items that fit well with the past and lead well into the future. Of these requirements, the first, the presence of active interest, is a necessary condition, but not of itself a sufficient condition. Granted a reasonably high interest and challenge, the teacher will seek the third factor, the highest possible promise of values. Preferably, however, it will be the pupils who finally choose; for their cordial commitment is necessary, particularly at first, for any good hope of success.

4. This matter of commitment is so important as to demand emphasis. The individual pupil inevitably will learn in the degree that he himself accepts the activity or the enterprise or the experience undertaken. The teacher will accordingly work, through the process of group discussion and choice, to get the individual learners and the class as a whole committed as wholeheartedly as possible to the activity chosen.

5. In connection with what has just been said, almost a variant of its outworking, the teacher will from start to finish encourage in the pupils as high a degree of self-directed responsible acting on thinking as it is possible to get. To feel one's self acting responsibly and so helping to create what is being done, and to do this in a way to deserve respect from others, is one of the very keenest of satisfactions; it almost certainly means strong commitment, and the learning that goes on in connection with it is likely to be very strong.

6. As the correlative of the last two items, learner commitment and responsible learner creating, the teacher's task becomes, as

previously stated, primarily that of guidance. The teacher will, to be sure, help the individual learner or the class as may prove necessary, but always so as to help the learners to help themselves. It is what pupils do of themselves that brings the best learning results, both in direct learning and in concomitant learnings. We can thus say, paradoxically, that the teacher's aim is to give as little help as possible, that is, to give the least degree of direct help consistent with the best personal work on the part of the pupils. (Even so the modern teacher works harder and continually helps pupils more than did the old type of teacher.)

7. In accordance with the foregoing, the teacher will as well as possible help the learners at each stage of the effort: (i) to initiate the activity (to form or choose the purpose); (ii) to plan how to carry the activity forward; (iii) to execute the plan; (iv) to evaluate progress during the activity and the result at the end. While all this is going forward the teacher will also (v) encourage the learners to think up and note suggestions or new leads for other and further work; (vi) help them to formulate these suggestions both for clarification of thinking and for later recall and possible use (perhaps writing them in a book or on the board for future reference); (vii) help pupils criticize their thinking en route or at the close, as may seem wise; and finally (viii) look back over the whole process to pick up and fix important kinds of learning involved as well as draw lessons for the future from both successes and failures.

INDOCTRINATION

In Chapter IX on "Respect for Personality" there was included a discussion on education *vs.* indoctrination. The present discussion carries the matter further.

In an earlier day practically everybody counted education to be exactly the process of fixing in the child what his guiding elders thought he should think and believe. The Alexandrian outlook proceeded rather consistently on this theory; and contending Western religions always have been—many still are—strong in practicing this kind of indoctrination. Under the influence of the Enlightenment and democracy, we began to see that to fix beliefs indelibly in the child is to enslave him to his teachers. In the degree that the child cannot, or will not, later re-examine such early implanted beliefs is he unable to think and decide for himself. He has then, in very fact, been enslaved. And any teaching which does not expect to upbuild in him, as fast as he can manage it, the tendency and capacity to think for himself is to that extent failing to respect his personality and, specifically, to help him build the character needed for democracy. No teaching is ethically defensible which knowingly and willingly hides from any person any matter within his grasp which will help him to think more adequately. So to teach is to fail of the ethical and democratic demand to treat the individual always as end and never as means merely.

That there are difficulties here cannot be denied. As parent or teacher I have to make decisions for those under my care on matters that they are not yet ready to decide, but which—in some sense at least—cannot now be postponed. Some writers have therefore said that all education begins in indoctrination and can only gradually move away from it. It is true I have to make temporary decisions such that my educative methods at that point may, to the undiscerning, look like indoctrination. Perhaps at the very beginning the difference is in intent only: "Do I or do I not mean by my teaching or other influence to indoctrinate this growing person to think as I decide?" If I mean not to indoctrinate him I shall, as soon and as fast as I can, explain the why of what I think and do, and let him in—as far as he is able—on the reasoning process at work. So from the earliest possible moment I bring him to expect reasoning to control both my thinking and his. And the older he gets, the more I shall expect him to act on reason and the more I shall help him to seek out the pertinent reasons and learn to obey them.

Curiously enough, some claim one exception to the rule against indoctrination, namely, that we must indoctrinate democracy, that this is too important a belief to leave to the choice of the immature mind. If we admit this one exception, then we must, in logical consistency, admit any other doctrine that the teacher or parent counts too important to endanger. It would be safer to say that democracy is so important that it must be understood and used intelligently and not applied blindly; and if it is to be used intelligently, it has to be learned thoughtfully. The practical answer would seem to be (i) that before our pupils can understand reasons for believing in democracy, we must none the less help them to live democratically, else they will not learn to respect each other or learn how to discuss intelligently, decide cooperatively, or execute with shared responsibility; but also (ii) we must, as soon and as fast as we reasonably can, have them consider the arguments for and against democracy and increasingly decide, each one for himself, on the merits of the case as he sees it, what he shall believe. To "indoctrinate in democracy" is both a contradiction of terms and a denial of the very democracy we profess to be teaching.

To this argument, academic freedom is, for older youth, the corollary. Jefferson's two statements previously quoted well present the fundamental position here:

> I have sworn on the altar of God eternal hostility to every form of tyranny over the human mind. (Letter to Benjamin Rush, September 23, 1800)
>
> This institution [the University of Virginia] will be based upon the illimitable freedom of the human mind. For here we are not afraid to follow truth wherever it may lead, nor to tolerate error so long as reason is left free to combat it. (Letter to William Roscoe, December 27, 1820)

The statement put forth in 1941 by the N.E.A. Committee on Academic Freedom, also quoted earlier, seems to say well what is more precisely needed here:

> Academic freedom is . . . in essence the freedom to study and learn, and to share with others the results of study. . . . It is thus intended for the good of students and of the public rather than for the personal satisfaction of instructors. . . . This practice of intelligent study is necessary to the proper working of democracy as of no other kind of society. . . . The justification of academic freedom lies . . . in its inclusive and unbiased study. If any teacher, by the way in which he teaches, either wilfully or carelessly permits some bias or prejudice of his own, or even the inappropriate expression of his reasoned convictions, persistently to mar the process of fairminded study on the part of those studying under him, he is to that extent damaging these students and in that same degree manifesting his unfitness to teach (116:4, 5, 8).

For the contrary view we have a D.A.R. official saying in 1923 that "academic freedom of speech has no place in school, where the youth of the country are taught and their unformed minds are developed." (33:57, 270) And in keeping with this view an official of the Daughters of Colonial Wars in 1940 spoke in condemnation of a certain textbook then in common use, complaining that this book "tried to give the child an unbiased viewpoint instead of teaching him real Americanism." And she went on to say that "all the old histories taught 'my country, right or wrong'; that's the point of view we want our children to adopt." (134: Feb. 20, 1940)

These latter quotations bring us to the second of our two problems:

CONTROVERSIAL ISSUES

Certain conservatively minded people are strongly opposed to having the schools consider any really controversial issue. Some of this opposition springs from resistance to change and some from the fact that in the Alexandrian type of school these opponents had attended all teaching was authoritarian; the school set out dogmatically in the book or lecture what the pupil or student should learn. Consequently they can hardly conceive any other way of teaching.

There are to be sure various kinds and degrees of controversial issues. Some matters, like the multiplication table, are fixed beyond any question. All such we shall teach unquestioningly, but understandingly; for it is intelligent persons and responsible citizens we wish to develop. There are other matters which school children have to take pretty much on authority, as the spelling of words and the facts of distant geography and history; but even in these, especially in such matters as geography and history, the wise teacher will seek as far as possible to make the pupils increasingly independent of the teacher and, especially, independent of particular books, by helping them learn to use various reference sources. For again, what we wish is to cultivate critical study and independence of thought.

There are still other matters which once were controversial but are now no longer so considered among competent teachers. We can conceive these once controversial issues on a scale: at one end, those most widely accepted by communities; and at the other end, those least accepted. As teachers we should deal differently with the different parts of the scale according to the temper of the community on the matter. Evolution, for example, is in some backward communities still rejected. In such a community we may decide to treat it as a truly controversial issue rather than as a matter no longer so taken (in this sense) by scientists. Instances of these once controversial issues are quite interesting. The earth we now know to be round, but it was not always so counted, as the Bible speaks of the "four corners of the earth." (Rev. 7:1) That the earth rotates daily on its axis and revolves annually about the sun was denied in 1633 by a group of church doctors: "the doctrine that the earth is neither the center of the universe nor immovable, but moves even with a daily rotation, is absurd." (qtd. in 133:20) That the earth is older than 4004 B.C. was once denounced—and still is by some—as antagonistic to revealed religion.

Finally we come to the really controversial issues, those issues concerning which a considerable number of thoughtful people hold contrary opinions. Most very live current problems may be expected to fall under this head. Some of these are so important that pupils or students of the proper age and development should study them, partly to understand the different positions taken and reasons therefor in order that each may form his own opinion, partly to learn, in the only possible way, how to deal intelligently with as yet unsolved social problems. In the degree that a problem is properly to be counted controversial will the true teacher refuse to let his own position prevent those under him from thinking fairly for themselves regarding it. The teacher must know that on such issues he is a public servant. He is not there to gain converts to his partisan cause; he is there to help those under his care learn to think reliably for themselves.

In the matter of controversial issues teachers must understand that, however or whatever they teach or refuse to teach, they are none the less necessarily promoting one kind of society in preference to all others. If they refuse to teach controversial issues in any effective way, they are thereby educating either to uncritical acceptance or to uncritical rejection of new proposals; either of these is an education to inferior citizenship. That many people prefer youth to be so educated is only too true. The true teacher, however, cannot yield to such a reactionary attitude; he must educate those under his care to the best independent thinking he and they can effect. To this conclusion we seem inexorably led by our study of the philosophy of educative method and democratic teaching.

CHAPTER XXIII. *Curriculum-Making*

THE discussion of curriculum-making as a separate topic at this point has certain disadvantages. Much of what needs to be said has, by implication, been given in preceding chapters. Nevertheless the topic must be treated on its own; it cannot be left simply to the implicit references previously given.

CONTRAST BETWEEN THE OLD AND THE NEW CURRICULUMS

In what follows it is the general curriculum of the elementary and secondary school that is primarily under consideration, the curriculum expected of all to prepare pupils generally for all-round living. The theory of this is quite different from that of a curriculum of specialization, as for example the professional curriculum preparing for law or medicine or engineering. The elementary school is given exclusively to general education. The secondary school, as will appear later, desirably includes both general education and specialization, and so also should the liberal arts college. As will later be brought out, the curriculum in general education is distinctively psychological in its construction, that is, it is specifically concerned with the needs of the individual learner; the specialized curriculum pays more attention to a fixed and logically organized body of subject matter. This distinction, however, belongs to the new view of education; the old curriculum was consistently "logical" both in content and arrangement.

The old outlook, as has already many times been stated, assumed that education consists precisely of the acquisition of preformulated knowledge presented to the learner either in textbooks or orally by teachers (or parents). It further assumed that acquiring the assigned content would build the desired mind in the learner. On the basis of these assumptions the old curriculum is *the requisite content of knowledge arranged systematically (logically) for progressive acquisition.*

This content was assigned for compulsory acquisition in the elementary and secondary schools, typically by "lessons," less often by lectures. Success of acquisition was tested, again typically, by daily recitations and at longer intervals by examinations; and success consisted, again typically, in ability to give back in words what had originally been assigned. The period primarily in mind for the actual functioning of the education was the life after school days were over.

As has been suggested in previous discussions, this older conception of education limits man and his educated life predominantly if not solely to intellect and counts memory as the primary means to intellect building. Behavior as such (beyond the behavior of proper study and recitation, obedience to teacher, and noninterference with the school process) had no place in this curriculum. Specifically, no consideration whatever was given to the conception of "the whole child"; nor to the conception of cumulative concomitant learnings, still less to the fact that these learnings are always in process, for good or ill. As against the various modern demands for the exercise of behavior traits in order to build them as traits into character, the assumption of this older intellectual memory type of curriculum was that if a child learned the right formulated statement, he would at the right time obey that statement and perform its content—a supposition everybody has always known to be in great measure fallacious if not entirely so.

The new curriculum outlook is so different from that just described that many brought up on the old, and familiar only with it, simply cannot understand the new. The way these people misconceive the new, and the absurd caricatures of it they readily accept and report, seem incredible. On bases discussed at length in previous chapters, the new curriculum makes at least six assumptions:

1. Education for the purpose here in mind is the effort of the adults in charge to guide the child's development and learning so that he may grow up to take his proper place in society and himself live the good life.

2. Each learns what he lives as he accepts it to live by, and he learns it in the degree that he accepts and lives it.

3. What one learns he builds, in corresponding degree, at once into character.

4. "The whole child" is always involved, and many cumulative, concomitant learnings are always in process.

5. From these various considerations the school should be *a place of living*, living of the kind to help build the desirable all-round character to serve the all-round good life.

6. Teaching exists to cultivate this quality of living in those taught.

With these presuppositions before us, *the new curriculum becomes the total living of the child so far as the school can influence it or should take responsibility for developing it.*

By contrasting the two italicized definitions of the old and the new curriculums we see the essential difference. The old consists of a systematically arranged *content of formulated knowledge* which the learner is to acquire. The new consists of *the total living of the child* so far as the school can affect it, living of a kind to build the desired all-round character. The *old* seeks *knowledge* and vaguely hopes that somehow from this the good life will ultimately follow; the *new* seeks as its *immediate* aim the *highest and finest quality of living* that it can help effect, relying on the fact that if children do really live *this quality of life* they will in that degree build the *same quality of character;* for they do learn what they live and what is truly learned is therein built into character.

MAKING THE NEW CURRICULUM

If the desirable type of curriculum is desirable living, how is this curriculum made? Who makes it? What respective parts in this process belong to teacher and to pupils? And how do superintendent and supervisor get into the picture?

These questions (except the last one) were substantially answered in the preceding chapter on teaching. The parts played by superintendent and supervisor we postpone to the next chapter. A further study of the parts played by teacher and pupils may help to make the theory clearer.

Since the pupils will learn what *they* live as *they* accept it and *in the degree* they accept and live it, it is *their* living which is to be sought, the finest quality of living that teachers and pupils together can effect—create or contrive or develop. But if the pupils are to learn the fine qualities of this living—and build these into character—they have to *live* precisely these fine qualities and *accept them in their hearts* to live by; and besides, the degree in which these qualities are learned and so built into character will depend on the degree in which they are accepted and lived.

These things mean *negatively* that the teacher cannot simply order or direct the living. In that case it would not be truly lived by the pupils, especially as to the finer qualities. Imagine a teacher ordering a pupil to appreciate a poem or a Beethoven symphony or a Rembrandt and threatening him with punishment if he does not appreciate it by next week! Or similarly ordering a pupil to regret *in his heart* having struck the first blow in a school fight! We have previously seen that, as "the quality of mercy is not strained" [comes not by constraint], so is it with all fine qualities of living, all spiritual matters, whether under the head of the true or the beautiful or the good. These have to come as real responses from the learner's own soul to something seen and felt by the learner himself. To say this is of course to state the rub, the issue, the crux, of the new curriculum-building: How can teachers bring to pass such finer living?

These same things mean *positively* that the teacher's proper work is to help pupils so live that the living itself will call for, evoke, and include a fine quality of responses. Such responses, being felt, accepted, lived, will be built into character.

And here is where the constructive part is played by the pupils, the teacher guiding. Suppose some actual situation confronts the class which allows, but does not of itself require, a fine quality as the next step. The teacher asks for proposals as to the next step. Some boy makes a proposal of lower quality than the teacher thinks need prevail. The teacher will then ask whether other proposals are suggested. Perhaps among others comes a proposal the teacher thinks would be a real advance, but not too great an advance for the class to take. The teacher directs attention to the several proposals and calls for a discussion as to their merits. In the discussion the merits of each proposal are considered, with the teacher helping as needed, but with the pupils encouraged to do as much as the quality of class thinking and background allows. During the discussion the teacher can himself make proposals, and if nothing worthy had come from the pupils he should do so. If a proper educational atmosphere has been built, pupils should be accustomed to speak freely and to feel both openness to teacher suggestions and values and at the same time the full conviction that the teacher will not dogmatically insist on his own point of view.

Suppose the question at issue is one on which teacher judgment should prevail, in that the proposal favored by the pupils is not feasible for them at their stage of advancement or for some other reason is clearly undesirable; then the teacher should recognize this and say so. But the teacher should be extremely sensitive to the danger of letting his authority too often be the deciding consideration, lest pupils build resistance to his suggestions and fail to build the disposition and ability themselves to make thoughtful choices. So far as possible the teacher will try to make the merits of the better proposals—those of the pupils or his own—so to stand out that they will be seen and supported—at least by the more discerning and better disposed pupils and by as many of the others as feasible. The class then, on the whole, will probably accept the better proposal, from whatever source, on its true merits as they themselves now see and appreciate these merits. What the teacher does here is not to load the dice in favor of some particular choice he had arbitrarily or partisanly made or even in favor of a choice that, in common with practically all good and discerning adults, he believes good. No, what he does is to try to get the merits discussed and to get a proposal accepted which both pupils and teacher could stand back of, with the pupils participating in such way as to feel the choice was made on its merits and to learn to do thoughtful choosing.

Can we say that this procedure gives the final and absolutely reliable answer as to the best proposal? The answer of course is no. But the procedure does help to develop a technique of group discussion and decision; such procedures not only will help these young people in school but also will help them in later life to confer with other adults in reaching as reliable answers as human ingenuity can effect. And the class can feel that it made the decision. This commits them and helps the further effort and its resulting learning.

What has just been said does not mean that the teacher may not properly take a positive part in the class enterprise. When necessary he will make definite proposals and defend them. In fact, he will at times be compelled to make the decision and enforce it. But the statement above was intended to bring out two points: one, that strongest learning results in the degree that the pupils themselves think and decide responsibly; two, that learning how to think together, exchange ideas, make choices, is a very important type of learning—in fact in the long run may be the most important to come from their experience. If the teacher is satisfied that the *direction* of the learning now in process is good and sound, he will leave as much of the responsibility to the pupils as he reasonably can. But, he will intervene by question or other guidance to help the pupils think and decide better than they could do without this intervention. As a rule, with any enterprise of the pupils it is more important that they think responsibly than that the particular enterprise as such attain the highest measure of objective success. It is the pupil responses, their thinking and feeling, that build character; and these rather than success of the specific enterprise must constitute the teacher's principal aim.

LEARNING CONTENT BY LIVING IT

As some read the preceding paragraphs, they will say, "Well, it all sounds fine, but it does not tell me what I want to know. Certainly you do wish your pupils to learn to read and write, to know arithmetic and geography and history. How can a beginning child *live* reading? Or an older child *live* the multiplication table? How can I get him to *respond in his heart* with the multiplication of fractions? I don't see it. What is the specific content of the living you are talking about?"

The questions are proper and must be answered directly and squarely. I will have my primary children gradually *live* reading. To begin with, each one will, for example, have his name on his cabinet, where he keeps his various school possessions. His name he will soon learn to recognize along with the names of the others near by. There will also be a bulletin board on which announcements that concern the school are daily written. Those who can, will read and live these announcements. They will also read them to the others not yet able to read, who will likewise live them. Accounts of pupils' own experiences in school and out will be written in their presence, on paper chart or blackboard, for them to read. Stories they make up will similarly be written out and read. In these and other ways written matter will play an increasing part in their lives, and those who cannot read will by these means increasingly wish to read. With such a foundation attitude we will begin consciously to teach reading more directly, but always on the basis that the children do actually live it.

As to the multiplication table, my pupils will not see any such table until they themselves perhaps *live* the making of it. They will, however, *live* numbers as these enter into their other living. I will be on the lookout for opportunities to help them experience the arithmetic (living arithmetic, not formal arithmetic as such) already in their daily living—for example, arranging the proper number of chairs needed, ordering milk for lunch, giving out supplies, and the like. If a process seems needed, such as "carrying" in addition, in order to prosecute the task they are otherwise engaged in (and if I think they are advanced enough to take it in), I will show them how to operate the new process. If I have so far managed wisely and they are in fact psychologically "ready" for the operation of "carrying," most if not all will listen eagerly and do their best to catch on. To make sure they get it I will give some other instances for them to practice on. A few will fail to get the operation this time. I will try to manage so that these are challenged to try next time, not discouraged by failure this time. The next time most of these will get it. Those who still fail I will study, perhaps to postpone for these individuals for a while any further efforts at "carrying," perhaps to give them some special lessons in it. Somewhere along the road we will set up a store and sell school supplies for actual money. Obviously, only those pupils able to figure the money involved can act as sales people.

By learning in such ways, real and meaningful to the children, they will, before they get through the elementary school, read and write and cipher better than they would have done under the old way of teaching. And they will similarly know more geography and history and be more interested in these areas of study. They will besides, as a rule, be more interested in reading books and in writing letters and other accounts of what interests them; also, as a rule, they will show more initiative and be more creative in everything they do, more persistent in the face of difficulties, more secure and better poised as persons. But in getting these things done I shall not teach subjects, that is, not have textbooks in arithmetic or geography or history with daily lessons assigned. In time, suitable reference books will be published along these lines for the various age levels. Until that time comes pupils read existing textbooks as reference books.

All of this requires creative ingenuity on the part of teachers, but this is part of the satisfaction the new type of school gives—this and the further satisfaction resulting from noting the growth of individual pupils. The eager response of pupils to such treatment is one of the keen joys of life to teachers who have helped such responses into being. To develop that eagerness into an abiding personal characteristic, and not kill it as the old generally did, is indeed a lasting and worthy satisfaction.

BUT DON'T CARICATURE THE METHOD

It would be most misleading to allow any reader to think that such a regime means—to use the words of a widely known educator now deceased—that "the natural longings and instincts of the infant have been exalted as the sole guide for his development of mind and character." Such a saying is one of the incredible caricatures referred to above. If any teacher does so manage children it is because he does not understand the philosophy and theory of the new procedures. The author would not be so rash as to say no teacher ever has so misunderstood. In that case the warning above is directed to such a teacher. But by far the greatest number of such caricatures come from the fictitious conceptions of people who have never studied what goes on in a better school, who have never grasped the significance of differing aims and procedures because these are so different, and who therefore look only with eyes and minds attuned to the old. Such people are frequently more concerned to see any lack in the new than to admit the many incontestable defects in the old.

As stated earlier the teacher remains in charge and retains full control; but he knows that any steady diet of commands and compulsions fails both as regards the ordinary school learning and if possible even more as concerns character building. Most of this topic has already been discussed in the three chapters on purpose, coercion, and interest. Because we start with the child's existing interests, avoid coercion, and guide his developing purposes and interests, this does not mean that the teacher abdicates or takes only the child's impulses as guide. Certainly not! It simply means that the teacher starts at the only real available starting point, namely, with the child as he now is, and so guides the child's best available interests as, on the one hand, to utilize his fullest learning potentialities and, on the other hand, to develop these in every way possible toward higher and finer interests. Such a program is simply the most promising means for developing the best possibilities available in the child, upbuilding him into ever fuller democratic control of his own behavior and choices. Instead of representing an abdication of discipline, this is, in the degree attained, the utmost realization of the ideal discipline, namely, self-discipline. And studies show clearly that the child is in no way disadvantaged as to learning most of the subject-matter sought by the old—that in fact he usually learns it much better.

VARIOUS QUESTIONS CONSIDERED

This new curriculum is for many still so strange that some additional discussion may help to make it more meaningful. Three specific matters in connection with it will be considered.

1. *All-Roundedness.* A varied but all-rounded life is desirable both from the individual and the social point of view. The question here is what the school can do to effect such all-roundedness. What does the teacher do? What do the pupils do? Because the teacher is older and more experienced, he must be the chief and guiding factor in effecting this all-roundedness. The teacher's "map of values," continually criticized through personal reading as well as in teachers' meetings, must be his guide. If the class, by the accident of previous choices, has been tending toward a one-sided emphasis to the exclusion of other matters desirable and fitting for children of this stage of development, then the teacher must begin to emphasize the hitherto excluded aspects. By suggestions and questions he can generally lead the class to see other possibilities and choose along the needed lines. If the class is old enough, they should be led to

join in considering this precise problem of avoiding one-sidedness. As an extreme matter, the teacher can refuse to accept a choice of the class; but if the teacher is alert and aware of the various possibilities suited to the children, this is usually unnecessary. A steady diet of refusal and prescription and the class will become antagonistic, with concomitant learning thereby hurt. On the whole, if the teacher is properly observant, no serious one-sidedness will appear, even temporarily. He can guide to wider considerations but still let the class be the determining factor in the choices made. In fact here as elsewhere the teacher must chiefly beware lest the pupils yield too easily, and so come too much to rely on the teacher's suggestions rather than learn themselves to reach out and to make responsible choices.

2. *Conscious Ideals as Aims.* Take, for example, the matter of spelling. Most of those who have had full opportunity to learn and still tend to spell badly do so because they do not much care whether they spell badly or not. The teacher who meets such spelling difficulties should get each individual to study his own misspellings and so take care of his particular failures; but this is not enough. If we do not also develop in each pupil a definite ideal of and active interest in correct spelling, over and above these particular misspelled words, we shall probably not get even these misspelled words well learned; still less shall we succeed in having him care for the other spellings he will later meet. In other words, if we had to choose—as we do not, for it is no "either-or" matter—between developing the conscious ideal of correct spelling and teaching the correct spelling of specific words, we had better develop the ideal; it is the best single promise of both. Fortunately we can teach both the ideal and the actual spellings together; and each, properly taught, helps teach the other.

It need hardly be said that this same discussion holds for other instances where ideals are involved. We work on the specific instances as we meet them; but through these, and always, we work even more strenuously to develop the overruling ideal. It is through this that we best build effective dynamic character. We cannot teach all the individual ways of doing everything right, the task is too great, the particular ways of going wrong are too many; but the number of ideals is much smaller, we can in reason attempt at least the most important of these. One ideal well taught can carry the responsibility for innumerable particular instances of appropriate procedure.

3. *Continuous Growing as the Aim.* Without especially arguing the matter, the old education accepted its values as practically all "deferred values." What was learned was primarily for use in adult life; it had admittedly little direct application in the life of the child as child or even of the adolescent as adolescent. There are even yet adults who still defend this practice for the young; but few if any of these are willing, in the thick of their own adult life, to practice it on themselves. How many adults try to learn anything except what they now need or believe they will need or are otherwise interested in? Adults learn much, but seldom if ever on the basis they were taught in school, by rote memorizing, on the word of someone else that they will later need it. Instead, they learn now because they feel a need or an interest now. Self-directed life runs itself on a different basis from the old school and always has; and this self-directing life basis of learning is exactly what is found in the new education; for it was from life as actually run that the new education got its model and theory.

The conception of continuous growing founds itself on the further conception of the growing interest span or, perhaps better, interest-planning span. A one-year-old child does not look far into the future. His interest-planning span is measured in minutes. His ten-year-old brother, however, will plan for days and even weeks ahead. In a few more years this brother will plan far ahead, will perhaps be considering his life work, debating whether to begin upon "preliminary medicine" with the ten or twelve years of professional preparation involved. Educatively it is unfortunate and generally hurtful when a child has to work beyond and outside of his interest span. Everything previously discussed about learning—how purpose and interest contribute and how hurtful concomitants may be learned—comes forward to protest against making the learner work on such "deferred" values. This phrase, *deferred values*, let it be clearly understood, refers to values felt by the adult in charge, but not yet by the young learner. The old education acted as if no other values were worth considering; as the essayist and critic, Arthur Clutton-Brock (1868–1924) said, "the young must accept what they are taught or they will learn nothing."

It is exactly at this point that the old and the new outlook lock horns. The eminent educator referred to a few pages back discussed the same thing under the head of discipline. He sneered at "sentimental imitations of philosophy" which decry "discipline as something unnatural, abhorrent, and to be avoided." Such ideas meant, he said, that "the world of human experience was to be put aside and a world of the ego substituted for it." This is one further instance of the caricatures discussed above. A current writer, LeComte du Noüy, similarly spoke of "a right and moral discipline," which, he said, "must be imposed on a child from tender childhood, we mean the cradle." It is "a gross error," he believed, to say that such a child cannot learn discipline; "a child of three months can learn perfectly. . . . It is not necessary for the child to understand, it is even necessary that he not understand." The technique of such training for small children should be "the same as employed to train animals." This "creates conditioned reflexes and gives excellent results." (126:207, 209, 210, 213)

It suffices perhaps for the present to say that the whole trend of current professional thinking on the care of childhood goes counter to this animal treatment of human infants. Thorndike some years ago stated the position here upheld: "The discipline from enduring the disagreeable seems to be far outweighed by the discipline from working with an interested will along lines that fit one's abilities." (156:XXV:143)

The conception of continuous growing gives us perhaps the answer to the problem that this older point of view felt. It brings together and utilizes all the discussions previously given on learning and with these the conception of the growing interest span. The teacher looks ahead and guides the present living, with its inherent learning, towards its present stage of character building, with the more distant future in mind as the basis of guidance. Any advances in insight or knowledge or skill or self-control made by the children in this particular living experience come through the resulting learning stored up in character. Character is thus increased and improved by these advances; the child is accordingly ready for further and additional advances in quality and range of living through the next learning experience. As this is continued day by day, month by month, year by year, young childhood grows successively into older childhood, early adolescence, later adolescence, early adulthood, fully developed adulthood. Each advance makes the next step possible. The process is continuous.

Developing what has just been said, the teacher looks ahead at each stage and guides present living so that this continuous growing may be true growing toward desirable goals. Does this mean that the teacher—or anyone else—chooses the future for the several individuals and guides each toward a goal prechosen for him? It does not; democracy rejects such external choice and previously made decision. The inclusive, desirable democratic goal is that each individual shall grow more and more into adequate self-direction, a self-direction which takes other people and the conditions of living duly into account and acts accordingly. As Herbert Spencer stated a century ago, "the aim . . . should be to produce a *self-governing* being; not to produce a being to be *governed by others*." (151:212; italics in original) Toynbee has recently commented, "The criterion of growth is progress toward self-determination." (165:208) And Dewey: Education "is that reconstruction or reorganization of experience which adds to the meaning of experience, and . . . increases ability to direct the course of subsequent experience." (44:89*f*.) Elsewhere he says: "Children in school . . . must be allowed to develop active qualities of initiative, independence and resourcefulness." (53:304) The teacher in guiding the day-by-day growth of those under his care looks thus *immediately* to present living, *mediately* toward the intervening process, and *remotely* to adult life. The intervening process must be the kind to grow step by step into the desired kind of adult living.

This is a true democratic process. The teacher works on the living present with two things always in mind: (i) these children are persons living now as truly—though not as completely—as ever they will live; and (ii) what they live today should rank high to them in present quality of living, while at the same time today's living and learning should so develop them in insight and character that tomorrow will see them one step further toward more adequate self-control of the process of living. Thus they develop step by step toward the full possibilities of adult life. Under the first of these two guiding aims—that the pupils live truly as persons today—the teacher will understand, following an extension of Kant's democratic dictum, that today's living for these children is always to be considered as an end in itself and never as means merely; but under the second aim he will recognize that the present living is to be more than *merely* an end in itself; it is also to be means toward the fuller living which tomorrow—and increasingly the future—will demand. The child possibly understands and feels the present as end only; the teacher sees the present as both end and means. In time, the child, when further along, can share with the teacher also in seeing both.

Desirably, in no part of the learning process (curriculum) is the child to work at what are merely deferred values, chosen by another and imposed upon him without his seeing meaning for himself in them; but with his growing interest-planning span he looks further and further into the future as he fits ever more distant means and steps into his increasingly more elaborate planning.

Only as the learner himself accepts the predominance of the broader view over the hitherto narrower, will advance in moral outlook and dignity of thinking take place. So much for the conception of continuous growing.

THE SECONDARY SCHOOL CURRICULUM

It was explicitly stated above that the whole time of the elementary school is to be given to what is increasingly called "general education,"—the education that all should have to fit them as well as possible for full living, full living now of a kind to add continually to growing and richness of living as the years advance. This general education, whether in the elementary or the secondary school, should, it appears, be under one teacher. Departmentalized work in the elementary school inevitably approximates a modern type of Alexandrian school, conceiving education primarily as the acquisition of subject matter; and in addition it represents a factory-like specialization rather than the desired integrated living. The modern type of elementary school class under one teacher will be run on an activity basis, teaching no subjects as such but using in the living of the children the desirable content of the ordinary school subjects.

But the secondary school is in one important respect essentially different from this elementary school. It must serve two functions. The secondary school must continue the general education for all, for this must go on all through high school and even into college;

and it must besides provide a beginning specialization. Our civilization is based on a division of labor, and a beginning must be made at this specialization during the adolescent period in preparation for what is to follow.

We have thus far had much more experience with the Alexandrian type of secondary school than with the modern type. So that what is here suggested must be held as tentative, subject to further experience in the area. What is suggested is simply the author's best thinking to date in the light of all available facts and theory.

The part of secondary education devoted to the common or general education—here called the core curriculum—should, for each grade or division of grade as numbers may demand, be in charge of one teacher, a teacher especially prepared for this particular work. The class should not be large, twenty-five or thirty, so that this core teacher may know each pupil as an individual person. The proportion of time properly to be given to the core work is still uncertain, but for the seventh grade from half to three-fourths of the day would seem a fair amount, with this decreasing gradually to half the day or possibly somewhat less in the twelfth grade. Considering the importance of this part of the work and the amount to be done, these time allowances seem not too high. This core teacher will teach along the same lines as were followed in the elementary school: the activity program; no subjects as such, though rich content of study about living problems; no curriculum fixed in advance, though constant painstaking planning and evaluation with reference to needs of the group. It might be well for a good core teacher to stay at least as long as two years with a class in order that individual pupils may be better known and guided as persons.

The specialized work of the secondary school, at least until we can have more experience in core work, might well stay much as it now is except as to method of teaching. What each pupil should choose as his specialization would depend on a variety of factors: on plans for the future as to vocational work, whether he is to go at once to work after high school or attend college for professional preparation or prepreparation; on interests of the pupils; on college entrance requirements (for those colleges which have not yet digested the Eight Year Study). It is contemplated that, as a rule, there would be no separate high schools for vocations or science or music and art or liberal arts, but that pupils of all types should attend the same schools, mingle indiscriminately in the core, and separate as may be wise on the specializations. This seems by all odds the most democratic arrangement, the one least likely to foster divisive cleavages.

The teaching in the specialized work as far as possible should be remade on the general principles of teaching hitherto discussed. So far, in the typical American high school, the teaching has adhered much too closely to the Alexandrian model, with far too little attention to life as the basis of learning. On the program herein proposed teaching in the several specialized departments would be appreciably more enjoyable than is now usual; for the classes would be composed typically only of those who for special reasons choose the work, thus excluding many now forced to enroll. It would be better if those preparing to teach specialized subjects did not as now major under subject matter professors, but rather in teaching of their subject or area. As a rule such subject-matter professors fail to appreciate the fuller and truer aim of modern education and tend often to indoctrinate their students against the modern point of view.

THE COLLEGE CURRICULUM

While college education is not primarily in mind in this book, it is in principle included though but little discussed.

What has just been said about general and specialized education for the high school will hold in part for the college, with, however, more to be said. The college curriculum, it appears, should recognize four fairly distinct divisions, each with a primary aim: (i) the general or core work aiming at the general or inclusive or common education of all; (ii) the vocationally directed work—direct vocational education and preprofessional preparation for later study of medicine, law, engineering, or the like; (iii) special interests, usually nonvocational, as literature or music or art or economics, typically a specialization in what is given more generally under (i); (iv) work experience required of all but adapted to each. These we take up in order.

1. *General Education.* This may properly take two-thirds of the freshman year, half of the sophomore, a third of the junior, and a fourth of the senior. As at present conceived, this might profitably include five areas: (i) One is work in a course concerned with un-

derstanding people, or psychology and living, or some such area, a course which would help all students better to understand themselves and others; the course would also give special attention to personal difficulties or problems of students which if not adequately cared for might lead to personality problems. This area would be emphasized in the freshman year. (ii) Another is citizenship—a study of the problems facing the modern citizen, with as much commitment to responsible citizenship as can be effected by the college. This might be emphasized in the sophomore and junior years. (iii) Still a third area is the spirit and philosophy of modern science—something emphatically different from what is commonly got from a year of laboratory science, though it might include laboratory work. This might be emphasized in the sophomore year. (iv) A fourth is enrichment of the quality of living so far as this can be effected by the study and practice of literature, drama, art, and music. This may come the last three years. (v) Finally, there is the development of a personal philosophy of life, something emphatically different from what is commonly got in a course in the history of philosophy; this should permeate all the work of the core and everything else, but may well be emphasized in the senior year.

In the teaching of this general work the intent should be to get as far away from the Alexandrian method and as deep into the living-and-learning method as college conditions, revised and reconstructed therefor, will permit. With the proper conviction and effort on the part of instructors much can be accomplished along these desirable lines, especially if the preparation of college teachers can be shifted from the present emphasis on research to actual preparation to teach. Surely those in charge of this general work in the college should have special preparation for it—now seldom or never available in existing institutions.

2. *Vocational Preparation or Prepreparation.* This does not here call for much consideration, except to say that it should be consciously conducted in the light of what is going forward under general education, so as to support it and not oppose it as now is too often the case. It may be noted here that preparation for the existing type of graduate school belongs under this head of vocational preparation, namely, preparation for research.

3. *Special Interests.* These will usually represent further and more specialized treatment of the interests cared for more generally under

General Education. These, too, should be taught on the living and learning basis rather than on the more common method of lecturing, which, as the poet Auden says, is for the lecturer too often "talking in someone else's sleep."

4. *Work Experience.* Such activity is being increasingly adopted in colleges as part of the conscious effort to guide and direct the process of growing up. Modern home life, especially under city conditions for the better-to-do, can easily fail to give sufficient experience in the work of the world or indeed in seeing what practical life outside the home is like. Many girls, through early marriage especially, would, without such "work experience," fail ever to grow up in this respect. Many of the more protected boys will find work experience during their college days an excellent preparation for the more strenuous business demands ahead; and if, as here intended, college help is given in seeing meanings in their experience, these boys will perhaps see significance which protected homes have not shown them.

It is from such considerations that the practice of providing "work experience" is growing as a definite part of college work. To be most educative the work undertaken should, under guidance, be individually chosen. The college should have a competent person in charge to manage the whole enterprise, helping students find suitable opportunities, helping the individual to meet his needs, getting reports on how the individual student fulfills his task, making the pertinent information known to the other college instructors that they may help the students under them to digest their work experience and incorporate its results into their further thinking and acting.

These suggested heads and emphases in college work are but a few of the suggestions pertinent to college teaching from the "new" outlook on education. The chief and most urgent need is to release the American college from the Alexandrian grip. Until this is better done than hitherto, we shall continue to hear of college teachers saying that college work would be fine if it were not for the students.

CHAPTER XXIV. *School Management and Administration*

THE two preceding chapters, on teaching and on curriculum-making, have anticipated in a measure the problems belonging here. In those chapters, however, it was the part played by the individual teacher that mainly concerned us. Here we assume all of that and go on, as it were, from teachers confronting pupils to systems of schools as such, to teachers confronting each other, to schools as units in themselves facing their obligations, and to the school system with its officers and broader relationships and duties.

In each school, the principal and the teachers work together, work with administrative staff and janitor too, and in a very significant sense work with the parents—all primarily to educate the pupils. But all of these people also truly work to educate each other, primarily for better teaching, but with effects that reach further. Whenever people associate, they stimulate reactions in each other; and these reactions, as we know from Chapter XVII, bring educative effects which register themselves as character. At this point, democracy and ethics become concerned, as always where the acts of one person affect the living of others. Is this school run with the conscious democratic intent to let each one—teacher and janitor and official—live freely and truly as a person and therein build himself as well as possible into the finest and richest character and personality of which he is capable? Or is it run autocratically in disregard of what happens to the interests, lives, and personalities of those affected?

Similar questions present themselves regarding the superintendent and the system as a whole. We ask regarding the superintendent and his staff, working directly under the authority of the school board (and so, ultimately, under the people), first of all, how well they serve the cause of educating pupils. For whether we consider the superintendent, or his staff, or the separate schools, or the school board, the primary and guiding concern of organized education is the proper development of the pupils. *Everything connected with the whole school system centers in this one thing, the educative development of the pupils.* For that, the budget exists; for that, everything is done that is properly done; for that, the superintendent receives his salary, a larger salary than the others get because—it is believed—this differential best promises to promote the purpose for which he is paid, namely, to advance the better education of the young. The success of the system under every head is finally to be tested by the effects of the actual teaching on the young, the effects of that teaching directly in the characters built and ultimately in the lives they live now and later because of the way they were taught.

In the following two ways, then, does the *educative effect* stand as the aim and test of all that is done in the school system: first, the educative effect on the pupils, as the dominant and guiding aim of the whole system; second, the educative effect and the life effect, considered socially and ethically, of every act by and in the system in its relation to all affected. With the measuring rod thus furnished us, we are ready now to study the various problems of school management and administration.

PROBLEMS CLOSE TO TEACHERS

1. *Class Size.* At an earlier date a class size of forty pupils was considered proper. Now, however, the best judgment seems to put the number at about twenty-five, with thirty as a maximum. A few private schools have had classes smaller than twelve, so small, in the judgment of the writer, as to lose the highly desirable factor of group influence on the individual pupil.

It thus appears that two opposed considerations work together to determine desirable class size. On the one hand, the smaller the class, the better the teacher can study the individuals so as to adapt the work better to the special needs of each. If nothing else counted, this might lead to the ratio of one pupil to one teacher, and some might quote James Mill and his son John Stuart to illustrate. On the other hand, a necessary part of growing up is to learn to work with others in associated effort. And besides, as every discerning teacher knows, the comrades of a pupil have great weight in helping him decide his acts; properly guided, this influence of the group can greatly facilitate many desirable learnings.

If, then, we put together these two opposed considerations, each pupil must have others to live and deal with, but the class size must not be beyond the teacher's ability to manage effectively for each pupil. These considerations, in the light of experience to date, seem, as indicated, to suggest a class size for elementary and secondary school alike of not less than twenty and not more than thirty, with twenty-five as the present-day ideal. Preschool classes, however, must be smaller for best work.

2. *Curriculum-Making*. The discussion in Chapter XXIII put the making of the actual curriculum under the guidance of the class teacher. It is clear, however, that full realization of the proper curriculum concerns at least the entire school. What any one teacher does this year is, on the one hand, conditioned by what was done by and with this class in preceding years; and what is done this year will, on the other hand, similarly affect what succeeding teachers can and must do. In other words, these considerations make the full curriculum the concern of the whole staff of the school.

While the full staff will thus discuss the whole curriculum, this does not mean that the group should dictate a curriculum to the individual teacher—the living and learning type of curriculum cannot be made by dictation. However, from the fuller discussions of the group the individual teachers will better understand the process of growing as a whole, so that each may better fit his particular year's work into the all-round whole. Some specific projects or units of work can wisely be repeated with different learning results at different maturity levels, others perhaps will hardly bear repetition. Discussion of such points should give the individual teacher wisdom from the experiences of others higher up and lower down in the class age scale in order to make the current year's decisions more intelligent. Again, almost all important conceptions and attitudes must be cumulatively built during many years of the learner's experience. Probably anything less than a whole-school attack on character building will of necessity be spotty and inadequate. Here, too, full discussion up and down the line can give sensitivity and guidance to individual teachers. Also certain new proposals may require full discussion before all the strong and weak points can be made evident. In these and various other ways the whole staff can profitably discuss curriculum-making, although the individual teacher and class together make the effecting decision.

3. *The School's Map of Values.* Williams James says that philosophy is "our more or less dumb sense of what life honestly and deeply means. . . . It is our individual way of just seeing and feeling the total push and pressure of the cosmos." (87:4) We may say from this that the educational map of values, discussed in the preceding chapter, is the aggregate of what education "honestly and deeply means" and specifically what it is driving at, the all and sundry that education should seek to accomplish with the pupils.

While each teacher will and must make his or her own map of values, it is a subject which in one form or another should continually come before the school staff, and the aggregate staff of the system, for consideration of new points of view and revision of the old. An early fall meeting might be devoted to a symposium on new points of view, new insights, new values seen, from the various educative experiences of the summer. Each teacher should be open-minded enough to hear of new ways of thinking and teaching, so as always to be engaged in revising his map of values. To keep growing is the surest sign of life; and all growth, it appears, comes by one's reaction to new stimuli. And shared discussion is a potent means of getting new stimuli and aid in criticizing both new and old ideas.

4. *A Continuing Record for Each Pupil.* In an older day the only records kept were the class marks turned in and the records of promotions. These were, to be sure, supplemented by the voluntary memories of the teachers. Now we believe a folder should be kept for each pupil in a central office, perhaps the principal's, in which information regarding the child is accumulated as long as he is in school. Successive yearly records of various kinds should be placed there to show any inquiring teacher somewhat of the character and possibilities of the pupil. Indications of the pupil's particular interests, his home background including significant experience and problems, any incidents regarding life outside school which are revealing, his relations with other children, discriminating

specimens of class work, personal accounts by the teacher of the pupil's performance, an intelligent account of strengths and weaknesses with specific instances, results from standardized tests, judgment of the guidance expert (if such be available)—such items as these cumulatively kept will help each succeeding teacher to know the child better. If a particular difficulty arises, restudy of the folder may throw new light on the problem. The best kind of data to put in such folders can well be a matter of staff discussion through the years.

5. *Reports to Parents.* The customary use of report cards seems very doubtful. These are usually made to report the pupil's success in recitation and examination. In other words, the customary report card is part and parcel of the old notion that education consists in the acquisition of subject matter—a point of view this book rejects. Such a report card serves to keep alive this old point of view in both parents and teachers as well as to build it up in the rising generation.

But worse still, this old-type report card serves to build up a wall of separation between teacher and pupils, especially pupils whose reports are not acceptable at home. Also they often build or increase a like opposition between child and exacting parents. Fortunately, reports are being devised that lessen and perhaps avert the evils associated with the old; but mutual conferring is, as will in a moment appear, perhaps the best of all.

That parents wish to get reports is natural. If, however, they could see the price in the way of antagonisms and anxieties of children exacted by the old-type reports they might feel different. The best conclusion seems to be to abolish the old way of reporting. The most promising means of keeping parents informed is one of the type now used by many schools—a conference once or twice a year between teacher and parent in which both contribute their insight as to the child's progress and needs, and plan together lines along which special help or stimulation to growth can be given at home and at school. What counts most in education is as accessible to discerning parents as to teachers, namely, the emerging in the child of improved behavior (deeper sensitivity and insight, better controls, finer interests, and the resulting development of character and personality). If the teacher, because of deeper study into child growth and behavior, has insights or techniques which can help parents to understand and deal more wisely with children, the conferences provide opportunity to share them for the benefit of the child; but the gaining of understanding should be a two-way process. Parents and teacher should cooperate to these ends, and desirably there should be such a relationship of confidence between teacher and parents that both alike feel sure that if either has significant knowledge the other would wish, it will be given. In particular if any problem should arise with either in which the other can probably help, teacher and parent should talk it over constructively. This policy of mutual trust and appropriate conference may not always be feasible, but it seems the desirable goal toward which to work.

6. *Marks.* The discussion on this practically repeats that just given on reports to parents. It seems equally certain that marks as such do more harm than good. They, too, direct attention unduly to learning for recitation and examination purposes, rather than for life and for character building. Also their tendency is to alienate teacher from pupils and to set one against the other. The emotions which marks arouse are generally bad. In the upper part of the class, marks often lead to hurtful competition; for all concerned, pupils, parents, and teachers, they tend to distract from the inherent worth of what is being studied; for the lower half of the class, discouragement and antagonisms are the common results. When we put schooling on a living basis, we do not care for marks. No parents think of marking their own children. If they should, the alienating effect would be most obvious. And if the two parents were to keep marks against each other, the effect on family unity would be disastrous. When life is on a truly friendly basis, marks for report purposes seem quite out of place.

7. *Honor Rolls; Prizes.* These relics from the past likewise do more harm than good. Specifically, so far as they stimulate activity, they shift effort from the basis of the intrinsic reward of work consciously well done to the basis of external reward obtained by satisfying someone else, which is not a desirable foundation for character-building. Further, they generally stimulate only the few, and those the ones that need it least; most pupils soon conclude that they have little or no chance. The safest rule, it appears, is to abolish all such artificial incentives and try to see that each pupil is stimulated to put his best into his work, with the full recognition that

good work will be seen and appreciated by others. The studies by Hartshorne and May* show that in schools run on progressive lines there is less disposition to cheat than in schools run on the old basis of opposition between teacher and pupils. Here is one bit of pretty good evidence against artificial incentives such as marks, report cards, prizes, and honor rolls.

8. *Promotion.* This is a conception based purely on the graded school theory of apportioning the subject matter over the several years of age or class levels. As soon as we adopt the "whole child" theory of education, promotion ceases to be pertinent. Each child is to be put where he can work best with the others. This will usually be on the basis of social age. If any reader feels troubled at giving up the conception of promotion, let him ask himself what promotion can mean for children not yet in school. Should this two-year-old be promoted to be three years old or kept back a year? What would the mother do differently whether she did or did not promote the child? Such questions are seen at once to be preposterous. Is it not clear that as soon as education is put on a life basis, promotion simply ceases to have any desirable meaning? On the other hand, for the child to be with a group in which it can have security and stimulation and a feeling of self-respect is exceedingly important.

Many teachers will, however, ask about those older boys who still cannot read. The question is a good one, but failure of promotion is apparently not the answer. Many studies seem to show that, even as regards learning subject-matter, failure to be promoted does not help matters. At the end of the year the failed child, in addition to having suffered humiliation and alienation, has in most cases learned no better or worse than if he had been promoted. The answer as to inability to read lies elsewhere, probably in the beginning of teaching reading. To force a child to try to read before he is psychologically "ready" for reading is practically certain to result in failure at reading, with various emotional difficulties added besides. The same thing is likewise true for beginning arithmetic. The marvel is that the old formal lessons in reading and arithmetic did no more harm than appears. Pushing children beyond what they are

* "A long series of experiments" seem to prove that "progressive methods are more likely to foster situations in which honest behavior is the natural result than are more conventional methods."—Hugh Hartshorne, *Character in Human Relations* (New York, Scribner's, 1932), p. 226.

"ready" for and punishing them or shaming them for the consequent failures—these are among the chief sins of the old-fashioned school.

But as things are now teachers can expect to have a number of pupils who don't read well or seem not to read at all. (Have we ever tried them on comic or mystery stories?) The answer is not to demote them and further shame them and antagonize them; this means almost certainly that they will become truants, or, if they can, drop out of school—in this case we "demote" them to be *citizens* instead of pupils! Rather, the answer is to help them to feel accepted in the group, to find easy reading materials of interest to them in order to build up their reading ability, and otherwise do what we can to build up their quality of living.

In this connection the practice of keeping a teacher with a given class only one year may well be questioned. Some primary schools have their teachers run a cycle of three years, with upper kindergarten, first grade, and second grade successively under the same teacher. Other schools follow the same plan for the three first grades. On either basis the teacher can better learn the pupils' personalities and better undertake long-term planning for those few who need very special treatment. A contrary practice of semi-annual promotions exactly denies the advantages of better personal acquaintance and better long-term planning—a sufficient argument to banish this now out-of-date method of adapting the program to individual differences.

CERTAIN WIDER PROBLEMS OF MANAGEMENT

There are yet other problems of school management to be considered.

1. *Homogeneous Grouping*. This was vigorously advocated some twenty years ago, principally on the promise of taking better care of individual differences in the acquisition of subject matter. We have previously considered, and rejected, the theory that education consists primarily of the acquisition of knowledge. But on any basis the homogeneous grouping breaks down. First, pertinent studies show that it is literally impossible to group individuals homogeneously. No matter what specific basis of grouping be chosen, the group is still not homogeneous. No known effort of grouping will take care of all significant individual differences. Even if it were

possible, to learn to *live* with the various degrees of ability is a necessary part of life. In addition, every effort at homogeneous grouping under any name leads in effect to the official labeling of the third group as "dumbbells." This is heartless if it can be avoided; it is indefensibly hurtful when we consider the full facts. Fortunately, the newer theory of the educative process does not depend on "homogeneous" abilities to make it work. So the effort to secure "homogeneous grouping" becomes needlessly artificial. The problem is otherwise to be attacked.

2. *The "Platoon" Plan or Departmentalized Teaching.* The idea of a departmentalized elementary school was vigorously advocated in certain quarters some twenty or thirty years ago before the activity school and the idea of integrated living had won their present acceptance. The reasons for wishing such a regime were, partly, to give fuller use of the school plant and so house two schools in one building, partly to secure, as its advocates hoped, better standards of subject-matter acquisition. Such a school procedure we must reject; it practically prevents best teaching on a living basis. The arguments for better use of the school building have likewise failed to win acceptance. Few—practically none who study the question—now defend departmentalized teaching for the elementary school.

3. *Community Relations; Socially Useful Activities.* Our ultimate aim in education is such continuous development of the individual pupil as will lead him eventually into the fullest and finest quality of available living, both social and individual. But there can be no adequate development to full social living of the desired quality except by *living* the responses that are to be learned and built into abiding traits and ideals. This means that the school must develop community relations of a kind to provide opportunity for living all kinds of desired social responses. Clearly the degree of such active community relationships will increase with age and maturity. The youngest will visit and observe; what they do will mostly be limited to action among themselves. Older children can go further into the community, while still older ones can engage in obviously socially useful activities. These fuller activities will serve best if they are associated with adult citizen effort at community service. For high school pupils to feel that they are sharing with adults in deliberation and decision as well as in serving is

most educative. And this means real sharing in decisions. As John Dewey has said in another connection: "There can be no stable and balanced development of mind and character apart from the assumption of responsibility." (47:135*f.*)

What these community relations mean for the future development of the school, we are just beginning to imagine. They may lead to the entire transformation of the school as we now know it. In any event, they beckon us on toward an alluring vista of wider educative activity.

4. *Group Tensions; Better Human Relations.* The world still stands appalled at the Nazis' treatment of minority peoples, growing out of their selfish doctrine of racial superiority. When we consider their actual treatment of the Jews, with intent to destroy them altogether, and their other plans, ruthlessly begun, of reducing Poles and Czechs to a permanent status of social inferiority, we stand aghast.

But we of this country have to think twice if we would see such behavior in its full light. Our record is not good, as the Japanese during the war continually told the peoples of Asia and Indonesia, and as the U.S.S.R. now tells the world. We too have within this country those who hold indefensibly to the doctrine of racial superiority, as well as those who wilfully discriminate against groups within our borders.

Science tells us that, so far as can be judged on evidence, the very term *race* has no meaning apart from certain outward physiological features such as color of skin, texture of hair, and facial configuration; that psychologically, no racial differences have been found; specifically, that the Jews (where they wish it) do constitute a cultural and (often) religious group, but (whether they wish it or not) are not a race or racial group; that the Negroes are, in all known psychological respects, natively equal, as a group, to any other, as are also the Mexicans, the Indians, and all those other groups which immigration has brought to this country.

It is a sad and regrettable fact that the English-speaking peoples are, of all groups in the world, most given to prejudice against other peoples strikingly different from them in looks or manner of living. Being prejudiced, they easily believe evil of these groups that are different, that their ways are pernicious, and that they are natively inferior; and these prejudiced ones are easily persuaded to deny to peoples thus stigmatized the rights they claim for themselves and their equals. Thus arises one of the most disquieting problems that face our people.

Our historic American documents, notably the Declaration of Independence and the Constitution of the United States with its successive amendments, now recognize no differences of legal status among the constituent groups in the population. All rights and privileges are asserted to hold equally for all, irrespective of race, color, religion, sex, or origin. Concurring to the same effect are our other great historic documents—Lincoln's Gettysburg Address, Wilson's Fourteen Points, the Atlantic Charter, the Charter of the United Nations. These great historic documents taken together state, we may say, the nationally professed ideals of our people.

To like effect stand other significant elements in our tradition: our social ethical ideals; the great social philosophy we call democracy; the principles of ethics and morals as generally understood by the most competent writers on the subject; and still further the widely accepted principles of religion as propounded in the Judaeo-Christian tradition. These concur in what is called the Golden Rule: As we would that men should do unto us, so should we do unto them.

Thus our science, our stated social philosophy, our accepted ethics and religion, all agree in rejecting group discrimination: science finds no innate racial or group differences; the legal rights and privileges which we as individuals cherish for ourselves apply equally to all; our moral and religious principles demand that we reject intolerance and discriminations against anyone because of the group to which he belongs. If any person is criminal or ill-mannered, he may be refused for the time the privileges which otherwise he could claim, but this can be justified only because of his personal behavior, not because of the group to which he belongs. Even so he must be accorded the fair and just treatment which is the right of all, he must be dealt with only in a way that respects the best self in him and besides promises to bring him under the control of that best self.

These are high ideals. Though not all among us appreciate them fully or accept them to act on, they remain the best authenticated ideals of the American people.

When ideals are thus authenticated, they thereby become ideals to guide education. It becomes our duty as American educators to try to bring up American youth to understand these ideals and the grounds on which they claim our loyalty and our active obedience. This is not to say that we should indoctrinate youth even with these ideals. We cannot indoctrinate—teach unthoughtful acceptance—and at the same time be true to democracy or to our highest ethics. Even these ideals, crucial though they be to the continuance of democracy, must come within the ultimate framework we are trying to build—that each person must inquire, weigh, and decide for himself. Democratic freedom, as we have previously seen, demands that the individual be truly free to decide what he shall believe. The school's role is to help youth, as best we can, learn to understand the pertinent facts and their implications, to reason *fairly* and to decide honestly. Beyond that we cannot go as regards beliefs.

But as regards the behavior of man to man and child to child, it is the task and duty of education to take positive steps. It cannot allow positive discrimination in school. It must besides do its best to bring all to see and appreciate how others feel when they are discriminated against and to act in a way to lessen such discrimination as far as can be done; it must avert or abolish all such discrimination if possible, and lessen what cannot be averted or abolished. The facts as to racial differences must, moreover, be taught as other scientific conclusions are taught, and their bearings on proper human relations seriously studied. For all our people, young and old, must learn to act in the light of known facts, not by ignorance.

In addition, we who teach must understand that discriminations are often the results of slights and sneers previously experienced by those who now discriminate—the practice of "scapegoating." If we do not understand this, we shall attack certain manifest discriminations in less than the wisest way.

It is a very serious problem which thus faces our country and its schools. If we are to exert our full and proper influence in the world, we must ourselves rise above the bias and discrimination all too common among us. If we are to live up to our ideals, we must free ourselves from such bias and discrimination. Strange as it may seem, only recently has the American school become actively sensitive to this problem as one of its vital tasks. If we believe in ethics, we must accept its solution as an urgent duty.

PROBLEMS OF ADMINISTRATION

Where school management leaves off and school administration begins, it is neither easy nor necessary to state; but certain problems remain to be considered which we may call administrative.

1. *The Work of Supervision.* In an older day school supervisors —in some places called school inspectors—served mainly to see that the authoritative regulations were met, that the required course of study was followed, and that teachers taught as they were expected to teach. Such inspectional service was often dictatorial, and teachers on the whole disliked both the service and officials.

Where the newer point of view has been consistently accepted, the supervisor, now often called a "helping teacher," plays a very different role. As the new type of teacher guides the pupils without ordering them and the pupils in their turn feel that the teacher is "on their side," so also is it with the modern type of supervisor. He or she guides where guiding seems needed, but mainly works "on the side" of the teacher. Perhaps the main service of today's supervisor is twofold: on the one hand, to help steer the in-service study programs with a minimum use of authority and a maximum encouragement of teacher leadership; on the other hand, to help new teachers find themselves in their work. Of course, with educational theory in transition, an abiding task of the supervisor is to mediate constructively between the incoming and outgoing theories and their respective advocates—a difficult but a necessary task.

The chief work of the supervisor when things are going well is to promote and encourage new and better ideas of teaching within the staff. Certain teachers have got new ideas at summer school and would like to try them; others have read certain new books; still others have conceived new ideas or contrived new developments of ideas already in use. The supervisor can do no more effective work than give sympathetic encouragement and help. To aid such new ideas sprout and grow, to arrange for observation and discussion of the work of other teachers doing similar work, to help discuss experiments discerningly and sympathetically—nothing can keep a system more fully alive than such services.

One negative word. It was once common to have subject-matter supervisors, as in geography or English or nature work. These clearly belong to the outworn subject-matter theory of education, and have therefore no proper place in the living-and-learning type of school system. A music or art supervisor seems to stand on a somewhat different basis; but even these must consider themselves not as inspectors or governing authorities, but as consultants and helping teachers. Specifically, these must not, as was once true in small systems, do the main teaching along these lines.

2. *High-School Problems.* The more essential problems of the high school have already been considered. Here it will suffice to call attention to one or two special problems.

In some of the larger cities very large high schools are to be found. Such size seems educationally of doubtful value. The personal touch, the sharing of problems both among pupils and among teachers, becomes increasingly difficult as the school gets increasingly large. The community connection, too, tends to become more tenuous. From the educational point of view the principal should come to know intimately every teacher and at least most of the leading students. These considerations seem to suggest 3,000 pupils as the upper limit for a high-school enrollment, with less than this as desirable.

A second point. Many cities have different kinds of high schools —academic high schools, various kinds of trade high schools, and perhaps a music and art high school. A close study of such a system will often show that there is really an X-Y-Z grouping here, with the lowest ability pupils shunted off into some trade training for which they may have neither interest nor aptitude. The argument from expense must be conceded some weight here; not every 3,000-pupil high school can economically afford all the different types of vocations the city might wish. Democracy, however, must object to a regime which encourages some students to look down on others, and also, if possible, democracy must refuse to deny any students the education they individually need. As far as feasible all different types of students should associate together in the core curriculum work and separate only to meet specific individual needs. This argues for the "cosmopolitan" high schools as the standard type; though in any one system these need not all offer the same vocational opportunities.

3. *Transfer to Another School System.* Some have objected to the activity theory of the curriculum on the ground that it increases the difficulty of transferring pupils from one system to an-

other. But the argument really works the other way. If all systems were run on the basis herein discussed, transfer would be much easier than it is on the old basis. On the old basis the second system must by chance have essentially the same course of study as the first, with even the same time sequence, in order to facilitate transfer. This coincidence is rare. On the curriculum basis herein discussed transfer presents practically no problem. In school systems taught on the activity basis, a transfer pupil will be assigned to a class of the same maturity level as he had left. When the next activity is taken up, if it is relatively new to all, he is at once on substantially the same basis as the others.

4. *Rural School Consolidation.* Many states in this country have "the district system" managed in such a way as to retain many very small country schools. That a school may be educatively too small follows at once from the argument made above against too small a class size. Consolidation of such small schools into larger units seems indisputably required.

But it does not follow that all separate rural schools should be consolidated; or that the larger the consolidation, the better the resulting education for the children. There is positive danger of real educational loss when children are taken needlessly out of their own communities and away from their own parents. What was said earlier about community relations can be elaborated here. If parents, teachers, and children can work together to improve school, home, and community, the resulting education can be of very high quality, even though the school, the home, and the community be otherwise very poor. In fact, in some ways the more backward the community the greater the opportunity of the school to educate its pupils by having them work constructively and creatively with the parents to improve home and community. Anyone who has seen the work of the rural schools out from West Georgia College at Carrollton–Oak Mountain, Sand Hill, and Tallapoosa–will be ready to believe that a consolidation which removed these pupils from their community contacts would have greatly hurt both schools and communities. The conclusion would seem probable that where the school has enough pupils to constitute an effective working group and where parents can be induced to cooperate, good teachers will make consolidation unnecessary and undesirable.

With the type of high school herein advocated, substantially the same argument against unnecessary consolidation would appear to hold. The size of the student body would, however, need to be appreciably larger than in the case of the elementary rural school.

In considering consolidation it should not be overlooked that for certain types of experience and study, children of several age levels can work effectively together, thus reducing the needed number of classes and so lessening one argument for consolidation. This would hold true for the elementary school and for the core work of the high school. All schools, it may be added, should arrange for more inter-age pupil activity than is now common. A proper education demands it.

5. *Centrally Administered Examinations.* Such examinations, more common abroad than here, are administered by an authority other than the teacher or teachers of those examined. With the coming of standardized tests, such centrally administered examinations became for a while very common in American city school systems. One of the chief claims made for such a practice is that it maintains standards throughout the system. Before we grant such a claim, we wish to be sure as to what particular standards are maintained and at what price. By price we mean, of course, the effects of such examinations on the other-than-subject-matter learning of the pupils and on the subsequent teaching.

This writer visited a certain small school system in a mid-western state and found in the superintendent's anteroom one whole wall made into a blackboard. On this appeared the results of a recent system-wide examination in arithmetic. The results for all the third grades were scored there side by side for all comers to see, and similarly for each of the other grades. Is it unreasonable to suppose (i) that the teachers studied these comparative results? (ii) that the third-grade teacher whose children did the worst determined that this would not happen again, and accordingly set out to drill on arithmetic as never before? (iii) that anything not to be included in this and other subject examinations would be given less attention than would otherwise have happened? (iv) that the long-run natural result of such an examination system is to destroy much of if not all the finer educative efforts whose results are not to be shown by such examinations?

If there is a more effective way of reducing education to mere formalism and of eliminating all the finer parts and aspects of a proper education, this writer does not know what it is. New York State with its "regents examinations" of secondary schools is one of the few states in this country which has such a system. The bad effects are apparent to any open-minded study. Best thinking is against it for the reasons suggested above.

PROBLEMS OF THE SCHOOL SUPERINTENDENT

Some twenty-five years ago a published school survey laid down certain "essentials" of an effective system of schools. In the judgment of today it would be difficult to find a clearer statement of how *not* to administer a school system. The account begins by likening a system of schools to the human organism, with the brain as "the central administration"; "the nerves, the supervisory force"; and "the fingers and hands" as "the teachers." It was then explicitly stated that for "the system" to "be effective" the central administration should "in careful and detailed fashion . . . determine the purpose of the process," work out "the content, arrangement, and order of the curriculum," develop and provide "the materials of instruction" and determine "the methods . . . by which the curriculum may best be presented to and mastered by the pupils." "These," it stated, "are some of the problems of the brain of the organism." And it was further stated that "without the solution of these problems, the fingers and hands do not know how to work most effectively" or "the nerves to give [the proper] impulses." And it went on to say that "the fingers and hands, the teachers" are "to carry out the plans of the central organization"; and "the nerves . . . are useful only in so far as they facilitate the work of the teacher or carry messages to and from the central organization. Their task is to keep the work going . . . see that the direction of the work is right, and keep the central organization in touch with the work that is going on." (27:135*ff.*)

This was written in 1922. It states precisely one attitude then very common in school administration practice, an attitude derived from a then common big business procedure and applied with a minimum of modification to the school system. This same attitude, somewhat modified perhaps, holds even today in too many school systems. The reader is asked to recall the previous discussions on democracy, on respect for personality, and specifically the demand for judging institutions by their educative effect on the individuals affected. Such an administrative system as that sketched in the quotation cannot stand the tests we have thus previously laid down. First, it is antidemocratic. Here "the brain" at the top does all the thinking and makes all the decisions; these it hands down through obedient "nerves" to obedient teaching "fingers and hands" at the bottom, at no point allowing the latter any share in the process. In a truly democratic system all members of a system will share in determining the policies that are to govern. We saw at the beginning of the chapter how the superintendent and the system are always to be judged by their educative effect on all in the system, not only on the pupils but also on the teachers. In the words of John Dewey:

> Full education comes only where there is a responsible share on the part of each person, in proportion to capacity, in shaping the aims and policies of the social group to which he belongs (52:209).

And further: "No matter how wise, expert, or benevolent the head of the school system, the one-man principle is autocracy." (59:IV:195)

TEACHERS' SHARE IN POLICY-MAKING

From the foregoing considerations the definite principle follows that teachers should by law have the explicit right to share with the school administration in determining policies that concern their welfare and their work. Decision regarding such sharing cannot be left to the judgment either of the superintendent or of the school board; at least the minimum provision should be fixed by law. In this, conscious distinction is made between policy-making and the execution of policies; it is the former and not the latter which the superintendent should share with the teachers. In a very small system, the superintendent may meet for the discussion of policies in regular session with all the teachers. Where numbers forbid this, the teachers must elect representatives to meet with the superintendent, representation being apportioned appropriately among the different kinds or types of teachers—preschool, elementary, junior high, senior high. For some purposes the janitors should be present and share both in discussion and decision.

How superintendent and teachers will actually share in making joint decisions has not yet been crystallized into any set pattern. Awaiting such extended experience, it seems wise to confine attention here to general principles. The following, for example, should be considered:

1. Provision establishing shared policy-making should be so clearly defined that any antagonistic superintendent will be unable to prevent the actual practice.

2. The sharing in policy-making should reflect the fullest spirit of democracy and respect for personality of all involved.

3. No policy should be adopted which unnecessarily limits the freedom of individual teaching.

This third principle follows directly from the fact that teaching is the supreme instance of creative artistry; it deals with the most infinitely delicate of all artistic media; and its results, for good or ill, are the most significant within the range of human effort. Unless clearly necessary, no policy should thwart the maximal individual responsibility in this supreme art.

THE SUPERINTENDENT'S NEED FOR AN ADEQUATE PHILOSOPHY OF EDUCATION

We saw at the beginning of this chapter that the criterion for judging everything done by and in the school system is its *educative effect*, primarily on the pupils, secondarily on the staff. This educative effect becomes then of necessity the proper end and aim of the superintendent's work; he is to be judged by his success in attaining this end and aim. Decision as to which specific educative effects to seek is necessarily a matter of one's philosophy of life; decision as to educative methods to be used is, as we saw in Chapter XXI, a problem for the philosophy of educative method. It follows at once that for the discharge of the duties involved in determining both ends and means the superintendent must have an adequate philosophy of education. Otherwise he will be inadequate to the duties involved in his work.

This argument may be elaborated as follows: (i) the superintendent is, and of right must be, the guiding head of the school system; (ii) any defensible guidance implies both adequate understanding of ends primarily sought and also sufficient appreciation of suitable means to permit the contrivance and direction of steps necessary to attain the ends; (iii) the values at stake in the superintendent's work are primarily the character and personality traits of the individual persons affected by the educative process of the school system; (iv) on the aggregate personality traits thus developed in all concerned depend the future of our civilization. In other words, the superintendent is responsible for the best possible guidance of the varied educative efforts of his entire system toward the finest possible conception of the good life; and in this guidance his perception and appreciation of the values involved, both as to means and ends, constitute the chief factor in success. Without such perception and appreciation of the values involved his guidance would be blind and uncertain.

It is not here claimed that an adequate philosophy of education suffices to constitute all that the superintendent should know and be—far from it; but it is claimed that such a philosophy must furnish the essential and dominating guide of all that he does as superintendent, whether he be talking to the teachers, or to a parent, or to the janitors, or to his architects, or to the school board, or to the citizens at large. What the superintendent stands for and how intelligently and how strongly he stands for it—these are the factors that strategically determine the effectiveness of the school system. As is the head, so in time is the system.

As Whitehead says, "If my view of the function of philosophy is correct, it is the most effective of all the intellectual pursuits." (173:x) Chesterton says, in a statement widely quoted through William James's writings, "We think that for a landlady considering a lodger it is important to know his income, but still more important to know his philosophy. We think that for a general about to fight an enemy it is important to know the enemy's numbers, but still more important to know the enemy's philosophy." (24:5) H. A. Overstreet says it thus: "The totality of one's loyalties is one's philosophy of life. . . . A philosophy of life is one's world outlook. It is the way in which one regards things . . . the values one sets upon them. . . . It is clear from the above that the most powerful factor or force in one's life is one's philosophy." (157:IV:2) And John Dewey observes: "If we are willing to conceive education as the process of forming fundamental dispositions, intellectual and emotional, toward nature and fellow men, philosophy may even be defined as *the general theory of education.*" (44:383)

The superintendent above referred to who had covered the wall of his anteroom with the arithmetic marks of his different schools had a poor philosophy of teaching method. He had not perceived that he was so stressing the formal results of arithmetic as to lessen and thwart the finer values possible from better teaching. Similarly, some twenty or thirty years ago certain dissertations purported to prove that a class of sixty could be taught as effectively as a class of thirty. During the depression of the 'thirties a certain superintendent accepted these findings and increased the class size in his system from a prior regulation of thirty to the new rule of fifty. This was a case where the writer of the dissertation, his professor who accepted the dissertation, and the superintendent who changed his regulation class size, alike failed in philosophy. They accepted the idea that education consists of the learning of formal textbook content. They disregarded such important factors as the personal creative work of pupils and the necessity for teachers to know them as individual personalities and so give them the chance to live and study as individuals. Specifically, they disregarded the concomitant learnings and fixed their attention exclusively on the formal school work. Again, some twenty years ago a published article stated that "the most effective device that can be applied to learning is to increase the amount of drill or practice. The prime function of motivation is to make the drill or practice palatable." (96:XX:34: Jan. 1929) The authors of this article experimented with the learning of grammar, the pupils learning the words to recite them. When the chief experimenter was asked whether the pupils whose greater drill showed greater learning had or had not learned to speak and write as the grammars directed, the answer was that he was not concerned with this. His definition of learning had been the ability to recite the words substantially as given in the book. Thus again an inadequate philosophy of education disregarded both the practical test of learning and also the concomitant learnings.

If the superintendent's philosophy of education does not suffice to see through such bad reasoning as that found in the three foregoing instances, then his system fails of adequate teaching and so of the desired educative results.

FEDERAL AID TO STATE PUBLIC EDUCATION

First a glance at history. Up to 1914 the support given by the national government to public education was largely in the form of land grants. As each new state was admitted from 1802 to 1845 the sixteenth section of each township of nationally surveyed land was reserved for school support. From 1848 this amount was at first doubled and later still further increased. In 1862 the land-grant college fund was provided. This was offered to each state then in the Union at the rate of 30,000 acres for each representative in Congress, and was to support a "college of agriculture and the mechanic arts." Additional direct funds were later added for these colleges.

In 1881, and later, Senator Blair from Vermont made a notable effort to get Federal funds to help support public schools in the separate states; but so great was the fear of national interference in state affairs that the effort came to nought. In 1914 Congress passed the Smith-Lever bill in support of extension teaching in agriculture and home economics in rural areas, a truly great innovation. In 1917 the Smith-Hughes act provided national funds for the preparation of teachers of agriculture, trades, industry, and home economics and for the support of secondary school teaching along these lines. This was the first direct appropriation of funds by the national government for the current support of any phase of the state public schools. Since 1917 many efforts have been made to secure Federal aid for the general support of state public education, but so far in vain. In common opinion three considerations have mainly blocked this measure: (i) the fear of Federal control over, or at least undesirable interference with, the state management of public education; (ii) the opposition of the wealthier states to greater taxation when all or most of the tax money would go to other states; (iii) the opposition of the friends of certain nonpublic schools to Federal aid unless their schools also share in the aid.

The argument for Federal aid is itself simply stated and, taken alone, appears convincing. Federal aid is but the logical extension of principles now all but universally admitted in support of local and state public education. The argument advances in three steps.

1. Our Part I discussions of democracy, respect for personality,

and the obligation to social morality support the conclusion that any local community is under obligation, according to its financial ability, to offer to all its youth at least a minimum standard of free compulsory schooling. Otherwise some of the rising generation would, from parental poverty or negligence, probably fail of proper education; and because of this the individual would probably suffer in his living and the community itself would suffer a correlative lowering of effective citizenship with hurt to all.

2. If public education is good public policy for the separate communities of a state, it is similarly good public policy for the state to provide equalizing funds so that the poorer communities may be able to bring their schools up to the minimum standards necessary for proper education. This is so not only for the sake of the poorer communities, but also because the young people of the poorer regions tend, on growing up, to seek more promising opportunities; and the more attractive, wealthier regions will accordingly suffer if these migrants represent lower standards of either living or efficiency or citizenship. Also, wherever they live, they vote and thus share in making public policies. Good public policy thus joins with democratic justice and fair play in demanding that the state maintain good standard schools throughout its territory.

3. Exactly the same logic holds for the nation. If the community ought to educate all its citizens; if the state should therefore equalize educational opportunity throughout its domain, at least to an adequate minimum of schools for all its communities; then also should the nation by Federal aid equalize an adequate minimum for all the states. Good national policy thus in its turn joins justice and fair play and national advantage in demanding Federal aid for state public education.

So much for the argument in favor of Federal aid. Now for the arguments against such aid.

1. The fear of national control or of national interference in state and community self-control is not to be idly dismissed. All should understand the dangers involved in order to take wise precautions against them.

The danger most feared is the possible threat to local and individual responsibility and initiative. Nothing is more important than this, both to long-run effective democracy and to intelligent progress. Probably the greatest danger facing both democracy and fine quality of individual living is the threat, the world over, to individual initiative and personal responsibility which comes from increasing bigness and its tendency to dictate individual action. We see this alike in the increasing role of government, in the growing size and complexity of industrial organizations, and in the spread of ideologies favoring collective action and centralized force. That bigness properly directed can often mean efficiency of material output seems highly probable. On the other hand, it is undeniable that an essential ingredient in the desirable quality of living is individual freedom of initiative, thought, and decision. The saddest sight in the world is the police state of Communist Russia, willing to seek equality of material goods at the expense of individual freedom!

Moreover, local autonomy in school control has been an important factor in developing American public interest in education. Few if any countries of the world manifest more effective interest than ours in the education of youth, and no country equals this one in interest devoted to the study of education. Even more certainly has local autonomy helped to build our outstanding interest in the study of education. Local autonomy has meant that success of a school official in one system or institution has led to calls to some more important system or institution. This might develop simply personal ambition on the part of the administrator. But ideas also spread in this same way from one system or institution to another. Perhaps even more important, local autonomy means a greater opportunity to experiment. A professor of education in a nationally known university has every reason to believe that a worthy new idea which takes root in the mind of one or more of his students may sprout the next year in some school system or college perhaps a thousand miles away. Such local freedom to experiment results in far and away more experimentation, and consequently more study and development of educational theory, than is possible where all the schools of a state or nation must, if they change, change all at once. Certainly a school man or educational theorist can have far less hope of spreading practical school ideas in a country like France or the U.S.S.R. or Argentina, where a single system dominates all. The undertaking is too great, too difficult for a single individual to attempt. And for all the commanding quality of French intellect, it has added but little to modern educational theory.

Do these considerations mean that we must oppose Federal aid? Not at all. But they do mean that we must know the danger and guard against it. Some regulations the Federal government may properly demand of the states receiving Federal funds; but these should not be such as to interfere with any proper local freedom. As to debatable issues, the Federal Office of Education (or Department of Education when it comes) should expect to rely on persuasion to improve practices, not on Federal regulations.

2. The argument that the wealthier states should not be asked to tax themselves to benefit the poorer we have really answered in the opening discussion. Federal aid is the proper third step in developing our American public education. As matters now stand, certain poorer states are already appropriating a greater proportion of their per capita wealth than are the wealthier states. These poorer states simply are not able, on any reasonable reckoning, to support a proper standard of education. They need help and should have it for the reasons previously given. Moving about is so common and relations between states so widespread that the cause of one state is here also the cause of us all. Any backward group hurts all the rest, culturally, politically, and even financially. The long-range good of the whole country calls for the adequate education of the whole people.

3. The third line of opposition to Federal aid is indirect and conditional. Certain groups interested in securing direct or indirect public support for nonpublic schools have been unwilling to vote for Federal aid unless provision were made at the same time to aid their schools.

It seems hardly necessary to consider this argument in the light of the recent Supreme Court decision. No public money can, in accordance with the Court's interpretation of the Constitution, be appropriated directly or indirectly to support of any religion. But it may be well to add the argument against separation of our people into distinct and abiding groups, as would tend to be true if public funds were given either to private or to parochial schools. It seems much better for all the population to mingle together in one system of public education. For any group to separate itself, either for social prestige or for religious purposes, is to introduce into America the lasting divisions in the population which curse certain European countries. The success of democracy depends on the ability of ideas to spread through the population on merit alone. Separating groups lessens the probability of such spread. The democratic aim must be to bring people together into one effectively communicating whole.

The conclusion seems clear that we should have Federal aid to equalize more nearly public school education throughout the country. Such aid should be given solely to tax-supported, publicly controlled, public education, and should carry no Federal control beyond seeing that the money is distributed without discrimination to all affected.

CHAPTER XXV. *Character Building*

A PERSON's character is the organized aggregate of his tendencies to behavior—specifically, his tendencies to regular and predictable behavior. In the degree, then, that one has character he will tend to behave—think, feel, choose, act—in accordance with the personality patterns he has accumulated (learned) through the years. We thus say of a certain person that kindliness or considerateness is "characteristic" of him. If we then hear that this person has acted harshly, we say that is "not like him."

To appraise one's character in this way indicates the assumption, suggested in the opening sentence, that a character is an organized, interactive whole. And this seems demonstrably true. All parts and aspects of a well-built character do cooperate in the service of its accepted underlying principles of action. This action as a whole gives, as we saw earlier, efficacy to the act; but, with principles also involved, it does more than that, it gives *appropriateness of action*, appropriateness to fit the principles of action previously organized into the character.

Thus in each act there are involved all of one's habits, dispositions, and tendencies, each according to the degree of its pertinence to the matter at hand. Each one accordingly feels as it is "like him" to feel, including of course his peculiar impulsiveness and "aberrations"; he thinks out of his own specific insight and understanding; he acts morally according to what he accepts as right to do; his motor habits come into action in accordance with their previously organized connection with his feelings and thoughts. This is character in operation.

It is, then, the internally organized aggregate of all one's habits—insights, dispositions, any psychological tendencies—which constitute his character, which make him what he is as an individual. The Oxford English Dictionary defines character as "the aggregate of the distinctive features of anything," "the sum of the moral and mental qualities which distinguish an individual." Each real character is thus necessarily unique. It is the fact of the interpenetration of habits (taking habit in its broad sense) which makes character possible, the fact that all work together and that each affects the others. In fact John Dewey says that "character is the interpenetration of habits," having just asserted that "were it not for the continued operation of all habits in every act, no such thing as character could exist." (46:38) To say that "all habits" thus operate "in every act" may appear a bit strong; but when we consider how habits do act, the assertion seems justified. It is out of this fact that we can have regularized, predictable behavior.

It should not be misunderstood from the foregoing discussion that character alone is the sole source of behavior; the environment is also a true factor, as we shall later consider in some detail. In a true sense, character and environment are, so to say, mother and father of behavior. That is, character is, as indicated, the psychological structure which sums up in one organic whole all of the individual's prior experiences, and out of which, in its interaction with the environment, behavior emerges.

Character is, as we saw above, regularized. It may of course be regularly bad as truly as regularly good. However, in the more usual sense, a man of character is a man with tendencies toward worthy behavior. Webster's *Dictionary of Synonyms* gives the quotation: "When we say of such and such a man that he has . . . character, we generally mean that he has disciplined his temperament, his disposition, into strict obedience to the behests of duty." Bertrand Russell speaks to the same effect of the achieved "power of pursuing a distant object steadily, foregoing and suffering many things on the way. This involves the subordination of impulse to will, the power of directing action by large desires even at moments when they are not vividly alive. Without this, no serious ambition, good or bad, can be realized, no consistent purpose can dominate." (143:170*f.*)

What is the relation of character and personality? Are the two identical? Or do they need to be distinguished? Character is the inclusive term which takes in all aspects of the organism's behavior in relation to itself and its environment; it is the habit aspect of the whole, recognizing that habits are not merely motor or physical, but mental and emotional as well. In other words, as indicated earlier, character means the sum of all one's tendencies to regularized and predictable behavior, which includes the personality.

Personality is an aspect of character, and accordingly is distinguishable from character. Personality is the self-conscious, self-directing self. Though the term is less inclusive, personality is the central and crucial essence of character, the self as it feels and thinks about itself, about others, about things, about values, all in terms of the interrelations of the person with his environment.

Thus any discussion of character necessarily includes personality. But certain aspects of personality-building require special treatment and will therefore be discussed in a separate chapter. Here will be discussed the building of the character and the desirable content to be built into character.

HOW CHARACTER DEVELOPS

Character is not, as some have thought, inborn; it is individually achieved. It is developed from the original equipment one has at birth. At the beginning the infant is much like a sensitive plant, with little if any consciousness, no self-consciousness, and nothing properly to be called character. The process of achieving or building character is that of effectively accumulating and organizing successive learnings. The first habit formation may begin even before birth and so on a relatively unconscious level. After birth, learnings slowly accumulate to form the beginning of an organization, out of which comes consciousness in a fuller sense. In time, especially as language begins, the self-other process discussed in Chapter III comes into operation and from this develops self-consciousness. Now the individual acts not only consciously, but self-consciously, aware both of what he does and that he is doing it. Out of this fact, as we saw further in Chapter VIII, come in turn accountability, responsibility, and conscience; so that prudence and morality have now begun to function and grow.

But suppose we go more slowly through this process. Even during the first baby stages, before self-consciousness, the child is taking on meanings, dispositions to act in certain ways, attitudes toward himself, toward others, toward life. Though not aware in any self-conscious sense of how he is feeling and learning to behave, he is building unconsciously a basis for character which may be highly significant for the character he will later build self-consciously.

Even when the child attains early self-consciousness, in the sense of knowing what he is doing and that he is doing it, he will in most cases be acting chiefly on impulse, with little control of impulse by thought; he is not yet a self-governing, self-determining person—not yet a character in the true, full sense; his behavior is instead determined largely by impulse or by someone else who intervenes. He has not reached the stage to choose in the light of his own thinking and control. Certainly he has not yet reached the stage to examine critically what he wishes to do and to stand for before the world.

The earlier growth as a person, from birth on, came by living through experiences and responding with feelings, new meanings, increasing skills. Growth in character comes as the child himself begins to make choices on his own (or as nearly as he can manage). Even in the early impulsive-choice stage, it is now *he*—the person in a beginning sense—who is intervening to make situations go as he wishes. If he were to develop no further in character-building, he would continue, as do many adults, to act chiefly on impulse, with no criticism of his impulses. In that case he would carry an inadequate "character" through life, despite its bad effects on others and very often on himself.

But if as the child matures physically he is also helped to mature as to character, he will learn to take thought and so restrain some impulses; beforetimes others have restrained him, now he learns, in varying degrees, to restrain himself through his own thought and choice of results. But if he is to build character, the character out of which he will act when not managed by others, he must build it himself. Character, as has been said, "cannot be given to the individual, nor memorized into him, nor trained or inculcated into him in the direct sense; but it can be fostered by the provision of such conditions for his living as direct his sensitiveness and responses into this distinctive way of behaving." The problem of character-building thus relates itself to this educative living and asks how to foster and guide it. The individual must build desirable character, if at all, only by himself *choosing* to act in desirable ways, by accepting in his heart that these are desirable ways and that he wishes to live by them. *His* character, accordingly, manifests itself by what *he* chooses to be and to do, by what *he* values. As Wordsworth said: "So build we up the being that we are." The actual process is one of development through behavior; and this development is precisely one of learning. We conclude thus far that not only does the individual build his own character, but that he builds it by behaving that way.

To build character, then, the individual must face many situations where he himself does the choosing. As long as someone else manages and directs him, (socially essential as this may be at times), he is not himself choosing, he is not exercising constructive choice and so is not building proper character. If he is to learn to subordinate present impulse and habit to broader or deeper good he must himself see the broader good as under these circumstances the right thing to do; and so accepting, he must do it. Thus it is that one grows in character. Others may help, teacher or class or both, but the person himself has to see and accept. It is out of these internal conflicts between present impulse and broader purpose that character is built. Present impulse and existing habits pull the individual in one direction; the broader purpose pulls in another direction, with the consequent demand for remaking the behavior pattern. In the degree, then, that the new broader impulse wins out, the person will rebuild or develop his character. The first victory may not suffice, it usually does not; successive victories are generally necessary in order to fasten the new pattern—thinking, feeling, impulse, and movement—firmly into a reliable habit. Only when the new has become so firmly imbedded, so thoroughly digested, that the self now identifies itself fully and cordially with the new—only then has the new pattern of behavior, the new addition to character, been truly achieved. In this achieving the appropriate new behavior has become regularized; others can now expect it to recur.

At a higher level, character is *critically* adopted behavior built into effective psychological structure. A person has such a character in the degree that he acts from *critically* accepted principles. Kant speaks of this level when he says, "Character means that the person derives his rules of conduct from himself and from the dignity of humanity." The processes of building such critically made principles of action and of fitting habits of conduct into them are mutually interactive, each helps the other into fuller being and action. Thus is the higher character achieved.

IMPACT OF THE SURROUNDINGS ON CHARACTER

That the surrounding culture in considerable degree shapes to its model the characters growing up in it has long been noted. The less the group members question their specific culture, the more completely will the rising generation accept it as it is. Primitive groups do very little questioning; they are highly insistent on the *status quo*. The young accordingly tend to accept the group culture as one whole. We sometimes wonder how they "swallow" such—to us—"curious" ways and beliefs. In contrast, we have seen how Athenian Greece led the world in questioning the home culture. In time the youth of that culture grew up with as creative and inquiring minds as the world has ever known. The practice of criticism is, however, far from universal today in even the most highly cultivated societies. The importance of criticism is, nevertheless, beyond doubt. On it depends the quality of character to be developed by the youth of that society—whether inquiring, creative, and constructive, or docile, submissive, and stereotyped. On it, in addition, depends the future of any given society.

In the civilized world today any given social group distributes itself on a scale of disposition to question. At the top of the scale are those most disposed and best prepared to question; these have accepted their beliefs only after the closest criticism. Such characters have strong convictions where there is adequate basis for such; but even these they hold subject to possible modification as new facts may appear or better insight is gained. These persons at the top of the scale are "reasonable," that is, open to argument and reason as adequate cause to re-examine may appear. At the bottom of the scale just the opposite holds. The persons here hold stubbornly to what they first learned, or, if they change, they change not so much by reason as by emotional whim; they have not learned how to judge critically. These can hardly be said to have characters in the authentic sense of the term. Their beliefs were determined by others or by tradition, they have little if any power to criticize them. In between these two extremes we find varying degrees of openness to argument mingled with varying degrees of stubbornness, that is, varying degrees of established character.

Two points concern us here: first, the degree to which any culture tends to build unquestioning acceptance of its tradition, as contrasted with a disposition to question and re-examine what has been handed down; second, the relative types of character resulting from each tendency. The finer quality character, it seems clear, is one which holds its beliefs and convictions as a result of reason, not because of authoritarian tradition. In Chapter XIV it was pointed out that each older adolescent should critically re-examine and reappraise the various principles of thought and ways of life that he had in childhood "swallowed whole," so to say, on the authority of his elders and of established practice. After such reappraisal the adolescent may or may not accept what he previously believed; but in either case what he now believes is his own in a sense and degree not previously true—it is held now on consciously recognized and chosen grounds, it is accordingly both more serviceable when used and is besides better suited for further development as future need may arise. It is more serviceable, because being now better understood it can be applied more intelligently to the various life situations that arise. It is better suited to further development, because being consciously held on known grounds it can be more readily revised and built anew as new situations demand and as new related thoughts are found to join constructively with this.

However, in spite of all we can do by way of re-examination and reappraisal, none of us will achieve complete freedom from our specific cultural limitations; the civilization in which we grow up will in some measure predispose us to its ways of life and thought. Anthropology shows how universal has been this effect. Our own civilization still tends strongly in this direction, character-degrading as the tendency is if carried far. This is present not only in the lower levels who so misbuild the minds and characters of their children; many in the middle and upper groups fear to have their sons and daughters question values taught them in youth, lest on examination these values be no longer cherished. This age-old tradition is still very strong. To these people, and to many organized groups among us, education is still essentially indoctrination, inadequate as such a conception is for life in a changing world.

To be critical of our existing culture and civilization is not to deny the thesis of Chapter VI that, as we now judge values, the service performed for us by our culture is absolutely essential. Without the culture achieved by our predecessors and by them handed down to us we would now be little better than beasts, more intelligent than the rest, but beasts still. The indebtedness we thus owe we can never forget, but this in no way detracts from either the propriety or the necessity to criticize the civilization we now have.

If it were reasonable to believe that civilization has, however, achieved absolute truth on social and moral matters, opposition to re-examination and reappraisal would be more logical and perhaps in certain respects defensible. But no modern-minded civilization can admit such a claim in its behalf. If we are to help build the kind of characters needed, we have to recognize that weaknesses exist both in our personal outlooks and in our civilization, and that even the most adequate of our present beliefs will need to develop as conditions of life change. We must therefore educate our youth to the ability and disposition to study our civilization so as to find these defects and remedy them. No other type of character can serve either the individual or the common good. To take any other position is to hide one's head, ostrich-like, in the sand. Such a policy can lead only to unhappiness and eventually disaster. Whitehead speaks strongly on this point:

> When one considers . . . the importance of this question of the education of the nation's young, the broken lives, the defeated hopes, the national failures, which result from the frivolous inertia with which it is treated, it is difficult to restrain within oneself a savage rage (172:22).

THE TYPE OF CHARACTER TO SEEK

Answers to this inquiry will, of course, depend on one's deeper values, on the kind of personal and group living basically desired for self and for society. To love and desire democratic living means to seek the development of one type of person; to love and desire any kind of nondemocratic living would mean a different choice, a choice to fit the kind of living desired. This book has been built around acceptance of and concern for democracy, thus certain choices as to character must of necessity follow.

This does not mean a blueprint either of character or of civilization; for each is inevitably entangled in the changing future, and that future is in its details forever unpredictable. It does, however, mean planning for a growing character, increasingly able as events develop to reshape both itself and the surrounding civilization. The test of such growth is, as Toynbee says, its "progress toward self-determination," each—both individual character and civilization—alike progressing toward ever more adequate self-determination, a self-determination which knows increasingly better *what* it does and *how* and *why*, with ever more effective regard for the good of all concerned. Specifically, the ultimate test of the good character is its effectiveness in bringing the good life, not simply to the individual himself but also to all concerned. From this point of view the good character is exactly the correlative of ethics and the good civilization; and both the good character and the correlatively good civilization taken together constitute precisely the inclusive bifocal aim of education.

This then becomes the stated aim of character education: to build a character which by its conscious choices brings the good life ever more effectively both for itself and for civilization.

What, in more specific detail, does this mean as to the character to seek? Traits previously discussed will be brought together here to indicate directions of growth. That individuals will differ in degree of attaining these traits does not deny their applicability to all and hence their validity as goals for education to seek.

We wish, for the individual's own happiness and social fitness, a well-adjusted personality. Without this all else is endangered. We wish, as befits democracy, a self-determining person, one not tied to the dictates or direction of others, one who can himself make worthy and rewarding choices, choices for his own living and for the common good. He must then act thoughtfully, not impulsively or selfishly; he must be disposed to study before he decides what to do: he must know how to use resources, books, or people, know how to confer with others and profit by their ideas and suggestions. He must be able—at his level of ability and maturity and in proportion to what is at stake—to weigh and evaluate the various factors involved, in other words to "think critically." He must like to learn, to find out, to add to his existing insight, to get to the bottom of things. For in our kind of world to accumulate knowledge and insight is, for the thoughtful, a life-long task and duty; and, besides this, to be curious, to like to learn, adds much to the content and enjoyment of one's personal living.

This growing youth must also be helped to build creativeness in his attack on life's problems and situations, rather than simply following the crowd. He must, too, be morally sensitive to the needs and values of others; not selfish but disposed to act out of concern for others and for the common good. He must learn to live happily and fruitfully with his fellows, enjoying his relations with them as they work together for interests and purposes in common. Also he must build interests worthy and meaningful to him; for by increase of interests he adds not only to the richness of his life's content and satisfactions, but to his service to the group. Finally he must develop a disciplined self, build "moral backbone," the steady disposition to act on what study indicates as right and to persevere until he has done what he should.

THE SCHOOL'S PART IN CHARACTER-BUILDING

To describe in any fullness the school's part in the development of character would require an entire book on method. The aim here will be to sketch such a method from the point of view of the philosophy of education involved. Certain underlying principles of psychology will first be given and then certain problems likely to arise in connection with them will be considered.

As indicated earlier, character cannot be given, either peaceably or forcibly, to another. Each one builds his own character, and from his own innermost heart. Others, however, can help, fruitful conditions can be named and fostered.

The building of some kind of character, good or bad, strong or weak, is always in process. Each act, each decision, each impulse accepted for action, leaves its effect. As James said in a previous quotation, "We are spinning our own fates, good or evil, and never to be undone. Every smallest stroke of virtue or of vice leaves its [impress]." The problem is how to foster desirable character, how to bring about such living as will, through the principles of learning previously discussed, bring into active being the strong, worthy character.

Seven principles of living and learning seem especially applicable in such character-building:

1. To build any desired trait of character, the individual must *live* that trait: he must behave that way and in a setting which he feels properly calls for that behavior.

2. The individual must accept this new behavior as his own, his way of behaving for this kind of situation. Otherwise he will not so learn it as to build it into effective character.

This means that to learn initiative, self-direction, or responsibility, one must *live* that way. To learn to make decisions, to act on thinking, to evaluate wisely and objectively, one must engage in these precise processes; and through it all he must accept in his heart that such behavior is right for him, is his chosen way of behaving.

3. To foster the inner essence of character-building, that is, the acceptance by one's innermost being of the new behavior, requires the closest attention on the part of teacher or parent to child attitudes and feelings; for these are the crucial factors involved, they determine what the individual will accept as his way of living. To feel that his own values are slighted makes the person less disposed to be considerate of others; it also makes him less inclined to accept better standards that are being fostered. Hostility to the teacher or to the school or to what is going on in school shuts off desire to try. Accumulation of such antagonistic feelings adds in time to a person's characteristic attitudes and values.

4. As the individual grows in maturity he must more and more see and accept the conscious *why* of what he does; otherwise intelligent self-direction is not being built. (We must, however, not expect younger children to think *much* of *why* they act. This kind of learning comes but slowly; to push it too fast is to hinder, not help.)

5. Strength of character results in the degree that there is (i) clearness of decision to act and (ii) internally supported vigor of effort to carry out the decision, especially vigor of effort in spite of continued difficulties and discouragements.

6. The more the new behavior is felt by the individual to be essential for carrying out of purposes important to him, the more surely will the foregoing principles be acted upon.

7. Close attention should be paid to all cases of difficulty in living up to accepted standards, as well as to cases of internal conflict over new standards to be accepted. In such cases help may be needed (i) to clarify thinking and remove conflicts as to what to do and why; and (ii) to encourage all concerned, both individually and collectively, to live as well as possible up to the results of their own highest thinking.

It may be well to repeat in another way what has just been said. School life must provide many situations where the child can make choices of a kind to count toward moral character development. It is not enough for him to choose whether to draw a bird or a fish (though not to allow this might bring hurtful antagonisms), for this makes no difference to other people and probably not much difference to the child's life as he sees it. If he is to learn to make choices that make life better for himself and for others, he must practice making worth-while choices and do this under conditions in which others can help him improve his standards. Only in this way can there be real hope of his learning to take wider considerations into account and act accordingly.

The school situation and atmosphere must be such that, on the one hand, the pupil will feel free to do his own best thinking and acting and, on the other, will be challenged so to think and act. If he feels hostile, tense, inclined to sabotage, he is not likely to work constructively with the rest and may even prefer to interfere with and disrupt their activities. If he feels that what is going on doesn't make any difference anyway, he will hardly feel challenge in it or accept responsibility to make it succeed. So that the cultivation of a really constructive atmosphere is perhaps the first crucial task of school and teacher—an atmosphere of friendly group relationships to open the pupil's heart to constructive thinking and acting. Out of this can come the easy exchange of helpful ideas, the feeling of hearty acceptance of responsible effort, and a growing regard for good standards of workmanship and proper behavior toward others.

In order to accomplish the desirable atmosphere just discussed, teacher and pupils have to work together. The pupils will immediately affect each other probably more effectively than will the teacher. We saw earlier how the social setting is, in the judgment of John Dewey, "the greatest force in shaping the dispositions and attitudes of individuals." But it is the teacher who must guide and steer the group process in school. Many of the most desirable character traits require years of widening experience for their adequate development. The teacher must know and appreciate the full-grown traits; the pupils have yet much ahead of them to experience and digest. It is in this situation that the teacher's guidance is essential.

And further, for best growth the young must get the *idea* of the next advance. To bring an idea to conscious awareness is usually an essential prerequisite to getting it accepted as a principle of behavior. And to get this conscious awareness two things seem necessary, a practical experiencing of the new principle and the naming of it. The Alexandrian education seemed to think that giving the name would give the idea. It is impossible to get an idea apart from actual experiencing. The children must thus get the idea of finer ways of living; for example, that responsible self-direction is a more desirable way of living than being managed by others. Once they get this idea and can talk about it together so as to look consciously at the working of the principle in action, then they are far readier to accept the principle to act upon. And similarly for the principle of working for the common good; though this may take longer to accept and will probably require more skillful guidance. Many children, it seems fair to assert, have never had their attention called to this regard for the common good, much less considered it on its merits, even though they are often scolded for not acting on it. In all such matters, let it be repeated, mere naming does not give the idea. Preaching, verbal admonitions, may do more harm than good. It is living a thing that prepares for naming it. He who finds himself and others living for the common good is ready for the idea, for the naming of the principle. The class can then discuss the principle on its merits, and the influence of public approval can be exerted. It is in such ways that conscious character traits can be built.

KNOWLEDGE AND CHARACTER

Some will ask whether this kind of character-building, if fitted into the total school program, will not crowd out other desirable parts of the present program; specifically, whether knowledge of the usual sort will not be lost. The point is important. The building of knowledge and thought are important school aims.

There are two lines of answer. First, the character stressed in this book as the aim of education is the intelligent character, one able to think adequately before it decides to act. Thus to think intelligently the individual must have a wide range of effective knowledge, and this the school must help him get. The second line of answer is to distinguish two kinds of knowledge: type 1 and type 2. Type 1 is what we were considering in the preceding paragraph—knowledge which actually functions in life to help carry it on better. Much of this is never written down in books; certainly most people have never learned from books how to get on with other people, how to get about town. Type 2 is such knowledge as is usually found in textbooks and other scholarly works. This second type may, especially for some, become type 1; that is, it may be tied meaningfully into a person's thinking so as to be used to add content and richness to life. But type 2 may, and this is true for many, remain merely as information, held as such but not really used in conducting life. Some to support their ego may exhibit this information before others, to let it be seen that they have it; but this is merely a vain show, it is no true functioning of the information as serving life's purposes.

Knowledge as organized in textbooks and as presented in the old-line school was almost entirely pure type 2. It was learned that way and for many, probably for most, it stayed type 2. The old school knew no other way of teaching. The new school wishes *as much knowledge as possible* of the sort to help life go on better, to make life more meaningful, to deal with life more intelligently. The new way intends accordingly to have knowledge learned on the basis of its present functioning in the life of the learner. It believes that knowledge is easier and better learned this way and is far more likely to be used, and that knowledge better learned and used in life furnishes the best basis for further learning.

For youth to learn in this way requires a new and different method of teaching. What we wish is knowledge built into effective character; and this the assignment-memorizing-examination-passing procedure does not furnish. It is actual living properly guided that alone can build knowledge into adequate character.

CHAPTER XXVI. *Emotional Adjustment and Education*

THIS topic is, as history goes, new to the educator. For only within the present half century has study of emotional problems, of "personality adjustment," been sufficiently advanced to warrant acceptance by the practical educator as a proper object for his concern and effort. Following the impact of Freud (1856–1939) and other students of the problem, it begins now to appear that, as regards conscious school education, attention to the demands of normal emotional adjustment should—along with character-building—take priority over all other specific educational aims. For, without proper emotional adjustment, little else avails in life. And the problem concerns not simply individuals. Society is increasingly finding that emotional problems arising from our modern industrial civilization affect the health of society as such. It is another instance of the principle that we are all members one of another.

However, acceptance of responsibility for problems of emotional adjustment is very uneven within the teaching profession. At the moment, acceptance is most pronounced as regards younger children and lessens in general with the increasing age of the learner. In the typical high school and college, teachers tend to ignore the matter, partly because the idea is too new, partly because the traditional commitment of teachers for these ages has been almost solely to subject matter and its acquisition.

Recognition that *behavior is caused* and that *personality maladjustments are learned* constitutes the twentieth-century contribution to an understanding of emotional problems; and this insight gives helpful clues both to positive procedure for building wholesome personality and to the more difficult problem of how to treat maladjustments. It is the importance of these two problems which demands a place for this topic in any adequate philosophy of education. No aim for education is more vital or essential than the proper care of the emotions, the building of properly adjusted personalities.

EMOTION IN GOAL-SEEKING BEHAVIOR; VARYING RESIDUAL EFFECTS

We have seen in preceding chapters how emotion is in truth an organic resource which when properly used serves to increase the effectiveness of behavior. Because, biologically, man is a goal-seeking organism, structure and function have been built to this end. Let some stirring situation confront him, either as threat or as hope; desire then arises, and to attain this desire man sets up an end or goal and devises means which promise the attainment of the goal. Suppose a measure fails and the enterprise is threatened. If the man has sufficient desire and strength of character, he will—unless reason forbids—renew the attack either by hitting harder or by devising more promising means. In the end success or failure attends the effort.

Let us now review the steps in this analysis to see just how emotion serves at the various successive steps. At the very first, when the situation emerges—it may emerge slowly or it may burst upon the person—feeling will arise according to the impact the situation makes on him, and this feeling, in the degree of its strength, will stir him to act. If the situation is not unusual and involves neither special threat nor specially inviting possibility, the feeling aroused will be one of mild interest. But suppose a very threatening situation suddenly emerges. If the person involved is quite emotional, the feeling aroused will likely be very great, so great as probably to interfere with wise and thoughtful consideration of what to do. If the person is well-balanced and thoughtful, the sudden trouble may stir him, but he will probably try to think things over before he determines his action. And after he has thus waited and thought, his emotional stirring may calm down a bit as he understands the situation better, or it may continue and even increase as he sees the seriousness of what is involved. His revised feeling of the importance of the matter at issue will probably stay with him throughout all the rest of the experience as a constant urge to furnish appropriate care and effort at each succeeding step.

When the personality is healthy and the effort successful, each step is accompanied by an emotion of interest in the measures taken and a concern to make the effort succeed. This accompanying interest in the effort itself is a definite satisfaction at the time, and when success is attained (if it is) there is further satisfaction as the person perceives the outcome fitting his aim. Such satisfactions from specific successes accumulate to give an abiding feeling of confidence that one can safely undertake such efforts; and this feeling of confidence is itself a satisfaction in the degree that it is achieved. Suppose, however, an important step should so fail as to threaten the success of the whole enterprise. The thoughtful man (of strong character) will feel his emotion stirred by this threat and will give greater thought and care and, if need be, expend stronger effort to get the enterprise going successfully once more. In the end, if full success is attained, the emotion as urge to act will disappear; instead a resulting emotion of satisfaction at success will emerge, with probably some addition to the person's long accumulating sense of confidence in himself as able to manage the ordinary situations of his life. If other persons cooperated, there will be additions to the person's estimate of them according to the kind and degree of helpful cooperation they gave. If instead the final result was failure, the resulting emotions would be practically the opposite: the urge which had supported the continued effort may remain waiting another chance; there may be feelings of humiliation and discouragement; with regard to those who cooperated there will or will not be appreciation, depending again on the kind and degree of cooperation they gave.

MEANING OF EMOTIONAL ADJUSTMENT AND MALADJUSTMENT

We saw just above how varying emotions accompany the successive stages of the typical goal-seeking effort. It is from these manifestations that we get definitions of adjustment and maladjustment. If in a particular effort satisfaction results, this satisfaction can accumulate with others like it into an abiding confidence that one can work successfully along this particular line. A general accumulation of such confidence gives poise of character. If, in addition to confidence in himself, the person has built also satisfying feelings of appreciation for fellow workers and confidence in them as persons of kindliness and integrity, then in this respect, too, is his personality better adjusted. If as time goes on there continues to be accumulated a wholesome emotional outlook, we say that the person has a well-adjusted personality. His emotions arise at the right time and they help him succeed better at whatever he is doing. Neither lack of confidence in himself or others nor warped attitudes toward life prevent him from facing life situations squarely and as wisely as he is able.

But suppose instead of success there is failure, such repeated failure that the person cumulatively builds an abiding distrust of himself and disbelief in his ability to accomplish his undertakings. This "inferiority complex," as it is often called, will henceforth come forward to keep him from trying his best. His emotion, instead of spurring him to greater effort, as it does with the well-adjusted personality, now tells him that it is no use to try, that he always fails. This man's emotion now enters to thwart effort; it hurts, not helps. Any person who has built such a hurtful emotion is by so much maladjusted.

Because this discussion is so crucial to our topic, it may be well to repeat parts of it with elaboration. The dominating characteristic of the normal organism is, as stated, to behave, to act, so as to meet and control the confronting situation. In such behaving the organism acts as a cooperating whole, with thinking, feeling, and physical motion all inextricably intermingled, each of these functions cooperating with the others. Thinking, for example, not only guides and directs the whole effort but, besides, it relates all this to the longer life and larger world whole of which this one experience is but part. To act without proper thinking is to act impulsively; to act on thinking is to act on one's best judgment. Thus, if life is to go well, thinking must control what is being done. Habits and skills must work under the control of thinking; otherwise, the person will not be acting intelligently. Effort, too, must go on in accord with judgment in spite of external hindrance and opposition, in spite of internal fatigue and tendencies to discouragement or the like. Here emotion, if it is wholesome, serves not only by adding to the content of life (allowing the individual to enjoy what he does), but also by helping the organism to fight better, whether the enemy be external hindrance or internal weakness. In this fight, properly adjusted emotion helps by adding genuine strength and continuity to what is otherwise being done.

But—to repeat—if emotion is to help and not hurt the proper effort of the organism, it must obey and support thinking. If emotion fails to subordinate itself to proper thinking, either by supplanting the thinking in deciding what to do or by refusing to shift as thinking shifts, then the proper effort of the organism is by so much thwarted and the resulting action becomes inappropriate. It is to such a state of the organism, wherein emotion thwarts intelligent action, that we give the name of personality maladjustment.

CERTAIN COMMON TYPES OF MALADJUSTMENT

To understand better the difference between adjustment and maladjustment of personality it may be well to consider several common types of maladjustment.

1. *Insecurity*. This is an abiding feeling, acquired from experience, that one does not have a safe base from which to face life. It may be begun in earliest infancy if the mother fails to manifest enough love and tenderness in feeding the child or otherwise caring for it. It easily develops if the father or older children so tease the child as to make him feel unsafe. It may develop in school if other children seemingly receive more favored treatment or if the child has difficulty in making a satisfactory place for himself in the group. It is a maladjustment in the degree that because of it the child hesitates to take a normal part in surrounding life. This is in fact one of the more common of the serious maladjustments, and the "mother," so to say, of many others.

2. *Inferiority Complex*. This is the cumulative effect of repeated failures such that from them the child has come to feel insecure, to shrink from normal relationships, and to distrust the effectiveness of his effort. Such a child will refuse to try where he could succeed. It is a clear case of maladjustment: it is an emotional learning which interferes with appropriate behavior. This is one of the most hurtful of personality maladjustments.

3. *Attention-Seeking*. It is the abnormal seeking of attention that here concerns us, where the person seeks undue attention or intrudes himself unduly. There is, of course, a proper practice of attention-

seeking. The infant who cries, for example, when he finds himself in seeming need, is using his only resource to attract necessary attention. To seek attention is, in fact, a proper procedure for anyone who finds himself in need.

Excessive attention-seeking, however, is a very common manifestation of insecurity. If a child gets less than normal satisfaction from life relationships, outside of school or inside, and so feels unhappy and insecure, his efforts to compensate, to secure satisfaction, may take the form of attention-seeking. Failure on the part of teacher or parent to recognize the cause of the behavior, to see that the child needs recognition and satisfaction rather than scolding, is one of the commonest failures in insight. It is the child with spirit who, if he feels left out, seeks to attract attention, to gain recognition. and so to remedy his situation. This behavior is more wholesome than the tendency to shrink into himself, withdraw into unhappiness and insecurity.

Many sorts of factors may cause attention-seeking. Deprivation of ordinary enjoyment, overprotection, oversupervision, are common causes. The first-born who feels neglected in favor of his newly born brother or sister may develop the habit. In fact, attention-seeking, while one of the milder maladjustments, is one of the most common. It should also be recognized that attention-seeking may be a result of overindulgence. The point to understand clearly is that the behavior is caused, and that study of each case is necessary to determine the particular cause. Then measures appropriate to the cause should be taken—to counteract the feeling of neglect or to break down expectation of indulgence. Most adults in their effort to overcome this maladjustment tend to overstress indulgence as a cause and to ignore the normal demand for legitimate attention.

4: *Withdrawal.* By withdrawal is meant the tendency of the individual to withdraw into himself instead of to engage in the give-and-take of ordinary group life and to make efforts to work out situations as he would like them to be. It arises out of difficulty of making life come out as he wishes, usually because of repeated unsatisfactory efforts to do so. The tendency to withdraw is very widely overlooked by adults because it gives no trouble. It passes as "goodness" or "mere shyness," with failure to recognize that such goodness or shyness can be a sign of serious difficulty, that it can constitute a more serious type of behavior than attention-seeking or other such forms of aggressive behavior in which the person works out his feelings rather than internalizes them.

Undue timidity may be one manifestation of withdrawal—a shrinking from taking normal part in surrounding situations and from making efforts to control such situations. A certain amount of timidity need not, of course, be disturbing; but it is something to watch. It at least represents lack of confidence, quite differentiable from unassuming self-confidence and poise. The quiet child who prefers solitary amusements to association with others or prefers helping the teacher to playing with other children or prefers much study of lessons to normal childhood activity and fun; the good child who never causes trouble because he never deviates from expectations; the child who easily acquiesces in the teacher's ways or the plans of other children—these are children to observe with care in order to discover the *cause* of their behavior.

A frequent manifestation of withdrawal is daydreaming. This trait, like any manifestation of withdrawal, also comes from failure to secure sufficient satisfaction in ordinary living. In daydreaming the person, instead of making the healthy response of searching for an effective way to get what he wants, seeks "escape," indulges in the unhealthy response of *imagining* ("daydreaming") a satisfying situation and using the satisfaction from this imagined success as compensation for his actual lack. "Good" children often indulge in daydreaming, children who would not engage in attention-seeking or annoying behavior; and such children, too, are often overlooked because they cause no trouble to others. Some children resort to daydreaming as easier than facing the causes of failures which could be remedied by taking thought and making effort. In such cases they need help in attacking their problem effectively. Some other children whose lives present problems beyond their ability to cope with resort to daydreaming as an escape. These children need outside help to reduce the intensity of their problems. In either case it is essential to find the *cause* and make plans accordingly.

The Wickman study* found that teachers most frequently underestimated or ignored the seriousness of withdrawing behavior and instead focused their concern on aggressive or "annoying"

* E. K. Wickman, *Children's Behavior and Teachers' Attitudes* (New York, Commonwealth Fund, 1928).

behavior; the teachers' ratings, however, were the exact reverse of judgments of clinical psychologists, who rated withdrawing behavior as of highest seriousness. Since the Wickman study, insight along such lines has grown definitely among teachers. However, failure to recognize the real cause of behavior of this type, and therefore to count it as "good" behavior to be disregarded in favor of other more important concerns, is still widespread.

Many different kinds of maladjustment are recognized by psychiatrists, but they do not call for recognition here. In addition to the instances listed above, others may be named as inordinate hate or fear, an upsetting sense of guilt, over-anxiety. The normal person may entertain feelings which, from a certain logical point of view, belong in the same category with any of these disturbing feelings. But with the normal person the feeling does not so affect him as to make him act inappropriately. In fact, as we have already seen, feeling and emotion, when they act normally and properly, increase effort and enhance life; it is only the excessive and "undigested" emotion that remains with one to constitute maladjustment.

MALADJUSTMENT IS LEARNED

Two principles govern the modern treatment of personality adjustment: that behavior is caused, and that maladjustment is learned. If a child behaves badly, we can know that actual, and presumably ascertainable, causes lie back of the bad conduct. If the bad behavior is recurrent and persistent, some personality maladjustment is probably an essential factor. Since such maladjustment is no original feature of the personality structure, the conclusion appears obvious that it has been learned, even though some innate predisposition may have provided a "lowered threshold" in this direction. In the light of the step-by-step analysis given earlier, there appear two principal ways in which personality maladjustments are learned.

1. *Excessive Emotion.* If an aroused emotion be excessive, this may, by being thus too vividly lived, be so strongly learned as to remain, long after the particular experience has passed, as an abiding tendency to excessive emotion. If so, this extreme emotion thus becomes an abiding personality trait and as such will enter hurtfully—that is, as opposed to good reason—into succeeding experiences. In this way an excessive fright may remain for years to make a

child feel insecure and overanxious in situations similar to that which originally gave the fright. Life is therein by so much hurt. "The burnt child dreads the fire," is a folk recognition of this principle.

2. *Cumulative Emotion.* The more common cause, however, of maladjustments is the cumulative effect of successive instances of emotional learning. This is perhaps best seen in cases of repeated failure and frustration. If, as a result of failure or other frustration, the person takes away with him a small but persistent sense of personal failure or fear or hate or insecurity, this undigested residuum of emotion, whatever it be, will render the person more sensitive to the like emotion on a further occasion of failure. And if this new failure again leaves an undigested deposit, the second will unite with the first to form a still stronger emotional residuum. If this process be sufficiently repeated, the cumulative effect will be a personality maladjustment of unreasoning fear or insecurity or an inferiority complex, as the case may be.

All emotional maladjustments seem to come from one or the other of these two sources or a combination of both.

THREE INSTANCES OF DIFFERING EMOTIONAL OUTCOMES

Consideration of three specific instances may help to a better understanding of how different emotional experiences bring differing adjustment results.

1. A musically gifted high-school girl undertakes a difficult song, works at it assiduously, but in the end fails. What will she learn emotionally? What will be the effect on her personality?

The answer depends on the facts of the situation and how she responds to them. Suppose this girl's voice was in fact not equal to this particular song. If she has good help in appraising the experience, she may decide that she did in fact put up as good a fight as she reasonably could, but that with her voice she should not have made this particular effort. If she does so decide, in good faith and discernment, she may come out of the experience unhurt as regards her personality adjustment. True, she will henceforth know that her voice range is less than she had hoped, but she need feel no real discouragement under such circumstances. In fact, she is better off than she was at the outset; she has now "digested" her failure and initial discouragement with no general or inclusive loss of faith in herself. She can make a wiser decision next time and plan more intelligently for the future. In short, she has turned her failure into victory.

2. Another musically gifted high-school girl similarly undertakes a difficult song and fails. This girl, after thinking the matter over and consulting with older and wiser heads, decides that the failure was not necessary. While she had worked hard, she did not work wisely. She now believes, and justly, that a different practice procedure would probably have brought success. This girl is now wiser, and being wiser feels surer of herself. Feeling surer, she will next time try harder and along new lines. This girl, too, has specifically turned defeat into victory. She comes out with a better disciplined personality; her feelings are under better control. She is now more of a person.

3. The third possibility is of the negative sort. Either of these girls might, with less security to begin with or with bad advice, have come out with such a deep sense of failure as to be unable to "digest" her feelings of discouragement. Further brooding over the failure would, by cumulative learning, probably deepen the discouragement. Next time there would be less zeal and smaller faith, and consequently less effort and a greater likelihood of continued failure. Failure, if it comes, will add its cumulative effect; and an inferiority complex has been begun. Future efforts are to that extent doomed in advance. And the maladjustment is exactly this: that she has cumulatively built an aggregate of emotional discouragement which prevents her, when opportunity comes, from acting appropriately—up to her best effort. Her present emotion unfits her for proper effort.

WHAT EDUCATION CAN DO

Since maladjustments are learned, to do whatever is possible about them—both to prevent them and to cure them—appears to be a primary responsibility of education. A recent statement by Dr. E. T. McSwain appears pertinent at this point:

> I am a child. I am creating my emotional feelings and my mental abilities out of situations that adults provide for me. Daily I am creating the content of my future. How well prepared I will be to

> deal with the situations that will be encountered in the years ahead will be determined largely by the willingness of parents and teachers to understand what growing up means and their eagerness to provide for me the experiences and the materials that give me the opportunity to raise myself to an eventual higher level of mental and moral behavior (25: XXVI:403).

Educative effects begin in the home and continue in school and community. Three distinguishable types of personality adjustment problems accordingly present themselves: (i) the problem of avoiding maladjustment and, instead, building the healthy well-adjusted personality; (ii) the problem of aiding (curing) in home and/or school the milder, less serious cases of maladjustment; (iii) the problem of dealing with the serious cases of maladjustment. Problems (i) and (ii) as belonging properly to parents and teachers will be discussed here. Problem (iii), belonging properly to the psychiatric worker, will not be further considered.

1. *Building the Well-adjusted Personality.* The emphasis here is on positive measures, with only enough reference to maladjustment to see how to avoid and avert it.

The basis alike for building strong emotional adjustment and for avoiding maladjustment is to recognize that in addition to such bodily wants as hunger and thirst, there are certain personal wants or needs, insistent inner urges, such that to use them is to give vigorous expression to happy life while to deny them reasonable expression and satisfaction is to court positive maladjustment.

The more insistent of these urges are now fairly well recognized: (i) the craving for interesting and even exciting activity, (ii) the demand for security as against anxieties and fears, (iii) the desire for response (the most social of these urges), and (iv) the desire for recognition. These desires vary, to be sure, according to age and development, but in some form or other they are always present, awaiting but slight stimulation to be called actively and insistently into play. If denied natural expression and satisfaction, they will accumulate from experience to experience until they seriously interfere with desirable normal behavior.

Teachers and parents must recognize the serious demands which the existence of these urges makes on all who have to do with childhood and youth. In the past, little or no thought was given to this specific matter. From now on it becomes immoral for teacher or parent or group leader to fail to study seriously these urges so as (i) to know what they mean to the young; (ii) to recognize any maladjustment already begun because of lack or denial; and (iii) to deal appropriately, either personally or under expert guidance, with the situation that has developed.

Of the four urges above named, the first—the desire for activity—stands on a different basis from the other three in that it can, peculiarly as regards the school but also in the home, be used as leverage in meeting the others. That the healthy child craves activity of a kind interesting to him has been known from the beginning of time; but only within more recent years has this craving been recognized as itself a necessary, and therefore a proper and healthy, manifestation of life. In our social heritage, compulsory restraint of children was until recently the common procedure. Within the recollection of most now living, pupil initiative was distinctly repressed. In school even the youngest pupils were supposed to sit quietly, each at his individual desk, engaging in nothing more active or interesting than studying the next lesson in a book.

In contrast we have seen in preceding chapters how the newer school uses this craving for interesting activity as the primary basis of its teaching. In steering child life we begin with the child's desire for activity, especially with his desire for activity in behalf of personally felt interests. Typically the activity takes the form of the purposeful pursuit of enterprises either individually chosen or, more usually, group chosen. If the enterprise is a group choice the individual shares cooperatively in making it and so identifies himself with its fortunes. Reasonable success in such purposeful activities will be a strong factor in fostering desirable emotional adjustment.

Let us see how the carrying on of activities provides a means of meeting the other three basic needs mentioned above and also provides means for curing many mild disturbances that have already begun. As the need for security is one of the most basic requirements of human beings, so *insecurity* is one of the most common forms of maladjustment. By insecurity is meant, as was stated earlier, an abiding feeling, derived from experience, that one does not have a safe base from which to face life. In connection with the activity program, the teacher must give especial attention to the shy and retiring child, that he or she may find inviting opportunities for activity and so get used to living with the rest and sharing freely and happily in what is being done by the whole group. The teacher will at the same time seek to get this shy child working with others who will be most likely to show friendly "response" to the withdrawing one. Also the teacher will seek increasing recognition for the results of the shy one's work. For response and recognition rank along with security as essentials to normal adjustment. In all of this, success in what one undertakes is a most desirable concomitant. The teacher will thus be careful as to what this diffident one undertakes, seeing to it that it be well enough within reach for success to follow rather surely.

This emphasis on success for the early treatment of the shy child does not mean that pupils must never be allowed to fail. That would practically deny reality. Repeated failure, of course, is to be avoided because few can stand up under it; but normal failures may be distinct opportunities for the proper education of the emotions. The first and second cases of high-school music pupils illustrate how educative victory can be plucked from overt failure. To learn to study the causes of failure and to accept emotionally the results of such study is perhaps as valuable educatively as any of life's experiences. The teacher must be alert to see that failure is thus emotionally digested.

At this point consideration may well be directed again to what was said earlier about the inferiority complex and attention-seeking as common types of maladjustment. The discussions there given as to how these maladjustments arise carry positive suggestions for avoiding them and for curing them. In this sense everything said there is pertinent here.

A word may be necessary regarding certain more assertive and more capable pupils. There is a possibility that these may, by taking the leadership often and successfully, build in themselves the twin maladjustments of "attention-seeking" and conceit, and at the same time deny to others their fair share of opportunity at leading. This can be avoided if the teacher is alert to the danger. Avoidance of the element of competition is a very potent means of reducing the abnormal desire for attention. Care that leadership posts be wisely distributed will also help.

2. *Curing Minor Maladjustments.* This has already been discussed in the preceding section. Certain additional suggestions may, however, be added. It is, as stated above, only the less serious cases

of maladjustment that the ordinary teacher can hope to remedy unaided. And these we have with us in some measure possibly in every pupil or student.

Perhaps the most important factor is for the teacher to recognize that behavior is caused and so learn to diagnose pupils as to know what personality difficulties are thwarting normal work and development. At the present time many teachers are learning these techniques, and study in the field is making great advances.

Underlying all else, and this might just as well have been stated under the preceding subtopic, the teacher must know his or her own emotional weaknesses. In fact, it is much to be hoped that school authorities of the future will take this matter of teacher personality adjustment to heart to a degree not often found hitherto. The maladjusted teacher can cause more maladjustments than all other agencies can cure. The writer recalls a fifth-grade teacher he once had who did just this. Teachers' colleges must take this as a definite part of their study and work. Excessive maladjustment should disqualify for admission to a teachers' college. And all prospective teachers should be helped to overcome their emotional weaknesses. But for teachers in service, fair and considerate treatment of them as real persons, constructive school atmosphere, flexible curriculum to give teachers opportunity for personal creativity—these things and their like can prevent many emotional problems from developing through the years.

3. The writer believes and reiterates that a wisely directed school program of purposeful activities can make a great contribution toward caring for many lesser maladjustments. Some students of the subject will deny this; and the writer has to admit that at the present it is based more on faith than on established facts. But with the present undeveloped state of knowledge in this general area this faith seems the most promising line of action. This is not to say, of course, that the teacher is not to learn all that is reasonably available about maladjustments and use this knowledge for all it is worth.

Suppose, however, that a child has built an inferiority complex; what is the most promising treatment? Supposing the case is not so extreme as to demand referral to the expert psychiatrist, will not the best treatment be to get this child engaged in some interesting activity at which success is feasible? And to repeat this next time with another activity which again can have a successful outcome and appropriate recognition for achievement? Will not the cumulative result of such successive successes, duly appreciated by others, build a gradually increasing morale until this child ceases to feel inferiority before ordinarily difficult tasks?

And does not the same kind of treatment hold similar promise for various other not too serious maladjustments? On the day these words were written the morning newspaper told of a settlement-house theater in which children developed a confidence that served as a discipline for life itself. One eight-year-old, known in the community for annoying activities of doorbell ringing, turning on hydrants, pushing over ashcans, and so forth, came one day to ask: "If I had a part in the Christmas play what days would I have to rehearse?" He was told, and he accepted the part. After that his annoying activities were laid aside. He came promptly for each appointment to practice. On the stage he was no longer mischievous. "He wouldn't dream of upsetting the act, but played the part of a troubadour perfectly." To find satisfaction in a sufficiently engrossing purposeful activity seems both the surest cure for hitherto hurtful tendencies and the most promising road to proper personality adjustment.

CHAPTER XXVII. *The Esthetic in Life and Education*

How is philosophy concerned with the esthetic? To this question a preliminary answer was given in Chapter XI, where esthetic enjoyment was presented as a means of enriching life. Whatever concerns the aims of life, the quality of life, is properly involved in a philosophy of life and therefore in a philosophy of education.

The first inquiry here is how to understand, for the purposes at hand, the term *esthetic*.

MEANING OF THE ESTHETIC

The term *esthetic* has both a narrower and a broader meaning. The narrower meaning is the more conventional, and the broader the less usual. The narrower is closer to the meaning given by classical Greece, with its aristocratic disdain of manual labor, while the broader is more modern and democratic, more concerned to enrich life for all and not simply for the few.

Take, for example, the esthetic experience of a sunset, the perception and enjoyment of its beauty. This pleasure is located directly and immediately in the experiencing itself, and consists of what this experiencing in and of itself means for life, for the enhanced quality of present living. The beauty of the sunset thus enjoyed is, as Webster says of beauty in general, "that quality or aggregate of qualities in a thing which induces immediate and disinterested pleasure." The term *disinterested* as just used seems to mean that the pleasure is not concerned with further interests. In this enjoyment of the sunset is illustrated the action, as Webster further says, of "the beautiful as distinguished from the merely pleasing, the moral, and especially the useful." Certainly the enjoyment of a sunset is "immediate and disinterested," and there is in it no element either of morality or of the useful.

Had music, instead of the sunset, been chosen as the example, almost the same discussion would have followed. We value music—certainly in general—for the present enjoyment we get from it, not because it is otherwise useful. Music, however, has this difference from the sunset, that it is an art contrived by man for the purpose of arousing esthetic pleasure. Thus is illustrated in music the purport of the quotation from Walter Pater used previously in Chapter XI: "Art comes to you professing frankly to give nothing but the highest quality to your moments as they pass, and simply for these moments' sake." (131:252)

The esthetic pleasure is thus the same whether the thing experienced be of nature, as the sunset or the mountain view or the waterfall, or whether it be a work of art produced by the artist, as music or painting or sculpture or poetry.

Is enjoyment of the esthetic limited thus to the beautiful things of nature and to the "fine arts" so-called, namely, "painting, drawing, architecture, and sculpture, . . . poetry, music, dancing, and dramatic arts" [Webster]? The classical and conventional answers have tended to be yes. For a more considered answer let us accept the definition implied from all the foregoing, that the esthetic is any and every experience enjoyed directly for its own quality. And then let us ask whether there are not some experiences within human contriving, but still quite outside the "fine arts," which yield a true esthetic quality.

Consider a typical old-time artisan, a cabinet maker who earns his living by making neighborhood furniture. He has just finished a joint for a table he has under way and is now reviewing the joint. He perceives, and enjoys, its excellence. "It fits exactly," he says to himself. This is what he was trying to do and he sees that he has succeeded; and he enjoys the perceived excellence. Does his enjoyment consist of the money implications—that a good joint means a table well made and consequently a pleased customer and so in the long run more money income? No; his enjoyment at the moment is quite different. He is not now thinking of money. As a good workman, he has through the years developed ideals of workmanship and a love for his work. He tries in consequence to realize his ideals in the work he turns out. He notes that in this case he has realized, with fair approximation, his ideal of a joint—that is what gives him his present satisfaction. At another time, under different circumstances, he will think of money and of his reputation as a workman; but on this occasion, and for the time being, money is not in his consciousness. This time it is a matter of a good joint, with the consequent direct pleasure, enjoyed for its own sake, that he has made a good one.

Here we have the essential elements of an esthetic experience from a piece of work well done by a "mere artisan": (i) an ideal of good work, personal love of this ideal; (ii) consciousness that he had been seeking this ideal of good work; and (iii) a sense of satisfaction that he has now attained a fair approximation of the ideal. The esthetic in such instances is the pleasure inherent in the perceived realization of the ideal sought.

At the broadest, then, esthetic enjoyment is any and every experience directly enjoyed for its own quality. It is thus to be distinguished from any and everything valued because of its instrumental effect, or merely because of its promise for the future. Instances of the esthetic thus include the enjoyment of a sunset, a mountain view, music, paintings, sculpture, dancing, or anything enjoyed as beautiful, and every perceived excellence if appreciated directly for this quality of excellence.

Consider in connection with this discussion the words *beauty* and *beautiful*. Webster's *Synonyms* (p. 76) says that "aesthetic satisfaction is the content that accompanies the enjoyment of beauty for its own sake, and independently of all other considerations." The unwary who read this and go no further might suppose that esthetic satisfaction is limited to sense stimulation. But under the word *beautiful* (p. 110 of the same work) we find that "in general, . . . both in learned and in ordinary use, *beautiful* is applied to that which excites the keenest pleasure, not only of the senses but also, through the medium of the senses, of mind and soul." And then, as if the better to take care of the cabinet maker, the *Synonyms* goes on the say: "It [the term *beautiful*] commonly also suggests an approach to, or a realization of, perfection, often specifically the imagined perfection associated with one's conception of an ideal." And still further broadening the conception of the esthetic: "That is why *beautiful* is applicable not only to things that are directly perceived by the senses (as a *beautiful* woman; a *beautiful* scene . . .)

but to things that are actually mental constructions . . . as, a *beautiful* poem; a *beautiful* thought; a *beautiful* character."

A quotation from John Dewey will sum up the discussion so far as to the meaning of the term *esthetic*, specifically the effort here made to include the experiences of the artisan, or indeed of anybody, as possible instances of the esthetic: "Any practical activity will, provided it is integrated and moves by its own urge to fulfillment, have esthetic quality." (39:39)

How does art fit into the discussion thus far of the esthetic? In its wide sense *art* is skill or dexterity acquired by experience. In its narrow sense, it is (Webster) the "application of skill and taste to production according to esthetic principles; an occupation having to do with the theory or practice of taste in the expression of beauty in form, color, sound, speech, or movement." *Fine art*, which is art in a narrower and more explicit sense, is (Webster) "art which is concerned with the creation of objects of imagination and taste for their own sake and without relation to the utility of the object produced." The word *taste* is essential in the more restricted definitions of art as just given. William Hazlitt (1778–1830) gave this definition: "Taste is nothing but sensitivity to the different degrees and kinds of excellence in the works of Art or Nature." The *Oxford English Dictionary* says of taste that it is "the sense of what is appropriate, harmonious, or beautiful; especially discernment and appreciation of the beautiful in nature or art." Another source defines taste as "artistic judgment."

We seem led by these definitions to conclude that art and taste, while concerned always with the esthetic, tend to be restricted to the more refined instances of the esthetic.

Because two people can enjoy the same sunset or the same music or the same smoothly planed board or the same roast of beef, it is possible to use art as communication. So Rodin (1840–1917), the French sculptor, said: "Art . . . is the expression of thought seeking to understand the world and to make it understood." It was with this in mind, we may suppose, that I. A. Richards uttered the sentiment quoted in Chapter XI: "In the arts we find the record, in the only form in which these things can be recorded, of the experiences which have seemed worth having to the most sensitive and discriminating persons." (138:33) In connection with this point, John Dewey has said that "art is the most effective mode of communicating that exists." (39:286) And here is Robert Browning in the *Ring and the Book:*

> It is the glory and good of Art
> That Art remains the one way possible
> Of speaking truths.—Bk. xii, l. 842.

Because the emphasis just given is on art as communication, it does not follow that the message of the esthetic is purely or even predominantly intellectual in character. A sunset may be beautiful beyond compare, but no one can say it gives a message in words. It appeals to life, but not through the verbal intellect. And many insist that so-called "modern art" similarly appeals to feeling, not to thought as such.

VALUE OF THE ESTHETIC TO LIFE

Some, following the discussion given above, may wish to divide all value into the esthetic and the useful; others may rejoin that the useful is merely the promise of future enjoyment, the promise of what will later be present enjoyment, and that on this argument all final or actual enjoyment is esthetic.

But an entirely different line of thought is here proposed. It seems clear now that a much wider range of true esthetic enjoyment is open to people generally than many have hitherto thought. If so, does not society owe it to its members to explore such possibilities and find out what now thwarts the full realization of these potential pleasures? It may be possible by taking proper thought to start a new line of enrichment of our civilization. If so, then the final question for this chapter would arise as to the part that conscious education should play in such a program.

What possibilities are there for enriching life through extending the area of esthetic enjoyment? And what now thwarts the realization of such possibilities?

If we join to the discussion on the cabinet maker's esthetic pursuit of his ideals of workmanship a statement on art by Arthur J. Todd (1878–1948) we may get a promising lead. Says Todd: "Art is not a luxury; it is a spirit, an attitude. It is what makes life worth while. It is not things, but a life to lead. It is the mark of a fine discrimination of values." (163:544) If the word *art* of this quotation had been *the esthetic*, it might have seemed more closely adapted to the present discussion, but the distinction is perhaps not significant here.

As we think of a wider enrichment of life, we may say that the essence of the esthetic is the enjoyment following directly from perceived or felt excellence. (The word *esthetic* derives from the Greek word, *to perceive*.) To perceive excellence adequately requires proper taste, which Webster defines as "the power of discerning and appreciating fitness, beauty, congruity, symmetry, or whatever constitutes excellence," and the *Oxford English Dictionary* as "the faculty of perceiving and enjoying what is excellent." (To be sure, both these dictionaries stress in immediate connection with their definitions the hitherto dominant esthetic interest in the fine arts, in literature, and the like; but, even so, the actual words quoted reach beyond the fine arts, as the discussion of the cabinet maker clearly shows. We seem thus fully justified in carrying the esthetic into a distinctly wider area of life than the Greeks and their conventional followers have thought.)

Consider again the cabinet maker. If he is to live richly in and through his work, he must put heart and soul into what he does. In the degree that he does so, heart and soul will accordingly enter into each successive step of his endeavor. Success in each such step, as he notes his success and therein perceives the excellence of that step as fitting and promoting his ideal, will bring to him a resulting sense of joy and satisfaction. This joy and satisfaction, thus following perceived excellence, constitutes what we have defined as the esthetic emotion. What is true for the cabinet maker will likewise be true for anyone who works consciously at personally pursued purposes and ideals and puts heart and soul into what he does, and this holds over as wide a range as purpose can distribute itself—for carpenter, cook, farmer, housewife, merchant, teacher, lawyer, physician, statesman, poet, and (*sic*) child. It is the wholehearted pursuit of a purpose that makes the difference, the pleasure which comes from the successful pursuit of one's ideal.

As people seek the wider enrichment of life through the devoted pursuit of purposes, the question may be asked—and properly—whether all purposes yield the same degree of satisfaction. Do the cook and the poet stand at the same level? Carlos Baker in a discerning review of *The Poetic Image* by Cecil Day Lewis (123: Bk. Rev., Dec. 28, 1947), seems to think otherwise: "Next to a whole-souled act of worship, the poetic act is at its best the most profoundly satisfying of all the means which man has discovered." (99) People who are not poets may hesitate to accept so strong a statement, and still wonder about cook and poet. John Dewey perhaps gives us the hint of how to generalize here: "The scope of a work of art is measured by the number and variety of elements coming from past experiences that are organically absorbed into the perception had here and now." (39:123) That is, the satisfactions got will depend partly on the person and partly on the character of the work. Some lines of work admit of indefinitely many and refined elements, others are much more limited. As regards any rich line of work, people engaged in it will differ, according to ability and experience, as to the distinctions they make and the consequent number and character of the elements they bring to any one instance of perceiving and judging.

It seems justifiable, then, to conclude that one's life will be rich, satisfying, desirable, commendable in the degree that this life is given wholeheartedly to the pursuit of worthy purposes reasonably within one's range of capacity to attain. For a defensible richness of life, the purposes pursued must be worthy in the sense discussed in earlier chapters on morality, respect for personality, and democracy. Also, these purposes must be such that the person is thoroughly committed to them, as answering to the highest demands he can make upon himself. That is, they command his fullest interests, so that he will give heart and soul fully to their pursuit. Such a pursuit will, in the degree to which it is successful, be permeated by a continuing hearty enjoyment of the successive steps in the activity process, each an esthetic experience as above discussed. And the final outcome of the activity as a whole will, under the conditions named, be itself enjoyed in and of itself, that is, esthetically, as it is felt to be a fitting approximation to the aim originally chosen.

Certain points involved in the foregoing should be clarified. Some not accustomed to so broad and inclusive a use of the term *esthetic* may get the impression that we have somehow pulled a rabbit out of a hat, that we have managed to guarantee a whole happy life out of what is at most a limited part of the whole. No such claim is here made. Instead, attention has been called to an area of deep satisfaction, one open potentially to nearly everyone and reaching potentially into many facets of life. In the first place let it be noted (i) that the word *worthy* as used is broad enough to include all elements involved in the wise and proper choice of all conduct and life; (ii) that the word *wholeheartedly*—a strong word—is a condition applied to the pursuit of these worthy purposes; and (iii) that the phrase *reasonably within one's range of capacity* will, when joined with really wholehearted pursuit, prescribe limits which, when granted, go far to assure a preponderance of success for the individual purposes pursued. In other words, there is nothing of the magician's trick in what we have done. All that we have been concerned with is, first, to note and use the fact that one who really loves his work will seek excellence at each stage and on attaining at any step a reasonable approximation to his ideal will enjoy the (esthetic) satisfaction of this attainment; and second, to state the conditions under which one's work is socially worthy and is likely to be pursued with esthetic pleasure. These two conditions, if really met, will pretty certainly bring deep satisfaction in and for life. The present discussion, given under the head of the esthetic, has so far attempted no more than to call attention to the really wide range of that psychological term, a range wide enough to include the inherent enjoyment of every loving and successful effort.

However, granted that no rabbit has been pulled out of a hat, is it not still true, lamentably true, that many are practically denied such happiness? Do not many in our modern industrial civilization find that they seem condemned to unending drudgery in their daily work? We have in previous chapters considered this as a blot on our civilization and a denial of what we count right. Democracy demands that all have equal opportunity, so far as institutional arrangements can give such equality, at achieving satisfaction in life. Do all among us have equal opportunity at choosing purposes to pursue in life? Specifically, for example, does the man working on the Ford assembly line have as good opportunity at filling his life work with satisfaction from personally chosen purposes as has the designer of the plan for the automobile? The assembly-line worker has his day's work laid out for him by the assembly line itself: it tells him exactly what to do and when and how. The only choice he has is whether he will do what he is told or be dismissed. Certainly the satisfaction from perceived excellence in his personal work is small indeed. Contrariwise, the maker of the automobile plan spends his work time devising improvements, trying to create or invent new ideas. In other words, much of modern industry seems to deny to most workers any great measure of freedom to create or invent or even to choose.

Our civilization seems thus to deny the esthetic enrichment of life to a very large proportion of "working" people. Professional people are much more fortunate. For such inequality our industrial civilization stands at present condemned. In this situation we have a problem set for us which we cannot evade.

We cannot here consider the problem thus raised, but let us ask what education can do, within the range open to it, to enrich life through a better realization of its esthetic possibilities.

EDUCATION AND ESTHETIC VALUES

What can deliberate education do through school or otherwise to increase the direct enrichment of life through the esthetic? In general the answer will lie along two lines: one, the cultivation of interest and sensitivity (taste) for various forms of esthetic enjoyment; the other, the development of such interest in creative construction or creative arrangement as brings true esthetic enjoyment from surveying the sequence of successful stages of each endeavor as it develops. The person with such interest works devotedly to attain his ideals, and enjoys esthetically the several approximations thereto in the successive stages in the enterprise.

Three customary areas or sources of esthetic enjoyment were mentioned above: nature, the fine arts, and also other purposeful activities (outside of the fine arts) wholeheartedly pursued. We can consider in this order the work of education in these three areas.

1. How can education increase and extend the esthetic enjoyment of nature? While the recipient of such enjoyment may seem inactive, it is none the less true that he is positively active. Whoever really perceives, takes in and appreciates, such beauty reaches out actively in response to the beauty that nature offers. It is this active capacity so to respond that can be cultivated.

The school can cultivate this taste and sensitivity by exposing groups of children to nature under such conditions that they can enjoy its beauty or feel wonder at its marvels, and by encouraging those who feel the beauty or wonder to delight in their enjoyment and, so far as they can, give expression to it. What some thus feel and express, others will wish to see. However, care must be taken not to force either "enjoyment" or "expression," and also not to discourage and antagonize those who do not yet see or value what others report. Further, those who now see and feel beauty can be encouraged to make finer distinctions than hitherto. But here, as with all the finer things of life, pressure and compulsion will hurt rather than help. Taste and sensitivity can, by the principles of learning, grow only in the degree that the child himself responds with felt enjoyment (inner acceptance) to the newly sensed beauty or distinction. We can also help extend the range of enjoyment by telling where and how such esthetic experiences are available: for example, that certain flowers can be found at certain times and places; that the autumn leaves are very beautiful this week end at such a place within easy motor reach; that certain accessible mountain views are peculiarly rewarding. We can also call attention to the wonders of plant and insect life and the like. Seeing and appreciating these offers a further area of esthetic enjoyment.

2. The fine arts have been so much discussed by other authors that little need here be added. Taste and sensitivity in this area can be cultivated in much the same ways as we have just seen with nature. Possibly we must take even greater care here not to try to force or pressure the learner's enjoyment. If we act wisely, that is, if we do not begin too soon and do not proceed too aggressively, we can accomplish much. One further condition must be kept constantly in mind: not to build obedience to stated standards in place of personal enjoyment of actual beauty. School tradition makes for such obedience; we must work against it.

Within limits—and the possibilities are often greater than most recognize—we can cultivate a true interest in the amateur creation of art objects—painting, sculpture, poetry, drama. Both children and adults, when properly encouraged, can respond very significantly here. With such interest in creating there will almost surely come an increased appreciation of the masterpieces in the area. Also in this area, as with nature, it often helps to spread a knowledge of available masterpieces—a Gothic church not too far distant, a colonial building, certain special masterpieces in near-by art galleries.

3. Finally, what can education do to extend the range of esthetic enjoyment through purposeful activity outside of the area of fine arts? The answer is definite and significant: much in every way; no

aspect of life is excluded. Almost all the chapters of Part II of this book point the way. Whoever gives encouragement to the pursuit of chosen, worthy purposes, to building *internal* concern that these be pursued carefully, painstakingly, with increasing standards of excellence—that person is extending esthetic enjoyment. Everything done in school should lead in that direction. To build interests and cultivate the purposeful pursuit of these is to lay the basis for esthetic enjoyment through the pursuit of ideals as discussed earlier in this chapter.

The more fully the school can be a place of living, with intent to develop abiding interests to enrich life, the more surely will it care for the enriching of life through the esthetic. The point here is that this possibility of esthetic enjoyment is not restricted, as the classical outlook has considered, to the beauties of nature and the fine arts, but extends to any and every worth-while interest pursued so wholeheartedly that the person builds ideals for each stage of such activity and enjoys satisfaction from realizing these ideals.

To be sure, not all the interests developed in school can continue as main concerns in life. In our highly specialized civilization, many lines of esthetic enjoyment developed through purposeful activity in the school can continue in adult life only as hobbies. But even so, our civilization offers a far wider spread of leisure time than was ever before available. If this time be filled with a high esthetic quality of enjoyment, life is better in every way. And the opposite holds exactly true in its negative way: a low quality of leisure-time living lowers the quality of life for the individual and also the character of our civilization. As John Dewey has said: "Esthetic experience is a manifestation, a record and celebration of the life of a civilization, a means of promoting its development, and is also the ultimate judgment upon the quality of a civilization." (39:326)

But leisure time, important as are its potentialities, does not, as we have just seen, exhaust the possibilities of esthetic enjoyment in child life or in adult life. Some in the artisan world can, as we saw, get true esthetic enjoyment from their work, and most professionals have this possibility. And this is still not all. Every home owner and every housekeeper has a wide range of possible esthetic enjoyments. The lawn, the flower garden, interior decoration, table management, choosing if not making clothes, even cooking—these offer real esthetic possibilities.

And the greatest is yet to come. Everyone from later childhood onward faces true esthetic possibilities in the social and moral relationships of life. Take the matter of courtesy and refinement. A refined, heartfelt courtesy serves greatly to enhance reciprocally the quality of conjoint living. Manners have been called "minor morals." And an unidentified writer has said that "good manners represent the finest spirit of the race in its efforts to develop courtesy, kindness, sympathy, and all that makes for rich and fruitful human associations." Galsworthy is quoted as saying of a certain man: "He had that true refinement; he couldn't help thinking of others, whatever he did."

One final consideration will complete the topic and the chapter. The moral outlook has in it a true esthetic element. We saw above from Webster that taste is "the power of discerning and appreciating fitness, beauty, order, congruity, proportion, symmetry, or whatever constitutes excellence." Morality is certainly an excellence. The moral person is one who has developed such a taste for, and appreciation of, moral fitness, order, congruity, and excellence that behavior and attitudes embodying these qualities give to him immediate esthetic enjoyment. This is not to deny that one will need to reason about the probable outcomes of a contemplated act before one can decide what to do, or that appropriate moral obligation follows as well as precedes such study; but it is to say that the ideals of moral attitude and behavior should be so fully accepted and ingrained that their proper use brings this esthetic enjoyment. And it is further to say that education owes it to the individual and to civilization to help each one thus to develop and incorporate within himself these moral ideals. The more these can be built into the discerning active character of any growing person the finer and better for that person and for civilization.

PART 3
A Concluding Overview

CHAPTER XXVIII. *The Present World of Affairs: Meanings for Education*

THE educational outlook of each civilization, and of each nation, must be adequate to its specific practical situation. The aim of this chapter is to study the significant features of the present world of affairs, especially the bearing of certain economic and political features on the quality of the resulting living. The purpose of this study is to find what changes are needed in our educational aims and practices in order to secure better insight into, and control over, the forces which shape our civilization and determine its quality.

Various preceding chapters have anticipated aspects of this present study. The effort here made is to bring all these together in one consistent whole, with special reference to the educational bearings.

SOME BACKGROUND FACTORS

1. *The Long-term Revolution from Feudalism to Democracy*. The problems of this chapter can be better grasped if they are seen as part of a long-term and still developing revolution, namely, the gradual change from the feudalism of the Middle Ages to modern democracy. To be sure, many other features of our civilization have also been in the process of development during this period; for example the growing faith in free play of intelligence in place of the formerly prevailing authoritarian *a priori* deductive reasoning.

The term *revolution*, it should be noted, is used in two contrasted senses. In the older sense, a revolution is a forcible, perhaps violent, sudden overturn of a government or regime. The American Revolution is commonly so understood. In the other and newer sense, a revolution is a highly significant but gradual shift of fundamental institutional arrangements corresponding to a deep-rooted shift either of life conditions or of social outlook or insight. In any instance of this second type of revolution, the change of life conditions or of social outlook, as the case may be, is the significant cause of the institutional shift, though at the time that fact may not be well recognized. Thus, speaking of the American Revolution, John Adams asserted in 1815 that the "war was no part of the revolution; it was only an effect and consequence of it. The revolution was in the minds of the people, and this was effected from 1760 to 1775, in the course of fifteen years, before a drop of blood was drawn at Lexington." (4:116) To this may be added Noah Webster's assertion in 1787: "A fundamental mistake of the Americans has been that they considered the Revolution as completed, when it was just begun." (169:84)

From the point of view here accepted Webster's insight was more fundamental than Adams', though the latter's was truer than the common view. The American Revolution began long before 1760, though that date marks a sharp quickening of the process, and it continued long after the war was over. Further, the whole American Revolution is a constituent part of the long-term revolution under special consideration now. This more inclusive revolution began with the close of the Middle Ages and is not yet completed.

In feudalism the chief feature was the fixed levels or gradations in society, each level being fixed by heredity and so relatively unalterable. Not only was position on the social scale, with its accruing privileges, fixed beyond the usual reach of the individual to improve matters, but what to think and believe was likewise practically controlled by the dominant institutions of the period, with denial to the individual of any right to change the doctrines and ideas thus currently handed down. In other words, during the Middle Ages existing institutions came first and individuals only second, whereas in democracy institutions exist for the sake of the individuals concerned, to develop and express them and their values and ideals. And this medieval overlordship of institutions was made worse by the fact that in feudalism the upper classes had the right to exploit the lower classes in order themselves to live better.

Nietzsche (1844–1900), though living much later, stated very clearly the avowed defense of this feudalistic exploitation. "A good and healthy aristocracy," in his view, should regard itself "as the *significance* and highest justification" of society. It should "therefore accept with a good conscience the sacrifice of a legion of individuals, who, *for its sake*, must be suppressed and reduced to imperfect men, to slaves and instruments." And he adds that society does not exist "for its own sake, but only as a foundation and scaffolding" in order that "a select class" may "elevate themselves to their higher duties, and in general to a higher *existence*." (124:198*f*.)

It was against this general background of fixed privilege that the growing "liberal" movement increasingly demanded freedom and equality: freedom to think for one's self; freedom to work out one's own place in life; equality of opportunity in social, economic, and political affairs. Some of the factors that helped to bring the shift to democracy away from this feudalistic privilege and restriction of thought were considered in Chapter VII. New trading opportunities brought wealth to people previously denied it, and so helped to upset the old feudal order. The Renaissance (Revival of Learning) opened the intellect to a wider range of interests and led many intellectuals to think for themselves. The Reformation went further towards democracy (James Russell Lowell said that Puritanism, "believing itself quick with the seed of religious liberty, laid, without knowing it, the egg of democracy." [125:C:168: Jan., 1865]) The discovery of the New World opened new economic and political possibilities. The growth of science was most important in giving to man a new and assured faith in himself and accordingly led to the widespread use of inductive reasoning in place of the previous general faith in *a priori* reasoning. The British "Revolution of 1688" helped to destroy among the American colonists any lingering faith in the divine right of kings, and at the same time their frontier freedom was preparing them for independence and the Declaration of 1776.

The seventeenth and eighteenth-century Enlightenment strongly influenced the doctrines of American democracy, especially the thinking of such men as Franklin, Jefferson, Mason, and Madison. To this fact, it appears, we are indebted for the most liberal features of the Declaration and Bill of Rights in the Constitution. Jefferson's use of Enlightenment ideas was especially constructive. Immediately after the signing of the Declaration he set to work in Virginia to eradicate, as he said, "every trace" of "ancient or future aristocracy." To this end he proposed four lines of attack: the repeal of the laws of entail, which kept property perpetually in "the family"; abolition of primogeniture, whereby the oldest son must receive a disproportionate share of the paternal estate and so perpetuate "the family" as such; legalizing the right to freedom of conscience, with separation of church and state; and the establishment of a system of general education. All except the last objective Jefferson secured. In further support of the new outlook, the Constitution of 1787 stipulated that the new government should grant "no title of nobility." In these ways did the founding fathers seek to eliminate feudalism and a hereditary aristocracy from America.

However, we will go wrong if we think that this early effort to secure freedom and equality accepted democracy as we now understand it or that it even called itself a democracy; neither was true. The term *democracy* during the colonial regime was held in bad odor, so brought down from the days of the Greeks. Nor was equality expected consistently for all. Though John Locke, as we saw earlier, claimed that all men are born "free, equal, and independent," he had no apparent wish to extend suffrage to all; it came there only some two centuries later for all males and a half century later still for females. Similarly Jefferson claimed in the Declaration that "all men are created equal" and that governments derive "their just powers from the consent of the governed"; but at the adoption of the Constitution only about one in five of male white adults were authorized to vote. It took some fifty years to extend suffrage to practically all male white adults. After the Civil War suffrage was opened to Negro males; and only some fifty years after that, to women equally with men. This bit of history is a clear illustration of the fact that the emergence of democracy, even in the areas here considered, has been a long-term gradual process, not a sudden or catastrophic affair; and more remains to be done before full democracy is achieved.

2. *Property Rights vs. Human Rights.* Under the earlier laissez-faire outlook a certain sacredness was attributed to the right to property which seems far from obvious to us now. Then the right to property seemed, to its supporters, absolute: it could yield to nothing else; if humanity suffered through its enforcement, that was just too bad. Now we think that no rights are absolute as over

against the good life of the people affected. Justice must prevail, justice as the equilibrium between opposing rights.*

In keeping with this former acceptance of the absolute character of the right to property we find John Adams saying: "The moment the idea is admitted into society that property is not as sacred as the laws of God . . . anarchy and tyranny commence." (166:99:767). In further support we find Justice Van Orsdel of the District of Columbia Court of Appeals, in dissent from the minimum wage law, saying: "It should be remembered that the three fundamental principles which underlie government, and for which government exists, are the protection of life, of liberty, and of property. *The chief of these is property.*" (118:XXVII:92; italics supplied) Vice Chancellor Berry of New York said as late as 1938 that freedom of speech is "a qualified constitutional right" inferior to such "inherent rights" as "acquiring and possessing property." (119: Sept. 29, 1938) Joseph N. Choate arguing against the income tax law of 1894 said: "I thought that the fundamental object of all civilized government was the preservation of the right of private property. . . . If this law is upheld, the first parapet would be carried, and then it would be easy to overcome the whole fortress on which the rights of the people depend." (153:225*f.*) In 1935 a statement by the Union League Club of New York included the following words: "One of the essential rights necessary to human welfare is the individual right to own property; . . . The rights of the individuals must not be subordinated to the demands of any group." (123: Oct. 11, 1935)

How different men react to the controversy set forth above appears from the opposed statements of two clergymen in the same issue (May 10, 1934) of a magazine:

> Rugged individualism is a worn out doctrine, whose birth place was hell, whose father is the devil, and whose history is suffering and human misery.

* "Justice is the constant and enduring will to give to every man his right." Opening words of Justinian's Institutes (533 A.D.)

Shakespeare put it thus:

> . . . right and wrong
> (Between whose endless jar justice resides).
>
> —*Troilus and Cressida,* Act. II, sc. iii

Immanuel Kant said: "Justice is the external liberty of each limited by the liberty of all others."

> These propositions [the drastic limitation of wealth and income by estate and income taxes] are all Socialistic and Communistic. These two systems have this in common—they are both atheistic. But this is God's universe. He rules (176:XVII:251, 248).

A soberer statement is made by Professor James H. Tufts:

> Exclusive reliance upon the profit motive and upon the supreme importance of wealth tends to distort the prospect for life as a whole (54:488).

As opposed to the demands for an absolute right to property voiced above we find the United States Supreme Court deciding in 1934 (291 U.S. 502):

> Government cannot exist if the citizen may at will use his property to the detriment of his fellows, or exercise his freedom-of-contract to work them harm . . . (p. 523)
>
> A State is free to adopt whatever economic policy may reasonably be deemed needed to promote public welfare (p. 537).

We may then let this decision of the Supreme Court settle for us the legal problem of "property rights vs. human rights." But the matter has further bearings to be considered.

3. *Our Changing Social-Economic Scene.* In a true sense the past two hundred and more years of social-economic history belong together. We have seen how much our country is indebted to Jefferson and his fellow workers for abolishing the legal bases of a hereditary aristocracy. True, we still have informal remains of the older feudalistic granting of hereditary privileges, even though these are not legally supported in the old sense. In another respect—necessarily, it seems—we have not followed Jefferson. As Jefferson compared this country with Europe he hoped that nothing would lead us away from our then predominantly rural and agricultural life and economy. Cities he mistrusted; he had seen too many evils in the big cities of Europe. He also mistrusted any large-scale industrialization.

But even before Jefferson's death in 1826 three interacting and overlapping movements had begun to lead America away from the simple rural and agricultural life; (i) spread of the laissez-faire economic doctrine; (ii) acceptance of its natural result, *individualism;* and (c) the *Industrial Revolution.* These three movements had already begun in Western civilization and would in the end lead America at least partly away from Jefferson's hopes. The social-economic and social-political effects of these movements are so great that we must consider them here in order the better to understand the problems of our day and what we can do about them.

1. *Laissez-faire* is "the doctrine which demands the minimum interference by government in economic and political affairs." It began as a natural and proper reaction on the part of the mercantile community against the detailed and exacting restrictions earlier laid by various European countries on industry and commerce. The doctrine assumed that the self-seeking interests of individuals would in the matter of trade and industry suffice to lead society to the highest attainable good. We saw earlier (Chapter VII) how Alexander Pope (1688–1744) anticipated this position in his assertion that in such affairs God "bade self-love and social be the same." Adam Smith (1723–1790), also quoted earlier, counted that in such action man was led "by an invisible hand" to this good result. Edmund Burke (1729–1797) was more explicit: "The benign and wise Dispenser of all things obliges men, whether they will or not, in pursuing their own selfish interests, to connect the general good with their own individual success." (9:44) The physiocrat, Mercier de la Rivière (1720–1794), stated the same doctrine in more mundane and perhaps more convincing terms: "Personal interest compels each man vigorously and continuously to perfect and multiply the things he seeks to sell. He thus enlarges the mass of pleasures he can produce for other men in order to increase the mass of pleasures other men can produce for him in exchange. The world thus advances of itself." (61:XIII, 598)

It is easy to understand the appeal of this doctrine in the eighteenth-century climate of opinion, with its disposition to view nature and its inherent workings in a romantic light. Freedom from artificial interference had then a powerful appeal. The history of the doctrine, however, well illustrates the statement made earlier in this chapter, that ideals must be revised in terms of the way they work out. That freedom and liberty constitute a true ideal for life is clear, but freedom is no absolute; nor does the laissez-faire practice bring good only. To determine what corrections must be made in order to take care of all the factors involved—that is an unending task. Fortunately, what corrections are now called for need not be decided in this book. Educators must help those under their care to study any crucial problems of civilization—but it is not for educators as such to manage the social-economic situation.

2. In studying *individualism*, it is necessary at the outset to distinguish two conceptions of the term which more or less overlap. One stresses the individual as the proper unit of regard and concern and counts that institutions exist to develop and express the individuals composing the group. Democracy at its best accepts this position. The other conception of individualism is less admirable. Following Newtonian science, it looks on human individuals as the atoms of society, each at bottom existing in and of and for itself; and further, following hedonistic ethics, it counts that in this society, composed of atomistic, egoistic individuals, each is, and defensibly should be, concerned primarily, if not solely, with his own welfare. As an instance of atomistic individualism we found John Stuart Mill in Chapter VII saying:

> Human beings in society have no properties but those which are derived from, and may be resolved into, the laws of individual men.

Such a statement from so discerning a thinker astonishes us of today who have accepted the organismic conception of human psychology and social organization. We now believe that the individual-in-his-social-milieu is the only individual that exists.

Laissez-faire economics proceeds as if the second conception of individualism holds, counting that, in the exchange of goods between A and B, A serves B's purposes and B serves A's purposes, and that no more need be asked. The tendency thus to ally the upholders of laissez-faire with the hedonistic (selfish) ethics was previously noted in the quotation from Bentham that "man, from the very constitution of his nature, prefers his own happiness to that of all other sensitive beings put together." (12:X, 80)

This combination of laissez-faire with a selfish, atomistic individualism resulted in two tendencies. One was to say that the state should not act positively for the common good, indeed that business and business men could properly disregard any socially hurtful effects resulting from business practice; the other was that success in money making was the only thing needing therein to be considered. Two problems at once arose: (i) how to maintain an effective democratic freedom for the economically weaker individual in the face of an industrial regime growing ever more inclusive in its reach and having great power; and (ii) how to effect a true democratic equality of opportunity for all as against the threats of a still remaining feudalism of wealth. These two problems grew out of a proper concern for human living as such. Against these threats to individual welfare the state must act. Laissez-faire and individualism do not take adequate care of the lives of all. An effective regard for everyone becomes thus a positive duty of government.

3. The *Industrial Revolution* represents the most distinctive external manifestation of modern life. It arose from the substitution of machine production for hand production. This advance at once permits large-scale production under one management, and the advantage is great. The economy of machine production per unit of man power is startling. The cotton gin made it possible, we are told, for one man tending a machine to separate as much lint cotton from the seed as could 28,000 men working simply with their hands. Similarly, one man tending spinning jennies can turn out as much yarn as could 45,000 women with spinning wheels. And the results on life have been equally startling. For example, in a lesser area, "two centuries ago, not one person in a thousand wore stockings . . . now, not one person in a thousand is without them." (61:12, 305c)

Such possibilities, where realized, have transformed "a people with peasant occupations and local markets into an industrial society with world-wide connections." It has made possible, for the first time in history, enough production in this country to bring comfort and decent living to all.

But the Industrial Revolution has at the same time brought many new problems to the world. For one thing, as the great depression taught us, we are now all dependent on the proper working of one inclusive economic order. In this way it has "substituted unemployment for famine as the nightmare of mankind." (61:12, 306a) For another thing, as factories and industrial corporations have got larger, decisions have receded further and further away from the individual worker. Directive plans are handed down from above, so that the individual worker feels more and more reduced to the part of a mere cog in a great machine. This gives us the problem of "the little men in big societies and in big organizations lost in the frustration of impotence to guide their own destinies." (63:

March, 1949, p. 7) Out of such problems has come the apparent opposition of interest between labor and management—certainly the greatest single domestic problem of our times.

Another result of the Industrial Revolution is the great modern city. This, in contrast with the close and intimate family and community life which formerly prevailed, carries a serious threat to the proper working of society. The wholesome educative influences formerly carried on by the family and small community are now greatly reduced. In that older time education for life was inherent in life itself. Children worked with their parents to make of the family an almost sufficient economic unit. It was easy for all to see what was needed at any point; for nearly the whole process was carried on in the family or openly in the community, as in the village grist mill or the blacksmith shop. Not only has the Industrial Revolution taken this type of economic life from the family; but now the big city threatens still further the reduction of family life almost to disintegration and the consequent further lessening of its educative influence. The urban father is typically away from home all the working day. The mother and children not only do not share in his work, as formerly the boys at least did; but now for the most part they never see the father's work nor meet his business associates. The father and his associates live in a separate world. Moreover, the children, who know their mates mostly in school, know but little of each others' parents. The result, in the larger cities, is that the father and his friends, the mother and her friends, the children and their friends, tend to form three distinct groups, having very little to do with each other. Life is fragmented, so that the city child sees it whole with difficulty. The danger from this is that the individual city child will grow up to be a fragmented personality, neither socially intelligent nor socially disposed.

4. "*The Evil That Men Do Lives after Them.*" The growth of civilization, as we have just seen, has been no uniform or consistent affair. At any one time the past deeds of men, both bad and good, interpose to shape the present. Specifically, many of the world's greatest present problems are caused by the evil remnants of past unethical and undemocratic policies and deeds which intrude themselves as factors into current affairs. Some of these remnants, these evil interferences of the past with the present, we wish now to study.

As indicated earlier, the outstanding problem facing our half of the world is the attitude of the U.S.S.R. and its aggressive effort to bring the whole world to its point of view. The present controlling attitudes and beliefs of those now in power in Communist Russia constitute an outstanding instance of such evil remnants. The present attitudes and beliefs of the Communist leaders were developed during the long underground fight to overthrow the selfish dictatorship of old Tsarist Russia. This dictatorship was so repressive and so stubborn that it developed, in irreconcilable opposition, the extreme attitudes now found in the Politburo of the U.S.S.R.: absolute dogmas that know no yielding either to argument or to compassion, the belief that the end justifies the use of any means, the conscious rejection of all moral restraints in dealing with opponents, reliance upon force and lying propaganda in preference to the free play of intelligence, acceptance of the dictatorial police state, total disregard of the rights or feelings of every opposition.

Thus is clearly illustrated the principle set forth previously, that it is the stupid and reactionary insistence of the selfish privileged on keeping their outmoded privileges which brings about violent revolutions. Those at the top in Tsarist Russia held on so stubbornly to their selfish, oppressive privileges that they bred by reaction the revolution under Kerenski and the more extreme and violent revolution of the Bolsheviks in 1917. In this instance is further illustrated the inescapable fact that humanity is one: the whole world now suffers because the privileged classes in old Russia were so stubbornly insistent in holding on to their selfish advantage. And a third principle is also illustrated: that a good cause, here the uplifting of the Russian underprivileged, may be sought by bad means—in this instance the police state and the dictatorial denial of real liberty.

A further instance in which the past has left hurtful remnants of old conflicts to plague the present is France. The French Revolution was brought on by widespread reaction to the selfish blindness of the privileged upper classes and the unreasoning support given these privileged ones—at least as seen by Voltaire, Diderot, and their co-workers—by the established clergy. Reason and fair play had been denied legitimate sway. And since the Revolution, France has failed to digest this old conflict. This fact, it seems fair to believe, entered crucially both into the choice of Petain as the ruler of France after the debacle of World War II and into his subsequent subservience to the Germans—with the evil results which France and the world now recognize. One can but wonder how much the extreme Alexandrian type of French education has been a factor in this failure to digest the Revolution during the century and a half intervening. An education which stresses intellect and memory to the utter exclusion of any form of consideration of either individual or social behavior (except for study and examination purposes); which expects school work to take little or no account of current social and political life and problems; which magnifies the external written examination to the point of being the final, if not the sole, test of success in school work—such an education must tend, it would seem, to develop non-cooperating individualists unfitted by knowledge or interest to deal as citizens with practical social and political problems. Certainly the ancient division among the French people has operated on many crucial occasions to keep France in conflict with itself. This past of France has thus hurt not only France but the cause everywhere of opposition to Nazism and Fascism.

In our own country we find a third instance of hurtful attitudes handed down from wrong decisions and deeds of the past: the present denial of equal rights and opportunities to Negroes. We now hold it as a most extreme violation of fundamental human rights to seize helpless natives in Africa, bring them by force to this distant country and here sell them (including their children after them)—sell them as if they were a material commodity, sell them into slavery, a slavery which regarded them "as so far inferior that they had no rights which the white man was bound to respect—bought and sold and treated as an ordinary article of merchandise and traffic, whenever a profit could be made" (Dred Scott decision). No wonder Thomas Jefferson said as he thought of slavery, "I tremble for my country when I reflect that God is just." (90: Query XVIII, Manners) George Mason, another leader in the Virginia democratic movement, said that "such a trade is diabolical in itself and disgraceful to mankind." (55:XII:363)* We have in-

* Mason said this when he refused, after having been a most active member of the 1787 Constitutional Convention, to sign the resulting Constitution because of its compromise on the slave trade and other matters.

deed advanced greatly since these quoted words of the Dred Scott decision; but the country as a whole has still far to go in the matter of respecting humanity in the person of the Negro. We have outlived the past, but hurtful remnants of the old attitudes still linger among us.

A further instance in which the sins and errors of the past still trouble us is anti-Semitism. Many there are among us who profess to accept ethics and democracy but still deny equality of rights and opportunities to Jews. The earliest anti-Semitism began some fifteen hundred years ago with the dogma, now denied by all right-thinking people, that deviants from the religion of the dominant group should for that reason be denied equal privileges with the rest. When at long last mankind recognized that it could no longer in decency accept this virulent zeal for persecuting those who differ from the prevailing religion, then the religious anti-Semitism gave way to an equally indefensible racial anti-Semitism, alleging that Jews belong to a distinct and inferior race. This position reminds one of the Holy Roman Empire, which was neither Holy nor Roman nor an Empire. So far as science can tell us, there are no pure races; the Jews are not a race; and there are, psychologically, no known differences between racial groups. What remains of anti-Semitism is a mixed aggregate of past prejudices. These are kept alive in those who hold them by failure to outgrow, on the one hand, the childish fear and suspicion of others counted to be different from "us" and, on the other hand, the childish, bad logic of ascribing the bad deeds of any one out-group member as a trait to all the members of that group. On this last point the prejudiced ones say: If one of our group does wrong, *he* is a bad man; if one of the out-group does wrong, *they* are like that. This prejudice of anti-Semitism started long ago at the close of the Roman Empire; it now remains as a mere superstition, but active enough to bring inner hurt to those who hold it and outer serious wrong to one of the most effectively useful group of citizens we have. In this we have a fourth regrettable instance of a past evil handed down to plague the present.

There are yet other prejudices within our American life which have their roots in a now outgrown past. We must study and understand all such, partly to insure to them a fitting burial, partly to combat the charge that we have lost our faith in ethics and democracy, partly to guard ourselves against repeating similar pregnant evils in our own time and in our own country.

Have we now among us any privileged ones who, like the old Tsarist Russians, are breeding irreconcilability on the part of others by denying to them the fair and equal treatment they demand for themselves? The Irish were so treated in their homeland for some seven hundred years; the resulting hatred and irreconcilability will stay with the world to its hurt for many, many years to come. Do we wish to build such abiding attitudes of antagonism in our Negroes? In our Jews? In the Mexicans who have crossed our borders to live among us? Are other minority groups being denied their just rights? And what about religious antagonisms? Do we wish to cultivate these and so fragmentize our nation in the way we now see prevailing in Quebec and Belgium and France?

These are some of the questions we face as we observe how "the evil that men do lives after them."

IDEALS THAT HAVE EMERGED

What characteristic ideals seem to be emerging from this long-term revolution, as feudalism yields progressively to democracy? These ideals, it may be noted are progressively formulated by creative and sensitive leaders of social-moral insight as they seek to guide the evolution of civilization to its highest development. Such ideals, it is true, must be formulated progressively. Evolving historic experience is necessary to correct earlier and inadequate conceptions and hopes. But ideals, if they are to serve effectively, have to be consciously formulated. When so formulated, they clearly give better guidance; for then men can quote them and urge obedience to them. Also, only when so formulated can the ideals themselves be adequately criticized to improve them as they are critically judged with reference to the aims and goals of current conduct.

The principal ones of our resulting ideals are easy to name: liberty, equality, respect for personality, personal responsibility for the common good, personal integrity, acting on thinking, the free play of intelligence. All of these, except personal integrity, have been previously discussed, but an additional word or two here may help.

Of these ideals, that of liberty stands perhaps closest to the desires of the ordinary man and so will, under favorable conditions, grow into an insistent conviction and attitude. The wish to be free comes early and easy, at least among us—to be free from interference, from control by others, to be free to purpose at will, to pursue one's purposes—such freedoms and their like form the basis for the ideal of liberty. Mencken, distinguishing freedom from liberty, thus words the ideal for the individual: "Freedom in thought, the liberty to try and err, the right to be his own man." (168:370)

The ideal of equality arises perhaps in its earliest form when one child contrasts the apparently unequal treatment he receives with that accorded to another child. One principal service of the ideal of equality is to limit the doctrine of liberty. We have seen previously from Norman Angell that "when all demand complete freedom, none has any." The actual conflict between freedom and equality we saw in the discussion of individualism and in the earlier discussion of the socio-economic scale as creating a very acute domestic problem which our civilization now faces.

Respect for personality is too new a term and too abstract a conception to have built for itself a comparable place in popular American thought with that given either to liberty or to equality. In a way it includes the content of both of these and yet more. Respect for personality demands consideration for each person because he is a human being. The human individual has a self-other and self-conscious character or being; he can thus think about himself in relation to others, can think about the comparative treatment he is receiving, can feel and know that he is feeling, can conceive of other and better experiences. Because the normal human individual is capable of such comparative thoughts we must, to use Kant's words, treat each one "always as end and never as means merely."

Acceptance of personal responsibility for the common good appears, perhaps of all these ideals, least "natural" to the human individual. It is, however, a clear necessity for any decent social life. Unless a clear working majority of the group consciously accepts this responsibility, social life defeats itself. The necessity to develop the ideal of responsibility for the common good as a strong working attitude and habit is perhaps the present greatest need in our social life. The school must, as we shall in a moment consider, accept this particular task as a dominant aim.

Personal integrity is another strongly needed social ideal and virtue. The bigness characteristic of our civilization, bigness of business organization, bigness of cities, bigness of schools—all these make their mass demands in a way which threatens to overwhelm the individual as such. Bigness and the mass mind thus fight against personal integrity. By personal integrity we mean, specifically, such things as a sense of honor, adherence to honesty in all affairs, acceptance of obligations—for example, the obligation to respect other personalities and their rights. Integrity is the necessary basis of happy and effective human relationships. Without this, people cannot believe in each other, cannot trust each other, cannot truly cooperate. A person of true integrity will stand firm against assaults and against temptation; he cannot be bought, he will not be seduced, he will not yield to his own selfish impulses and desires.

The two ideals of acting on thinking and the free play of intelligence belong together. Acting on thinking—acting only after a study of probable effects—is the single best rule for effective behavior. The free play of intelligence must be accepted as the final resource to tell us what to think and do. In the degree that people accept both principles to act on them will civilization take a great step forward.

Clearly a higher type of democracy is here envisaged than we have yet achieved; but many—the wisest and best among us—have personally accepted these ideals to govern their lives; and their wider use can be spread.

THE RESULTING SOCIAL OBLIGATION

When we consider correcting the various evils confronting our modern civilization, we must distinguish between the part of this corrective process to be carried out by society at large and the part belonging primarily to education. Discussion of the latter we postpone to the end of this chapter; the social duty we consider now, but in a limited way.

The aim in considering these social problems here is not to present solutions; that would be beyond both the ability of the author and the scope of this book. Rather is the principal aim at this point to see the demands these problems make upon education, so that educators and teachers may better conceive the current task of conscious education; for this seems the best hope for meeting our mounting load of social problems.

It will thus perhaps suffice to list *seriatim* six of the principal problem areas considered at the close of Part I and suggest, regarding each, its principal demands upon education.

1. *The Problem of One World, of War and International Responsibility*. Another war would be disastrous in the extreme. The creation of such one-world arrangements as will abolish war and establish abiding peace is of supreme importance. To succeed with this problem will, it appears, require of the world, to an unprecedented degree, both ingenuity and good will. At the close of World War I our country did not have the necessary will. We refused to join the League of Nations; with what result we now see. This time we must not fail. As a proper social ethics limits the freedom of the individual citizen, so must a proper world order limit national sovereignty. But the needed limitation as yet meets strong resistance. Possibly it will require another generation before we can gain the necessary insight and good will. If so, the clearer are the demands on education. It must raise up a generation equipped with the needed insight and will.

2. *What System of Economy?* We saw in Chapter XIV that we now have in this country, and generally in the world, four types of economy simultaneously in operation: (i) unregulated private enterprise; (ii) publicly regulated private enterprise; (iii) state socialism; and (iv) communism. Our problem then is not so much which of these to adopt as what proportion of these will best serve human welfare.

Toward the close of World War I, as we saw in Chapter X, Nicholas Murray Butler (whom no one can accuse of "radicalism," to say nothing of "Communism") said, surprising as it may be, that "the mental attitude of the man who works with his just accumulations [a euphemism for "capitalist"] must be changed so far as to put production for use or for enjoyment in the place of production for mere profit." And to clinch the matter he added: "Production for profit alone is plainly an inhuman undertaking; it can and does close its eyes to human exploitation, to human suffering, and to human want." (123: Feb. 17, 1918)

More recently Mr. Justice Douglas of the United States Supreme

Court has declared that "the human welfare state is the great political invention of the twentieth century." And it seems a fair conclusion that this phrase, "human welfare state," does indicate a definite trend in American political and economic thinking today. Something like this becomes increasingly the accepted aim of thoughtful, humanitarian people. But even if all accepted this aim, there would still remain many serious problems to solve. We can produce enough for all, but we have not solved the problem of distribution, as we saw in considering hereditary poverty. We have only well begun solving the labor-management problem, as is obvious to all. We still have the problem of determining when striking should be illegal. We have not learned how to prevent depressions. Inflation becomes at times a serious threat.

These are a few of the more serious economic problems which the nation must learn to solve. Our schools must build people equipped in mind and attitude to attack these problems and their like.

3. *The Individual in Modern Industrial Society*. It is commonly stated that universal suffrage became the rule during the period of Andrew Jackson. This is in a sense true, but we still have restrictions, as we saw above, against Negroes in various states. The poll tax also works to reduce the proportion of voters. The welfare of the common man is never secure when suffrage is limited; for suffrage is "the right preservative of all other rights."

But the future holds other serious threats to individual freedom. We are now dependent on the good working of our economic system. This must be made safer against depressions. However, even if the worker could know that no depression could ever come, he still would not be free. Too often he has to work according to plans handed down from above, plans in which neither he nor any of his fellows has been consulted. The laborer's work brings more material goods to him than was true a century ago, but he now has less freedom than his farmer ancestor. So far as his work goes, he is less of a person. As we concluded in Chapter xiv, independence and self-respect and contentment have in serious degree decreased for many among us; restlessness, craving for excitement, and a feeling of not counting have increased.

Can education solve these problems? We cannot say what the future holds; but we can say this much: Education must accept the task of preparing the minds and hearts of the rising generation to feel these problems and to become intelligent about them. Possibly we can solve them all; some, possibly, we cannot. But we must build the proper attitudes and insight and methods of study to save as much for life as possible.

4. *Democracy and the Social Scale*. Discussion of this question need not here be repeated, more than to say that in this problem democracy itself is at stake. We must learn how to deal with the socially hereditary evils of poverty, ignorance, and crime. Our high schools and colleges must so guide those under their care that they will graduate able and disposed to deal constructively with this most disastrous of our domestic problems. It looks as if there always will be a lowest level; but the present level of the bottom must be greatly raised, and flexibility of movement upward on merit must be greatly increased.

5. *The Quality of Personal Living*. This problem calls for very serious advanced study to find how far our institutional arrangements hinder the finest development of personal living and refinement. We are told that there are some 20,000 liquor stores in our country and only 5,000 book stores. Those who drink much seek mainly to forget what life otherwise gives them. Of the common use of leisure it has been said that "the wage-slave enjoys temporary release from slavery by having other slaves provide him with amusement and entertainment." This is of course not a fair statement of all entertainment, but there is too much truth in the suggestion. Meanwhile the discussions of Chapters XIV and XXVII offer some suggestions which the schools can consider. Hitherto the Alexandrian outlook has tended to lead too much toward the ivory tower. We saw in Chapter XVI Irwin Edman saying that for some individuals culture is "a combination of elegance and nostalgia, of preciousness and disdain"; and that for such it is "an elegant escape into beautiful anachronisms." This is exactly what we do not wish.

6. *A Working Philosophy of Life*. If there is any one thing that present-day man needs, it is an adequate philosophy of life. In this country many have given up the authoritarian theological philosophy of their fathers, whether Protestant, Catholic, or Jewish, and have not yet found "assured objects of allegiance" to take its place. If education at its upper levels has any one inclusive task, it is to help people find defensible ground on which to stand and

from which to face the world. In this, as always in true education, it is not indoctrination we seek—exactly the contrary. Our task as educators is to help those under our care to think things through for themselves. We guide to better study but not to the answers we have personally accepted. Bronson Alcott was quoted earlier as saying: "The true teacher defends his pupils against his own personal influence." (168:728). It is wider and deeper independent thinking we must seek as we guide towards the building of an adequate philosophy. Without such a philosophy the individual has no adequate basis for guiding his life.

WHAT EDUCATION SHOULD DO

Wherever a problem of life makes such a demand on education as to affect the aims to be pursued or, correlatively, the methods to be followed, there the philosophy of education is concerned. In the preceding parts of this chapter many life problems are indicated which make such demands on the aims of education.

First, and most generally, these problems concern the sensitive citizen. They are problems which affect crucially the common everyday life of a large proportion of citizens. Society must face them and somehow dispose of them. Every normal child who grows to maturity will have to face the duties of citizenship. Each such growing person must then, if he is to do his part in life, become increasingly sensitive to the problems he will likely face as citizen, become intelligent regarding such problems, become disposed to accept his responsibility in connection with them, and acquire skill in attacking and solving such problems cooperatively with his fellows.

How good teaching can bring about such results we have discussed in preceding chapters. It should, however, be noted that while the consideration of a particular problem may not at the time require prolonged study, the building of the four general traits just named will require years. It should also be repeated that no suggestion is here made to give the pupil or student "the correct" answer to any of these problems. The omission is intentional. In no controversial issue should the teacher assume to give "the answer," and so close off the necessity for further study. Instead, the aim is to encourage each learner to do his own thinking, to grow in disposition and ability to think for himself. We do all we can to help his thinking but not in such a way as to direct the process toward our answer. No indoctrination truly educates to democratic independence of personality, and it is this true democratic education that we seek.

Second, the beginning will usually be with certain local problems and recently emerging social issues, which because of current general interest, have particular appeal to the students. These problems should receive special treatment. They should be so studied as to show their significant connections with past history and the wider setting. Their peculiar and close-at-hand interest should furnish a springboard from which to approach, later, certain other more complex problems. For each stage of development there is a limit beyond which we should not at the time try to make pupils go, but beyond which they must ultimately go if they are to be intelligent in the general citizenship field.

Finally, we must realize that the philosophy of life discussed above is all the time in actual process of building by our students. For good or ill every insight they get, every valuation they make, every decision they reach, will enter as constituent factors into the actual social philosophy they are building. Realizing this, we must do our utmost to help them think and judge carefully, objectively, inclusively, and reliably. Again, we are not to guide them toward our personal answer, but to the most careful thinking and judging they can do. What the students are to think, what decisions they will reach in these controversial areas, is for them to decide. The result we seek is a person able and disposed to think for himself and act in accordance with his best thinking.

CHAPTER XXIX. *Correlatives: Philosophy of Life; the Educative Process*

THE aim of this concluding chapter is to review critically the educational program of Part II in its relation to the philosophy of life developed in Part I. The purpose of the proposed program is, as stated at the beginning of Part II, to implement and realize the philosophy of life. In order to see whether this purpose has been attained, this chapter will first review briefly the chief elements in the philosophy and then, on the basis of these, face the inclusive question: Does the educational program meet satisfactorily the demands made upon it by that philosophy? Is that program such that the philosophy can permeate and work through it to shape and direct its various procedures to the life-enriching ends set forth in the philosophy?

BASIC VALUE-ASSUMPTIONS

First should be stated the basic value-assumptions inherent in the philosophy of life presented in Part I.

1. *The Living of People Is the Primary Value.* In the working out of this value, in the effects of any proposal on the living of all the people, is found the criterion for all else.

2. *The Good Life Is the Inclusive Aim.* The good life means the life good to live as good music is music good to hear. Without the life-good-to-live nothing else has meaning. In the degree that the content of the good life is defined, in like degree has been stated the content aims of ethics, of democracy, and of education.

3. *Morality Is a Social Necessity.* To act morally—to act in the light of effects on the future and on others—follows as an essential obligation from the two preceding values. If quality of living of

people is the paramount value; if enriching the quality of life be taken as the criterion of endeavor; if, in addition, we live in a world where all are tied together, with acts of each affecting all—then acceptance of moral obligation becomes essential to satisfactory social living. Only on such a basis can we have a decent civilization.

4. *Democracy Is the Chosen Way of Life.* Democracy includes "government by the people," but reaches beyond the compulsion of government to the active outworking of *respect for personality* wherever found. It includes *liberty*, *equality*, and *regard for the common good.* Democratic liberty is limited by democratic equality; there must be equal rights for all, and this requirement limits liberty for any one individual to that consistent with equal liberty for others. Each democratic right brings also its corresponding duty. Regard for the common good is necessary, otherwise rights are reduced to selfish privileges, the denial of democracy.

STRATEGIC GUIDING PRINCIPLES

Next are stated certain strategic guiding principles offered by Part I to Part II. These represent the best known conclusions of expert opinion in the respective areas. As such they can be verified by similar study of others.

1. *Man Is Best Conceived as a Goal-Seeking Organism.* As such he behaves in order to secure the ends or goals he values. The older philosophy thought of man primarily as *Homo sapiens*, stressing therein his intellect and its use for contemplation and this contemplation as man's highest end and endeavor. The older philosophy was ignorant of and so disregarded his biological character as an organism essentially fitted for and concerned with seeking goals and achieving its values in living itself.

We now see that out of man's capacity for *goal-seeking behavior* arise his *wants* and *efforts;* and out of these come his consciously chosen *ends* (goals) and *means.* Because ends *conflict*, man is led to *weigh* his goals against each other. When this is done *critically* enough, *values* emerge. Out of the further critical study of values, *philosophy* arises.

2. *Man's Capacity for Conscious Experience and Consequent Civilization Depends on His Socially Acquired Selfhood.* Man is born little more intelligent than a sensitive plant; but he can learn.

As he learns to associate with others and to talk, he comes in time to see in *others* what he first saw in himself—for example, hunger and pain—and similarly to see in himself what he first saw in others—such as pouting and fretting. Self and other thus mutually help each other into a better understanding of other and self. Most importantly, both factors grow together in the child's mind to form his self-other compounded selfhood. He now increasingly sees himself as others see him—in a word, he is now a *self-conscious* being. Out of this come in order consciousness of himself as doing and effecting; then of being *held to account* for what he does; then, later, his sense of *responsibility;* and finally his *conscience.*

It is out of such developments that man has studied what he and others do and so has devised language, tools, institutions—in a word, civilization.

3. *Change Is Inherent in Human Affairs.* The older philosophic outlook decried and belittled change; the new recognizes change as a strategic and pervasive factor in all human affairs. Indeed, increasingly rapid change is perhaps the most characteristic feature of modern life. In the nineteenth century progress was assumed to be inevitable. Now, though progress along nearly any specific line appears probable in the degree that it is explicitly sought, total net progress seems hard to prove and possibly not certain.

Acceptance of the modern conception of inherent change requires also recognition of uncertainty regarding the future. While there are many well-established uniformities in nature, we cannot in an infinitely complex universe know for certain the outcome of any specific event. As Whitehead says, "each event is a process issuing in novelty." (171:303) So that outcomes are fixed not in advance, as the fatalists have held, but only within the actual eventuation itself. This absence of antecedent fixation has great significance. Because outcomes are not predetermined, intelligence finds its opportunity to shape human affairs, personal accountability has meaning, morality is possible. To say it differently, without this freedom from antecedent fixation, neither conscious human endeavor nor moral obligation could have meaning or a defensible place in life.

4. *The Free Play of Intelligence Is Our Final Resource.* Still another meaning emerges from the twin facts that change is inherent in human affairs and that outcomes depend on the type of inter-

vention by men—that use of intelligence is obligatory if life is to go on well, if outcomes favorable to men, individually and collectively, are to be achieved. By intelligence, both individual and group, we mean the capacity to learn and use this learning in behalf of ends sought. Though man's native capacity forms the essential basis, effective intelligence is built up from experience, from study of situations, search for means of control, testing results by their consequences. In other words, methods of using intelligence must be studied by intelligence. That this may be successfully done intelligence itself must have free play to apply itself to any and every problematic aspect of any and every experience. This free play of intelligence becomes our "sole ultimate resource" to tell us what to think and do.

5. *Probabilities Furnish Our Guide in Thought and Act.* Although there are many reliable instances of uniformity in nature, it is never possible in a particular case to be sure we know all the factors at work. So that, as stated above, any specific event is always uncertain as to outcome. As Dewey says, "all action is an invasion of the future, of the unknown. Conflict and uncertainty are ultimate traits." (46:12). The best we can do, then, is to act on probabilities.

6. *Men Need a Philosophy of Life Based on Thoughtful Study.* "Socrates," as Cicero told us in *Academica*, "called philosophy down from the heavens to earth, and introduced it into the cities and houses of men, compelling them to inquire regarding life and morals and things good and evil." And men must so inquire. To live contradictions or indefensible choices either within the soul or in the world outside is by so much to make life thwart life. We must try, then, to make life a defensible whole, value and aim fitting with value and aim without final contradiction; and each individual must try to unify himself within in accordance with this defensible aggregate of values and aims. Philosophy exists to help men in both these efforts. Philosophy is accordingly both criticism and the criticism of criticism; first, criticism of life with its various contending goods and values to find what to accept and support, and second, criticism of this criticism, that all may be done with deepest insight.

Such a philosophy is an eminently practical matter. As Chesterton said, "for a landlady considering a lodger it is important to know his income, but it is still more important to know his philosophy."

(24:5) Philosophy, however, is not only immediately practical; it reaches still farther into life. Says E. A. Burtt in his *Metaphysical Foundations of Physics:*

> In the last analysis it is the ultimate picture which an age forms of the nature of the world that is its most fundamental possession. It is the final controlling factor in all thinking whatever. (p. 3).

And Thomas E. Shields:

> A man's philosophy, by imperceptible degrees, colors the whole of his life and affects his attitude toward all things in heaven and on earth. In like manner the prevalent philosophy of a people gradually transforms all their social institutions (147:22*f.*).

With these demands and guiding principles from the philosophy now before us we are ready to evaluate the educational aims and procedures of Part II with reference to their promise to implement these demands. Three definite lines of inquiry seem indicated: Is the learning-teaching theory given in Part II defensible? What specific educational aims are necessary to implement the given philosophic demands? And, finally, how appropriate are the education procedures of Part II to attain these aims? Specifically, is the educational program such that the accepted philosophy of life can effectually permeate it to shape and direct its procedures to the best known ways of managing life?

Is the Learning-Teaching Theory Defensible?

Seven distinct items in this theory will be considered here in order:

1. *We Learn What We Live.* This principle follows from any adequate study of the behavior process. A child's behavior vexes his teacher and she scolds him. What does the child live in this experience? He lives all the thoughts and feelings that come to him, directly or indirectly, in response to the scolding. What does the child learn? He learns just so much of these thought and feelings as stay with him to come back into his life to help shape it and give it content. In a word, he learns in greater or less degree just what he lives.

Or again suppose a more complex situation, one complex enough to demand the conscious choice of an end or goal and appropriate means. To choose these effectually the person must, as he chooses, keep in mind the specific *character of his situation* and the *degree of its importance*. But to *keep in mind* the "character of the situation" and its "degree of importance" so that these play their proper role in the choice is exactly to illustrate the definition and the proper functioning of learning. These things—the character of the situation and its degree of importance—had been "learned" at the first or they would not have stayed with the person to re-enter his experience and play there their proper role. And they were "learned" as and because they were thus "lived."

The same would hold for each new step in the experience. What is done in one step and what resulted would again be held in mind as the next step was decided upon. Clearly, then, things are learned as they are lived, as they play their role in actual experiencing.

2. *The Direction of Learning Is Determined by the Direction of Its Acceptance for Expected Future Use.* Whatever the scolded child felt in the preceding item, he learned, as he accepted it, either not to behave that way again to his teacher or to feel irritation and resentment at being scolded. In either case the direction of learning fitted the direction of his acceptance. In the other instance, the more complex one, if one of the foregoing steps should fail when attempted, the person will learn *not to use* that measure again, at least for just such a situation. In other words, as regards direction the person learns it as he accepts it for expected future use. He may decide that he can never use it; if so he learns it that way. Or he may decide that this measure will serve some other end or this end under other circumstances; if so he learns it as he accepts it for these possible future uses. This is the consideration which determines whether one learns from an experience *to do* the like again or *not to do* it.

3. *The Degree of Learning Depends on the Degree of Acceptance and Living.* This has been thoroughly discussed previously and from observed facts we cannot doubt its defensibility.

4. *Concomitant Learnings.* This also has been sufficiently discussed previously.

5. *Cumulative Learnings.* This principle, too, is amply supported by the observed facts.

6. *Generalizations Are Seldom Directly Transferable.* This principle makes so crucial an attack on the older textbook-lecture-examination theory of teaching that we must examine it carefully.

It is not true that no generalization can be transferred from one person to another. What is true is that such a transfer is possible only when the recipient's experience in the area of application is sufficiently full and varied to allow him to think intelligently about the various possible applications. Mary's mother can tell her that this bottle holds poison and "you mustn't touch it." Even young Mary can henceforth avoid the poison by avoiding the bottle; that much she can understand and do; but she probably gets a very inadequate conception of poison. Later, however, when Mary first meets prepositions in her old-fashioned grammar, neither textbook nor teacher can at first tell Mary what a preposition is sufficiently well for her thenceforth to recognize a preposition at sight. This generalization like nearly all generalizations of complex matters cannot be transferred directly.

This principle constitutes one of the most crucial differences between the old and the new outlooks. The old, from its very beginning, consisted essentially of the effort to transfer knowledge and wisdom to the young by the device of having them "learn" (memorize) the formulations given in textbooks and lectures. The new asserts that for a generalization to be effective it must be made by the one who is to use it, and for this he must have adequate variety of experiences. Even when using knowledge from books about objects distant in time or place, the learner will, typically, generalize from several different treatments; so that even here he has a basis for making his own generalizations.

7. *The Doctrine of Interest.* This constitutes a further crucial difference between the old and the new theories of education. The old knew that it could not typically expect interest, and accordingly disregarded interest in its typical working procedures. For the new, however, interest is basic: without the support of interest some of its most desirable aims cannot be realized—e.g., concomitant learning in the way of character traits, citizenship traits, morality, responsibility, and the like. Such aims cannot be achieved by the routine or mechanical behavior common in schools, and certainly not by pressure or force. The building of taste and fine spirit and worthy, unselfish concerns can be achieved only on a basis of active interest in these values. Moreover, as regards the customary "knowledge" sought by schools, the new finds this is much better learned when an "active and interested will" is at work in the pupil. For

the new, then, the presence of interest gives the best promise of learning of all constructive types and provides besides the best promise of "leading on," in school and out. No one who, in objective spirit, has really compared the results of the two—learning with interest and learning without interest—can doubt that the factor of interest is a significant one to be taken into account and incorporated into educational procedures wherever possible.

What Specific Educational Aims Are Necessary to Implement the Accepted Philosophy?

No more will be attempted here than to state briefly the more strategic aims which, if attained, promise to implement the philosophy set forth with fullness in Part I and in brief at the beginning of this chapter.

To fit these aims into the larger whole, it may be well to recall the three successive aims which actual education must pursue simultaneously: the immediate aim, the intermediate aim, and the remoter aim. The *remoter* and inclusive guiding aim of education is to rear the young *to live the full good life*, both individual and social. The *intermediate* aim is to build such character in the young as will guarantee, so far as this is possible, that they *can* and *will* live the desirable good life. The *immediate* aim is such living on the part of the young as will, by their resulting learning, build the needed character.

Discussion of the content of good living, the immediate aim, does not belong in this discussion. At this point it is character that concerns us, and more specifically a strategic list of the needed traits of character. The older education professed the same *remoter aim* for education as that given above, but it mistakenly rejected character as its guiding aim, counting instead that acquiring knowledge and ideas *about* the good life would suffice to *effect* the good life. The new education, by contrast, knows that merely having ideas *about* a desirable line of conduct does not of itself bring about that conduct. Actual effective character has to be built, character which values such conduct and acts it out. Only on the basis of strongly built habits and attitudes can effective behavior be expected, habits and attitudes built into traits on the basis of conscious acceptance and acting on thinking.

The following eight traits of character are proposed as strategically important and representative of any proposed complete list that might be offered:

1. A normally adjusted personality.
2. Practical common sense in facing the varied situations of life.
3. Acting on thinking. This includes (i) sufficient sensitivity to note situations properly calling for thought; (ii) the habit of stopping, as needed, to think; (iii) an increasing range of appropriate knowledge to think with; (iv) skill in thinking to a reliable conclusion; (v) disposition to act as thinking has decided.
4. Commitment to and skill in cooperative group discussion and decision, as a means both to improvement of ideas and to carrying them out in life.
5. Regard for the rights and feelings of others; in one word, respect for personality, beginning with one's fellows close at hand and extending gradually to all more distant.
6. Attitudes of responsible citizenship; regard for the common good. Here again these begin close by but extend gradually to the larger and distant groups.
7. A variety of interests and sources of finer enjoyment.
8. Ideals, standards, and principles of action, beginning again with matters close at hand but going on ultimately toward a philosophy of life.

These eight objectives seem to promise implementation of the accepted philosophy of life.

How Adequate Are the Proposed Educational Procedures to Attain Their Aims?

We come at last to the crucial evaluation of the proposed educational procedures: Do these procedures promise to build the traits of character necessary to meet the demands set forth in the philosophy of life? More specifically, are these procedures such that an adequate philosophy of life can permeate them and work through them to shape and direct their efforts to the building of the traits needed to manage life properly?

What are these teaching procedures? They may be summed up under the following four principles:

1. Count that the school is properly a place of living. Work for the finest quality of living that teacher and pupils can together devise, reaching out as much as feasible into the community.

This means that the curriculum is this fine quality of living as chosen by the pupils under teacher guidance (and, if need be, direction); that in the elementary school and in the "general" education of the high school ordinary school subjects as such are not taught; that marks are not kept nor formal report cards given.

2. Let the principles of interest and purposeful activity set the predominant pattern.

Start where pupils are in interest, but guide so as to build new interests, new knowledge, skills, attitudes, etc.

Stress pupil purposing, initiating, creativity, and responsibility.

As a rule use no compulsion and no punishments (though emergency situations may of course demand positive teacher control).

3. Run everything on a basis of democracy and respect for personality.

Begin where pupils are in maturity and character, but lead always as fast and as far as possible to best possible practice and commitment thereto.

4. Work in season and out, depending on pupil maturity and development, for the finest and most inclusive aims of life, these to be increasingly exemplified in everything done in school and out.

Do these procedures promise to build the various strategic traits of character? The answer seems yes; but let us consider.

1. Do these four procedures promise a well-adjusted personality? The answer is that these are exactly the procedures advocated by the experts in the field for the building of normally adjusted personality. The teacher works to make each child feel secure, to get each one actively and creatively at work along lines at which he can achieve success. Each child is treated with respect as a person. For pupils suffering maladjustment, these procedures promise enough successful normal living to overcome much if not all of their difficulties. Even very serious cases may show significant improvement.

2. Will the procedures help pupils to build practical common sense for facing life's practical demands? Again the answer seems

yes. Taking the school years together, the pupils will face many and varied aspects of life, far and away more than in the conventional school. And the pupils will be expected to face these situations in a practical first-hand way. Surely, no other school program offers so much in this respect.

3. Will the pupils learn to act on thinking? If there is anything that the new will seek, certainly this is it. Each succeeding activity will afford a new chance to think and act. To be sure, this is a highly crucial demand on the school, probably the most crucial of the eight, unless the eighth rivals it. The school will stand or fall by its success under this head. Indeed, acting on thinking is the one necessary means for attaining practically all else.

What about the range of knowledge essential to think effectively? Critics who see that school subjects are not taught as formerly often ask about the knowledge and skills resulting from these newer procedures. The answer again seems clear. Every close study so far made shows the learning in the newer schools to be at least equal to the records of the older type school and for the most part superior. The judgment of this writer is that the more thoroughly the new is tried, the more will its superiority appear in meeting the requirements of knowledge and skill, while in the other respects of character and attitude the superiority of the new will be far greater.

4. In the matter of skill in group discussion and decision making, there can be no doubt. The old largely ignored this; the new makes this its chief procedure.

5. In the matter of learning respect for the rights and feelings of others, the old—so far as it depended on recitation and examinations—took no positive steps in the matter. The new makes this an essential aim in everything done. And, further, the old with its avoidance of communication and shared activities in school, offered small opportunity to practice respect; the new expects all to be working together in such a way that innumerable opportunities will arise for social dealings and accordingly for active practice in personal relations. With the teacher alert to what is at stake here, there is every opportunity to build an active respect in each child for all the other personalities.

6. Is there opportunity to build attitudes of responsible citizenship, including an adequate regard for the common good? This, it must be admitted, is an aim difficult of achievement; but the proba-

bilities all lie with the new procedures as against the old. We saw previously that Spaulding's study of the New York State high schools showed positive decrease in regard for the common good with advancement through the high school. The Eight Year Study showed exactly the opposite, namely, positive advance for graduates of the newer type school; and the more thoroughly the new differed from the old, the greater was its superiority in this respect.

7. As to building a variety of interests and sources of finer enjoyment, an analogous discussion to that just given will hold.

8. Ideals, standards, and principles of action are of necessity built out of the person's own experience, out of his own thinking, feeling, inner acceptance. Everything said above about the nontransferability of generalizations holds distinctly here. These can be best built under wise teacher guidance in connection with actual experiences conducted under the rule of acting on thinking. In a word, guidance is an important aid, but the actual building is by the person's thinking on his own experiences, especially those experiences in which he has a responsible share in management.

In one word, the principle of responsible pupil activity, under wise guidance, seems to furnish the best means, if not the only safe way, to achieve these eight desired traits. It thus appears that the teaching procedures do answer to the accepted philosophy; the procedures, fairly executed, do lead toward the aims of the philosophy.

Will, then, these teaching procedures succeed? What can make them succeed? What does a philosophy of life have to do in the situation?

These are probably the most searching, the most crucial questions of all in this book. The answer to them depends on one factor. In the degree that the teacher has a defensible working philosophy of life and sees its various bearings on the teaching to be done, in that same degree can and will that teacher—if normal and sufficiently skillful—succeed in guiding his pupils to build the traits discussed above. The philosophy will permeate everything done. The same holds for principal, for supervisor, for superintendent: in the degree that these have an adequate philosophy of life and let that philosophy permeate all they do, shaping and directing each step taken, in like degree may we expect proper character and personality effects to follow in all affected.

Schools of education should make it their guiding aim that all under their care build effectual working philosophies of life and education. All else done in education depends on this.

So we reach the end. Do schools professedly run on the basis herein advocated really measure up as claimed above? In answer, it may serve to quote the recent words of the man who has made a greater number of thoroughgoing surveys of school systems than anyone else in our country, Professor George D. Strayer. It may not be amiss to say that earlier he was skeptical of the new. Professor Strayer is quoted as saying:

> People who criticize modern education just don't know what children are doing in schools today. . . . In the fundamentals children today are doing much better than their mothers and fathers or grandparents did. They are reading more and they read better; they spell better and they are as competent in the fundamentals of arithmetic as any other generation, and they write better and more interestingly than their parents did (123:Apr. 24, 1950).

He had previously reported in 1944 from his survey of the New York City schools:

> Every member of the survey staff visiting schools in the City of New York has noticed that, where the development of the activity program is well under way, overt acts of misbehavior seldom occur, that in these schools the working morale of the pupils is high, and that emotional conflicts and tensions have all but disappeared. On the other hand, these evils are still prevalent in most schools which have not undertaken the new program—in some of them alarmingly so (121:29).

Add to the foregoing the findings of the previously noted Eight Year Study (made at a cost of over $600,000) of 1,475 college students coming from the newer type of schools: "Consistently higher academic averages and more academic honors . . . clear cut superiority in . . . the willingness and ability to think logically and objectively, and active and vital interest in the world about them . . . [were] more frequently concerned with . . . the importance of assuming their share of responsibility . . . more often cooperative, tolerant, and self-directing." (23:173*f*.) Putting together all these and other like findings, it seems fair to conclude that the new outlook furnishes appreciably better teaching procedures than the old.

REFERENCES CITED

1. Adams, George P., and Montague, Wm. P. (eds.), *Contemporary American Philosophy* (New York, Macmillan, 1930)
2. Adams, Henry, *Education* (Boston, Houghton Mifflin, 1918)
3. Adams, John, *Works* (Boston, Little Brown, 1851)
4. Adams, John, and Jefferson, Thomas, *Correspondence* (Wilstach ed.; Indianapolis, Bobbs Merrill, 1925)
5. Alexander, Thomas, *The Prussian Elementary Schools* (New York, Macmillan, 1918)
6. American Academy of Political and Social Science, *Annals* (Philadelphia)
7. American Antiquarian Society *Proceedings* (Worcester, Mass.)
8. *American Scholar: a Quarterly for the Independent Thinker* (Phi Beta Kappa, New York)
9. Archbishop's Fifth Committee, *Report* (London, 1918)
10. *Atlantic Monthly* (Boston)
11. Baldwin, J. Mark, *Individual and Society* (Boston, Badger, 1911)
12. Bentham, Jeremy, *Works* (Edinburgh, Tait, 1843)
13. Boas, Franz, *The Mind of Primitive Man* (New York, Macmillan, 1938)
14. Bradley, F. H., *Ethical Studies* (London, King, 1876)
15. Breasted, James H., *The Dawn of Conscience* (New York, Scribner's 1934)
16. Brown, Elmer E., *The Making of Our Middle Schools* (New York, Longmans Green, 1902)
17. Burke, Edmund, *Works* (London, Bohn, 1854)
18. Bury, J. B., *A History of Freedom of Thought* (London, Williams and Norgate, 1920)
19. Bury, J. B., *The Idea of Progress* (New York, Macmillan, 1932)
20. Butler, Samuel, *The Way of All Flesh* (New York, Macmillan, 1927)
21. Caldwell, Otis W., and Courtis, S. A., *Then and Now in Education* (Yonkers-on-Hudson, World Book, 1924)
22. Carlyle, Thomas, *Past and Present* (New York, Scribner's, 1918)
23. Chamberlin, Dean, et al, *Did They Succeed in College?* vol. IV of Adventure in American Education (New York, Harper's, 1942)
24. Chesterton, Gilbert K., *Heretics* (New York, John Lane, 1905)

25. *Childhood Education* (Washington, D.C.)
26. Childs, H. L. (trans.), *The Nazi Primer* (New York, Harper's, 1938)
27. *Christian Education in China* (New York, Foreign Missions Conference, 1922)
28. Collings, Ellsworth, *An Experiment with a Project Curriculum* (New York, Macmillan, 1923)
29. *Common School Journal* (publication discontinued)
30. Compayré, Gabriel, *Histoire critique des doctrines de l'education en France* (Paris, Hachette, 1882)
31. Condorcet, Marquis de, *Esquisse d'un tableau historique des progrès* de l'esprit humain (Paris, Bibliotheque Nationale, 1886. 1st ed. 1794)
32. Conklin, Edwin G., *Heredity and Environment* (Princeton University Press, 1929)
33. *Daughters of the American Revolution Magazine* (Washington, D.C.)
34. Dealey, J. Q., and Ward, L. F., *Textbook of Sociology* (New York, Macmillan, 1905)
35. *DeBow's Review* (publication discontinued)
36. Dell, Floyd, *Were You Ever a Child?* (New York, Knopf, 1919)
37. Denton, Daniel, *A Brief Description of New York* (New York, William Gowans, 1845. 1st ed. 1701)
38. DeTocqueville, Alexis, *Democracy in America* (New York, Colonial Press, 1900. 1st ed. 1835)
39. Dewey, John, *Art as Experience* (New York, Minton Balch, 1934)
40. Dewey, John, *Characters and Events* (New York, Henry Holt, 1929)
41. Dewey, John, *A Common Faith* (New Haven, Yale University Press, 1934)
42. Dewey, John, (ed.), *Creative Intelligence* (New York, Henry Holt, 1917)
43. Dewey, John, *Culture and Industry in Education*, reprinted in Teachers College Bulletin, Tenth Series, No. 10 (March 1, 1919)
44. Dewey, John, *Democracy and Education* (New York, Macmillan, 1916)
45. Dewey, John, *Experience and Nature* (Chicago, Open Court, 1925)
46. Dewey, John, *Human Nature and Conduct* (New York, Henry Holt, 1922)
47. Dewey, John, *Individualism Old and New* (New York, Minton Balch, 1930)
48. Dewey, John, *Interest and Effort in Education* (Boston, Houghton Mifflin, 1913)
49. Dewey, John, *Liberalism and Social Action* (New York, Putnam, 1935)
50. Dewey, John, *Logic: The Theory of Inquiry* (New York, Henry Holt, 1938)
51. Dewey, John, *The Quest for Certainty* (New York, Minton Balch, 1929)

52. Dewey, John, *Reconstruction in Philosophy* (Boston, Beacon Press, 1948. 1st ed. 1920)
53. Dewey, John, and Dewey, Evelyn, *Schools of Tomorrow* (New York, Dutton, 1915)
54. Dewey, John, and Tufts, James H., *Ethics* (New York, Henry Holt, 1932)
55. *Dictionary of American Biography* (New York, Scribner's, 1928–36)
56. Dodd, Agnes F., *Early English Social History* (London, Bell, 1913)
57. Drake, Durant, *The New Morality* (New York, Macmillan, 1928)
58. *Educational Review* (publication discontinued)
59. *Elementary School Teacher* (publication discontinued)
60. Eliot, George, *Romola* (Garden City, Doubleday Page, 1901)
61. *Encyclopedia Britannica* (14th edition)
62. *Encyclopedia of the Social Sciences* (New York, Macmillan, 1930–34)
63. Federal Council of Churches, *Information Bulletin* (New York)
64. Ferrer, Francisco, *Origin and Ideals of the Modern School* (New York, Putnam, 1913)
65. *The Forum* (New York)
66. Fosdick, Dorothy, *What is Liberty?* (New York, Harper's, 1939)
67. Fowler, Thomas, *Progressive Morality* (London, Macmillan, 1884)
68. *Frontiers of Democracy* (publication discontinued)
69. Goodsell, Willystine, *The Problems of the Family* (New York, Century, 1928)
70. Hall, Bishop Joseph, *A Recollection of Such Treatises as Have bene heretofore Severally Published and are now Revised* (1614)
71. *Harper's Magazine* (New York)
72. Hartshorne, Hugh, *Character in Human Relations* (New York, Scribner's, 1932)
73. Hayes, Carlton, J. H., *History of Modern Europe* (New York, Macmillan, 1916)
74. Hegel, Georg Wm. Friedrick, *Philosophy of History* (New York, Willey, 1944)
75. *Helvetic Confession, The Second*, 1566
76. *High School* (publication discontinued)
77. *High School Quarterly* (publication discontinued)
78. Hobbes, Thomas, *The Leviathan* (London, Routledge, 1885. 1st ed. 1651)
79. Hogben, Lancelot, *The Retreat from Reason* (London, Watts, 1936)
80. Hurley and Eagan, *The Prophet of Zion-Parnassus* (Richmond, Va., Presbyterian Board of Publications, 1934)
81. Hutchins, Robert Maynard, *The Higher Learning in America* (New Haven, Yale University Press, 1936)
82. Inge, William Ralph, *More Lay Thoughts of a Dean* (New York, Putnam, 1932)
83. *International Conciliation* Document (Carnegie Endowment for International Peace, New York)

84. *International Journal of Ethics* (publication discontinued)
85. James, William, *Memories and Studies* (New York, Longmans Green, 1911)
86. James, William, *On Vital Reserves* (New York, Henry Holt, 1911)
87. James, William, *Pragmatism* (New York, Longmans Green, 1907)
88. James, William, *Talks to Teachers on Psychology* (New York, Henry Holt, 1899)
89. James, William, *The Will to Believe, and Other Essays* (New York, Longmans Green, 1923. 1st ed. 1897)
90. Jefferson, Thomas, *Notes on the State of Virginia* (Boston, Lilly and Wait, 1832. 1st ed. 1784–85)
91. Jefferson, Thomas, *Writings* (Ford, ed., New York, Putnam, 1894)
92. Jefferson, Thomas, *Writings* (H. A. Washington, ed., New York, John C. Riker, 1853–55)
93. Jefferson, Thomas, and Cabell, J. C., *Early History of the University of Virginia* (Richmond, Randolph, 1856)
94. Jennings, H. S., *Prometheus* (New York, Dutton, 1925)
95. Johnson, F. Ernest, *Church and Society* (New York, Abingdon Press, 1935)
96. *Journal of Educational Psychology* (Baltimore)
97. Kant, Immanuel, *Fundamental Principles of Metaphysics of Ethics* (Abbott trans. New York, Longmans Green, 1895. 1st ed. 1785)
98. Laplace, Marquis de, *A Philosophical Essay on Probabilities* (trans. by Truscott and Emery. New York, Wiley, 1902. 1st ed. 1814)
99. Lewis, Cecil Day, *The Poetic Image* (New York, Oxford, 1948)
100. Liard, Louis, *L'enseignement supérieur en France, 1789–1889* (Paris, Colin, 1888–94)
101. Lincoln, Abraham, *Life and Works* (New York, Current Literature Publ. Co., 1907)
102. Lippmann, Walter, *A Preface to Morals* (New York, Macmillan, 1929)
103. Locke, John, *Essay Concerning Human Understanding* (1690)
104. Locke, John, *Two Treatises on Government* (1689)
105. McGiffert, A. C., *The Rise of Modern Religious Ideas* (New York, Macmillan, 1915)
106. MacIver, R. M., *Community* (London, Macmillan, 1917)
107. Mandeville, Bernard, *The Fable of the Bees* (Edinburgh, J. Wood, 1772). The quotation is from the *Essay on Charity Schools.* The first paragraph has not been located in this edition of the Essay, but seems authentic.
108. Mansfield, Edward D., *American Education* (New York, Barnes, 1851)
109. Marcus Aurelius Antoninus, *Meditations* (trans. by John Jackson. Oxford, Clarendon Press, 1906)
110. Milton, John, *Areopagitica*, in *Of Education, Areopagitica the Commonwealth* (Boston, Houghton Mifflin, 1911. 1st ed. 1644)

111. Monroe, Paul, *Source Book of the History of Education* (New York, Macmillan, 1901)
112. Montaigne, Michel de, *Essays* (trans. by George B. Ives. New York, Heritage Press, 1946. 1st ed. 1580)
113. Muirhead, John H., *Elements of Ethics* (New York, Scribner's, 1892)
114. Napoléon I, *Correspondence*
115. Napoléon I, *Paroles au conseil d'etat*
116. National Education Association, *Principles of Academic Freedom* (Washington, National Education Association, 1941)
117. *New Era* (London)
118. *New Republic* (New York)
119. *New York Post* (New York)
120. New York, State of, *Ecclesiastical Records of the State of New York* (Albany, 1901–06)
121. New York, State of, *Report of the New York City Sub-Committee of the Joint Legislative Committee on the State Educational System* (Legislative Document, 1944, No. 60)
122. *New York State Education* (Albany, N.Y.)
123. *New York Times* (New York)
124. Nietzsche, Friedrich, *Beyond Good and Evil* (trans. by Zimmern. New York, Modern Library, n.d., 1st ed. 1885)
125. *North American Review* (publication discontinued)
126. Noüy, Lecomte du, *Human Destiny* (New York, Longmans Green, 1947)
127. Ogburn, Wm. F., *Social Change* (New York, Huebsch, 1922)
128. *Open Court* (publication discontinued)
129. Ortega y Gasset, Jose, *The Revolt of the Masses* (New York, Norton, 1932)
130. Otto, M. C., *Things and Ideals* (New York, Henry Holt, 1924)
131. Pater, Walter, *The Renaissance: Studies in Art and Poetry* (New York, Macmillan, 1888. 1st ed. 1873)
132. Paulsen, Friedrick, *German Education* (trans. by Lorenz. New York, Scribner's, 1908)
133. Pearson, Karl, *Grammar of Science* (New York, Macmillan, 1911. 1st ed. 1892)
134. *Philadelphia Record* (Philadelphia)
135. Piaget, Jean, *Moral Judgment of Children* (New York, Harcourt Brace, 1932)
136. Prescott, Daniel A., *Emotion and the Educative Process* (Washington, American Council on Education, 1938)
137. *Reader's Digest* (Pleasantville, N.Y.)
138. Richards, I. A., *Principles of Literary Criticism* (London, Kegan Paul, 1925)
139. Ross, E. A., *Principles of Sociology* (New York, Century, 1922)
140. Ross, E. A., *Social Control* (New York, Macmillan, 1915)

141. Rousseau, Jean Jacques, *Emile* (trans. by Payne. New York, Appleton, 1892. 1st ed. 1762)
142. Ruskin, John, *The Crown of Wild Olive* (New York, Thos. Y. Crowell, 1891)
143. Russell, Bertrand, *Why Men Fight* (New York, Century, 1917)
144. *Saturday Review of Literature* (New York)
145. Schneider, Herbert W., and Clough, Shepard B., *Making Fascists* (Chicago, University of Chicago Press, 1929)
146. *Scientific Monthly* (Washington, D.C.)
147. Shields, Thomas E., *Philosophy of Education* (Washington, Catholic Education Press, 1917)
148. Smith, Adam, *The Wealth of Nations* (1776)
149. *Social Frontier* (publication discontinued)
150. Spaulding, Francis T., *High School and Life* (New York, McGraw Hill, 1938)
151. Spencer, Herbert, *Education* (New York, Appleton, 1860)
152. Spencer, Herbert, *Social Statics* (New York, Appleton, 1865. 1st ed. 1851)
153. Strong, T. G., *Joseph H. Choate* (New York, Dodd Meade, 1917)
154. Sumner, Wm. G., *Folkways* (Boston, Ginn, 1907)
155. Tagore, Rabindranath, *Personality* (New York, Macmillan, 1917)
156. *Teachers College Record* (New York)
157. *Thinker* (publication discontinued)
158. Thorndike, Edward L., *Adult Learning* (New York, Macmillan, 1928)
159. Thorndike, Edward L., *Education* (New York, Macmillan, 1912)
160. Thorndike, Edward L., *Original Nature of Man* (New York, Teachers College, 1913)
161. *Times Educational Supplement* (London)
162. Titchener, E. B., *An Outline of Psychology* (New York, Macmillan, 1896)
163. Todd, Arthur J., *Theories of Social Progress* (New York, Macmillan, 1918)
164. Todd, John, The Student's Manual (Northampton, Mass., Hopkins Bridgman, rev. ed. 1859)
165. Toynbee, Arnold J., A Study of History (abridged by Somerville. Oxford University Press, 1947)
166. *U. S. Supreme Court Reports*
167. Van Doren, Mark, *Liberal Education* (New York, Henry Holt, 1943)
168. *Webster's Dictionary of Synonyms* (Springfield, Mass., Merriam, 1942)
169. Webster, Noah, *A Collection of Essays and Fugativ Writings* (Boston, Thomas and Andrew, 1790)
170. Wesley, John, *Works* (New York, J. & J. Harper, 1826)

171. Whitehead, Alfred N., *Adventures of Ideas* (New York, Macmillan, 1933)
172. Whitehead, Alfred N., *Aims of Education* (New York, Macmillan, 1929)
173. Whitehead, Alfred N., *Science and the Modern World* (New York, Macmillan, 1925)
174. Whitman, Walt, "Song of Myself," in *Leaves of Grass* (New York, Aventine Press, 1931)
175. Winthrop, John, *Life and Letters, 1630–1649* (Boston, Little Brown, 1869)
176. *World Tomorrow* (publication discontinued)

INDEX